Blockchain and Cryptocurrency: International Legal and Regulatory Challenges

The University of Law
133 Great Hampton Street
Birmingham B18 6AQ
Telephone: 01483 216041
Email: library-birmingham@law.ac.uk

Birmingham I Bristol I Chester I Guildford I London I Manchester I York

Blockchain and Cryptocurrency: International Legal and Regulatory Challenges

Dean Armstrong QC
Dan Hyde
Sam Thomas

Bloomsbury Professional

LONDON · DUBLIN · EDINBURGH · NEW YORK · NEW DELHI · SYDNEY

BLOOMSBURY PROFESSIONAL
Bloomsbury Publishing Plc

41–43 Boltro Road, Haywards Heath, RH16 1BJ, UK

BLOOMSBURY and the Diana logo are trademarks of
Bloomsbury Publishing Plc

British Library Cataloguing-in-Publication Data

A catalogue record for this book is available from the British Library.

ISBN:	PB	978 1 52650 837 9
	ePDF	978 1 52650 839 3
	ePub	978 1 52650 838 6

Typeset by Evolution Design and Digital Ltd (Kent)
Printed and bound by CPI Group (UK) Ltd, Croydon, CR0 4YY

To find out more about our authors and books,
visit www.bloomsburyprofessional.com. Here you will find extracts,
author information, details of forthcoming events and
the option to sign up for our newsletters.

Dedications

This book is dedicated to my son, Freddie Armstrong, who is the inspiration for all that is good in my world.

It is also for my mother Merle, father Paul, sister Paula, and for Oliver and Anna, whose love, help and support is without equal.

This book is dedicated to my wonderful family, especially my parents Terence and Shirley for their unflinching support in everything I do, brother Philip, and for Imogen Darcy, a remarkable girl who defied all odds.

For Mia Grace, my favourite person in the whole wide world.

About the authors

DEAN ARMSTRONG QC

Dean is a highly experienced practitioner who has been involved in some of the highest profile cases of the last decade. Dean heads the cyber team at 36 Commercial, part of the 36 Group barristers Chambers.

Dean is one of the UK's leading authorities on cyber law. Co-author of the first comprehensive textbook on the subject, he has advised international banks, large financial institutions, blue chip companies and major players in the not-for-profit sector. He is an expert in areas such as GDPR (General Data Protection Regulation), the impact of Brexit on data regulation, and how international firms should manage data across the world.

He is a regular commentator on legal matters both for Sky and BBC on television and radio and has recently been a contributor on cyber matters on BBC Business breakfast briefing.

He has a City background, having been employed by blue chip corporates and major City solicitors and has advised on mergers and acquisitions, directors' and shareholders' rights and obligations, and set up the regulatory regime for a major multinational company. The combination of City-based advisory experience and high-level advocacy makes him suitably placed to lead in high-profile contentious and non-contentious matters.

PROFESSOR DAN HYDE

Dan writes, lectures and practises innovative law. A pioneer of the law as it applies to emerging tech, he is a leading cybersecurity lawyer and advised the Law Commission on its recent review of cybersecurity and data protection law in the UK. He delivers talks around the world, is a Visiting Professor of Law at Queen Mary, University of London and has authored/co-authored textbooks on cybersecurity and data regulation. He is a partner at international law firm Penningtons Manches Cooper and has been instructed in a number of high-profile, ground-breaking cases which involve cyber and emerging tech regulation.

An Officer of the International Bar Association's Business Crime Committee, he has been described by the Legal 500 as "a lawyer of the highest calibre". Dan's commentaries on legal developments have broadcast on national and international television and radio and been published by the quality press. Dan is interested in entrepreneurship and, for relaxation, plays squash and practises martial arts.

SAM THOMAS

Sam Thomas has written and advised on every aspect of cyber law and regulation, from jurisdictional issues in the online environment to government oversight of cryptocurrency and initial coin offerings. Before being called to the Bar in 2011, Sam worked in the financial sector, as a broker for indices, commodities and treasuries. Consequently, Sam brings a practical insight with his robust legal analysis.

Acknowledgements

Our thanks go to Alexandra Minnis and Hugo Brown for their excellent research, to Shyam Thakerar and Kartikeya Sharma of 36 Commercial for their valuable additions and suggestions to the text, and to Richard and Jill Dutton of The Elias Partnership for their help with Chapter 9.

Acknowledgements

Contents

About the authors   vii
List of abbreviations   xv

CHAPTER 1   INTRODUCTION   **1**

The Internet of Things   2
Blockchain   2
Distributed ledger technology   2
Regulatory and legal challenges   3
Smart contracts   5
Decentralised autonomous organisations   5
Global regulation   5
Initial coin offerings   5
Natural resources industry   6
General Data Protection Regulation   6

CHAPTER 2   WHAT ARE BLOCKCHAIN AND CRYPTOCURRENCY?   **9**

Blockchain   9
    Introduction   9
    Characteristics of DLT   14
Cryptocurrency   15
    Introduction   15

CHAPTER 3   REGULATORY AND LEGAL CHALLENGES   **25**

Regulatory challenges   25
    Cryptoassets   25
    Regulation of cryptoassets   26
    Regulation of DLT   27
Legal challenges   27
    Criminal   27
    Money laundering   28
    Data privacy/protection   30
    Does a user's public key constitute 'personal data'?   30
    Ownership of IP of information contained in the blockchain   31
    What is the legal status of decentralised autonomous
        organisations?   32
    Is the data on the blockchain 'property' for the purposes of the
        Law of Property Act 1925?   33
    Jurisdictional issues   33
    What is the effect of this?   33
Contracts   34
    Smart contracts – what are they?   34
    Who are the parties to a 'smart contract'?   34
    What are the benefits of a 'smart contract'?   35
    What are the ingredients for a 'smart contract'?   35
    Is a 'smart contract' sufficient to govern a contractual
        relationship on its own?   35
    Where does the liability fall under a 'smart contract'?   36

CHAPTER 4 GLOBAL REGULATION: UK AND EU MEMBER STATES   **37**

Choice of jurisdiction   37
Declaration for European Blockchain Partnership   38
     The EU Blockchain Observatory and Forum   38
Regulation in the UK   39
     What are the requirements of being an authorised person?   41
     How is currency regulated across the EU?   41
MiFID II controversies   42
Regulation in other European jurisdictions (case studies)   44
     Estonia   44
     France   44
     Malta   45
     Jersey   49

CHAPTER 5 GLOBAL REGULATION: NORTH AMERICA   **51**

Canada   51
Mexico   53
United States   55
     Licensing   57
     Money transmission laws   58
     Regulatory guidance   58

CHAPTER 6 GLOBAL REGULATION: THE REST OF THE WORLD   **61**

Introduction   61
Divergent philosophies on cryptocurrency and blockchain regulation   64
     China   64
     Gibraltar   66
     Hong Kong   67
     India   67
     Israel   69
     Japan   69
     Kazakhstan, Belarus and Estonia   70
     Kyrgyz Republic   70
     South Korea   70
     Russia   71
     Switzerland   71

CHAPTER 7 INITIAL COIN OFFERINGS   **73**

Introduction   73
     What is an ICO?   73
     What is the regulatory picture in the United States?   74
Investment companies   77
     What is the regulatory position in the UK?   79
     How might ICOs be regulated in the UK?   80
Restrictions of marketing an ICO which is a CIS or an AIF   85
The limited approach of the European Union   85
The Chinese case study of prohibition   89

CHAPTER 8   THE INTERNET OF THINGS   93

Introduction   93
    What is the IoT?   93
    Security problems with the IoT   95
    How does a director mitigate this security concern?   97
    Who owns the data collected through the IoT?   98
    UK regulation of the IoT   99
EU regulation of the IoT   104
    How does GDPR apply to the IoT?   105
    Will the ePrivacy Regulation apply to the IoT?   107
    What is the Cybersecurity Certification Framework?   108
    Why does the Network Infrastructure Security Directive
      ('NISD') not apply to the IoT?   113
US regulation of the IoT   113
    So who owns the data?   117

**CHAPTER 9   RIGHT TO BE FORGOTTEN AND RIGHT TO
            ERASURE**   119

Introduction   119
    Right to erasure   120
    Right to be forgotten   120
    Fundamental issues with right to erasure/right to be forgotten
      and their enforcement   120
    Methods of data protection and data privacy   123
    What are the effects on compliance if data is pseudonymised?   124
The right to amendment   125
    Other DLTs and GDPR compliance   125

CHAPTER 10   NATURAL RESOURCES   129

Introduction   129
    Is blockchain the answer to the 'trilemma'?   129
Regulatory reform   131
    What is the key regulatory question?   131
    What other regulatory issues need to be addressed?   131
Decentralisation   132
Areas of application   133
Non-renewables and intermediaries   134
Renewables and electricity   135
Case studies   136
The reality   138
Digitisation   139
    Information storage, transparency and real-time tracking   139
    Distributed technology and the energy market   140
    Obstacles for blockchain in the natural resources industry and
      energy sector   143
    Blockchain as a disruptive technology   143
    Legal issues   144
    Current regulation   144
    Strong and weak smart contracts   145
    Data privacy   147

Public or private   148
Addressing some of the unique challenges of the natural
     resources industry   149
Solutions, opportunities for regulation and conclusions   151
The legal status of data   153
A possible blueprint for regulation   154
Moving forward   154

**CHAPTER 11   DECENTRALISED AUTONOMOUS
ORGANISATIONS: REGULATION AND LIABILITY   157**

Understanding decentralised autonomous organisations   157
The legal status and other issues around DAOs   159
Risks   160

Appendix 1   General Data Protection Regulation   163

Appendix 2   Cryptoassets Taskforce: final report (October 2018)   287

Appendix 3   Cryptocurrencies and blockchain – Legal context and
implications for financial crime, money laundering and tax evasion
(European Parliament, July 2018)   345

Index   *347*

List of abbreviations

AIF	alternative investment fund
AIFM	alternative investment fund manager
AIFMD	Alternative Investment Fund Managers Directive
AML	anti-money laundering
BYOD	bring your own device
CDD	customer due diligence
CEA	Commodity Exchange Act
CFD	contract for differences
CFTC	Commodity Futures Trading Commission
CIS	collective investment scheme
CJEU	Court of Justice of the European Union
DAO	decentralised autonomous organisation
DDoS	distributed denial-of-service
DLT	distributed ledger technology
DPA	Data Protection Act 2018
DPIA	data protection impact assessment
DPO	data protection officer
DSP	digital service provider
EMIR	European Market Infrastructure Regulation
ENISA	EU Agency for Network and Information Security
ESMA	European Securities and Markets Authority
EWF	Energy Web Foundation
FCA	Financial Conduct Authority
FDA	Food and Drug Administration
FSMA	Financial Services and Markets Act 2000
FTC	Federal Trade Commission
GDPR	General Data Protection Regulation
ICO	initial coin offering OR Information Commissioner's Office
ICT	information communications technology
IoT	Internet of Things
MiFID	Markets in Financial Instruments Directive
MiFIR	Regulation on markets in financial instruments
MLAT	Mutual Legal Assistance Treaty
MLD4	Fourth Anti-Money Laundering Directive
NISD	Network Infrastructure Security Directive
OES	operator of essential services
OTC	over-the-counter
P2P	peer-to-peer
PEP	politically exposed person
PoA	proof of authority
PoS	proof of state
PoW	proof of work
RAO	FSMA (Regulated Activities) Order 2001
SEC	Securities and Exchange Commission

Chapter 1

Introduction

1.1   It was observed by Albert Einstein that 'we cannot solve our problems with the same thinking we used when we created them'. Mr Einstein also noted that 'if you can't explain it to a six year old, you don't understand it yourself'. Both of these statements ring particularly true in the context of this book. We have strived to elucidate blockchain, cryptocurrency and the new thinking that these topics represent whilst always keeping in mind that it should be explained in a way that anyone, including a six year old, would understand. In our view, far too many books and articles discuss emerging technology in a way that baffles rather than enlightens and we hope that the book achieves the right balance between innovation of thought and clarity of explanation.

1.2   We are entering what has been referred to as the Fourth Industrial Revolution or the Second Machine Age. The Third Industrial Revolution and First Machine Age arguably began in the 1950s with the advent of digitalisation and technological progress that was so significant and complementary as to radically shape the world from what had gone before. That technological progress continued apace into the Fourth Industrial Revolution to the point where the level of digitisation and computing heralded global frontier-less interconnectivity and breakthroughs in emerging technologies such as artificial intelligence, robotics, quantum computing, the Internet of Things and decentralised consensus via distributed ledger technology. There are valid arguments that this new Second Machine Age is witnessing an era of technology that can both assist and undermine humanity, with artificial intelligence capable of replacing areas of human cognitive endeavour and cybercriminals utilising technology as a tool for harm.

1.3   The scope of this work is limited to blockchain (which is a type of distributed ledger technology), cryptocurrency, the Internet of Things, and ancillary concepts such as decentralised autonomous organisations that required inclusion for the reader to have a comprehensive appreciation of blockchain, cryptocurrency and the international regulation and challenges that apply. It was simply not possible in a book of this length to forecast and examine every regulation or future challenge; whilst blockchain and cryptocurrency are not new, it is estimated that the zenith for their true potential might not be realised until 2027. On the near horizon, one can expect huge changes across a variety of sectors. It is projected that by 2020 some 31,000,000,000 devices will be connected to the internet worldwide, rising to more than 75,000,000,000 by 2025. Whilst analysts predict that smart cities, connected health and industrial devices will be at the forefront of this growth, a multitude of other sectors will be involved too.[1]

---

1   Louis Columbus, 10 December 2017, Forbes, 'Roundup of Internet of Things Forecasts'.

1.4   Such levels of interconnectivity will bring huge benefits and advances in life and health, but they will also generate risk through the creation of an enlarged attack surface for criminal hackers to exploit, with the potential to take control of entire homes or fleets of vehicles. The enlarged attack surface would similarly facilitate the malicious distribution of ransomware across multiple systems and interconnected devices. The Internet of Things will result then in both significant gain and significant pain, with jurisdictional issues where national or state borders are crossed by cyber criminals oblivious to traditional physical borders.

THE INTERNET OF THINGS

1.5   The Internet of Things is to be found in **Chapter 8** where our examination includes an explanation of what the Internet of Things actually is, the security problems that surround it, how these might be mitigated, and a consideration of who owns the data and the regulation that might apply.

BLOCKCHAIN

1.6   Blockchain, the underlying technology for cryptocurrency, has become synonymous with Bitcoin and is a buzzword that is casually thrown around but often misused and misunderstood. There is no single, universal definition of blockchain and it need not have an associated cryptocurrency. There has been academic debate around the terminology of blockchain and support for the view that blockchain vocabulary is so treacherous because it is a fluctuating, evolving inter-disciplinary technology that is hard to pin down. The terms of reference have also become contaminated from businesses' attempts to use language that attracts investment. Changes in the language around blockchain technology are largely due to a mix of substantive reasons (such as an actual technological difference) and non-substantive reasons (such as the marketing goals of businesses). It also 'takes time for people to figure out how to talk consistently about a new topic, and many times, we never do'.[2]

DISTRIBUTED LEDGER TECHNOLOGY

1.7   This book aims to inject some consistency in clarifying what blockchain, a type of distributed ledger technology ('DLT'), is and how it operates. In **Chapter 2** the authors provide an explanation of DLTs, and explore the differences between private DLTs and public ones, of which blockchain is the most well-known. We then explore how blockchain is being applied to cryptocurrencies, and consider whether 'currency' is the best definition for assets such as Bitcoin and Etherium.

---

2   Angela Walch, 'The Path of The Blockchain Lexicon', 36 *Review of Financial and Banking Law* 713 2017 p 728.

REGULATORY AND LEGAL CHALLENGES

1.8   Following the explanation of blockchain and cryptocurrency, **Chapter 3** then looks at how they are regulated, and current and future challenges. The topics covered are various and include the different categories of cryptoassets, which broadly fall to be categorised as tokens of exchange, security or utility and, dependent on the categorisation, the regulatory treatment that will apply. Legal challenges are also discussed, and these legal issues arise from the broad spectrum of laws, from criminal to cybersecurity, data protection to property and contract to jurisdiction.

1.9   The much-publicised criminal aspects of cryptocurrency and the future policing of blockchain are of particular importance and deserve attention. It should first be understood that blockchain has benefits as well as disadvantages, from a crime enforcement perspective. The downside for enforcement is that, by its very nature and construction, blockchain cuts intermediaries (such as banks and financial institutions) out of the loop.

1.10   Cryptocurrencies were developed on a blockchain platform that operates on a peer-to-peer basis, sending encrypted payments direct from the sender to the beneficiary. The direct transmission method means that banks are not involved. The end-to-end encryption means that the parties to the transaction and the transactions themselves can be shrouded and invisible to outsiders. Police, creditors or other parties seeking to identify the transactions or the transacting parties cannot look to a bank or other financial entity to request or compel information, because they do not hold such information. For the police, these traditional routes of financial investigation will disappear.

1.11   How will the police identify participants in a blockchain that isn't public? Without a visible target, they cannot employ cyber investigation tools under the Regulation of Investigatory Powers Act 2000, such as Section 49 Notices that allow them to serve a notice forcing an individual to divulge information (such as a password or encryption key) or face imprisonment if they fail to comply. Other tools, such as court contempt orders, are usually best applied where the party is identified and ordered to perform an action (such as disclosure) or face imprisonment for contempt. Yet, even where a party can be identified, these powers would have limited effect where a decision is made to keep the cryptoassets hidden, giving preference to gain over pain.

1.12   Common law remedies, known as Norwich Pharmacal Orders,[3] and injunctive relief are both able to require third parties to disclose information and may be of some use if a third party with relevant knowledge can be identified, but this presents as a high hurdle. To add to this, the advances in encryption technology and the means to protect anonymity or falsify identity will potentially make the blockchain harder to govern and police where there is a concerted

---

3   See Simon Bushell and Gary Milner-Moore, *Disclosure of Information: Norwich Pharmacal and Related Principles* (2nd edition, Bloomsbury Professional, 2019).

attempt to remain anonymous. Yet there are strong counter-arguments to all of this.

1.13 Firstly, money laundering is hardly new and already rampant in many jurisdictions, and this was achieved with fiat currency (that is, real currency). Historically, money launderers and criminals have used offshore banking systems and banking regimes that enable the proceeds of crime to be untraceable or registered to a trust or entity that conceals the true ownership. This is a battle that is still being fought and arguably lost.

1.14 Blockchain will present new problems but, throughout history, the law and its enforcement have evolved to meet new challenges. The advent of mobile communication devices and the internet caused similar upheaval, as law enforcement struggled to match phones and IP addresses to users. Anonymous communication and criminality across national borders is nothing new. The police and courts have innovated to keep up.

1.15 Secondly, blockchain has an advantage that flows from the immutable nature of its transactions: because there is no centralised power, there is an improved, inbuilt honesty; this means, in practice, that opportunities for fraud and deception are reduced. Because a *public* blockchain[4] creates an immutable audit trail of each and every transaction, where it *is possible* to identify the parties, there will consequently be a money trail that is the antithesis of encouragement to the money launderer. If one can obtain a given cryptocurrency address, then Blockchain enables the tracing of each and every transaction across the chain to the first transaction. That address stays with the user; if you can identify him or her, then you can identify every transaction they have been involved with when using that address.

1.16 In addition, where the parties are anonymous or visible, the police would likely be able to investigate criminals at points where they sought to convert fiat currency into cryptocurrency and then cryptocurrency to fiat currency. These jumping on and off points provide the police with traditional investigation opportunities. In essence, the focus would be on tracking the movement of cryptocurrency as it leaves a cryptocurrency exchange, and vice versa. The police and investigation agencies in the UK and around the world are developing software and systems to gather and share blockchain intelligence. The borderless nature of blockchain actually provides an advantage, because police from different jurisdictions will not need to request the assistance of foreign law enforcers (known as 'Mutual Legal Assistance Treaties' or 'MLATs') in any blockchain investigation, as there are no borders within blockchain. MLATs simply are not needed. Once law enforcement can access the blockchain, there are no third parties or foreign states to hamper the investigation.

---

4 See **Chapter 3** for the explanations as to types of blockchain.

SMART CONTRACTS

1.17   Smart contracts, self-executing pieces of computer code, are another means whereby blockchain might reduce the opportunity for fraud, by removing the involvement of the human mind and automating the execution of agreements. These smart contracts are explained in **Chapter 3** and examined in further detail in **Chapter 11** within the context of decentralised autonomous organisations.

DECENTRALISED AUTONOMOUS ORGANISATIONS

1.18   A decentralised autonomous organisation ('DAO') is a computer program that has no manager or leader. It involves users, and it runs on a peer-to-peer network. A peer-to-peer network means that each computer receives information from every other machine on the network rather than from one big central server. The collective contents of the network are at the command of each connected machine and enable the direct exchange of services or data between computers. In such an environment, service desktops and personal computers that make up a network become equal peers that contribute some or all of their resources to the overall computing effort.

1.19   In a DAO a set of users connect and interact with one another pursuant to a protocol which is programmed through code and is enforced on a blockchain. DAOs are autonomous; they remove the human mind from the equation, as human intervention is not required in any way. That removal of human intervention reduces the common ingredient of crime – that is, the human mind.

GLOBAL REGULATION

1.20   The global, borderless nature of blockchain means that, in our view, any book limiting itself to looking at it through a local domestic prism fails its readers. Moreover, regulations and the acceptance of blockchain and cryptocurrencies vary so widely between countries and states that one should examine each in turn. To this end, we have provided separate regional chapters for the UK and EU (**Chapter 4**), North America (**Chapter 5**) and the Rest of the World (**Chapter 6**). Each chapter contains a country-by-country (and state-by-state for the US) discussion of the regulations and challenges for the countries/states within that region. We identify the front runners and explain why those jurisdictions provide clear advantages for cryptocurrency and blockchain enterprises.

INITIAL COIN OFFERINGS

1.21   **Chapter 7** focuses on the use of initial coin offerings ('ICOs') an area that has generated a huge amount of controversy. $7 billion worldwide was raised via ICOs between January and June 2018, yet less than half of all ICOs survive four months after the offering,[5] while almost half of ICOs sold in 2017 failed by February 2018.[6] The concern around ICOs stems from their history of use as vehicles for fraud and we consequently explain their regulation and examine whether they are, on one view, an ingenious new method for raising capital away from structured funding or, on another, a method to extort money from naïve speculators.

NATURAL RESOURCES INDUSTRY

1.22   Blockchain technology will likely have an impact across almost every aspect of the natural resources industry, and **Chapter 10** is devoted to studying the potential impact on natural resources. The potential benefits range from real time data registry as gas and oil come out of the ground, or electricity is produced, to the possibility of peer-to-peer energy selling, disintermediation and the creation of a smart energy grid. These benefits are often, and first by the Energy Web Foundation, grouped under the headings of:

- decarbonisation;

- decentralisation;

- digitisation; and

- democratisation.[7]

1.23   These four interconnected categories are often defined as the long-term aims of blockchain implementation in the natural resources industry, and we discuss the possibilities as well as the regulation that is needed to help address the world's natural resource problems.

GENERAL DATA PROTECTION REGULATION

1.24   Finally, no book dealing with regulation after 25 May 2018 could be considered complete without mention of the General Data Protection Regulation ('GDPR' – see **Appendix 1**). On that date the GDPR came into force across Europe (including the UK) but impacted on every business worldwide that handles the personal information of European citizens. It mattered not where the business (or the personal data) was situated, only that it was the personal data of Europeans. In the scramble to comply, many reorganised their storage

5   Kharif, Olga, 'Half of ICOs Die Within Four Months After Token Sales Finalized', Bloomberg, 9 July 2018: www.bloomberg.com/news/articles/2018-07-09/half-of-icos-die-within-four-months-after-token-sales-finalized (last accessed 2 March 2019).
6   Hankin, Aaron, 'Nearly half of all 2017 ICOs have failed', Fortune, 26 February 2018: www.marketwatch.com/story/nearly-half-of-all-2017-icos-have-failed-2018-02-26 (last accessed 2 March 2019).
7   Basden, J. and Cottrell, M., 'How Utilities Are Using Blockchain to Modernise the Grid', *Harvard Business Review*: https://hbr.org/2017/03/how-utilities-are-using-blockchain-to-modernize-the-grid.

systems and set up new organisational policies to ensure this data was collected, processed, retained and erased in accordance with the principles of the GDPR; this meant there had to be a legitimate basis for dealing with such data and that it was not kept for longer than necessary, and it was erased when required, to include at the request of a data subject.

1.25 What few failed to appreciate was how blockchain could comply with the GDPR and whether rights given to individuals could be consistent in the context of blockchain. **Chapter 9** looks at the tension between the rights to deletion and erasure, as enshrined in the GDPR, and the practical difficulties that might need to be addressed to comply.

1.26 We hope this book educates and informs but, most of all, we hope that it sparks new thinking about how we can solve old problems in new ways. Welcome to the revolution.

Chapter 2

What are blockchain and cryptocurrency?

BLOCKCHAIN

Introduction

2.1   The rise of decentralised ledger technologies ('DLTs'), the best known of these being blockchain, is part of the technological revolution that is proceeding apace. There are potentially far-reaching issues with the ability of DLTs and blockchain to be compliant with recent data regulation; however, the use of blockchain is growing by the day, not least in the area of cryptocurrencies.

2.2   On 17 December 2017, Bitcoin, a decentralised virtual cryptocurrency, soared above $19,500 ($19,783.06) to reach a record high. This came only three months after Jamie Dimon, the Chairman and CEO of JP Morgan Chase, described the currency as a fraud that would blow up, and was only useful 'if you were a drug dealer'.[1] What is clear is that the blockchain, and the creation of cryptocurrencies, has the potential to create huge profits for those willing to speculate on the technology, but also considered by many as a 'bubble' or a scam which requires further regulation.

2.3   The use of blockchain, however, is not limited to the underlying technology that facilitates cryptocurrency transactions. Blockchain can be used for far more purposes, ranging from registering intellectual property to voting. Its increasing prevalence in a wide range of industries across the world, and its seemingly non-exhaustive list of uses, means that states and authorities must continue to adapt regulatory frameworks in order to ensure that DLTs are used in a safe, consistent and transparent way.

2.4   Blockchain was created in response to the global financial crisis, in an aim to solve the double-spending problem. The potential of DLTs has arguably not yet been realised and there is a need for exploration into the legal consequences of its use. The World Economic Forum conducted a survey in 2015 and found that respondents thought the tipping point for blockchain was most likely to occur in 2027 (WEF, 2015). Considering blockchain was invented in 2008, so has already existed for a decade, it is interesting to see how its potential may not be reached

---

1   Monaghan, Angela, 'Bitcoin is a fraud that will blow up, says JP Morgan boss', *The Guardian*, 13 September 2017, www.theguardian.com/technology/2017/sep/13/bitcoin-fraud-jp-morgan-cryptocurrency-drug-dealers (last accessed 25 October 2018).

until 2027 due to its complexity, a lack of understanding and the use of legacy systems within companies that may not integrate or work with blockchain.

2.5   In this chapter, we provide an explanation of DLTs, and explore the differences between private DLTs and public ones, of which blockchain is the most well-known. We then explore how blockchain is being applied to cryptocurrencies, and consider whether 'currency' is the best definition for assets such as Bitcoin and Etherium.

How does the blockchain work?

2.6   All DLTs share common characteristics. There are digital ledgers that evidence transactions between two parties who usually do not know each other. They engage in a peer-to-peer ('P2P') network via connected computers. True to its aim of decentralisation, the network reaches a consensus on which transactions are valid without reliance on a middleman.

2.7   There are principally three means of reaching consensus:

1   proof of work ('PoW') (the basis for Bitcoin and Ethereum);

2   proof of stake ('PoS'); and

3   proof of authority ('PoA').

2.8   Proof of work consensus or verification is used by Bitcoin and Ethereum, and is discussed later in this chapter in more detail. Transactions are verified together (by the proof of work mechanism known as 'mining') and added to the chain of blocks, thereby creating a blockchain. The blocks are connected by cryptography, meaning that it cannot be tampered with or changed once another block is added to the chain after it. The details of the transaction are visible; however, the identities of the parties are represented by their usernames. This combination is one of the reasons that blockchain use is conducive to those with the best and worst intentions.

2.9   The data within the chain is secure from attack, to a considerable degree, because the cryptography ensures that the transaction is permanent and tamper-proof. This is what makes the blockchain 'immutable' unless an attacker can influence 51% of the participants. The blockchain data is downloaded onto thousands of computers who are on the participating network. In order to influence 51%, a huge amount of processing power would be required; however, it is conceivably possible. An actor who could influence 51% of the network could rewrite previous blocks or 'double spend' by repeating transactions. The constant updating of new transactions, over a large number of servers and processors, also has an environmental impact. The amount of electricity required to run the Bitcoin network is comparable to the total energy used in Ireland.[2]

2   Faridi, Omar, *Proof of Work (PoW) vs. Proof of Stake (PoS)*, 4 March 2019, www.cryptocompare. com/coins/guides/proof-of-work-pow-vs-proof-of-stake, last accessed 18 April 2019.

2.10   Proof of stake verification requires an actor to deposit a certain sum, either in the relevant cryptocurrency or in a traditional currency equivalent, in order to be entitled to verify whether a block is valid. In 2013, the Nxt platform, followed by other second-generation crypto networks, such as Peercoin, began experimenting with proof-of-stake-based consensus as a way to secure and verify transactions on blockchains. As its name implies, network participants looking to validate and generate blocks on PoS networks must first stake a certain amount of their funds. The benefit to verification is that, once a new block is validated or created, the actor verifying the block is rewarded through earning new cryptocurrency.

2.11   VeChain (denominated in VET), a semi-decentralised supply chain management solution, requires block validators (referred to as Masternodes) to hold a stake in the VeChain platform. The minimum stake amount is 25 million VET (approximately $116,000) in order to be eligible to become a Masternode candidate on VeChain. Users can also stake lower amounts, such as 15 million VET, and still be able to perform certain network management duties. Nodes that stake at least 15 million VET can expect to earn a fixed 5.81% in VET tokens as a return on their investment.[3]

2.12   Proof of stake networks are 'semi'-decentralised, rather than fully decentralised, because there is still a reliance on a trusted third party, albeit that the third party is fluid and can change. In most PoS networks, the deposit or stake is locked-away so that network managers are discouraged from engaging in dishonest behaviour. Should a validator try to introduce fraudulent transactions on a network, then they risk losing their staked amount in addition to other privileges. Proponents of PoS-based consensus argue that this is a more effective way of managing decentralised cryptocurrency platforms. The amount of energy (electricity) in a PoS system is far less, because there are fewer actors able, and required, to validate blocks. Theoretically, PoS systems are also susceptible to 51% attacks.[4] External attacks are less of an issue for a PoS system; however, these networks are more susceptible to dishonesty from those holding a stake.

2.13   In a proof-of-authority-based network, transactions and blocks are validated by approved accounts, known as 'validators'. Validators run software allowing them to put transactions in blocks. The process is automated and does not require validators to be constantly monitoring their computers; however, it does require maintaining the computer (the authority node) uncompromised. Consequently, the PoA model is suitable for public and private blockchains.[5]

2.14   Holding the position as a validator is incentivised through reputation, with validators keen to maintain their position. This is considered to be an

---

3   Ibid.
4   If a single actor owns 51% of a proof of work blockchain, they could potentially manipulate the blockchain dishonestly.
5   Hose, Adam, *Rolling your own Proof-of-Authority Ethereum consortium*, Enuma Technologies, https://blog.enuma.io/update/2017/08/29/proof-of-authority-ethereum-networks.html, 29 August 2017.

improvement upon PoS, where the stake of two actors may be equal but their total financial position within a system may be unequal. However, PoA only allows non-consecutive block approval from any one validator, meaning that the risk of serious damage is centralised to the authority node which, if compromised, could undermine the entire system.

2.15   Once a transaction has been validated by the network (whether by PoW, PoS or PoA), it gets posted onto the digital log.

2.16   There are two types of blockchain:

1   permissioned or private; or

2   permissionless, also known as public.

2.17   In the latter, visibility of the transaction and participation can be restricted. Most corporate entities use private blockchains.

2.18   As has been seen, the decentralised technology keeps an anonymous record of transactions across the network that is replicated across every computer that uses the blockchain, therefore rendering it virtually impenetrable and infinitely more secure. Each block usually contains four pieces of information:

1   the hash of the previous block;

2   a summary of the included transaction;

3   a time stamp; and

4   the validation (PoW, PoS or PoA) that secured the block.

2.19   A PoW or PoS consensus blockchain is, therefore, difficult to undermine, due to the lack of a 'centralised point of vulnerability for hackers to exploit and each block includes the previous block's hash', making any attempts to change the transaction 'easily detectable'.[6] Its secure nature has also even maintained the anonymity of its creator(s), Satoshi Nakamoto.

2.20   Each blockchain user has a public key, usually a string of letters and numbers, and a private key, effectively a password. The combination of the public and private keys allows the identity of the individual to be known, but the private key decrypts the data held. As stated above, in public blockchains, anyone can engage with a node with use of the relevant software. This allows the data to be read by anyone using the appropriate software. If private, the blockchain runs on a private network and an administrator allows individuals permission to gain access to a node.

---

6   McKinlay, J., Pithouse, D., McGonagle, J. and Sanders, J. (2018) 'Blockchain: Background, Challenges and Legal Issues'. Available online at: www.dlapiper.com/en/denmark/insights/publications/2017/06/blockchain-background-challenges-legal-issues/.

2.21   The issues surrounding compliance with recent changes in data regulation, most notably the General Data Protection Regulation ('GDPR'), are dealt with in **Chapter 9**; however, it is important to stress that there are challenges which are inherent in the concept of a decentralised ledger being compliant with a Regulation aimed at traditional centralised models. For example, who is the data controller? Can one be readily identified in this system? For example, it may be possible in a private blockchain to identify a central figure who is the data controller, but a public blockchain will have no such central figure. In such a scenario, where would the obligations imposed by the Regulation land? On each node? This is a major challenge to these types of DLTs, of which blockchain is one, and the best known.

How does blockchain impact intellectual property?

2.22   The trust that the blockchain provides is native to the technology and could have impacts on intellectual property offences. For instance, the Copyright, Designs and Patents Act 1988 outlines that copyright is an intellectual property right and that, as creators, you can stop people from stealing or copying:[7]

> 'the names of your products or brands; your inventions; the design or look of your products; and the things you write, make or produce.'

2.23   The creators of different kinds of work therefore have the right to control the ways in which their material is being used. As the blockchain can store the title of ownership of intellectual property, it can be protected, and individuals can control their own content.

> Example
>
> Imogen Heap, the musician, uses the blockchain digital ledger to store information about artists' songs and to facilitate trackable payments. This highlights the practical use of blockchain with regard to potentially stopping/ reducing unauthorised downloading of music.

2.24   The blockchain's ability not only to store information but also to track assets and information makes intermediaries, such as banks, potentially redundant. However, as will be discussed below, the use of public blockchains in the financial world, has, in our view, too many regulatory challenges to be part of the culture going forward. It will, in a defeat for the purists, mean that private, permissioned blockchains will be in widespread use, thus requiring some form of central administration.

---

7   www.gov.uk/intellectual-property-an-overview.

What is distributed ledger technology?

2.25　　Distributed ledger technology ('DLT') 'is a type of technology that enables sharing and updating of records in a distributed and decentralised way. Participants can securely propose, validate and record updates to a synchronized ledger (a form of database), that is distributed across the participants'.[8]

2.26　　'A DLT platform can be used like any conventional database that sets out who owns what, or who did what', and it can store a huge range of data.[9]

What is the difference between blockchain and DLT?

2.27　　Essentially, blockchain is a form of DLT. Blockchain uses a certain method of storing data in 'blocks', with each block being linked to another cryptographically. The blockchain only allows data to be added to the existing chain and does not permit the alteration or deletion of previous 'blocks'. Blockchain and DLT are often used interchangeably, but this is technically incorrect and, although many of the characteristics are the same (such as decentralisation and transparency of the recorded ledger to users), blockchain is simply a type of DLT that has come to prominence through the increasing use of cryptocurrencies such as Bitcoin.

2.28　　DLT does not take a particular form and there are many different types of platform. All types of DLT, though, share the same common features set out below.

Characteristics of DLT

2.29　　DLT has these four common features:[10]

1　　Data distribution – the participants in the ledger have a copy of the ledger and can access the data stored on it.

2　　Decentralisation – participants are allowed to update the ledger, subject to the extent of control and processes that have been agreed.

3　　Use of cryptography – this is used to identify and authorise participants, as well as confirm data records and facilitate consensus.

4　　Programmability/automation – code can automatically implement the terms of an agreement by triggering predetermined responses to certain actions. These are called 'smart contracts' and are discussed later in this chapter.

8　*Cryptoassets Taskforce: final report – October 2018* (HM Treasury, FCA and Bank of England), 2.1.
9　Ibid, 2.2.
10　Ibid, 2.3.

2.30   Although blockchain has myriad practical uses, blockchain, the most well-known DLT, is becoming synonymous with cryptocurrency, in particular Bitcoin. In order to better understand the use of blockchain, it is helpful to understand its use within cryptocurrency and, more fundamentally, whether cryptocurrencies are, in fact, a 'currency' to be regulated.

CRYPTOCURRENCY

Introduction

2.31   The international trade in US Dollars is approximately \$5.3 trillion dollars per day, and the foreign exchange (Forex) market in terms of trading volume is four times the combined gross domestic product (GDP) of the entire world.[11] To provide some context, spending one dollar (\$1) every second, it would take you 31,688 years to spend a trillion dollars, and 126,118 years to spend the daily value of the Forex market.

2.32   Although the trade in currency is big business, 85% of the global Forex market consists of trades in just seven pairs of currency.[12] In many instances, these trades are speculative, potentially based upon market movements, Central Bank actions or perceived consumer confidence, but often simply guesswork.

2.33   What then is the potential for cryptocurrencies? Is the perceived value of Bitcoin merely a speculative bubble or is there intrinsic worth to cryptocurrency? This chapter seeks to assist by providing the legal and regulatory context in which cryptocurrencies are traded within this jurisdiction and abroad.

What is a currency?

2.34   Before leaping into the legal and regulatory context, it is important to have an understanding of currency. It is arguable that cryptocurrencies are not, in fact, currencies; rather, that they are properly classified as commodities.

2.35   The following table provides six steps to understanding currency:

---

11 BrokerNotes, 50+ Forex & Trading Industry Statistics & Trends, https://brokernotes.co/forex-trading-industry-statistics (last accessed 25 October 2018).

12 The major trading pairs are considered to be US Dollars with the currencies of seven other developed nations: EURUSD, USDJPY, GBPUSD, AUDUSD, NZDUSD, USDCAD, USDCHF. Trading pairs which do not involve US Dollars are called crosses, for example EURGBP or GBPJPY. Crosses involving the Euro will often be referred to as euro-crosses: BIS, Triennial Central Bank Survey of Foreign Exchange and Derivatives Market Activity in 2007 – Final results, 18 December 2007 www.bis.org/publ/rpfxf07t.htm (last accessed 25 October 2018).

SIX STEPS TO UNDERSTANDING CURRENCY		
1.	What is a currency?	Currency, or money, is a medium of exchange. Although traditionally coins or banknotes, currency is now a system of money (monetary units) in common use within a nation or trading area.
2.	Why do we need a Central Bank?	A Central Bank guarantees the value of the currency within a system.
3.	What is the value of money?	Previously, Central Banks guaranteed the value of a coin or banknote against a weight in gold (The Gold Standard). Since 1971, when the United States left the Gold Standard, currencies have been valued against other currencies in a floating exchange rate.
4.	What if a currency cannot be converted internationally?	When there are no restrictions on trading a nation's money, the currency is considered to be fully convertible and the value can be easily determined against any other currency (think USD, EUR, GBP). When international investment into a country is controlled but domestic trade is freely permitted, this is called partially convertible. A conversion rate for individuals or companies can often be determined, but the true value of money may be maintained at a false level against other currencies. For example, special approval is required to convert Indian Rupees into certain currencies. When neither individuals nor companies are permitted to convert currencies, this is a non-convertible system (North Korean won). These countries will often artificially maintain the value of their currency.
5.	How do Central Banks control the value of money?	A Central Bank (or the Government which it represents) can use monetary policy to influence the value of money in comparison to other currencies. A Central Bank can raise interest rates (the cost of money) to encourage foreign money (capital) to enter into the system. This will raise the value of the national currency. Conversely, interest rates can be lowered to devalue a currency.
6.	What about printing money?	Central Banks could physically print money to lower the interest rate. However, there is a delay and cost to physically printing notes or forging coins. In practical terms, Central Banks will buy government or other bonds (debt) to release money into the economy.

2.36   Early virtual currencies created in the late 1990s, such as Flooz and Beenz, relied upon a company (Flooz.com and the 'Bank of Beenz') to guarantee the value of the units exchanged. In principle, therefore, it was not dissimilar to a 'traditional' currency with a Central Bank confirming that these units, if acquired in a trade, could be exchanged again or changed into another currency (eg US Dollars).

2.37   The 'virtual' Central Banks also had another function. Unlike a coin or note, which is lost once exchanged (it is physically handed over to the other party), there is nothing to prevent a virtual currency from being double-spent. If a virtual currency consists of a piece of code, there is nothing to prevent a user from recreating that piece of code and simply spending it again. The virtual Central Bank prevented this double spending by logging all trades on a central server, and could therefore monitor whether a trade was genuine.

2.38   Current cryptocurrencies such as Bitcoin and Ethereum are different. These do not rely upon a trusted third party to guarantee the value of the unit or to confirm the legitimacy of a trade. Instead, each currency movement forms part of the blockchain, with 'miners' used to confirm that a transaction is genuine. This is a significant difference from a 'traditional' currency and the early virtual currencies.

What is a cryptocurrency?

2.39   A cryptocurrency is a digital or virtual currency designed to work as a medium of exchange. It uses cryptography to secure and verify transactions as well as to control the creation of new units of a particular cryptocurrency. Essentially, cryptocurrencies are limited entries in a database that no one can change unless specific conditions are fulfilled.

2.40   Bitcoin is currently the most well-known cryptocurrency in circulation, and utilises the blockchain to avoid the need for a Central Bank or trusted third party.

How Bitcoin works in six easy steps
1.	A Bitcoin (₿) is a unit of currency worth approximately £4,128.60.[13] Smaller denominations of Bitcoin are millibitcoin (mBTC), and satoshi (sat). A millibitcoin is 1,000th of a Bitcoin (0.001 or approximately £4.13) and a satoshi is a 100,000,000th of a Bitcoin (0.00000001).
2.	All Bitcoin transactions are recorded on a public ledger called the 'Bitcoin Blockchain'. The Bitcoin Blockchain is not held on a single server, rather on a network of communicating nodes. The transactions are in the form: Payer X sends Y bitcoins to Payee Z.
3.	Every transaction within the Blockchain can be traced back to the 'Genesis Block', which was created on 13 January 2009, at 18:15:05. The Genesis Block is the block number 0.
4.	A Bitcoin is composed of a chain of digital signatures formed of transactions leading back to the Genesis Block (0). To transfer a

13 As at 1 April 2019. The value of Bitcoin is notoriously volatile. Consequently, this is an approximate value at the time of writing.

	A Bitcoin is composed of a chain of digital signatures formed of transactions leading back to the Genesis Block (0). To transfer a Bitcoin, Payee X sends a 'hash' (the existing chain of signatures in their possession) with their own (X's) signature (private key) to Payee Z's public key. This transaction then becomes the new hash. Payee Z signs this new hash with their private key when a new transaction takes place.
4.	All new transactions are timestamped and broadcast to the network nodes. The network nodes group the transactions into a 'Block' and seek to validate the transaction through a proof of work ('PoW').
5.	Every 10 minutes, a node will find a PoW and will broadcast the Block to the other network nodes. The Block is accepted if the transactions contained are valid, and have not been double spent. If Payee X has sent their hash to another payee (other than Payee Z), the nodes will reject the block.
6.	An accepted Block is added to the Blockchain. Acceptance by the nodes is through using the previous Block as the new hash, against which all new transactions will be conducted. This process of validating and creation of Blocks is 'Bitcoin mining', and prevents double spending of Bitcoin. The process of Bitcoin mining generates a reward for the miner, who is paid in newly created Bitcoin.

2.41 On 31 October 2008, Satoshi Nakamoto, the creator of Bitcoin, released an essay titled 'Bitcoin: A Peer-to-Peer Electronic Cash System'. He described within his essay a method for creating a decentralised currency, which did not rely upon a Central Bank or trusted third party.

2.42 The essay is a scholarly work, which provides the mathematical justification for decentralised cryptocurrency (Bitcoin), but it also provides a visual representation of Bitcoin transactions:[14]

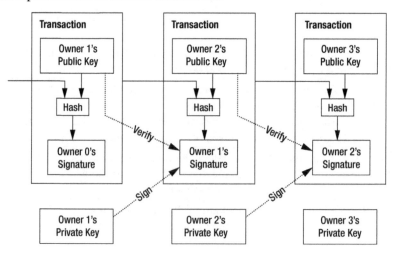

14 Nakamoto, Satoshi, 'Bitcoin: A Peer-to-Peer Electronic Cash System', 31 October 2008 (https://bitcoin.org/bitcoin.pdf), p.2

2.43   The method that Satoshi Nakamoto describes is synonymous with the explanation for the use of blockchain earlier in this chapter. Each transaction consists of a previous hash (which leads back to the Genesis Block (0)), the private key of the seller (password), and the public key of the buyer (username). This transaction becomes a new hash which is then verified by the private key (password) of the buyer. Multiple hash transactions are brought together into a Block which then needs to be verified.

2.44   The first ever Block (1) used the Genesis Block (0) as its hash. After there were sufficient transactions using the Genesis Block (0), these new hash transactions were grouped together to form Block 1. Verification is an important step, otherwise a seller could sell a Bitcoin to multiple buyers.

2.45   Verification is undertaken by 'bitcoin miners'.

What are people 'mining'?

2.46   'Mining' is a little of a misnomer, as the actions undertaken by a 'miner' would be more properly characterised as 'confirming'.

2.47   Before transactions can be broadcast to the network, they need to be confirmed. A bitcoin miner confirms a transaction by considering the hash which is contained (remember, each transaction consists of a previous hash (which leads back to the Genesis Block (0)), the private key of the seller and the public key of the buyer – see **2.43** above) and working back through the blockchain towards the Genesis Block. If the hash is consistent with previously broadcast Blocks on the Bitcoin blockchain, the transaction is confirmed by a PoW.

2.48   Bitcoin miners are rewarded for their PoW by being issued with newly generated Bitcoin.

2.49   The original Block (1) required very little processing power in order to generate a PoW. The hash(s) used within this Block (1) was the Genesis Block (0). Therefore, bitcoin mining could be undertaken on home computers using minimal processing power and energy (electricity).

2.50   However, since January 2009 the number of transactions have increased exponentially. It would be impossible to trace each transaction through to the Genesis Block. Instead, bitcoin miners work through the hash transactions until a satisfactory comparison has been made with a reliable time-stamped Block. A real world example of a reliable time-stamped Block would be the use of a newspaper in a photograph. All other information within that photograph can reliably be assumed to be correct, as it contains the dated newspaper, with the relevant headlines. Regardless, even working back to a reliable Block now requires a huge amount of processing power, and corresponding energy, to provide a PoW.

2.51   A Block which has been confirmed becomes the new reliable time-stamped Block (the photograph with the next day's newspaper captured within it) against which future transactions are completed. The Block against which the most transactions are completed becomes the longest, and the network considers the longest blockchain to be correct.

Is a cryptocurrency a currency?

2.52   In September 2017, a London property developer, The Collective, said it would allow its tenants to pay deposits in Bitcoin and would soon accept rent payments in cryptocurrency. The very next day, entrepreneur Baroness Michelle Mone OBE indicated that properties within development Aston Plaza, Dubai, could be purchased using Bitcoin. However, despite these very limited examples, Bitcoin is not used for the purchase of items. Arguably, therefore, Bitcoin fails in being a currency because it is not a 'medium of exchange'.

2.53   In part, this is due to the pragmatic exchange of Bitcoins and/or the volatility of the currency. Practically, buying a pint of milk in a local shop could be overcome; however, using a volatile currency means that, on Monday, the milk may cost 50 pence but, on Tuesday, it could cost anywhere between 41.64 pence and 62.70 pence.[15] This volatility may seem insignificant on a single low-cost item but, when scaled-up to commercial levels, it would simply be economically unviable to risk using Bitcoin to purchase items.

Is Bitcoin a commodity?

2.54   On 10 December 2014, the Chairman of the Commodity Futures Trading Commission ('CFTC') in the United States, Timothy Massad, declared that Bitcoin fell within the definition of a commodity under the Commodity Exchange Act ('CEA'):

> 'While the CFTC does not have policies and procedures specific to virtual currencies like bitcoin, the agency's authority extends to futures and swaps contracts in any commodity. The CEA defines the term commodity very broadly so that in addition to traditional agricultural commodities, metals, and energy, the CFTC has oversight of derivatives contracts related to Treasury securities, interest rate indices, stock market indices, currencies, electricity, and heating degree days, to name just a few underlying products.
>
> Derivative contracts based on a virtual currency represent one area within our responsibility. Recently, for example, a SEF registered with us made such a contract available.'

---

15 On 14 September 2017, Bitcoin fell by 16.72% when Chinese authorities indicated a plan to shut down domestic digital currency exchanges; and, on 20 July 2017, Bitcoin increased by 25.4% when an agreement was reached regarding Segregated Witness, or SigWit, the scaling of Bitcoin's payment system: Gulker, Max, *Bitcoin's Largest Price Changes Coincide with Major News Events About Cryptocurrency*, American Institute for Economic Research, 26 January 2018, www.aier.org/article/bitcoins-largest-price-changes-coincide-major-news-events-about-cryptocurrency (last accessed 17 February 2019).

2.55   The declaration indicated that the US CFTC had jurisdiction over a virtual currency when it is used in a derivatives contract, or if there is fraud or manipulation involving a virtual currency traded in inter-state commerce.

2.56   On 7 March 2018, US District Judge Jack Weinstein confirmed the position and ruled that the CFTC had standing to bring a fraud lawsuit against New York resident Patrick McDonnell and his company Coin Drop Markets.[16]

2.57   However, the clear declaration by the US CFTC is somewhat complicated by the position taken by the European Union. The European Central Bank has classified Bitcoin and cryptocurrency as a convertible decentralised virtual currency; but, in July 2014, the European Banking Authority initially advised European banks not to trade in virtual currencies until a statutory regulatory regime was in place. There is currently no specific regime with regard to cryptocurrencies.

2.58   On 22 October 2015, the Court of Justice of the European Union ('CJEC') ruled that 'The exchange of traditional currencies for units of the "bitcoin" virtual currency is exempt from VAT' and that 'Member States must exempt, inter alia, transactions relating to "currency, bank notes and coins used as legal tender"'.[17] Consequently, the CJEC judgment considers bitcoin a currency as opposed to being a commodity.

2.59   Whether cryptocurrencies are currencies or commodities is moot, and may change over time. The important aspect to consider is less whether, academically or historically, Bitcoin is a currency or commodity but rather, pragmatically, whether it can be used as a medium of exchange and how it is regulated within the various jurisdictions over which it is traded.

Is the future Libra Coin?

2.60   In June 2019, Facebook announced that it was launching a new cryptocurrency, the Libra Coin, which would be supported by a permissioned blockchain. Facebook hoped to launch the currency in 2020 with a trusted private network of 100 companies responsible for posting transactions without the need for an independent validation system. The Libra Coin is anticipated to employ a hybrid PoS/PoA system, which is fully backed by a combination of bank deposits and treasuries from high-ranking central banks. The Libra Association is a 28-member, independent non-profit based in Geneva, Switzerland, which will oversee major decisions about the digital coin. Deposits will be generated

16 CNBC, *Virtual currencies are commodities, US judge rules*, 7 March 2018, www.cnbc.com/2018/03/07/cryptocurrencies-like-bitcoin-are-commodities-us-judge-rules.html (last accessed 17 February 2019).
17 Court of Justice of the European Union, Press Release No 128/15, Judgment in Case C-264/14, *Skatteverket v David Hedqvist, The exchange of traditional currencies for units of the 'bitcoin' virtual currency is exempt from VAT*, https://curia.europa.eu/jcms/upload/docs/application/pdf/2015-10/cp150128en.pdf, 22 October 2015.

through investors, with a minimum $10 million investment to join. Non-profit members, such as financial inclusion group Kiva, will be permitted to join the trusted companies without investment.

2.61   The stated objective of the initiative is to launch a new global currency which would ultimately be used, via a standalone App, to purchase goods and services via Facebook, Facebook Messenger, and WhatsApp. It is also said to have the backing of the Visa and MasterCard payment networks as well as PayPal, Uber and eBay. Proponents of the initiative state that the new 'coin' will not create any new money, but the backing fiat currency would act as a reserve, allowing the digital partner to be used on the internet with the resulting fall in transaction services.

2.62   Corporates have issued forms of coin before (JP Morgan or JPM Coin being one example), but Libra Coin appears to be significantly different. The stated aim of Libra Coin is to produce a global currency – in other words, to be used as a medium of exchange rather than a commodity upon which to speculate. Because it is being backed by Facebook, with the apparent support of Visa, MasterCard and eBay, this cryptocurrency may have the power to impact on traditional markets, without huge volatility, and to effectively be used on a day-to-day basis.

2.63   Critics have already raised some disquiet that data may be shared across services. Facebook will be a member of the trusted companies via Calibra, a newly created subsidiary that will offer a digital wallet for Libra. Individuals and merchants will be able to use Calibra to store, send and receive Libras, with Facebook able to potentially use this data created within Calibra for their own purposes. Facebook have pledged not to use Calibra data to improve ad targeting.

2.64   The supporters of Libra Coin have pointed to the advantages of the new coin in terms of opening more opportunities for online commerce, the scope for using for micropayments by those without bank accounts, and the attendant benefits in paying for digital content.

2.65   Understanding the regulatory environment, though, will be crucial to correctly predicting the success of Libra Coin. At the time of writing, it is anticipated that Libra Coin will be prohibited in India and China, excluding a third of the world's population from using the currency. Perhaps more significantly, upon the announcement of Libra Coin, Republican Maxine Walters, the Chairwoman of the US House of Representatives' Financial Services Committee, requested that Facebook halt development of the cryptocurrency:

> 'Facebook has data on billions of people and has repeatedly shown a disregard for the protection and careful use of this data. It has also exposed Americans to malicious and fake accounts from bad actors, including Russian intelligence and transnational traffickers. Facebook has also been fined large sums and remains under a Federal Trade Commission consent order for deceiving consumers and failing to keep consumer data private, and has also been sued by the government for violating fair housing laws on its advertising platform.

With the announcement that it plans to create a cryptocurrency, Facebook is continuing its unchecked expansion and extending its reach into the lives of its users. The cryptocurrency market lacks a clear regulatory framework to provide strong protections for investors, consumers, and the economy. Regulators should see this as a wake-up call to get serious about privacy and national security concerns, cybersecurity risks, and trading risks that are posted by cryptocurrencies. Given the company's troubled past, I am requesting that Facebook agree to a moratorium on any movement forward on developing a cryptocurrency until Congress and regulators have the opportunity to examine these issues and take action.'

The protection that the US House of Representatives needs to extend to investors such as Visa and MasterCard is likely to be minimal. However, the political appetite to protect smaller investors, and the privacy of consumers, may determine the level of regulation applied to Libra Coin and the future cryptocurrency market. Libra Coin may determine the future of cryptocurrencies, even if its development goes no further than an announcement in a White Paper. This book provides an understanding of the present regulatory context across the world to better predict future development.

Chapter 3

Regulatory and legal challenges

REGULATORY CHALLENGES

Cryptoassets

3.1   The Cryptoassets Taskforce Report published in October 2018[1] has set out what it envisages the regulatory challenges facing cryptoassets currently are, and what they will be. Cryptoassets are used, traded and stored both through blockchain technology and wider distributed ledger technology ('DLT'):

> 'A cryptoasset is a cryptographically secured digital representation or contractual rights that uses some type of DLT and can be transferred, stored or traded electronically.'[2]

3.2   Although not all DLTs use cryptoassets, their regulation is hugely important, as the creation, investment and trading of cryptoassets is what has led to the increasing prominence of blockchain and distributed ledger technology. The use of cryptoassets will no doubt continue to grow using this technological platform, and therefore how they are currently regulated and the potential legal risks they pose is vitally important for both UK and international markets.

3.3   The Taskforce has broken down cryptoassets into three broad categories:[3]

1   Exchange tokens – these are used as a means of exchange or for investment. They are most frequently referred to as 'cryptocurrencies' such as Bitcoin.

2   Security tokens – these are a 'specified investment' as set out in the Financial Services and Markets Act 2000 (Regulated Activities) Order 2001. They provide rights such as entitlement to a share of future profits or ownership. They may also be transferable securities or financial instruments under the EU's Markets in Financial Instruments Directive II.

3   Utility tokens – these can be redeemed for access to a specific product or service that will be provided by a DLT platform.

---

1 Cryptoassets Taskforce Report (October 2018), https://assets.publishing.service.gov.uk/government/uploads/system/uploads/attachment_data/file/752070/cryptoassets_taskforce_final_report_final_web.pdf. See **Appendix 2**.
2 Ibid, para 2.10.
3 Ibid, para 2.11.

Regulation of cryptoassets

3.4

> 'Whether and what regulation applies to a particular cryptoasset instrument or activity can only be decided on a case-by-case basis.'[4]

3.5   Therefore, cryptoassets that are being used to facilitate payment services may be regulated, whereas the cryptoassets being used as a capital-raising tool may not be.

3.6   The exchange of cryptocurrencies, such as Bitcoin, is unregulated, as the Payment Services Regulations 2017 only cover fiat funds and, as cryptocurrencies have not been recognised by the UK Government as being currency or money, such exchanges are unregulated.[5]

3.7   Conversely, where cryptoassets are used as an intermediary in cross-border transactions (eg GBP–Bitcoin–USD), these transactions will be regulated as money remittances under the Payment Services Regulations.[6]

3.8   Even if certain activities relating to cryptoassets are technically unregulated, the Financial Conduct Authority still expect businesses to comply with certain regulatory provisions that instil a more general ethos as to how businesses should conduct their activities:[7] the Principles for Business, the Senior Managers and Certification Regime, the System and Controls Provision, and the Financial Promotions rules all contain high-level rules and provisions that businesses and senior management members must abide by. For example, the Principles for Business contain 11 rules that all FCA-regulated businesses must adhere to, which includes when conducting any unregulated activities.[8]

3.9   The Taskforce has recognised that, when the regulatory perimeters were being drawn up for a business' financial activities, the use of cryptoassets was not considered.[9] Therefore, although certain regulations do cover the use of cryptoassets, it is more by chance that they do rather than being custom-made for them. This is, and will continue to prove, a problem for regulatory bodies and indeed everyone who uses cryptoassets, as many activities involving cryptoassets remain unregulated. The Taskforce has identified this issue but it remains to be seen exactly what will be done about it.

3.10   The Taskforce offers some insight into what is currently planned on tackling such regulatory gaps. For example, the 'FCA will consult on a prohibition of the sale to retail consumers of all derivatives referencing exchange

---

4   Ibid, para 2.26.
5   Ibid, Chart 2.A: Centralised and distributed ledgers, p 9.
6   Ibid, Chart 2.A: Centralises and distributed ledgers, p 9.
7   Ibid, para 2.29.
8   Ibid, para 2.29.
9   Ibid, para 2.32.

tokens, such as Bitcoin'. Further, the FCA and the Government will undertake further consultations during 2019 to consider how the regulatory perimeter can be, or whether it should be, extended to regulate for further uses of cryptoassets, such as initial coin offerings.[10]

Regulation of DLT

3.11   The Taskforce believes that the UK's regulatory approach to DLT is sufficient and well-suited to supporting its development in financial services.[11]

3.12   The Bank of England is confident that the renewed Real-Time Gross Settlement service (a service that holds accounts for banks, building societies and other institutions) will be compatible with DLT.[12]

LEGAL CHALLENGES

Criminal

3.13   It is difficult, when looking at illegal activity taking place on the blockchain, not to get bombarded with information regarding the use of bitcoin. Blockchain is very much in the shadows behind bitcoin and its notoriety.

3.14   As blockchain is still in its infancy (with regard to our overall understanding of it), a lot of the articles related to blockchain and criminal law focus on what blockchain could do. Therefore, it is relatively speculative.

3.15   As transactions can be sent/received anonymously, illegal activity could be taking place on the network without their identity being disclosed or apparent. The anonymity therefore carries potential for criminal secrecy.

3.16   Microsoft founder, Bill Gates, has recently commented on how the anonymity that cryptocurrencies, Bitcoin and initial coin offerings ('ICOs') offer can create difficulties for the pursuit of criminals by law enforcement agencies.

3.17   Bitcoin is not completely anonymous, as its value proposition includes 'censorship resistance'.[13] Due to Bitcoin lacking total anonymity, a preference for cryptocurrencies with 'privacy features that make them more difficult to track using blockchain analysis techniques' have developed, such as ZCash, Dash and

---

10 Ibid, paras 5.15–5.19.

11 Ibid, para 3.20.

12 Ibid, Box 3.J: Bank of England – RTGS renewal programme, pp 29–30.

13 Torpey, K. (2018), 'Bill Gates: I Don't Think Bitcoin's Anonymity Is A Good Thing'. Available online at: www.forbes.com/sites/ktorpey/2018/02/27/bill-gates-i-dont-think-bitcoins-anonymity-is-a-good-thing/#48e93a131395.

Monero.[14] Monero is now the 'fifth-largest by market capitalization'[15] and is used predominantly for dark web transactions.[16]

3.18   The argument, however, concerning the balance of anonymity and control is provocative:

- Do we want complete freedom and anonymity with regard to our financial activity?

- Conversely, do we want organisations, governments or security agencies to be monitoring all global financial activity?

3.19   These arguments are outside the scope of this work, but issues such as these are not new in terms of the effects of advancing technology. The law always has met, and will continue to meet, the challenges and it is not healthy for new technology to be spurned because of fears of how to deal with its consequences.

Money laundering

3.20   One of the single biggest areas cited, by those concerned with the proliferation of blockchain and the cryptocurrencies it supports, is that it will increase and facilitate money laundering. Leaving aside the obvious point that the very essence of blockchain is to create an immutable record of each transaction, some may argue that this is the very antithesis of the money launderer's desire; more and more research is being conducted into how blockchain can actually assist in anti-money laundering efforts.

3.21   The argument that the blockchain facilitates secret activity can be challenged in the very nature of the technology. Blockchain creates an immutable audit trail of every transaction recorded where, on a public blockchain, it is possible to identify the parties. This 'transparency', it is argued, is enhanced by the validation and time-stamping process.

3.22   Notwithstanding the regulatory challenges faced by public blockchains in particular, this argument, has, in our view, validity. Bear in mind that Bitcoin cannot currently run without blockchain technology and so it is right to point out that a time-stamped verified public online record is less attractive to a money

---

14 Fanusie, Y.J. & Robinson, T. (2018), 'Bitcoin Laundering: An Analysis of Illicit Flows into Digital Currency Services'. Available online at: https://cdn2.hubspot.net/hubfs/3883533/downloads/Bitcoin%20Laundering.pdf?__hssc=222901956.3.1516201470218&__hstc=222901956.b7d6531ad164bec182c043c05b5510ba.1516201470217.1516201470217.1516201470217.1&__hsfp=3478668143&hsCtaTracking=66a034a3-865d-481a-8e56-f510419fde74%7C840a3208-7448-4fe6-ad03-a3731f462b7d.

15 Rizzo, P. (2017) 'Drugs, Code and ICOs: Monero's Long Road to Blockchain Respect'. Available online at: https://www.coindesk.com/drugs-code-icos-moneros-long-road-blockchain-mainstream/.

16 Hodgson, C. (2018) 'Crypto Expert: The Anonymity of Cryptocurrency Users Will Not Last Forever'. Available online at: https://nordic.businessinsider.com/cambridge-academic-cryptocurrency-users-anonymity-will-not-last-2018-1/.

launderer than the deposit of cash in a bag at an isolated location. The verification process by miners, who have financial inducements to ensure reliability and security of transactions, should also not be ignored in this debate. It is fair to say that much of the bad publicity over cryptocurrency, but particularly over blockchain, occurred historically, when fear of potentially disruptive technology was at its highest.

Significantly, Silvio Schembri, Malta's Junior Minister for Financial Services, Digital Economy and Innovation, in stating that Malta has opted for legislation to manage the concern regarding fraudulent ICOs, expressed the following view, 'When certain countries say that cryptocurrencies are being used for money laundering or for terrorism (and the bad things associated with the black economy), I state the argument that money laundering is already being done with fiat. Furthermore, fiat is not traceable, while cryptocurrency is. Having said that, if the connectors and people behind a specific cryptocurrency have bad intentions, then yes, crypto can be used for harmful purposes' therefore 'having proper regulation that will not stifle innovation will address these issues'.[17]

3.23   In the light of the implementation of the fifth Anti-Money Laundering Directive, the Taskforce has confirmed not only that the UK will abide by the Directive but that it will go beyond its requirements, consulting on the following:[18]

- '• exchange services between different cryptoassets, to prevent anonymous "layering" of funds to mask their origin;
- platforms that facilitate peer-to-peer exchange of cryptoassets, which could enable anonymous transfers of funds between individuals;
- cryptoassets ATMs, which could be used anonymously to purchase cryptoassets;
- non-custodian wallet providers that function similarly to custodian wallet providers, which may otherwise facilitate the anonymous storage and transfer of cryptoassets. Consultation on this area will include considering technological feasibility.'

3.24   In addition, the Government will consider whether it will require firms based outside the UK to comply with these regulations when providing services to UK consumers.[19]

3.25   Time will tell whether the UK's ambition comes to fruition and if any of these steps are actually implemented and to what extent.

---

17 Wolfson, R. (2018), 'Silvio Schembri Explains How Malta Has Become The World's Blockchain Island'. Available online at: www.forbes.com/sites/rachelwolfson/2018/07/31/silvio-schembri-explains-how-malta-has-become-the-worlds-blockchain-island/#2fe2c532cad7.
18 Cryptoassets Taskforce Report (October 2018), para 5.7.
19 Ibid, para 5.8.

Data privacy/protection

3.26   What makes blockchain so unique and powerful is its permanency and the transparency it provides. Therefore, one can assume that it will naturally not be compliant with data protection laws. However, it is not as clear cut as this.

3.27   One first needs to assess whether 'personal data' is even being processed. Article 4 of the General Data Protection Regulation ('GDPR') defines 'personal data' as:

> 'any information relating to an identified or identifiable natural person ("data subject"); an identifiable natural person is one who can be identified, directly or indirectly, in particular by reference to an identifier such as a name, an identification number, location data, an online identifier or to one or more factors specific to the physical, physiological, genetic, mental, economic, cultural or social identity of that natural person.'

3.28   When a transaction is carried out on the blockchain, each user is identified by a public key. This key does not reveal the identity of the user, but the user's transactions can be monitored by reference to their public key.[20]

Does a user's public key constitute 'personal data'?

Example

The Court of Justice of the European Union dealt with a similar question in its preliminary ruling in *Patrick Breyer v Bundesrepublik Deutschland* (Case C-582/14 – 19 October 2016). In this case, one of the questions asked by the Federal Court of Justice in Germany was whether a dynamic IP address (one which is only held temporarily by a device when connected to a network) is 'personal data' even where further data held by a third party is necessary to identify the individual. The Court of Justice ruled that such data could be held to be 'personal data' in limited circumstances where legal means can be used to combine the data to identify an individual.

3.29   Drawing a parallel with the blockchain and the public key, it is arguable that the 'public key' can be considered 'personal data' as long as one has the lawful means to identify a user. However, as discussed elsewhere in this work, it is our view that public keys are pseudonymous data for the purposes of GDPR.

3.30   In certain situations, the identity of the user will be obvious, because he/she will have revealed himself/herself on purpose (for example, if he/she wishes to establish his/her IP rights). In such situations and in all others where

---

20 www.hlengage.com/_uploads/downloads/5425GuidetoblockchainV9FORWEB.pdf, p 9.

the blockchain is processing personal data, the strength of data protection on the blockchain will be called into question.

3.31 Due to the transparent nature of blockchains, all transactions executed via a smart contract 'are propagated across a peer-to-peer network, rendering them publicly visible to network nodes'. This has several legal effects. Smart contracts (discussed later in this chapter) may lack the required confidentiality and the necessity for either some data to be stored off chain, or the use of an administrator will be required to ensure compliance with regulation and to evidence the intentions of the parties.

3.32 Who is responsible for protecting data that is recorded in a blockchain, and who is responsible for complying with regulations such as GDPR?

3.33 The central tenet of principle which enshrines current data regulation is that compliance must be achieved by selected individuals. The primary responsibility is vested in the data controller. As has been alluded to, in a permissionless blockchain, this entity may be very difficult to detect. Who could it be? Would each of the individual nodes be a data controller? How, even if in practical terms, could that be achieved? Would obligations be able to be enforced? Would each node have to be forced into compliance? In the event of non-compliance of one, would that lead to the shutting down of each of the nodes? What about jurisdictional issues of such an attempt at sanction? Who is the appropriate supervisory authority to administer the fine?

3.34 All of these issues illustrate the difficulties of decentralisation and compliance with regulations aimed at centralised entities. It is easier when dealing with permissioned blockchains. This would allow the appointment of an administrator which could go some way to dealing with these concerns. That would, however, be contrary to the principle of decentralisation upon which blockchain technology is built.

3.35 The Taskforce has highlighted the potential incompatibility of the DLT in general with GDPR with regard to the right of erasure under Article 17. The ability of the blockchain and DLT to comply with GDPR and data protection laws has yet to be fully tested. For a full discussion of this topic, see **Chapter 9**.

Ownership of IP of information contained in the blockchain

3.36 The same issues relating to a lack of centralised governance apply in respect of public blockchain to ownership of the intellectual property of the transactional information in the nodes. This is not of simply academic importance, as legal issues in respect of ownership of data create rights and obligations. Blockchain technology, whilst it can allow for the secure distribution of content to authorised users, can also be an agent for distribution of material that infringes copyright. Who and where to sue are relevant considerations.

3.37   There is also the issue of how liability is attributed. For example, if there is an image stored on the blockchain, 'what liability is associated with a node's storage of that image – albeit in the form of an encrypted block on the chain? Is that direct copyright infringement? Contributory infringement?'.[21]

3.38   These are questions that do not have answers as yet and will, of necessity, have to be resolved by the courts at some point in the future.

3.39   The blockchain, however, can also provide significant benefits to intellectual property owners.

3.40   There are advantages to using blockchain in this field as well as the difficulties outlined above. Due to the immutability of blockchain, registration of work creates a full proof record of ownership. It also aids any subsequent licensing or assignment of the work, creating a permanent record in a similar way.

3.41   Using the Proof of Existence platform is a good example of the use of blockchain technology in order to evidence ownership. The process is achieved by the owner anonymously uploading a document, and a hash being generated providing proof of ownership, thus achieving an audit trail in the event of subsequent dispute.

3.42   Blockchain confirms who the creators are, when things were created, and puts it all in an immutable form so nothing can be edited or questioned.

What is the legal status of decentralised autonomous organisations?

3.43   Decentralised autonomous organisations ('DAOs') are used to execute smart contracts and record activity on the blockchain. For more information on DAOs, see **Chapter 11**.

3.44   They are therefore a quasi-tribunal in the event of a dispute. Whether they welcome that responsibility or seek the obligations it may impose is an unanswered question. What is their legal status? It is unlikely that they have any since they, in the absence of agreement, do not derive any from statute or case law. As we discuss below, the governance of the arrangements made under smart contracts is best catered for in an orthodox written agreement. A good example of the dangers of the use of 'unincorporated virtual organisations', such as DAOs, is set out below.

3.45   The 'SEC issues a Section 21(a) report of its investigation into an offering of digital tokens by "The DAO", an unincorporated virtual organisation … the SEC used the opportunity to warn others engaged in similar activities that

21 Ibid.

an unregistered sale of blockchain tokens can, depending on the circumstances, be an illegal public offering of securities'.[22]

Is the data on the blockchain 'property' for the purposes of the Law of Property Act 1925?

3.46   The key to this dates back to the definitions in the Law of Property Act 1925.

3.47   The definition of property contained therein is '"Property" includes anything in action, and any interest in real or personal property'.

3.48   Many property transactions have to be evidenced in writing. Is code 'writing' for these purposes? The Interpretation Act 1978 provides that '"in writing" includes typing, printing, lithography, photography and other modes of representing or reproducing words in visible form'. In our view, it must be so included as it is representing words in this context. In those circumstances, it is a reasonable argument to suggest that the data on the blockchain is a form of property and the code associated with it is the 'writing' required.

Jurisdictional issues

3.49   Public blockchains have nodes which are often located in various jurisdictions across the world. This feature, once again a badge of decentralisation, causes issues with recent data regulation. GDPR applies to the processing of personal data affecting EU citizens wherever the processing is taking place, as well as other EU-related jurisdictional provisions. The effect is that the Regulation will bite on blockchains with only passing links to the EU. However, once it bites, all of the issues relating to compliance are present. Further, all of the data transfer provisions, where minimum standards must be met, come into play. Whilst, again, a private blockchain may govern such transmission from a central point under binding terms and conditions, that is unlikely to be the case for public blockchains. The result, again, is a lack of ability to comply.

What is the effect of this?

3.50   The creation of rights under GDPR for data subjects of the EU includes ensuring consent for the processing of their personal data and ensuring data is minimised, amended or removed. The issue of consent, and effective consent to boot, can already be seen to be of the greatest difficulty in a public blockchain, because of the reasons already set out in this chapter. The issues of rectification

---

22 Polk, D. (2017), 'SEC Confirms That Some Initial Coin Offerings Are Illegal Unregistered Securities Offerings'. Available online at: www.law.ox.ac.uk/business-law-blog/blog/2017/08/sec-confirms-some-initial-coin-offerings-are-illegal-unregistered.

and erasure are fully set out in **Chapter 9**. Data minimisation is a central tenet of GDPR. It is, by its very nature, completely contrary to the principles behind a DLT. The obligation in Article 5 of GDPR to be highly selective in the purposes behind data collection, and the importance that no more data than is necessary is collected, are at odds with the aims of a continuously expanding DLT block system. Once again, the obvious tension between regulation designed for traditional centralised entities and the brave new world of decentralisation is seen here.

3.51   It is our view that there is a very strong case to be made to have an orthodox contract alongside any smart contract, to deal with issues such as jurisdiction, data collection and minimisation.

3.52   These jurisdictional and related issues once again fortify the argument that having a 'non-smart contract' alongside a smart one would greatly help clarify matters should a dispute arise.

CONTRACTS

Smart contracts – what are they?

3.53   A smart contract is a self-executing piece of computer code. It consists of a set of pre-defined rules that automatically enforce the terms of the contract. When X happens, Y automatically happens without any further action from the parties needing to be taken.

Who are the parties to a 'smart contract'?

3.54   The parties in a smart contract are those who are written into the code as being parties, as it would be in a normal contract.

3.55   There may be simply two parties to the contract (eg Buyer A and Seller B), or there may be multiple parties in addition to this (eg Shipper C and Manufacturer D).

3.56   A smart contract would work like this:

Example

Buyer A puts money into an escrow account for Seller B. Seller B is using Shipper C to deliver the products. When Buyer A receives the products, the money held in escrow will be released to Seller B and Shipper C. If the products are not delivered by the pre-determined date, then the money held in escrow will be returned to Buyer A or whatever else has been agreed between the parties if such a situation occurs. For example, Buyer A may receive a discount instead. After the transaction is complete, Manufacturer D is notified that it needs to create more of the same products to ensure there is sufficient stock in place.[23]

What are the benefits of a 'smart contract'?

3.57   It is said, with force, that smart contracts have the advantages of certainty whereby they are executed through a digital process and efficiency in removing intermediaries. That, whilst true, is also a potential source of weakness.

What are the ingredients for a 'smart contract'?

3.58   The normal ingredients to create an ordinary contract (offer, acceptance, intention to create legal relations, and consideration) are still needed to ensure that a smart contract is actually a binding legal contract. If any of these fundamental ingredients are not present, a 'smart contract' will be nothing more than a process which can be amended or altered by those who wish to do so.

3.59   However, there are additional factors that need to be taken into consideration when creating smart contracts: certainty of computer language, efficiency in terms of computer use, and sufficient security to thwart potential hackers. From a computationally effective point of view, these are all important. However, from a legal point of view, these features may not be of the utmost importance.

Is a 'smart contract' sufficient to govern a contractual relationship on its own?

3.60   Parties to a smart contract may intend, to use a term of art, 'to create legal relations'. They may assess that the stages represented by the code created cater for all potential eventualities. However:

*   How is jurisdiction to be addressed?

*   Who owns the data on the blockchain to which the smart contract may have regard?

*   Are the intentions of the parties sufficiently set out?

*   What happens if the factual situation requires a change to the contractual relationship?

---

23 Example adapted from www.ibm.com/blogs/blockchain/2018/07/what-are-smart-contracts-on-blockchain.

3.61   All of these matters are addressed in **Chapter 9**, but it is our view that smart contracts alone cannot be sufficient to govern complex international arrangements.

Where does the liability fall under a 'smart contract'?

3.62   Smart contracts, by their nature, should make it tougher for agreements to be breached, as the transactions are carried out automatically through the written code. Well-drafted smart contracts should cover all possible eventualities. However, it cannot be forgotten that smart contracts still require human input, at least at the creation stage, and it is likely that a smart contract will not be able to cover all scenarios that may arise.

3.63   For example, it may be written into the code that neither party will be liable for failure to meet their obligations in cases of force majeure or acts of God. However, the code might not state what such instances are, and it will still be between the parties to determine if such an event constitutes force majeure or an act of God. This is where 'non-smart contracts' can be particularly helpful (see above).

3.64   Further, in private law:

> 'the issue of liability needs to be addressed if the contract has been miscoded such that it doesn't achieve the intent of the parties … In addition, the parties will need to agree on applicable law, jurisdiction, general principles of proper governance, dispute resolution, privacy and the means of digital identity.'[24]

3.65   It will need to be agreed between the parties who is liable for the writing of the code. Law firms will most likely delegate this function to third-party tech teams. If the code is drafted so as to lead to unintended consequences for the parties, it could have a significant impact on the parties and the potential liability of the code writers. It is clear, therefore, that smart contracts cannot function properly in isolation without other written or oral agreements governing them.

3.66   The unique issues facing lawyers advising on arrangements based on smart contracts will require them to consider matters such as the ownership of data, IP ownership, jurisdiction and dispute resolution.

---

24 Deloitte (2018), 'Blockchain: Legal Implications, Questions, Opportunities and Risks'. Available online at: https://info.deloitte.com/rs/231-YWE-658/images/Blockchain%20WP%20 March%202018_.pdf.

Chapter 4

Global regulation: UK and EU member states

CHOICE OF JURISDICTION

4.1   Evidently, one of the chief issues which surrounds resolving a dispute in civil matters (as opposed to criminal) is who has jurisdiction when there are features of an action or actions which straddle different countries and jurisdictions. There has consequently developed a widely accepted practice of inserting a clause where the parties submit to the exclusive jurisdiction of a particular country. Once that has been freely selected, the courts, certainly in England and Wales, and in many other global jurisdictions, will be slow to interfere.

4.2   In a case decided in the UK, *Donohue v Armco Inc*,[1] the issue of the enforceability of exclusive jurisdiction clauses had to be decided along with several other matters not relevant for present purposes. That case concerned a group of companies incorporated in the United States and Singapore who appealed against the granting of an injunction restraining the prosecution of proceedings in the United States which arose from alleged fraudulent activity. The basis of the fraud was alleged to relate to a management buy-out which was governed by a sale and purchase agreement and two transfer agreements. Each of the agreements contained a clause purportedly giving exclusive jurisdiction to the English courts. Following the commencement of the proceedings in the United States, the defendant sought to invoke the clause and applied for an anti-suit injunction.

4.3   The House of Lords, the highest UK court (now the Supreme Court), allowed the appeal. At paragraph 24 of the judgment, Lord Bingham said:

> 'The general rule is clear: where parties have bound themselves by an exclusive jurisdiction clause effect should ordinarily be given to that obligation in the absence of strong reasons for departing from it. Whether a party can show strong reasons, sufficient to displace the other party's prima facie entitlement to enforce the contractual bargain, will depend on all the facts and circumstances of the particular case.'

4.4   In cases involving blockchain, with identical nodes across multiple locations, where information and property will transcend varied laws and territories, the advantage of inserting an exclusive jurisdiction clause should provide clarity as to the governing law and jurisdiction. That choice will, however, be complex, given the competing regulatory regimes, the need to factor

---

1   [2001] UKHL 64.

in the impact of cybersecurity/ data protection laws on the venture, and other legal concepts that may come into play in the eventuality of any dispute.

4.5   The welcome news is that a race has developed with jurisdictions seeking to be regarded as *the place for* blockchain, cryptocurrency and innovative tech business. That global race will likely lead to ever more inducements and an evolving regulatory and legal landscape that is increasingly certain and beneficial.

DECLARATION FOR EUROPEAN BLOCKCHAIN PARTNERSHIP

4.6   The Declaration for European Blockchain Partnership has now been signed by 24 countries:

Austria	Belgium	Bulgaria	Czech Republic	Estonia
Finland	France	Germany	Ireland	Latvia
Luxembourg	Malta	Netherlands	Norway	Poland
Portugal	Slovakia	Slovenia	Spain	Sweden
United Kingdom	Greece	Romania	Lithuania	

4.7   Greece and Romania have both joined since the launch.[2]

4.8   Lithuania was not listed on the European Commission's website as signing the Declaration; however, it is in the image from the signing ceremony and is listed on every other website. Therefore, we are assuming that Lithuania was missed out by mistake.

4.9   The Partnership aims to ensure that Europe continues 'to play a leading role in the development and roll-out of blockchain technologies':[3]

> 'The decentralised and collaborative nature of blockchain and its applications allows exploiting the full scale of the Digital Single Market from the outset. Close cooperation between Member States can help avoiding fragmented approaches and can ensure interoperability and wider deployment of blockchain-based services. The Partnership will contribute to the creation of an enabling environment, in full compliance with EU laws and with clear governance models that will help services using blockchain flourish across Europe.'[4]

The EU Blockchain Observatory and Forum

4.10   This body invested more than 80 million euros in blockchain projects. DECODE and MHMD are two key projects that have been invested in:

---

2   European Commission 2018, 'European Countries Join Blockchain Partnership'. Available online at: https://ec.europa.eu/digital-single-market/en/news/european-countries-join-blockchain-partnership.
3   Ibid.
4   Ibid.

- 'DECODE is a project exploring and piloting new technologies that give people more control over how they store, manage and use personal data generated online. It will use blockchain technology to create tools that will give people ownership of the data which they and the devices they own generate'.[5]

- MHMD: 'Medical data is generally stored in separate locations, and is not always easily accessible to patients and research institutions. It can be vulnerable to security breaches and identity theft – and at the same time scientists do not always have access to data for biomedical research and the development of new treatments. My Health My Data (MHMD) aims to use blockchain technology to enable medical data to be stored and transmitted safely and effectively'.[6]

4.11   They have allocated a further 300 million euros to invest in blockchain by 2020.

REGULATION IN THE UK

4.12   The trade and exchange of cryptocurrencies in the United Kingdom (UK) is currently unregulated.

4.13   In general terms, foreign exchange (Forex) brokers within the UK fall under the regulation of the Financial Conduct Authority ('FCA'). All regulated brokers are required to conform to FCA guidelines, by maintaining segregated accounts for client funds and company funds. The FCA further mandates that all regulated Forex brokers must maintain at least £1 million in operating capital, based upon the number of traders currently registered to their platform and depositing at their company.

4.14   However, the FCA has stated explicitly that cryptocurrencies are neither currencies nor commodities for regulatory purposes under the Markets in Financial Instruments Directive II ('MiFID II').[7]

4.15   If a company is dealing in derivatives based upon cryptocurrencies, or tokens issued through an initial coin offering ('ICO' – see **Chapter 7**), or arranging transactions in, advising on or providing other services that amount to 'regulated activities' in relation to these derivatives, FCA authorisation will be required. Examples of financial derivatives based upon cryptocurrencies include:

---

5   European Commission 2018, 'Blockchain to Give People More Control About their Data'. Available online at: https://ec.europa.eu/digital-single-market/en/news/blockchain-give-people-more-control-about-their-data.

6   European Commission 2018, 'Blockchain to Enable Medical Data to be Stored and Transmitted Safely and Effectively'. Available online at: https://ec.europa.eu/digital-single-market/en/news/blockchain-enable-medical-data-be-stored-and-transmitted-safely-and-effectively.

7   Financial Conduct Authority, *Cryptocurrency derivatives*, www.fca.org.uk/news/statements/cryptocurrency-derivatives, 6 April 2018.

- **cryptocurrency futures** – a derivative contract in which each party agrees to exchange cryptocurrency at a future date and at a price agreed by both parties;

- **cryptocurrency contracts for differences ('CFDs')** – a cash-settled derivative contract in which the parties to the contract seek to secure a profit or avoid a loss by agreeing to exchange the difference in price between the value of the cryptocurrency CFD contract at its outset and at its termination; or

- **cryptocurrency options** – a contract which grants the beneficiary the right to acquire or dispose of cryptocurrencies.

4.16 'Regulated activities' are defined within section 21 of, and Schedule 2 to, the Financial Services and Markets Act 2000 ('FSMA'), and include: dealing, arranging, managing or advising in investments.

4.17 Therefore, any person who wishes to undertake a regulated activity with regard to cryptocurrency derivatives must be registered with the FCA as an 'authorised person' or an 'exempt person'. Carrying out a regulated activity without being registered is a criminal offence for which the maximum sentence is two years' imprisonment, an unlimited fine or both.[8]

Are you buying or selling actual cryptocurrencies?	• Cryptocurrencies are currently unregulated in the United Kingdom. Actions which would otherwise be 'regulated activities' do not require registration if dealing with regard to actual cryptocurrencies. • If the underlying product is a derivative of a cryptocurrency FCA registration may be required.
What is the underlying product?	• Cryptocurrencies which form the basis of any of the following require FCA regulation: Securities; Instruments creating or acknowledging indebtedness; Instruments giving entitlement to investments; Certificates representing securities; Units in collective investment schemes; Options; Futures; Contracts for differences; Contracts of insurance; Deposits; or Rights in investments • Tokens generated through ICOs which form the basis of any of the above also require FCA regulation.
What activity am I performing in relation to the product?	• Conduct with regard to any of the following is a regulated activity: Dealing in investments; Arranging deals in investments; Deposit taking; Safekeeping and administration of assets; Managing investments; Investment advice; Establishing collective investment schemes; Using computer-based systems for giving investment instructions
Am I an exempt person?	• A list of those who are exempt is contained within the Financial Services and Markets Act 2000 (Exemption) Order 2001 • Exempt persons are clearly defined within the order and include, with regard to some regulated activities: municipal banks, enterprise schemes and charities. Unless you fall within the specified categories within the order FCA regulation is required.
How do I apply for FCA authorisation?	• Guidance with regard to FCA authorisation can be found on the FCA website: https://www.fca.org.uk/firms/authorisation/how-to-apply

---

8   See Financial Services and Markets Act 2000, ss 19 and 23.

What are the requirements of being an authorised person?

4.18   Authorised persons are required to abide by the provisions contained within the FCA Handbook: www.handbook.fca.org.uk/handbook.

4.19   These provisions are extensive and varied, depending upon the regulated activity within which the individual or company is operating. For example, a company which has formed a collective investment scheme ('CIS') for the purchase of cryptocurrencies would be required to consider the 'Specialist sourcebooks for Collective Investment Schemes'. However, a technology company which provides order routing, post-trade processing, or other services to those trading in cryptocurrency CFDs would be subject to a more light-touch regulatory scheme and would need to consider the 'Handbook Guides for Service companies'.

4.20   The FCA Handbook should be considered in some detail once an individual or company has determined that they are required to be an authorised person.

How is currency regulated across the EU?

4.21   The Markets in Financial Instruments Directive ('MiFID') is the EU legislation that regulates firms who provide services to clients linked to 'financial instruments' (shares, bonds, units in collective investment schemes and derivatives), and the venues where those instruments are traded.

4.22   Firms covered by MiFID will be authorised and regulated in their 'home state' (in the UK, the FCA is the regulator for authorisation under MiFID). Once a firm has been authorised, it will be able to use the MiFID passport to provide services to customers in other EU member states. These services will be regulated in their home state by the regulator in that member state.

4.23   MiFID requires firms to categorise clients as 'eligible counterparties', professional clients or retail clients, which have increasing levels of protection. An eligible counterparty (for example, an investment bank) has less protection under MiFID than a retail client. Clear procedures must be in place to categorise clients and assess their suitability for each type of investment product; however, only verified and appropriate investment advice, or suggested financial transactions, may be provided to any client, whether an eligible counterparty or retail client. The consideration of the client's best interest is captured within MiFID, which requires information to be recorded regarding accepting client orders, and how orders from different clients may have been aggregated.

4.24   On 20 October 2011, the European Commission adopted formal proposals for a Directive on markets in financial instruments repealing Directive 2004/39/EC of the European Parliament and of the Council ('MiFID II'), and for a Regulation on markets in financial instruments ('MiFIR'), which would also amend the proposed European Market Infrastructure Regulation ('EMIR') on over-the-counter ('OTC') derivatives, central counterparties and trade repositories. Both MiFID II and MiFIR entered into force on 2 July 2014. The initial date for implementation by the member states was 3 January 2017; however, in February 2016 the European Commission delayed this until 3 January 2018 to allow for the building of IT systems to enable enforcement of the new package.

4.25   In the context of a trade in a cryptocurrency future or CFD, MiFID and MiFID II have three practical applications:

i.   **Pre-trade**: MiFID requires traders to provide the best price for the product. Operators of continuous order-matching systems must make aggregated order information available at the five best price levels on the buy and sell side; and for quote-driven markets, the best bids and offers of market makers must be made available.

ii.   **Best execution**: MiFID II requires firms to take all sufficient steps to obtain the best possible result in the execution of an order for a client. The best possible result is not limited to execution price but also includes cost, speed, likelihood of execution and likelihood of settlement and any other factors deemed relevant. MiFID II's 'all sufficient steps' test sets a somewhat higher standard than the previous 'all reasonable steps' standard in MiFID.

iii. **Post-trade**: MiFID requires firms to publish the price, volume and time of all trades, even if executed outside of a regulated market, unless certain requirements are met to allow for deferred publication.

4.26   A company which trades CFDs is categorised within MiFID as a 'systematic internaliser'. A systematic internaliser is a firm that executes orders from its clients against its own book or against orders from other clients. MiFID treats systematic internalisers as mini-exchanges; therefore, they are subject to pre-trade and post-trade transparency requirements, as set out above.

MIFID II CONTROVERSIES

4.27   MiFID II took effect in January 2018, to improve the functioning of financial markets in light of the financial crisis and to strengthen investor protection. However, it has not been without its detractors. Within days of coming into effect, Intercontinental Exchange ('ICE') announced plans to transfer trading in 245 energy futures contracts from London to the US, putting transactions under the oversight of US, rather than European, regulators.[9] Some analysts believe the impact of MiFID II will lead to global investment research expenditures falling by as much as $1.5bn annually when the rules come into force.[10] This fall comes

---

9   Meyer, Gregory, and Stafford, Philip, 'London loses oil futures listings as MiFID II bites', *Financial Times*, 11 January 2019.

10 Pearlman, Elisabeth, 'Banks want to delay a key part of the MiFID II legislation ahead of next month's deadline'. Verdict UK. GlobalData PLC. 15 December 2017.

as a result of MiFID II severely restricting asset managers' ability to obtain investment research with client commissions.

4.28   However, it is the 'Commodity derivatives: introduction of position limits and reporting regime' which will most directly impact upon those trading cryptocurrencies. The position limits and reporting regime for commodity derivatives came into force on 3 January 2018 (see Articles 57 and 58 of MiFID II).[11] The regime aims to prevent market abuse and support orderly pricing and settlement conditions by improving transparency and oversight of financial markets.[12]

4.29   A 'position limit' is the maximum size of a position held by a person in any commodity derivative traded on a European Economic Area ('EEA') trading venue and economically equivalent over the counter ('EEOTC') contracts.

4.30   MiFID II requires competent authorities, in line with the methodology of the European Securities and Markets Authority ('ESMA'), to establish and apply position limits on the size of a net position which a person can hold at all times in commodity derivatives traded on trading venues and EEOTC contracts.

4.31   Competent authorities are required to set position limits for a commodity derivative as per Commission Delegated Regulation (EU) 2017/591. For certain new and illiquid contracts, a distinct approach will be taken, including the application of fixed position limits below certain liquidity thresholds.

4.32   In other words, if the liquidity in a cryptocurrency derivative is low, MiFID II will apply a specific limit to the position that a trader can take within that market. Exceptions can be sought but MiFID II prevents, for example, an individual from taking too great a long or short position on a Bitcoin future or CFD. At the retail level, this is unlikely to have a great impact but, where an investment bank or systematic internaliser is taking a position against their clients, the illiquidity of cryptocurrency derivatives may be relevant.

4.33   In addition to imposing a limit, MiFID II imposes a reporting regime. Position reporting obligations apply to all trading venues that facilitate the trading of commodity derivatives, including cryptocurrency derivatives, and all investment firms trading EEOTC contracts on these financial instruments. Within the UK, trading venues and investment firms can submit position reports through the Market Data Processor System operated by the FCA.[13]

---

11 Directive 2014/65/EU of the European Parliament and of the Council of 15 May 2014 on markets in financial instruments and amending Directive 2002/92/EC and Directive 2011/61/EU (recast) https://eur-lex.europa.eu/legal-content/EN/TXT/PDF/?uri=CELEX:32014L0065&from=EN.

12 Financial Conduct Authority, *Commodity derivatives: introduction of position limits and reporting regime*, first published: 23 May 2016, last updated: 6 April 2018, www.fca.org.uk/markets/mifid-ii/commodity-derivatives, last accessed 18 February 2019.

13 Ibid.

REGULATION IN OTHER EUROPEAN JURISDICTIONS (CASE STUDIES)

4.34   Clearly, the regulatory regimes will vary depending upon the jurisdiction.

Estonia

4.35   Estonia has embraced the blockchain and has moved government records and public services, including voting, to the technology. Significantly, with all of the data being on the blockchain, it is immutable and can only be changed by an authorised person. It is important to remember that Estonia, as part of the European Union, is bound by GDPR.

France

4.36   The French government is apparently resistant to cryptocurrencies, although it is considering the virtual currency position and considering whether it ought to adopt a regulatory regime. The regulators in France are concerned about the high volatility and unregulated nature of cryptocurrencies, but they do appear to be much more positive about the underlying technology. In November 2018, the French regulators, the Prudential Supervisory Authority and the Financial Market Authority issued notices to investors warning of the regulated nature of cryptocurrencies and noting that cryptocurrencies are not defined as financial instruments under French law and consequently fall outside the regulatory perimeter; they are not deemed actual currency ('legal tender') and are not under the regulators' supervision.

4.37   The tenor of the French view appears to be that Bitcoin or cryptocurrency cannot be considered a real currency or a valid means of payment under French law and that it is regarded as a vehicle for speculation, an instrument for illegal activity and money laundering. Significantly, the view seems to be that the conversion of cryptocurrency into 'real currency' should be considered a payment service which consequently could only be formed by payment service providers who were authorised and supervised by the regulator. The regulator (the ACPR) has acknowledged this position and confirmed that entities that engaged in the activity of habitually purchasing or selling cryptocurrency in exchange for actual legal tender must be licensed by them as payment service providers. That said, the regulator does accept that the purchase or sale of investments in cryptocurrencies currently operates outside of any regulated market in France.

4.38   However, the French view of blockchain, the underlying technology, is much more positive. There seems to be real enthusiasm for blockchain technology which could bring material changes to the financial sector as it has the ability to reduce costs and intermediaries. In 2016 an Ordonnance included provisions that permitted the use of blockchain technology for a bond called a 'mini bond'. This ordinance provided the first definition of blockchain in French law, and a further

Ordonnance in 2017 made it possible to use blockchain technology for a much broader range of financial instruments. (Ordonnance 2016-520 of 28 April 2016 permits the use of blockchain technology for mini bonds, and Ordonnance 2017-1674 of 8 December 2017 permits blockchain technology for a range of financial instruments.)

4.39   In France, there is a continuing struggle to decide how best to regulate cryptocurrencies because the current lack of regulation is considered unsuitable and there seems to be broad agreement on the necessity to minimise the legal uses of cryptocurrencies such as money laundering and to provide protection for investors. In March 2018, the Administrator of Economy and Finance announced an upcoming plan that would enable growth and transformation of companies to allow them to launch an ICO to demonstrate their seriousness to investors.

4.40   It is thought that moves in France have been coordinated with Germany, and there have been joint requests for discussion at the G-20 in order that coordinated initiatives are taken at international level. Capital gains from the sale of cryptocurrencies are subject to taxation, and these gains are taxed differently depending on whether the acquisition and sale of the cryptocurrencies is an occasional activity and thus treated as non-commercial profit, or a habitual activity treated as commercial profit. Cryptocurrencies must also be taken into account when calculating the basis for the French wealth tax, and the transfer of cryptocurrencies free of charge from one person to another may be subject to the gift tax.

Malta

4.41   Malta, like Gibraltar, is certainly a market leader when it comes to the cryptocurrency sector. It evidently decided that this was a niche through which Malta could attract talent by providing regulatory clarity and it has sought to label itself, with justification, as 'Blockchain Island'.

4.42   There are three key pieces of legislation:

(i)   the Malta Digital Innovation Authority Act;

(ii)   the Innovative Technology Arrangements and Services Act; and

(iii)   the Virtual Financial Assets Act.

4.43   The Malta Digital Innovation Authority Act ('MDIAA') establishes the Malta Digital Innovation Authority ('MDIA') and details how the MDIA is to promote blockchain in Malta. Significantly, the MDIA has a certification role, in that it certifies DLT platform software and the internal governance. Certification is seen as a means of guaranteeing certainty to consumers, and Malta also regulates to ensure that businesses who are accepted offer their services in a transparent and honest manner.

4.44   The Innovative Technology Arrangements and Services Act ('ITAS') provides criteria and requirements for registering to provide innovative technology arrangements and innovative technology services; these services and those providing them are all regulated by the MDIA. The ITAS allows for auditing and certification of not only software but also the architectures used to provide blockchain and associated smart contracts, token exchanges, decentralised autonomous organisations and beyond, extending to innovative technologies that require certification.

4.45 The Virtual Financial Assets Act ('VFAA') provides a regulatory framework to govern any enterprise that works either directly or indirectly with virtual financial assets. Virtual financial assets are widely defined to include ICOs, token exchanges, portfolio managers, custodian wallet providers, service providers, investment advisers and brokerages. It also provides requirements for white papers relating to ICOs and security token offerings (STOs) which must be delivered to the Malta Financial Services Authority ('MFSA'), and any prospective token issuer must appoint a virtual financial assets agent who must be approved by the MFSA, which is the regulator for the purposes of monitoring the reporting on token offerings.

4.46 These three Acts, together with the Electronic Money regulation, set out the four possible categories of Distributed Ledger Technology Assets ('DLT Assets'). The chief consideration is to decide whether any asset in question is within the VFAA and subject to being within the regulatory perimeter. To determine this, the VFAA allows the MFSA to conduct a Financial Instrument Test ('the Test') for the purpose of categorising a DLT Asset into one of the following categories of DLT Assets:

(i) electronic money;

(ii) financial instruments;

(iii) virtual tokens (or 'utility tokens'); and

(iv) virtual financial assets ('VFAs').

4.47 This set test serves to determine whether the DLT Asset falls to be regulated or, if outside the scope of the regulations, unregulated. The test is carried out on a case-by-case basis to ensure that a reliable determination is made. It will be a task of the VFA agent, together with the VFA issuer (if appropriate), to conduct this assessment with respect to a DLT Asset when:

(i) an issuer proposes to launch an initial offering of a virtual financial asset (IVFAO) to the public in or from within Malta;

(ii) an issuer admits the VFA to trading; and/or

(iii) a service provider is offering a VFA-related service.

4.48 The first stage is to decide whether the DLT Asset can be categorised as a virtual token and, if so, that it falls outside the scope of regulation. A virtual token is defined as a form of digital medium recordation, and its value application is restricted to the purchase of goods or services either within the DLT platform or within a limited network of DLT platforms but not DLT exchanges.

4.49   The next stage is that, if the DLT asset is determined not to be a virtual token, a decision must be made as to whether it falls within the scope of any existing financial services regulation. If the agent determines that the asset does not fall within that scope, the issuer/service provider would need to comply with the regime applicable to financial instruments or electronic money, depending on the particular characteristics.

4.50   If it is then determined that the asset does not fall within the scope of existing financial services laws, the token will automatically go to the last stage of the Test. The last stage of the Test determines whether the asset would be deemed to be a VFA and, as such, is due to be regulated by the VFAA.

4.51   If a DLT Asset is a VFA, service providers are required to abide by the provisions of the VFAA, or an issuer of an IVFAO offered to the public (in or from Malta) must register its white paper with the MFSA and that white paper must satisfy the conditions set out in the First Schedule to the VFAA. In addition, service providers that are named in the Second Schedule to the VFAA (these include VFA exchanges) offering a VFA service (in or from Malta) would be required to obtain a licence from the MFSA before contacting any operations.

4.52   The sale of cryptocurrencies or other tokens may fall to be regulated by Maltese securities laws, and each DLT Asset must be assessed to determine whether it falls within the scope of existing securities laws or the VFAA, or whether it falls to be unregulated. If the DLT Asset is within the scope of existing securities laws because it is within the definition of a 'financial instrument' pursuant to the Test, it must clearly comply with securities laws. In Malta, commodities laws do not apply to the sale of cryptocurrencies or other tokens.

4.53   As regards taxation, cryptocurrency falls to be treated in the same way as currency. The Income Tax Act makes a distinction between receipts that are income and receipts that are capital; those that are income are subject to Maltese income tax at a rate of 35% if the recipient is a person or body of persons or at progressive rates, up to maximum of 35%, if the recipient is a natural person. Gains that are of a capital nature are either subject to income tax at a rate of 35% or not taxable at all. Income is not defined, but the Income Tax Act sets out a non-exhaustive list of sources of revenue that are considered to be classified as income, such as gains or profits from a business, trade, profession or vocation. The Income Tax Act then goes on to exhaustively list capital gains that are considered within this scope of income tax. Cryptocurrency is not currently listed as an asset that is subject to income tax on any of its capital gains.

4.54   As regards applying the above to transactions in cryptocurrency, profits derived from a transaction would be classified as income of a trading nature, or income of a capital nature, depending on factors (to be determined subjectively on a case-by-case basis) such as the intention of the acquirer when the cryptocurrency was bought, the period of time that the cryptocurrency was held, the price at which the acquirer entered the market, the price trends at the moment of entry, as well as the prices of the disposal and price trends at the moment of exit.

4.55   Significantly, so far as duty is payable by the purchaser of cryptocurrency, there are currently no provisions in the Duty on Documents and Transfers Act which impose a duty charge on the transfer of cryptocurrency. In terms of value added tax, it is expected that the exchange of cryptocurrency for traditional currency, effected for consideration, would likely be treated as a supply of service and be VAT exempt. The Maltese tax authorities are expected to issue further guidance on income tax, duty and VAT in respect of cryptocurrency in the near future.

4.56   In relation to anti-money laundering requirements and anti-terrorism, persons carrying out a 'relevant financial business' or 'relevant activity' will be considered to be a subject person and must adhere to the anti-money laundering obligations. Issuers of cryptocurrencies and related service providers must adhere to anti-money laundering legislation because the VFAA provides that an issuer, a VFAA licence holder and a VFAA agent should be considered as a subject person. It should also be noted that the white paper, which must be registered with the MFSA for either an IVFAO to the public or admission on a DLT exchange, is required to include a description of the issuer's adopted white listing together, with anti-money laundering and counter-financing of terrorism procedures in terms of the Prevention of Money Laundering Act, together with regulations made and rules issued in relation to the prevention of money laundering. VFAA issuers, licence holders and agents will also be required to comply with any cryptocurrency guidance that may be issued from time to time.

4.57   In March 2018, the Malta Gaming Authority (MGA) provided guidance on the use of DLTs and cryptocurrencies in the gaming sector. There is currently the implementation of a sandbox environment which is to consider allowing the use and implementation of DLTs and virtual cryptocurrencies by gaming and gambling operators licensed by the MGA. In order to safeguard players, there are two distinct implementation scenarios that are deemed acceptable. The first is a single wallet system, in which the operator has a maximum of one wallet for every supported cryptocurrency, and players issue deposits to the address of that wallet and use of their account with the operator to notify that they have made a deposit from a certain wallet address. The second is a multiple wallet system, whereby an operator assigns a wallet for each currency to each player's account. The MGA only accepts this case if the operator has an intermediate wallet structure comprised of one of more wallets. Such an intermediate set-up would be to accept deposits from the players' personal external source of funds.

4.58   With the regulatory framework and the certainty created by the three legislative Acts, Malta is arguably pulling ahead of rivals such as Switzerland, Gibraltar and other countries that are seeking to position themselves as 'Crypto havens'. Malta's broad framework deals with ICOs, cryptocurrencies and exchanges, together with other blockchain technologies that are not necessarily financial in nature.

Jersey

4.59   Similarly to Malta, Jersey has taken advantage of the slow pace of larger European countries to regulate the market, and established itself as an offshore hub for cryptocurrency ventures as well as initial coin offerings ('ICOs'). Jersey's legal and regulatory framework in relation to blockchain and cryptocurrencies can be divided up into the following areas:

(1)   investment funds;

(2)   ICOs; and

(3)   virtual currency exchanges ('VCEs').

4.60   With regard to investment funds, the Jersey Financial Services Commission ('JFSC'), Jersey's regulator, approved the launch of the world's first regulated Bitcoin investment fund, GABI Plc. GABI Plc was approved as an 'Expert Fund'. Jersey Expert Funds can have an unlimited number of investors and are aimed at 'Expert Investors'. Expert Funds can be established quickly and cost-effectively but must comply with the Jersey Expert Fund Guide (the 'EF Guide'). The JFSC does not need to review the fund structure, documentation or the promoter; instead, the fund administrator certifies to the JFSC that the fund complies with the EF Guide and, once the certification and the fund's offer document are filed, the JFSC aims for a three-day turnaround on the application for approval. Only 'Expert Investors' are able to place money into this type of fund, and the definition of 'Expert Investor' is crucial.

4.61   An investor must fall within any one of the 10 categories, which include a person or entity: in the business of buying or selling investments; with a net worth of more than US$1m, excluding principal place of residence; with at least US$1m available for investment; connected with the fund or a fund service provider; or making an investment or commitment of US$100,000 or more (or currency equivalent).

4.62   Expert Funds are eligible to be marketed into the EU/EEA in accordance with the Alternative Investment Fund Managers Directive (AIFMD) through national private placement regimes and, when available, third country passporting.

4.63   In contrast, a Jersey Private Fund, which can have up to 50 investors, cannot benefit from AIFMD marketing into the EU/EEA unless JFSC consent is obtained. The extent of regulation then subsequently applied by the JFSC will depend on whether the fund is 'sub-threshold' or not. Private funds are sub-threshold when total assets are less than €100 million; or total assets are less than €500 million, provided that the alternative investment funds (AIF) are not 'leveraged' and no redemption rights exist during a period of five years following the date of initial investment. Sub-threshold funds do not have ongoing regulation.

4.64   Non-sub-threshold funds must, however, obtain an 'AIF Certificate' to permit EU/EEA marketing. The JFSC will assess the suitability of the fund's promoter, having regard to its track record and relevant experience, reputation, financial resources and spread of ultimate ownership, in light of the level of sophistication of the target investor group; and, where the fund is a Jersey entity, it must be regulated by the JFSC, in accordance with the AIFMD.

4.65 ICO issuers in Jersey must be a Jersey-based company. Before an ICO can be made, the JFSC requires the ICO issuer to obtain consent from the JFSC before it undertakes any form of activity and to comply with the JFSC's Sound Business Practice Policy. Relevant anti-money laundering requirements to purchase tokens from, or sell tokens back to, the issuer must be applied; and the company must appoint a Jersey-licensed administrator and maintain a Jersey-resident director on the board. The company must: be subject to an ongoing annual audit requirement; have procedures and processes in place to mitigate and manage the risk of retail investors investing inappropriately in the ICO; and ensure that retail investors understand the risks involved. This will include: preparing an information memorandum which complies with certain content requirements required under Jersey company law; ensuring that any marketing material is clear, fair and not misleading; and providing certain prescribed consumer warnings.

4.66 Consent from the JFSC will be granted in accordance with the statutory instrument governing the raising of capital: the Control of Borrowing (Jersey) Order 1958 ('COBO'). The type of COBO consent granted by the JFSC will depend on whether the token is categorised as a 'security' under COBO. The token will be classed as a security if one or more of the following characteristics are present: a right to participate in the profits/earnings of the issuer or a related entity; a claim on the issuer or a related party's assets; a general commitment from the issuer to redeem tokens in the future; a right to participate in the operation or management of the issuer or a related party; and an expectation of a return on the amount paid for the tokens.

4.67 Whether or not a token is a 'security' under COBO makes no difference as to the requirements imposed on an issuer by the JFSC, but it does allow for the token to be traded in the secondary market (for example, to be listed on the cryptocurrency exchange).

4.68 Virtual cryptocurrency exchanges (VCEs) are regulated under the Proceeds of Crime (Miscellaneous Amendments) (Jersey) Regulations 2016. VCEs are required to comply with the Island's laws, regulations, policies and procedures aimed at preventing and detecting money laundering and terrorist financing. The Regulations also make a VCE a supervised business and require VCEs to register with and be subject to the supervision of the JFSC. However, VCEs with turnover of less than £150,000 per calendar year are permitted to test VCE delivery mechanisms in a live environment without the normal registration requirements and costs.

Chapter 5

Global regulation: North America

CANADA

5.1   Canada is a country that permits the use of cryptocurrencies, though the permission is qualified because cryptocurrencies per se are not legal currency in Canada. In essence, digital currencies can be used for the purchase of goods and services both online and in physical stores where cryptocurrencies are accepted. Canada also permits the buying and selling of cryptocurrencies on open exchanges as cryptocurrency exchanges.

5.2   There is then a rather unusual situation in Canada because, whilst cryptocurrencies are not recognised as legal tender, it is still possible to operate using cryptocurrencies. Whilst Canada does not recognise cryptocurrency as legal tender, it does apply tax as it would to legal currency such that cryptocurrency is subject to Canadian taxation because the revenue agency defines cryptocurrency as a commodity such that its use is treated as a barter transaction. The approach is an interesting one because the definition of cryptocurrency transaction as a barter transaction has consequences in that, where a contracts for sale of goods is conducted using cryptocurrency, the consideration or value of the goods must be declared by the seller and this can result in a taxable gain. The taxable gain (or, indeed, a taxable loss) can be treated as taxable income or capital for the relevant tax payer.

5.3   The Canadian system also regards cryptocurrencies as within the definition of 'money service businesses' in relation to its anti-money laundering regulations. This means that obligations on organisations with cryptocurrency operations to register financial transactions and to conduct due diligence and make suspicious activity reports apply in the same way that they would in any other financial services transaction. Anti-money laundering regulations are extraterritorial, in that a cryptocurrency operation outside the borders of Canada will still be caught if related to goods or services aimed at goods within Canada.

5.4   A digital currency can be used to pay for goods or services and, in Canada, the rules for barter transactions apply. A barter transaction occurs when any two persons agree to exchange goods or services and carry out that exchange without using legal currency. By way of example, paying for movies with digital currency constitutes a barter transaction. The value of the movies purchased using digital currency must then be included in the seller's income for tax purposes. The amount to be included will be the value of the movies in Canadian dollars. Canadian Revenue Agency has also declared that goods and services tax/harmonised sales tax will apply to the fair market value of any goods or services that are bought using digital currency.

5.5   Because digital currency is treated as a commodity when taxes are filed, any gains or losses arising from selling or buying digital currencies must be declared. This is because any resulting gains or losses would constitute taxable income or capital for the tax payer. The Canadian Revenue Agency Interpretation Bulletin IT-479R (Transactions in securities) provides further detail to assist in determining whether a transaction falls to be income or capital in nature. That bulletin in general terms sets out that, when a tax payer does not engage in trading cryptocurrency and acquires such property for long-term growth, any gain or loss arising from this position of cryptocurrency would be treated as on account of capital. Where a tax payer engages in trading or investing in cryptocurrency, the gains or losses arising would be treated as being on account of income. The cost to the tax payer of property received in exchange for cryptocurrency (for example, this could be another type of cryptocurrency) should be equal to the value of the cryptocurrency given up as consideration. Note that the mining of cryptocurrencies can be undertaken for profit and, of course, as a business or as a personal hobby; if a cryptocurrency is mined in the course of a personal hobby, it would fall to be non-taxable. If the tax payer mines in the course of a business, that commercial income must be included in the tax payer's income declaration for the year and will be determined with reference to the value of the inventory at the end of the year.

5.6   It is because Canada treats cryptocurrencies including Bitcoin as 'money service businesses' for the purposes of its anti-money laundering regulations that companies dealing in cryptocurrencies are required to register with the Financial Transactions and Reports Analysis Centre of Canada to abide by money laundering compliance programs and to keep and retain records as prescribed by Canadian law. They must also submit suspicious activity reports by reporting suspicious or terror-related property transactions and determine whether any of their customers are politically exposed persons.

5.7   Canada published a draft version of stricter, upgraded cryptocurrency regulations in June 2018. The draft, titled 'Regulations Amending Certain Regulations Made Under the Proceeds of Crime (Money Laundering) and Terrorist Financing Act, 2018', provided that:

> 'Persons and entities that are "dealing in virtual currency" would be financial entities or other entities deemed domestic or foreign MSBs, as the case may be. These "dealing in" activities include virtual currency exchange services and value transfer services. As required of all MSBs, persons and entities dealing in virtual currencies would need to implement a full compliance program and register with FINTRAC. In addition, all reporting entities that receive $10,000 or more in virtual currency (e.g. deposits, any form of payment) would have record keeping and reporting obligations. These amendments serve to mitigate the money laundering and terrorist activity financing vulnerabilities of virtual currency in a way that is consistent with the existing legal framework, while not unduly hindering innovation. For this reason, the amendments are targeted at persons or entities engaged in the business of dealing in virtual currencies, and not virtual currencies themselves.'

5.8 The implementation and final version of these regulations are presently on hold but expected sometime in 2020. Cryptocurrency firms are undoubtedly hoping that the stricter regulations are not adopted, or that they are diluted, as they assert that tougher financial hygiene regulation is uncompetitive and damaging to Canada's pioneering reputation as one of the leading crypto markets.

Conversely, there is a counter view that the delay will be negative in allowing other leading crypto markets, such as Switzerland and Malta, to steal a march and lure crypto firms away to markets that offer certainty.

MEXICO

5.9 At the time of writing the regulatory position in Mexico is a challenging and complex one. Mexico was relatively quick out of the blocks and, in September 2017, it launched a project called 'Blockchain then HACKMX'; the chief objective of the project was to promote government digital innovation and to additionally tackle the issue of public corruption. Significantly, Mexico saw blockchain as a potential weapon in the fight against its corruption, with many experts believing it could add transparency and security to transactions and records that are exposed to the risk of corruption. Distributed ledger technology and blockchain were thought to be of great advantage because of the transparency they could bring, together with the network of integrity that should prevent corruption through the falsification of data. The fact that it would reduce the centralisation of power was seized upon as of particular importance to Mexico. In Mexico, corruption is generally recognised as having reached a high point, with a large majority (around 80%) of Mexicans perceiving their government and politicians as corrupt.

5.10 In March 2018, Mexico enacted the 'Law to Regulate Financial Technology Companies' which provided rules that applied to cryptocurrencies with a specified chapter on operations with 'virtual assets' otherwise known as cryptocurrencies. Virtual assets or cryptocurrencies are not legal currency but are defined as representations of value electronically registered, utilised and transferred by the public as a means of payment. This was the definition adopted by the chapter (Art 30), which also provided that Mexico's legal currency could not under any circumstances ever be considered a virtual asset, thus separating out legal currency from cryptocurrencies which could only be transferred electronically.

5.11 On its face, this was a positive development for cryptocurrency in Mexico. However, Mexico's central bank (Banco de Mexico) has been granted broad powers, under the Law to Regulate Financial Technology Companies, to regulate virtual assets which include:

(i) authorising financial companies to perform transactions with virtual assets;

(ii) specifying those virtual assets that financial companies are allowed to operate with in the country, defining their particular characteristics and establishing the restrictions and conditions that may be applicable to transactions with those specified assets; and

(iii)   imposing fines for unauthorised transactions using virtual assets.

5.12   In addition, all financial companies that carry out transactions with cryptocurrencies must disclose to their clients any risks that are applicable to these cryptoassets and must inform their clients in a plain and accessible manner, either through their company website or whatever other means they use to provide and promote their services, that:

(i)   cryptocurrency or a virtual asset is not legal currency and not backed by the federal government or by the central bank;

(ii)   that the value of cryptocurrencies is volatile;

(iii)   that, once executed, cryptocurrency transactions may not be reversible; and

(iv)   that technological, cyber and fraud risks are inherent in cryptocurrencies.

5.13   However, it is this power that was granted to the central bank that has now caused difficulties for cryptocurrency regulation in Mexico. The central bank has circulated new rules on cryptoassets that adversely impact crypto exchanges. The circular recently published (March 2019) in the Official Gazette of the Federation detailed cryptoasset-related provisions that would apply to the regulation of financial technology institutions. This stated that 'institutions may only enter into transactions with virtual assets that correspond to internal transactions, subject to the prior authorisation granted by the Bank of Mexico'. The provisions further stipulated that there would be no eligibility for obtaining the authorisation to directly provide clients with cryptocurrency exchange, transmission or custody services. To most observers, this will operate to effectively ban or prevent cryptocurrency exchanges operating, because the law requires a Mexican exchange to become a regulated financial institution if it is to operate legally. That said, once the licence is obtained, the exchange would not have the authorisation to then list any cryptocurrencies, which would make it legally impossible to operate an exchange in Mexico with this Bank of Mexico circular in place. The circular was subject to public consultation until early June 2019 but it does appear that the circular will be applied by the Bank of Mexico.

5.14   The rationale behind the circular was to prevent customers from being exposed to the dangerous nature of virtual assets on the grounds of their volatility and complexity. The effect, however, is that it prevents institutions from offering cryptocurrencies to end-consumers. This circular essentially stipulated that the Central Bank will not allow any cryptocurrency to be offered by regulated financial companies, and the Bank of Mexico consequently envisages blockchain and cryptocurrency as for use only in the internal operations of financial institutions.

5.15   The question is whether there is room for manoeuvre and whether the circular can be interpreted to enable cryptocurrency exchange. A particular thought has been given to the definition of a 'consumer' within the circular, and some legal experts in Mexico have stated that financial institutions and foreign trade companies do not come within the definition of consumer as defined within the circular and thus can operate freely with a cryptocurrency exchange. That said, even with the benefit of this interpretation of 'consumer', it is clear that under the circular any cryptocurrency exchange that wants to serve the end-customer or public would not be able to do so without a successful appeal whereby a Court suspended the operation of the Bank of Mexico circular and allowed the service to the end-customer.

5.16   For Mexico it is hoped that the present embargo can be removed. Mexico achieved impressive growth in its cryptocurrency market and, in a country where some half of the country's population (approximately 130 million) do not have a bank account, cryptocurrency was viewed as a viable means of plugging the gap to ensure everyone has the ability to remit payments. The role of the Mexican Central Bank as the regulator, and the fact that exchanges require the Central Bank's approval to operate it, is evidently a problem for Mexico. The Central Bank is not only the regulator but effectively the cryptocurrency lawmaker because, in Mexico, the law grants it the means of defining and determining which cryptocurrency and blockchain activities are permissible, and this has led to a conflict, with many seeing the bank's vested interest being incompatible with its role as the virtual asset lawmaker.

UNITED STATES

5.17   Blockchain and cryptocurrency regulation in the United States is anything other than united. Whilst the US Government has of late shown its backing for the development of regulation and governance within the sphere of technology and in particular blockchain, there are variations between states that pose hurdles to those trying to navigate the regulatory course in the form of clearing licensing hurdles that have been erected by individual states.

5.18   US Congress created the Congressional Blockchain Caucus to deal with regulation and law pertaining to digital ledger technology and cryptocurrencies. It was that body that, in September 2018, introduced three pieces of legislation: the Resolution Supporting Digital Currencies and Blockchain Technology Bill; the Safe Harbor for Tax Payers with Forked Assets Act; and the Blockchain Regulatory Certainty Act. Those three pieces of legislation sought to persuade the federal government to monitor blockchain entities that may or may not need to register as money transmitters (this is considered later in this chapter). Those Bills also provide taxation guidance. The present position is that digital currency in the US is treated by the IRS as property rather than currency (IRS Notice 2014-21 Guidance on Virtual Currency, March 2014). The IRS determination of cryptocurrency as property means that individuals and businesses must maintain detailed records of cryptocurrency sale and purchase transactions and will be liable for capital gains achieved through acquiring goods or services with cryptocurrency. Gains made on the sale of cryptocurrencies for cash will also be liable to taxation, as will the fair market value of any mined cryptocurrencies at the time of receipt. Where gains are from cryptocurrencies held as capital assets for more than a year, capital gains tax rates will apply for individuals, whereas income tax rates will apply if the period was one year or less. Further legislation came in the form of the Virtual Currency Consumer Protection Act and the US Virtual Currency Market and Regulatory Competitiveness Act, both of 2018. They seek to provide consumer protection and are particularly focused on cryptocurrencies and price manipulation. Significantly, for the purposes of financial crimes enforcement, virtual currency is defined as being 'a medium of exchange that operates like a currency in some environments, but does not have all the attributes of real currency'. In the US, therefore, cryptocurrency is not considered a currency and, as will be seen later in this chapter, is subject to a variety of controls dependent upon the state. There is no single, US-wide definition of cryptocurrency, which is variously referred to as virtual assets, virtual currency, cryptoassets, cryptocurrency, crypto, digital assets and digital tokens.

5.19   Plans are afoot to introduce federal legislation to develop a token asset class so as to facilitate the regulation of initial coin offerings ('ICOs'). The regulation of ICOs in the US is examined in some detail in **Chapter 7**. In the US the Securities and Exchange Commission ('SEC') has regulatory authority over the issue or resale of any digital asset, cryptocurrency or token that can be considered to be a security. Where any digital asset is considered to constitute a security, the issuer must either register the security with the SEC or offer it pursuant to one of the exemptions from registration. The present position is that, following the SEC's decision on Decentralised Autonomous Organisation ('DAO') – a term used to describe a virtual organisation embodied in computer code and executed on a Distributed Ledger or Blockchain – and it being determined that DAO tokens were securities to be regulated by the SEC, ICOs or token sales are treated as an investment contract which fall to be similarly treated as a security under Section 2(a)(1) of the Securities Act and Section 3(a)(10) of the Exchange Act. Moreover, the SEC decision emphasises that US federal security laws will apply to an ICO if it fails to be considered as an investment contract. This then means that ICOs require registration and disclosure and must meet the provisions under the Securities Act (for further details, see **Chapter 7**). Representative Warren Davidson has submitted a proposal that legislation be introduced to enable a new token asset class so as to better facilitate the regulation of ICOs. Given the current position, that would be welcome news. The sale of cryptocurrency in the US is only generally regulated in three situations. Firstly where it constitutes the sale of a *security* under federal or state law. This means regard must be had to both the federal (national) and local position. Secondly where local (state) law catches the sale as constituting a regulated money transmission and/or the underlying conduct is caught by federal law as constituting a money services business ('MSB'). It should be noted that MSBs (money transmitters) are regulated by the Bank Secrecy Act which imposes extensive anti-money laundering requirements designed to prevent the facilitation of money laundering or terrorist finance. Current guidance on the definition of an MSB (FinCEN 18 March 2013, G001) is that 'an administrator or exchanger that (i) accepts or transmits a convertible virtual currency or (ii) buys or sells a convertible virtual currency for any reason is a money transmitter under FinCEN's regulations unless a limitation to or exemption from the definition applies to the person'. Thirdly, cryptocurrency derivatives such as SWAPS, futures, options, and other such contracts that refer to the value of cryptocurrencies or cryptoassets that are considered a commodity, will fall to be regulated by the Commodity Exchange Act and the Commodities and Futures Trading Commission.

5.20 In the United States, there is both federal regulation of cryptocurrencies and state-level regulation. If there has been an attempt at creating a more stable platform for cryptocurrency and blockchain at a federal level, this is certainly not true of state-level regulation which is diverse and sometimes inconsistent. This flows from the differing attitudes and responses of the states to the emergence of cryptocurrencies: some have not implemented any laws to address cryptocurrency, whereas other states have sought to reject cryptocurrency platforms with hostile legislation, and there are those that are more positive and have enacted less restrictive legislations. It is helpful to understand in broad terms which states are in favour of cryptocurrency services, and the following sets out, on a Category 1 (best) to Category 4 (worst) basis, those states that are favourable through to those that are hostile:

- **Category 1** states (*those that are most positive*) include New Hampshire, Montana and Wyoming.

- **Category 2** states (*those that are not as positive as Category 1 but are still favourable*) include Illinois, Kansas, Massachusetts, Tennessee and Texas.

- **Category 3** states (*those that are restrictive, though not hostile, in their approach*) include Idaho, Hawaii, New Mexico and New York.

- **Category 4** states (*those that are heavily regulated through regulation and are effectively hostile*) are Alabama, Connecticut, Georgia, North Carolina, Vermont and Washington.

5.21 In order to understand the different categories, one first needs to understand the different regulations that can be imposed at state level. There are various regulatory methods that apply on a state-by-state basis in order to regulate cryptocurrencies. In brief, these are essentially licensing requirements, money transmission regulations and regulatory guidance. We shall deal with each of these in turn.

Licensing

5.22 States are able to force those providing cryptocurrency services to be licensed in order to operate in their state. Not all states have decided to follow this route, but the need to obtain a licence can be a difficult, if not insurmountable, hurdle and those states that are Category 3 or Category 4 can be viewed as those where it is difficult to operate. New York has a licensing approach whereby the New York State Department of Financial Services requires what is known as a 'BIT license'. The application procedure and the requirements in order to obtain a BIT license are stringent and demanding. In addition, the State of New York currently requires any virtual currency business to provide a surety bond, the amount of that bond to be decided on a case-by-case basis. There has been a bill introduced into the New York Senate that may result in an alternative to this regulatory licensing approach, but the New York approach is not particularly accommodating. Connecticut has also taken a licensing approach and it prohibits third parties selling or storing cryptocurrencies for others without a licence being granted. Similar to New York, Connecticut also demands a surety bond which is to be determined on a prescribed situational basis by the State Banking Commission. The Commissioner effectively determines the amount of the bond, based on the forecast profits. Georgia has also followed this approach by restricting the transmission of cryptocurrencies within its state without the granting of a licence, and the Georgia Department of Banking and Finance is authorised to regulate and provide rules around the transmission of cryptocurrencies.

Money transmission laws

5.23   Money transmission laws were enacted in order to prevent money laundering and are the equivalent in some respects of the UK's Anti-Money Laundering Regulations and Proceeds of Crime Act. There are 50 American states, of which 49 have passed their own Money Transmitters Act, and these Acts have been used by a number of states to apply to cryptocurrencies. Consequently, even though cryptocurrencies are not a currency, they find themselves within the definition of money transmission and are consequently governed by the Money Transmitters Act for that particular state. In practice, this will mean that, where there is a cryptocurrency transaction, it will fall under each particular state law that is engaged, and the transmitter must ensure that all requisite conditions are fulfilled – these can include a security or surety bond, applications and administrative fees. It has been suggested, and there is good ground to accept the argument, that some states have deliberately raised the criteria to such a level as to positively discourage cryptocurrency businesses from trying to operate in the state. Washington State and New Mexico include cryptocurrency within their definition of money transmission and require licences as well as bonds and other high-level compliance steps that are stringent and discouraging to cryptocurrency businesses. It can be seen from the levels of category which states are more likely to have stringent requirements. Montana is included as a cryptocurrency-positive state because it has not enacted any money transmission legislation and consequently cryptocurrency is not subject to any money transmission regulations. This chapter does not propose to detail the Money Transmission Laws for each and every state, but regard should be had to the categories set out above and, before any business is contemplated or conducted, regard should be had to the particular money transmission laws applicable in that state and the need to make an application and acquire a licence or provide a bond or security.

Regulatory guidance

5.24   In addition to regulation laws, individual states may also impose what is termed regulatory guidance in order to affect the ease or difficulty of conducting cryptocurrency business in that state. Regulatory guidance is no more than guidance, but Hawaii, for example, has regulatory guidance that it requires cryptocurrency businesses to be categorised and, depending on the type, additional requirements may apply, such as a requirement that fiat currency reserves must be held in addition to the cryptocurrency. Texas uses regulatory guidance such that the majority of cryptocurrency transactions are not considered to be money transmission unless a third party is involved, and Tennessee takes a similar approach. It is beyond the scope of this chapter to examine each and every state and its level of regulatory guidance, but this has been taken into account for the purposes of the categorisation set out above; again, if business is to be conducted in a particular state, regard should be had to the specific regulatory guidance that may be in place from time to time and that could affect the ease of conducting business there.

5.25   It is important to emphasise that the position at state level can change frequently and, as a result, states can rapidly move up and down through the categories. That said, it is thought that, because the categories generally reflect the attitude of the state towards cryptocurrency, the likelihood is that those that are positive will likely remain so and those that are hostile will similarly continue to be hostile, although this is an assumption and cannot be relied upon. Category 1 states have enacted laws and regulations so that the operation of cryptocurrency is excluded from its money transmission legislation. By excluding cryptocurrency from this legislation, it makes compliance far easier and encourages cryptocurrency business. Category 2 states are states where cryptocurrency has not been excluded from what is, in effect, anti-money laundering legislation but they have issued decisions or determinations that define cryptocurrency as being outside the definition of currency for the purposes of that legislation. Category 3 states are states where cryptocurrencies are deemed, whether by regulation, guidance or determination, to fall within the state's money transmission legislation and where they may additionally be subject to licensing requirements. Category 4 states are those that have expressly imposed laws that treat cryptocurrencies as money transmission for the purposes of their legislation and, in addition, have a licence model which has stringent requirements.

5.26   It is accepted that there are many states that cannot be easily categorised. For example, some states, such as California and Colorado, have issued no guidance at all and do not currently regulate. There are other states such as South Dakota where decisions are made on a case-by-case basis; in South Dakota, a business plan is required before a final decision will be made as to compliance with the state regulations and money transmission regulations. The likely result of such divergent state regulation is that cryptocurrency businesses will be naturally drawn to those states that are more favourable, and there will ultimately be concentrations of cryptocurrency and blockchain platforms in those Category 1 areas.

5.27   In the US, at a federal level, one could argue that the focus and attention has been given to protecting consumers and that the proliferation of diverse legislation at both federal and state levels, together with a lack of consistency and overlapping jurisdictions, has meant that the US is currently a complex regulatory maze. Cryptocurrency exchanges in the US have sometimes sought to establish offshore operations in order to ensure they are protected from the difficult and changing US regulatory landscape. At the time of writing, it is evident that the US is not competing with other jurisdictions that offer a more consistent and less demanding approach to compliance.

Chapter 6

Global regulation: the rest of the world

INTRODUCTION

6.1   Advances in IT and the advent of the internet brought with them a concern that data, and in particular personal data, must be secured and protected in order that its potential misuse and harm to individuals, organisations and states should be avoided so far as possible. The ensuing approach to security of data and the implementation of regulatory law, such as the General Data Protection Regulation ('GDPR') in all European states, brought with it much fanfare and the expressed hope that there would be a harmonisation of data protection and its governing laws around the world.

6.2   That, however, did not happen. GDPR was the first attempt at a unified law to govern the collection, control and processing of personal data. But law is rarely without politics, and politics can be geographically sensitive. Significantly, GDPR emphasised the rights of the individual citizen and the sanctity of that citizen's personal data. That recognition, of the individual data rights, runs root and branch throughout GDPR; from the need to show this individual has given active and demonstrable consent, through to the embedded rights of the individual data subject to ensure that organisations may only keep data for purposes specified in the regulations and that a data subject has a 'right to be forgotten'. This development, born out of the GDPR, was a European concept and sought to ensure that there was a sea change in the way that entities, who are subject to European jurisdiction, treat personal data. In short, organisations became mere custodians of someone else's valuable property (ie the individual's data) and they were required to deal with personal data in a way that was consistent with handling someone else's item of significant value. There were individual rights of redress built into the regulation, and evidence was required to show that dealings in personal data had been conducted appropriately by those custodians of data.

6.3   The worldwide perspective is particularly important because blockchain is, by its very nature, a global phenomenon. The nodes in a blockchain can be (and often are) in a variety of different countries (or different states of a country), so that the chain is worldwide. If each node in the blockchain is an exact replication, we will be faced with touchpoints that arguably engage that country/state's jurisdiction. The question will be which jurisdiction prevails or has primacy; or, conversely, does the blockchain have to comply with the laws and regulations of each and every jurisdiction it touches? It will be seen from the commentary below that there are significant differences in the treatment of cryptocurrency and blockchain from country to country, and the regulatory landscape is rapidly changing as jurisdictions consider their position vis-a-vis virtual currencies, the underlying technology and innovative tech. A word of warning: if the laws of a jurisdiction 'bite', regard should be taken of its wider laws, and not just its regulation as it applies to blockchain. Around the world there are different legal systems that have different treatments of contract law, ownership and title to property, as well as what may constitute a partnership, a corporate entity, a security etc; all of these are legal concepts that could be very important in resolving any dispute that might arise. For example, if there is a contest as to what has taken place pursuant to a combination of smart contracts executed without human intervention by what is effectively a decentralised autonomous organisation ('DAO' – see **Chapter 11**), how will issues around the contract's interpretation, parties, liability and legal status of the DAO be resolved? The resolution will depend on which jurisdiction's laws are applicable, given the global variance in approach.

6.4   In relation to blockchain, the jurisdiction's model of cybersecurity regulation, which definition should be taken to include information protection, will be of paramount importance. The treatment of information is likely to be central to any dispute that arises, and access to accurate information lies at the heart of a blockchain operation. It follows therefore that care should be taken to ensure that any engaged jurisdiction that might govern the use of data is compatible with the aims of the venture. By way of example, if a state regards all information within its borders as the property of the state and is able to trump the rights of the individual members, there could be insurmountable problems. That is not a far-fetched scenario; some state models effectively operate a principle of data sovereignty, whilst others consider that information ownership rights vest in corporations rather than individuals. In choosing the appropriate jurisdiction(s), regard must be had as to whether the governing law ultimately recognises and empowers the rights of an individual, corporation or state in relation to data.

6.5   Conversely, another crucial jurisdictional consideration is whether cybersecurity/data protection regimes can be complied with by the blockchain. This is dealt with in **Chapter 3**. In short, if the blockchain is to be public (non-permissioned), will it fall foul of the right to deletion and the right to be forgotten, as provided by the GDPR or equivalent regulation? This may be a more manageable problem for a private, permissioned blockchain, where compliance might be achieved by a side arrangement that is 'off chain', but a public scheme could find itself compromised ab initio by regulation that it cannot abide by, due to the immutable character of the blockchain.

6.6   In Europe, the rights of the individual in relation to their personal data were recognised as paramount. Yet those hoping for the rest of the world to adopt a similar approach, to establish a global uniformity on the regulation and fiscal treatment of information, were to be disappointed. See **Chapter 4** for a detailed treatment of the current regulation in Europe. The cybersecurity initiatives that resulted in cyber laws in China (see **6.11** onwards below), Russia and the United States (see **5.17** onwards) were not convergent or on the same philosophical plane. There was in fact a rejection of the European model of individual data protection values. In Russia, for example, the Russian Federation passed a law requiring personal data relating to Russian citizens to be stored on servers physically located within the country. For Russia, such information belonged to Russia and it would remain within its national borders. In Russia, the philosophy was not that the individual must be protected, but rather that it is for the nation state to regulate and that the state has sovereignty over data. The nation state's data sovereignty trumps the rights of an individual, in apparent contrast to GDPR.

6.7   China similarly commenced its own cybersecurity law on 1 June 2017. Prior to that date, any European model of personal data protection law had not been recognisable in China. Indeed, China had not previously passed any meaningful comprehensive data protection legislation that regulated the collection, control and processing of personal information. On 1 June 2017, the change of direction taken by China was to give a nod to the protection of an individual's rights but also to emphasise that the state has the ultimate interest in data and, similar to the Russian approach, that data is ultimately in the possession and control of the nation state. The Chinese state was empowered to conduct what were termed 'security risk assessments' to trawl through all data so as to allow extensive state intrusion which in turn enabled the state to control data. This control included forcing entities or individuals to physically store data within China if it was deemed to be critical information.

6.8   Whilst the Chinese approach had parallels with the Russian approach, the approach of the United States was different in that, whilst it recognised and granted individual rights in relation to data, those data rights were diminished by the repeal of regulations that required internet service providers to do more to protect the customer's privacy than websites like OfferEx, Google or Facebook. The initiative, founded during the currency of the Obama administration, had sought to restrict the ability of internet providers to use information such as location, financial information, information in relation to health and web browsing for advertising and marketing purposes. The rules then made it unlawful to use such information without obtaining appropriate consent. We note that the sale of personal information collected by a retailer is huge business in the US, and the US appears to have taken an approach which takes the rights in the interests of the corporate to the front and centre of its philosophy. In the US, it might be argued that, in relation to data protection, it was the corporations who scored a major victory. It would be premature, given the size and scale of the commercial value of the use and resale of personal data, to suggest that recent issues surrounding Facebook and Instagram suggest a retreat from this philosophy, but there is no doubt that there is a greater acceptance of the significance of the rights of individuals over his or her personal data.

6.9   The history of data protection and how regulation developed around it across the globe is most useful when we now turn to younger technology – in this context, blockchain and the financial system that sits atop it, namely cryptocurrency. It will be seen that there are similar differences in approach by the various nation states in their regulation of cryptocurrency. There are those states that allow cryptocurrency markets to operate but their regulation is effectively inactive so that they have not passed any crypto- or blockchain-specific legislation or regulation. In those cases, it is possible to trade in cryptocurrency markets but there is a complete vacuum of regulation. Other states not only permit crypto markets to operate but have created and enacted specific laws and regulations that shape the cryptocurrency sector. Lastly, there are those that do not allow crypto markets to operate or, if not enacting a complete ban, have taken steps to reduce the possibility of cryptocurrency markets within their jurisdictions.

DIVERGENT PHILOSOPHIES ON CRYPTOCURRENCY AND BLOCKCHAIN REGULATION

6.10   There are divergent philosophies in relation to cryptocurrency regulation and blockchain, in the same way that there were differences between countries and regions in their approach to cybersecurity and data protection regulation. This section sets out the regulation that exists (and, in some cases, where it does not exist) at this particular point in time and, so far as possible, how that regulation is likely to develop. In the same way that regional trends can be seen to emerge from the historical regulation of information technology, we hope to forecast the future treatment of cryptocurrency regulation where there are gaps or underdeveloped regulation. This list is not exhaustive but it covers the key jurisdictions at the time of going to press and provides global guidance when considering the important question: which jurisdiction is most conducive to developing new ventures in this expanding field? For regulation in the UK and Europe, see **Chapter 4**; and for regulation in North America see **Chapter 5**.

China

6.11   China falls into the category of a state that has not allowed cryptocurrencies and, rather than just failing to regulate it, has actively implemented laws to prevent any cryptocurrency activity to include declaring that initial coin offerings ('ICOs') are unlawful and prohibited and refusing to recognise cryptocurrencies as either a legal tender or (unlike, for example, Canada) able to be part of any barter or retail exchange programme; the expressed rationale is that the financial risks to the public and investors are great. That said, it is not illegal per se to hold, trade, buy or sell cryptocurrencies in China, but the ban on ICOs extends to exchange platforms that trade cryptocurrencies or provide facilitation services with the result that they cannot operate.

6.12   On 4 September 2017, the seven key constituent governmental bodies issued a Notice regarding Prevention of Risks of Token Offering and Financing. The notice banned all ICOs in China and ordered that any organisations or individuals who had previously completed an ICO to make arrangements including the return of token assets to investors to protect investor rights.

6.13   The notice essentially defined an ICO as an arrangement whereby fundraisers distribute digital tokens to investors who make financial contributions in the form of cryptocurrencies. The notice concluded that such a scheme constituted an unauthorised and illegal public financing activity, which involves financial crimes such as illegal distribution of financial tokens, illegal issuance of securities and illegal fundraising, financial fraud and pyramid schemes.

6.14   China has effectively sought to criminalise ICOs both at home and abroad since, pursuant to Article 6 of the People's Republic of China Criminal Law, where *any* of the criminal activities or results of such activities occurred in China, the crime is *deemed* to have occurred in the territory of China. This means that those outside China may be prosecuted under Chinese law which has extraterritorial effect. If the ICO involved alleged financial crimes based on Chinese criminal law standards, the promoters or organisers of those ICOs may potentially be subject to Chinese criminal liabilities if they are Chinese citizens. Even if they are not Chinese citizens, if overseas ICOs attracted Chinese investors, they may still potentially be subject to Chinese criminal liabilities.

6.15   The section of the notice that extended to crypto exchanges ordered that any so-called fundraising and trading platforms must not offer exchange services between fiat currency, tokens and virtual currencies or buy or sell tokens or virtual currencies, or buy or sell virtual currencies as a central counterparty or provide price determination or information intermediary services for tokens or virtual currencies. China also restricts and blocks internet access to the online sites of overseas cryptocurrency exchanges.

6.16   This is a complete reversal from the earlier period, around 2013, when China was regarded as a fertile and pioneering jurisdiction for cryptocurrency. We suspect that China's current view is also formed because it lacks faith in anything other than its own currency and, given the Chinese approach to state sovereignty, one would expect any digital currency to be solely under the power and jurisdiction of the state. Cryptocurrencies pose a threat to that philosophy and China is actively closing the lid on cryptocurrencies.

6.17   There is a complete ban on ICOs that use cryptocurrencies, and any attempt to do so would be illegal. The state has issued a set of ICO Rules and these impose restrictions not just on the ICOs themselves but also on the permission of cryptocurrency trading platforms. In effect, these prevent the sale, purchase or other related services around cryptocurrencies, and it seems that China has every intention of stamping out cryptocurrency trading.

6.18   Ironically, despite its attempts to prevent cryptocurrency trading, the People's Bank of China appears to be launching its own cryptocurrency. There are suggestions that the Governor has been conducting research in the currency and has established the Institute of Digital Money which sits within the People's Bank of China. The contradiction does, however, make sense when one takes account of the Chinese approach to data sovereignty, and sovereignty of the state in general, in relation to all matters fiscal and political. Cryptocurrency may well flourish in China but, if it does so, it will be as a mainstream government-backed currency and will be regarded as legal tender if it is issued only by the Central Bank and not by any other non-government-backed entity.

Gibraltar

6.19   In comparison, Gibraltar has actively legislated to regulate the operation of cryptocurrencies within its jurisdiction. It currently requires the registration of firms that use distributed ledger technology (DLT) to store or transmit value belonging to others. The registration process involves the Gibraltar Financial Services Commission ('GFSC') reviewing the application and, if satisfied that certain criteria are met, a licence may be granted, enabling the holder to operate a business using DLT.

6.20   On 1 January 2018, the government of Gibraltar introduced the Financial Services (Distributed Ledger Technology Providers) Regulations 2017, under the Financial Services (Investment and Fiduciary Services) Act. The aim of the legislation is to protect consumers, protect the reputation of Gibraltar as a well-regulated and safe environment for firms that use DLT, and enable Gibraltar to prosper from the use and growth of new financial technology.[1]

6.21   Under the legislation, those companies which seek to use DLT to store or transmit value must apply for a licence. The initial application assessment request carries a fee of £2,000 and, depending on the complexity of the application, as determined by the GFSC, the application for a DLT licence ranges from £8,000 to £28,000. The GFSC has a discretion to issue a licence if the applicant will comply with nine regulatory principles:

1.   A DLT Provider must conduct its business with honesty and integrity.

2.   A DLT Provider must pay due regard to the interests and needs of each and all its customers and must communicate with them in a way that is fair, clear and not misleading.

3.   A DLT Provider must maintain adequate financial and non-financial resources.

4.   A DLT Provider must manage and control its business effectively, and conduct its business with due skill, care and diligence; including having proper regard to risks to its business and customers.

5.   A DLT Provider must have effective arrangements in place for the protection of customer assets and money when it is responsible for them.

6.   A DLT Provider must have effective corporate governance arrangements.

7.   A DLT Provider must ensure that all of its systems and security access protocols are maintained to appropriate high standards.

8.   A DLT Provider must have systems in place to prevent, detect and disclose financial crime risks such as money laundering and terrorist financing.

---

1   Gibraltar Financial Services Commission, *Press Release: Distributed Ledger Technology (DLT) Regulatory Framework*, www.gfsc.gi/news/distributed-ledger-technology-dlt-regulatory-framework-270, 2 January 2018.

9. A DLT Provider must be resilient and have contingency arrangements for the orderly and solvent wind down of its business.

6.22 The United Kingdom, following Brexit, will provide a further interesting case study. At this time, MiFID and MiFID II have direct effect within the UK, and cannot be avoided. However, both Switzerland and Gibraltar exist within the single market, albeit not within the EEA. The UK could take a light touch approach, following the Swiss example, or could heavily regulate the cryptocurrency industry to generate revenue and to protect consumers.

Hong Kong

6.23 The blanket ban on ICOs bypassed Hong Kong, due to their separate political system from China, therefore resulting in crypto-related businesses moving to Hong Kong. However, like South Korea, Hong Kong is very aware of the risks that come with developing technology and plan to 'intervene when appropriate'.[2]

Blockchain remittances were successfully tested in Hong Kong through Ant Financial, a subsidiary of Alibaba.

6.24 However, in common with other jurisdictions, Hong Kong's regulators issued public warnings about crypto investments including ICOs, warning of risks and inviting investors to carry out due diligence. They urged market professionals to play their role in ensuring propriety over dealings in such financial instruments. They took active steps by sending letters to several crypto exchanges, warning them of the consequences of trading without a licence.

India

6.25 India has recently published a draft of National e-Commerce Policy. These proposals were being finalised in March 2019 and there is to be a three-year period for implementation. Further, there is currently, an Indian Data Protection Bill in existence.

6.26 The draft proposals make great play of a desire to achieve 'the protection of personal data and empower the users/consumers to have control over the data they generate and own'. They add that processing of personal data by corporations without explicit consent 'must be dealt with sternly'. However, the proposals then outline that it is 'vital that *we* retain control of data to ensure job creation in India'.

---

2 O'Neal, S. (2018) 'Hong Kong Continues Taking Regulatory Action, Hopes to Become International Blockchain Hub'. Available online at: https://cointelegraph.com/news/hong-kong-continues-taking-regulatory-action-hopes-to-become-international-blockchain-hub.

The proposals seek to create restrictions on cross border flows of data and envisage domestic alternatives to foreign based clouds and email facilities 'will be promoted'.

6.27   The draft envisages barring businesses from sharing the data of Indian users stored abroad even if consent is given. There are some exceptions but it is of note that social media companies and search engines will not be exempt. Indeed, it appears that, although not named, Amazon, Google and Facebook, will be specific targets.

6.28   Other significant features of the draft policy are that it will mandate all e-Commerce websites and applications available for downloading in India, to have a related business entity in India as the importer on record or the entity through which all sales are transacted.

6.29   Of huge significance to the direction of travel away from the European model of data regulation is the following quote 'the data of a country, therefore, is best thought of as a collective resource, a national asset, that the government holds in trust, but rights to which can be permitted'.

6.30   In a highly significant statement, the draft policy states that 'it is also important that government reserve the right to seek disclosure of source code and algorithms' from a regulatory perspective.

6.31   The significant take away from all of this is that India, as envisaged by the draft policy, firmly sees ownership of data as joint as between individual and state. This is a far cry from the European model.

6.32   It is to be noted that, as well as the draft policy, there is also, about to be debated before coming onto the statute book, an Indian Data Protection Bill. Echoing some of the principles behind the e-Commerce draft is the provision for data to be stored by data consuming entities on local severs. The test for determining the scope of data to be regulated by the Bill is data having 'connection with any business carried on in India 'or 'systematic activity of offering goods and services to data principals within India' or 'connection with activity which involves profiling of data principles within India.'

6.33   The Bill envisages keeping one copy of personal data stored on servers located in India, and critical personal data must be processed only in India. The term 'critical' will be determined at some later date. In what, at first blush, appears to be a contradiction, the Bill envisages that personal data, other than critical data, may be transferred outside India on the basis of approved contractual clauses or to countries approved by the Indian regulator. This lack of data liberalisation may hinder a digital economy which is currently on track to be valued at $1 trillion by 2022.

6.34   The proposals appear to, on the one hand, echo the European model of the sanctity of personal data but on the other, fall squarely into line with the Russian and Chinese model of the citing of data domestically.

6.35   Where does that leave the possibility of a consistent approach to data protection and management across the world? The potential problems seem to us to be many.

Israel

6.36   In accordance with its regulations, namely Supervision on Financial Services (Regulated Financial Services) Law 5776 issued in 2016, cryptocurrency is considered a financial asset in Israel for which the provision of Financial Services requires a licence. In addition to being licenced as a financial asset, trading in cryptocurrencies is subject to capital gains taxation. In order to apply for and be issued with a licence, one has to be an Israeli citizen or a resident who has reached the age of majority, is legally competent and who has not been declared bankrupt or in the case of a company, has not been required to dissolve. It is further required that a licensee must have a minimum specified equity and if an individual, not have been convicted of an offence that would render the licensee unfit to handle financial transactions.

6.37   Israel does not recognise cryptocurrencies as being actual currencies and the Bank of Israel recently declared that it would be difficult to devise regulations capable of monitoring the risks of such activity to the country's banks and their clients. Although cryptocurrencies are not recognised as currency or legal tender by the Bank of Israel, the Israel Tax Authority ('ITA') has proposed that payment by virtual currencies should be considered as a means of virtual payments and consequentially subject to taxation (Israel Tax Authority Circular number 5 of 2018).

6.38   Because virtual currency is viewed as an asset it is taxed so that unlike a regular currency the ITA will regard an increase in the value for cryptocurrency as a capital gain rather than an exchange fluctuation making it subject to capital gains tax. Individual investors will not be liable for VAT but anyone engaging in cryptocurrency mining will be classified as a dealer and consequently subject to VAT according to the Circular (Income Tax Ordinance). Anyone trading as a business will be classified as financial institution for tax purposes meaning that they will be unable to claim VAT on expenses but will be subject to an extra 70% profit tax applied to financial institutions. The ITA requires a declaration of transactions that involve cryptocurrency so that it can verify their existence and scope and calculate tax liability.

Japan

6.39   Japan has decided to regulate cryptocurrency. Since April 2017, cryptocurrency exchange businesses have been regulated by the Payment Services Act. This provides that cryptocurrency exchange businesses must be registered, must keep records, must take security measures and must take measures to protect their customers amongst other requirements. These cryptocurrency exchanges also fall within money laundering regulations.

6.40 The Japanese Payment Services Act defines cryptocurrency (although the term actually used is 'virtual currency') to be:

> 'property value that can be used as a payment for the purchase or rental of goods or provision of services by specified persons, that can be purchased from or sold to unspecified persons, and that is transferable via an electronic data processing system; or property value that can be mutually exchangeable for the above property value with unspecified versions and is transferrable via an electronic data processing system.'

6.41 The Payments Services Act also stipulates that cryptocurrencies are limited to property values that are stored electronically on electronic devices. This means that currency and currency denominated assets are excluded.

6.42 To operate a cryptocurrency exchange business in Japan, business operators must be registered with a competent local Funds Bureau. Business operators must be either a stock company or a foreign cryptocurrency exchange business that is a company and has a representative who is resident in Japan and an office in Japan. If there is no representative resident in Japan and an office in the jurisdiction then it will not be possible to comply. A foreign cryptocurrency business includes a cryptocurrency exchange service provider registered with a foreign government where that foreign country's law provides for an equivalent registration system to that used in Japan. This will necessarily limit the foreign cryptocurrency exchange businesses who are able to conduct business in Japan.

Kazakhstan, Belarus and Estonia

6.43 Kazakhstan introduced a blanket prohibition on products associated with the blockchain whilst Belarus took a totally contrary view and positively encouraged cryptocurrency initiatives including offering tax incentives to smooth the path.

Kyrgyz Republic

6.44 Interestingly, Kyrgyz legislation allows trade in cryptoassets but makes them subject to local taxation, money laundering and consumer protection law.

South Korea

6.45 Initially South Korea's regulators viewed the developments in cryptocurrency with caution. They were concerned about market speculation in the area and the corresponding possibility of the market overheating. They also shared concerns over illegal activity being masked by use of cryptocurrency. In

March 2018 the country's regulators banned foreigners and minors from opening new cryptocurrency accounts.

6.46   In January 2018, the South Korean government also 'announced a substantial tax levied on local crypto exchanges. Thus, all crypto trading platforms in the country are required to pay a 22 percent corporate tax and a 2.2 percent local income tax'.[3]

6.47   In May 2018, 'even South Korea's central bank began exploring the idea of using cryptocurrencies and blockchain … in order to meet their goal of a cashless society by 2020'.[4]

6.48   In July 2018, South Korean commercial banks sought to launch a blockchain-powered ID verification platform.

Russia

6.49

> 'On the 22nd of May, the Russian Parliament approved the first reading of new regulation for the cryptocurrency. The law will regulate the ICOs and cryptocurrencies defining both cryptocurrencies and tokens as property, as well as specifying the rules for interacting with crypto and blockchain-related technologies such as smart contracts and mining. Moreover, the new laws affirm that the Bank of Russia may restrict the number of crypto transactions for anyone who is not a qualified investor' (Zakharova & Ali, 2018).

At the time of writing, the legislation was waiting to be passed but was expected imminently.

Switzerland

6.50   Switzerland adopts a progressive approach towards cryptocurrency and blockchain technology, and has a permissive regulatory framework. This chapter concentrates specifically on cryptocurrency, with greater detail on blockchain use and regulation in **Chapter 1**. Switzerland, according to its Federal Council report, classifies cryptocurrency as a 'digital representation of a value which can be traded on the Internet but not accepted as legal tender anywhere'.[5] Switzerland, therefore, regards cryptocurrency as a commodity. Cryptocurrency and derivative exchanges are legal in Switzerland, subject to regulations. There

---

3   O'Neal, S. (2018) 'South Korea Reviews its Stance on Crypto to Become Blockchain Haven'. Available online at: https://cointelegraph.com/news/south-korea-reviews-its-stance-on-crypto-to-become-blockchain-haven.

4   Ibid.

5   Confederation suisse, *Federal Council report on virtual currencies in response to the Schwaab (13.3687) and Weibel (13.4070) postulates*, www.news.admin.ch/NSBSubscriber/message/attachments/35355.pdf, 25 June 2014, p 7.

are currently no cryptocurrency-specific regulations in relation to trading and offering in Switzerland, but cryptocurrency remains subjected to relevant existing regulations such as tax, money laundering and securities regulation.[6]

'13.2   Within Swiss law the regulation which applies to a cryptocurrency depends on whether it is classified as a 'payment token' (currency) or an 'asset token' (commodity). Payment tokens are intended as a means of payment whereas an asset token provides a debt or equity claim on the issuer. Asset tokens are analogous to equities bonds and derivatives and consequently are subject to the jurisdiction of the Swiss Financial Market Supervisory Authority ('FINMA') under the Financial Market Infrastructure Act ('FMIA'). Issuers of an asset token are subject to the requirements in the Swiss Code of Obligations.'[7]

6.51   The Swiss Banking Act will not generally apply to issuers of cryptocurrencies unless there is a promise to return the capital used to purchase the token with a guaranteed return. BitConnect would have fallen with the definition before its collapse on 16 January 2018.

6.52   Those who issue or manage a means of payment in Switzerland are a financial intermediary, which will be subject to Switzerland's anti-money laundering (AML) regulation. Cryptocurrency issuers, operators of an exchange, and custodian wallet providers, are therefore subject to this AML regulation.

6   Victor, *Cryptocurrency Regulations in Switzerland*, https://crushcrypto.com/cryptocurrency-regulations-in-switzerland/, 9 October 2018.
7   Federal Act on the Amendment of the Swiss Civil Code (Part Five: The Code of Obligations), of 30 March 1911 (Status as of 1 April 2017), www.admin.ch/opc/en/classified-compilati on/19110009/201704010000/220.pdf, last accessed 18 February 2019.

Chapter 7

Initial coin offerings

INTRODUCTION

7.1   The use of initial coin offerings ('ICOs') has generated a huge amount of controversy. A total of $7 billion was raised via ICO between January and June 2018 despite the volatile prices of cryptocurrencies. However, fewer than half of all ICOs survive four months after the offering,[1] while almost half of ICOs sold in 2017 failed by February 2018.[2]

7.2   Some investors have commented that ICOs represent the democratisation of structured funding. On 20 September 2017, CNBC reported comments made by billionaire Taizo Son, CEO at Mistletoe and younger brother of SoftBank founder and Japan's richest man Masayoshi Son:[3]

> '[ICOs are] very good because they democratize venture financing for not only professionals like venture capitalists, but also individuals can participate in exciting projects from start-ups to support.'

7.3   But, with a history of ICOs being used for fraud, scams and resulting securities law violations, are ICOs an ingenious new method for raising capital away from structured funding, or are they simply a method to extort money from naïve speculators?

7.4   This chapter first explains ICOs before looking at the legal and regulatory provisions in the United States (US), the United Kingdom (UK), and the European Union, before providing a brief overview of the position in China, where the state has acted to make ICOs illegal.

What is an ICO?

7.5   An ICO is a means of crowdfunding using cryptocurrencies. Although traditionally a public offering (crowdfunded), private ICOs are becoming more

1   Kharif, Olga, *Half of ICOs Die Within Four Months After Token Sales Finalized*, Bloomberg, 9 July 2018, www.bloomberg.com/news/articles/2018-07-09/half-of-icos-die-within-four-months-after-token-sales-finalized, last accessed 2 March 2019.
2   Hankin, Aaron, *Nearly half of all 2017 ICOs have failed*, Fortune, 26 February 2018, www.marketwatch.com/story/nearly-half-of-all-2017-icos-have-failed-2018-02-26, last accessed 2 March 2019.
3   Choudhury, Saheli Roy, *Billionaire CEO Taizo Son predicts that ICOs will come to dominate fundraising*, CNBC, 20 September 2017, www.cnbc.com/2017/09/20/ico-cryptocurrency-will-become-major-funding-source-billionaire-taizo-son-says.html, last accessed 27 February 2019.

common. In an ICO, 'tokens' or coins (technically also cryptocurrency) are sold to speculators or investors in exchange for legal tender or other cryptocurrencies such as Bitcoin or Ethereum. The tokens sold are promoted as future functional units of currency if or when the ICO's funding goal is met and the project launches. In some cases the tokens are required to use the system for its purposes, or may give holders voting rights that can be used to determine the projects into which funds are invested.

7.6   ICOs have most commonly been used as a source of capital for tech-based start-up companies. ICOs can allow start-ups to avoid regulatory compliance and intermediaries such as venture capitalists, banks and stock exchanges. The first ICOs fell outside existing regulations; however, since these initial offerings, state actors have been quick to either interpret existing regulatory provisions to include ICOs or, in some jurisdictions, such as China, they have created new legislative provisions to prohibit ICOs.

What is the regulatory picture in the United States?

7.7   It may seem counter-intuitive to begin with the regulatory landscape in the US before addressing the UK or the EU; however, without an understanding of the US perspective, it may be difficult to consider the UK.

7.8   On 25 July 2017, The Division of Enforcement of the US Securities and Exchange Commission ('SEC') investigated whether a German corporation, Slock.it, and its co-founders and intermediaries may have violated federal securities laws. Slock.it was a decentralised autonomous organisation ('DAO'), a term used to describe a virtual organisation embodied in computer code and executed on a distributed ledger or blockchain. The DAO was created with the objective of operating as a for-profit entity that could create and hold a quantity of assets through the sale of DAO tokens to investors, which would in turn be used to fund projects. The holders of DAO tokens stood to share in the anticipated earnings from these projects as a return on their investment in DAO tokens. In addition, DAO token holders could monetise their investments by re-selling the DAO tokens on a number of web-based platforms that supported secondary trading.

7.9   After tokens were sold, but before the DAO was able to commence funding, a cyber-attacker was able to steal approximately a third of the assets held by the DAO. The SEC decided not to pursue enforcement action against Slock.it, but importantly determined that DAO tokens were securities regulated by the SEC:[4]

> 'The investigation raised questions regarding the application of the U.S. federal securities laws to the offer and sale of DAO tokens, including the threshold question whether DAO tokens are securities. Based on the investigation, and under the facts

---

4   Securities and Exchange Commission, *Report of Investigation Pursuant to Section 21(a) of the Securities Exchange Act of 1934: The DAO*, Release No. 81207, 25 July 2017, pp 1–2.

presented, the Commission has determined that DAO tokens are securities under the Securities Act of 1933 ("Securities Act") and the Securities Exchange Act of 1934 ("Exchange Act"). The Commission deems it appropriate and in the public interest to issue this report of investigation ("Report") pursuant to Section 21(a) of the Exchange Act to advise those who would use a Decentralized Autonomous Organization ("DAO Entity"), or other distributed ledger or blockchain-enabled means for capital raising, to take appropriate steps to ensure compliance with the U.S. federal securities laws. All securities offered and sold in the United States must be registered with the Commission or must qualify for an exemption from the registration requirements. In addition, any entity or person engaging in the activities of an exchange must register as a national securities exchange or operate pursuant to an exemption from such registration.'

7.10   The decision remains important because it categorises ICOs or token sales as 'an investment contract', which falls to be treated as a security under section 2(a)(1) of the Securities Act and section 3(a)(10) of the Exchange Act.[5] Importantly, the SEC decision stresses that US federal security laws will apply to an ICO if it falls to be considered as an investment contract:[6]

'The Commission is aware that virtual organizations and associated individuals and entities increasingly are using distributed ledger technology to offer and sell instruments such as DAO tokens to raise capital. These offers and sales have been referred to, among other things, as "Initial Coin Offerings" or "Token Sales." Accordingly, the Commission deems it appropriate and in the public interest to issue this Report in order to stress that the U.S. federal securities law may apply to various activities, including distributed ledger technology, depending on the particular facts and circumstances, without regard to the form of the organization or technology used to effectuate a particular offer or sale.'

7.11   The impact of the decision is to require registration and disclosure which meets the provisions of the Securities Act. These include:

i.   **Registration with the SEC**: The Registration Forms that a company files with the SEC provide essential facts, including: a description of the company's properties and business; a description of the security to be offered for sale; information about the management of the company; and financial statements certified by independent accountants.

ii.   **Full and fair disclosure (a statutory prospectus)**: The registration provisions of the Securities Act contemplate that the offer or sale of securities to the public must be accompanied by the 'full and fair disclosure'

---

5   An investment contract is an investment of money in a common enterprise with a reasonable expectation of profits to be derived from the entrepreneurial or managerial efforts of others – See: *SEC v. W.J. Howey Co.*, 328 U.S. 293, 301 (1946), at 299: 'The "touchstone" of an investment contract "is the presence of an investment in a common venture premised on a reasonable expectation of profits to be derived from the entrepreneurial or managerial efforts of others.").' This definition embodies a "flexible rather than a static principle, one that is capable of adaptation to meet the countless and variable schemes devised by those who seek the use of the money of others on the promise of profits."'

6   Securities and Exchange Commission, *Report of Investigation Pursuant to Section 21(a) of the Securities Exchange Act of 1934: The DAO*, Release No. 81207, 25 July 2017, p 10.

afforded by registration with the SEC and delivery of a statutory prospectus containing information necessary to enable prospective purchasers to make an informed investment decision.

iii. **Disclosure of information about the issuer**: In *SEC v Cavanagh,* 1 F. Supp. 2d 337, 360 (S.D.N.Y. 1998), aff'd, 155 F.3d 129 (2d Cir. 1998), the Court held that SEC registration entailed the disclosure of detailed 'information about the issuer's financial condition, the identity and background of management, and the price and amount of securities to be offered'. This must be disclosed to the SEC and then to the public through the statutory prospectus.

iv. **Provide the material facts**: In *SEC v Aaron,* 605 F.2d 612, 618 (2d Cir. 1979) (citing *SEC v Ralston Purina Co.,* 346 U.S. 119, 124 (1953)) the Court determined that the statutory prospectus must provide the public with any information which might bear upon the value of the ICO or tokens offered: 'The registration statement is designed to assure public access to material facts bearing on the value of publicly traded securities and is central to the Act's comprehensive scheme for protecting public investors'.

v. **Offer is prohibited without registration and disclosure**: Section 5(a) of the Securities Act provides that, unless a registration statement is in effect as to a security, it is unlawful for any person, directly or indirectly, to engage in the offer or sale of securities in inter-state commerce. Section 5(c) of the Securities Act provides a similar prohibition against offers to sell, or offers to buy, unless a registration statement has been filed. Therefore, both sections 5(a) and 5(c) of the Securities Act prohibit the unregistered offer or sale of securities in inter-state commerce.

7.12 Issuers must register offers and sales of securities unless a valid exemption applies. The most common exemptions from the registration requirements include:

- private offerings to a limited number of persons or institutions;
- offerings of limited size;
- intra-state offerings; and
- securities of municipal, state and federal governments.

FACT BOX – REGISTERING AN ICO
Those issuing or offering to sell an ICO must be registered with the SEC unless an exemption applies. Registration includes the disclosure of information to the SEC and the issue of a statutory prospectus.
Registration statements and prospectuses become public shortly after the company files them with the SEC. All companies, domestic and foreign, are required to file registration statements and other forms electronically.
Issuing or offering to sell tokens associated with an ICO without registration (when an exemption does not apply) is **prohibited**.

INVESTMENT COMPANIES

7.13   In addition to requiring the registration of the ICO as a public offering, any company in the business of investing, reinvesting or trading in 'securities' (which would include ICO tokens) must register as an 'investment company' in accordance with section 8 of the Investment Company Act. Investment companies are subject to federal securities laws, including the Securities Act of 1933 and the Securities Exchange Act of 1934.

7.14   Investment companies are classified as management companies, unit investment trusts, or face-amount certificate companies. Management companies are divided into open-end companies and closed-end companies.

Glossary	
Investment Company	Section 3(a)(1) of the Investment Company Act defines an 'investment company' for the purposes of the federal securities laws. Section 3(a)(1)(A) of the Investment Company Act defines an investment company as an issuer which is or holds itself out as being engaged primarily, or proposes to engage primarily, in the business of investing, reinvesting or trading in securities (see Section 2(a)(36) of the Investment Company Act). Section 3(a)(1)(C) of the Investment Company Act defines an investment company as an issuer that is engaged or proposes to engage in the business of investing, reinvesting, owning, holding or trading in securities, and owns or proposes to acquire 'investment securities' having a value exceeding 40% of the value of its total assets (exclusive of government securities and cash items) on an unconsolidated basis.[7]
Management Companies	Structured as corporations or trusts, a management company's board of directors (or trustees) oversees the management of the company (see Section 2(a)(12) of the Investment Company Act). A management company's investment adviser (which is typically a separate entity, registered with the SEC) manages the company's portfolio securities for a fee (see Section 2(a)(20) of the Investment Company Act).
Unit investment trusts ('UITs')	Investment companies that do not have a board of directors, corporate officers, or an investment adviser. They generally invest in a relatively fixed portfolio of securities. UITs typically offer to the public a specific, fixed number of redeemable securities (or 'units'). UIT sponsors may maintain a secondary market for trading UIT units after the initial public offering (see Sections 4(2) and 26 of the Investment Company Act).

---

7   www.sec.gov/investment/fast-answers/divisionsinvestmentinvcoreg121504htm.html,   last accessed 28 February 2019.

Face-amount certificate companies	Investment companies that are engaged or propose to engage in the business of issuing face-amount certificates of the instalment type, or which have been engaged in such business and have any such certificates outstanding (see Sections 3(a)(1)(B) and 4(1) of the Investment Company Act). The term 'face-amount certificate' is defined in Section 2(a)(15) of the Investment Company Act. There are only a few face-amount certificate companies in existence today.
Open-end companies ('mutual funds')	Management investment companies that offer or have outstanding redeemable securities of which they are the issuers (see Section 5(a)(1) of the Investment Company Act). The term 'redeemable security' is defined in Section 2(a)(32) of the Investment Company Act. Mutual funds hold a portfolio of securities, typically managed by an investment adviser. Mutual funds generally offer an unlimited number of their shares to the public on a continuous basis.
Closed-end companies ('closed-end funds')	Management investment companies that hold a portfolio of securities managed by an investment adviser and include all management investment companies that do not issue redeemable securities. They usually offer to the public a fixed number of non-redeemable securities (see Sections 5(a)(2) and 23 of the Investment Company Act). Closed-end fund shares typically trade in the secondary market, usually on stock exchanges.

7.15   A foreign investment company, that is organised or otherwise created under the laws of a foreign country, may not register as an investment company nor publicly offer its securities through inter-state commerce in the United States, unless the company applies to the SEC for an order permitting the company to register under the Investment Company Act, and to make a public offering in the US.

7.16   The SEC may issue an order granting the application of a foreign investment company if the SEC finds that, by reason of special circumstances or arrangements, it is both legally and practically feasible to effectively enforce the provisions of the Investment Company Act against the company, and further finds that granting the application is otherwise consistent with the public interest and the protection of investors.[8]

7.17   Those considering the issue of an ICO in the US should first consider whether any of the exemptions apply. If the ICO is public and for-profit, registration with the SEC will likely be required. In addition to registering the ICO itself, the individual or company issuing the ICO will also need to be registered. Foreign companies will need to make a specific application to the SEC for an

---

8   Section 7(d) of the Investment Company Act.

order permitting the company to register under the Investment Company Act, and to make a public offering in the US. For companies incorporated in the UK, the granting of an order, although not a formality, is not impossible. Specific legal advice is likely to be required before an application is made.

What is the regulatory position in the UK?

7.18   ICOs **may** fall under the general prohibition contained within section 19 of the Financial Services and Markets Act 2000 ('FSMA'), which prevents any firm from carrying on a regulated activity in the UK unless it is authorised by the Financial Conduct Authority ('FCA') or exempted under FSMA. In order to undertake a regulated activity, the firm must be performing specified activities relating to specified investments, as defined in the FSMA (Regulated Activities) Order 2001 ('RAO'). Failure to obtain authorisation is a criminal offence, with a maximum sentence of two years' imprisonment, an unlimited fine, or both. Further, agreements entered into which are in contravention of the general prohibition may be void.

7.19   The confusion as to whether an ICO does fall to be regulated arises from a statement by the FCA on 12 September 2017, in which it issued a consumer warning on ICOs ('ICOs are very high-risk, speculative investments').[9] The FCA statement indicated that regulation could only be decided on a 'case by case' basis:[10]

'Whether an ICO falls within the FCA's regulatory boundaries or not can only be decided case by case.

Many ICOs will fall outside the regulated space. However, depending on how they are structured, some ICOs may involve regulated investments and firms involved in an ICO may be conducting regulated activities.

Some ICOs feature parallels with Initial Public Offerings ('IPOs'), private placement of securities, crowdfunding or even collective investment schemes. Some tokens may also constitute transferable securities and therefore may fall within the prospectus regime.

Businesses involved in an ICO should carefully consider if their activities could mean they are arranging, dealing or advising on regulated financial investments. Each promoter needs to consider whether their activities amount to regulated activities under the relevant law. In addition, digital currency exchanges that facilitate the exchange of certain tokens should consider if they need to be authorised by the FCA to be able to deliver their services.'

7.20   This rather opaque statement does not really provide any guidance on how an ICO might be regulated in the UK.

---

9   Financial Conduct Authority, *Statement: Consumer warning about the risks of Initial Coin Offerings ('ICOs')*, published: 12 September 2017, last updated: 27 February 2019, www.fca. org.uk/news/statements/initial-coin-offerings, last accessed 3 March 2019.
10 Ibid.

7.21 It is highly unlikely that tokens generated from an ICO would be considered by the FCA to constitute shares, as this would require the company offering the ICO to incorporate and have legal status. There is no parallel in the UK to the US concept of 'investment contracts' being securities. Therefore, unlike in the US, tokens aligned with an investment contract will not be classified as securities.

7.22 Conceivably, an ICO could be structured so that the token represents a digital loan rather than an investment in currency. In those instances, it is possible that an ICO could be considered to be a debenture ('instruments creating or acknowledging indebtedness' – see article 77 of the RAO). However, this would involve strict conferring of profit-sharing rights and, consequently, is again unlikely to arise.

How might ICOs be regulated in the UK?

7.23 Broadly speaking, if an ICO is to be regulated within the UK, it will fall to be regulated either as a collective investment scheme ('CIS') or an alternative investment fund ('AIF').

Collective investment scheme ('CIS')

7.24 A CIS is defined as 'any arrangements with respect to property of any description, including money', and is a specified investment in accordance with section 235 of FSMA:

> '**235 Collective investment schemes**
>
> (1) In this Part "collective investment scheme" means any arrangements with respect to property of any description, including money, the purpose or effect of which is to enable persons taking part in the arrangements (whether by becoming owners of the property or any part of it or otherwise) to participate in or receive profits or income arising from the acquisition, holding, management or disposal of the property or sums paid out of such profits or income.
>
> (2) The arrangements must be such that the persons who are to participate ("participants") do not have day-to-day control over the management of the property, whether or not they have the right to be consulted or to give directions.
>
> (3) The arrangements must also have either or both of the following characteristics–
>
>   (a) the contributions of the participants and the profits or income out of which payments are to be made to them are pooled;
>
>   (b) the property is managed as a whole by or on behalf of the operator of the scheme.
>
> (4) If arrangements provide for such pooling as is mentioned in subsection (3)(a) in relation to separate parts of the property, the arrangements are not to be regarded as constituting a single collective investment scheme unless the participants are entitled to exchange rights in one part for rights in another.
>
> (5) The Treasury may by order provide that arrangements do not amount to a collective investment scheme–

(a) in specified circumstances; or

(b) if the arrangements fall within a specified category of arrangement.'

7.25 In order to determine whether an ICO fulfils the definition of a CIS within FSMA, the issuer should consider four questions:

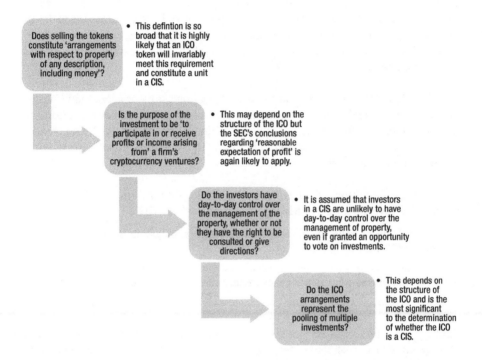

7.26 It is worth noting that, if these questions had been applied to the Slock. it DAO, it would have fallen within the definition of a CIS in section 235 of FSMA; in particular, the expected profits were to be pooled and the day-to-day management function of the DAO was in the hands of a few individuals rather than the collected investors, who merely had a vote over the direction of investments.

7.27 If an ICO meets the definition of a CIS, the person responsible will be carrying on a regulated activity of 'establishing, operating and winding-up' a CIS and would need to be authorised with FCA approval to carry on the activity.

7.28 Similarly, any company involved with an ICO, that falls within the definition of a CIS, would be undertaking arranging activities within the scope of the RAO, including:

i. fundraising for a specified activity;

ii. safeguarding and administering the fund; and

iii. discretionary management of assets.

Individuals and companies involved with the foundation of an ICO which meets the definition of an AIF may also need authorisation from the FCA.

Alternative investment fund ('AIF')

7.29　An AIF is a collection of investment undertakings that serve to raise funds from a number of investors. The purpose of AIFs is to allow investors to provide capital for a defined investment policy with the expectation of future dividends or economic gain (a hedge fund specialising in oil exploration products or rare wine would be an example of an AIF).

7.30　Most AIF assets are held by institutional investors or accredited,[11] high-net-worth individuals because of the complex nature and limited regulations of the investments. Alternative investments include private equity, hedge funds, managed futures, real estate, commodities and derivatives contracts. ICOs could fall within the definition.

7.31　The definition of an AIF can be found within Article 4(1)(a) of the Alternative Investment Fund Managers Directive ('AIFMD'):

'"AIFs" means collective investment undertakings, including investment compartments thereof, which:

(i)　raise capital from a number of investors, with a view to investing it in accordance with a defined investment policy for the benefit of those investors; and

(ii)　do not require authorisation pursuant to Article 5 of Directive 2009/65/EC;'

7.32　The authorisation mentioned within Article 4(a)(ii) is under the Undertakings for Collective Investment in Transferable Securities Directive 2009/65/EC ('UCITS Directive'). This is a consolidated EU Directive that allows CISs to operate freely throughout the EU on the basis of a single authorisation from one member state. In practice, the UCITS Directive requires a home state to authorise operators of a CIS. In the UK, authorisation is by the FCA.

7.33　An AIF is therefore an 'undertaking', regardless of structure, which 'raises capital from a number of investors, with a view to investing it in accordance with a defined investment policy for the benefit of those investors', and that does not fall to be authorised as a CIS. The definition is sufficiently broad to capture an ICO if there is a 'defined investment policy' and the profits raised are for the plurality of the investors.

7.34　The AIFMD is a regulatory framework for alternative investment fund managers, including managers of hedge funds, private equity firms and investment trusts. The AIFMD is EU legislation but was implemented in the UK on 22 July 2013.

---

11 'Accredited investors' are those with a net worth exceeding $1 million or with a personal income of $200,000 or more per year.

7.35   In the UK the AIF is not specifically regulated but can be authorised.[12] ICOs that fall within the definition of an AIF will likely be unauthorised. Regardless, the AIF manager ('AIFM') is required to be authorised. In addition, firms which act as depositories for an AIF are subject to depositary standards and an enhanced transparency regime through investor disclosure rules and mandatory reporting to competent authorities.

AIFM REQUIREMENTS[13]	
Authorisation	AIFMs must be authorised by the home state (in the UK, the FCA) as a fund manager under the full-scope AIFM or, alternatively, registration is subject to a lighter regime for AIFMs managing AIFs with 'assets under management' below certain thresholds. Sub-threshold AIFMs may not benefit from the AIFMD's marketing and management 'passports'; however, they have the right to opt in to full authorisation to access AIFMD passports.[14]
Conduct of business principles	There must be fair treatment of investors, with specific consideration to conflicts of interest, remuneration, risk management, valuation, disclosure to investors and regulators.
Regulated capital	An AIFM must define 'initial capital' and 'own funds' within the AIF. Professional indemnity insurance is required.
Safekeeping of investments	Depositories must be separate from the AIFM and are mandatory.
Controls over delegation	Certain tasks, including portfolio management and risk management, cannot be delegated.

7.36   Full-scope UK AIFMs are required to notify the FCA of material changes to the conditions for initial authorisation – in particular, material changes to the information provided at authorisation. A change should be deemed as material if there is 'a substantial likelihood that a reasonable investor, becoming aware of such information, would reconsider its investment in the AIF, including because such information could have an impact on an investor's ability to exercise their rights in relation to investment, or otherwise prejudice the interests of one or more investors in the AIF'.[15] Firms are encouraged to assess the materiality of the change being notified against this principle.

---

12 Certain investment funds can seek specific authorisation from the FCA, for example: an investment company with variable capital; an authorised contractual scheme; or an authorised unit trust scheme.
13 www.fca.org.uk/firms/aifmd.
14 www.fca.org.uk/firms/aifmd/uk-aifm.
15 Financial Conduct Authority, AIFM notifications, first published 8 June 2016, last updated 18 January 2019, www.fca.org.uk/firms/aifmd/notifications, last accessed 4 March 2019.

7.37 A firm which wishes to act as a depository for an AIF must seek permission from the FCA. A depositary of an AIF cannot be an AIFM or a CIS management company. The AIFM and the depositary of an authorised AIF must be independent of each other; however, the AIFM and the depositary of an unauthorised AIF can be separate yet connected entities in the same group, provided there is proper management and disclosure of potential conflicts of interest.

7.38 A full depository must be one of the following:[16]

'1.   an EEA credit institution

2.   an authorised MiFID investment firm which provides the services of safe-keeping and administration of financial instruments and which has own funds of not less than €730,000 under Article 28 of the CRD (2013/36/EU) (for a UK firm this would be an IFPRU 730k firm with permission to safeguard and administer investments)

3.   a firm which on 21 July 2011 had a Part 4A permission of acting as trustee of an authorised unit trust scheme or depositary of an open-ended investment company that in either case is a UCITS scheme

4.   another type of authorised person or an unauthorised person which will, if authorised as a depositary of AIF, only:

   a.   act as trustee or depositary for AIFs of the kind defined in FUND 3.11.12R (a PE AIF depositary), and/or

   b.   provide one or more depositary services to non-EEA AIFs.'

7.39 An authorised AIF can only use the firms or institutions listed at 1–3 above as a depository. An unauthorised AIF, into which ICOs (if regulated as an AIF) would likely fall, can have any of 1–4 as a depository. As an unauthorised AIF, an ICO could also have a 'separate yet connected entity' as a depository. An authorised person connected to the ICO could act as a trustee or depository if sufficient separation could be demonstrated.

7.40 A full-scope AIFM who wishes to market an AIF in the UK must apply to the FCA for permission. This permission can allow marketing to retail and/ or professional investors in the UK, but also to 'passport' so that an AIF can be marketed into the EEA.[17] A small authorised UK AIFM does not have an EEA right to market AIFs to investors in other EEA states, and must comply with UK marketing laws.

7.41 Companies seeking to market an ICO to UK investors can use the passporting provisions of the AIFMD if they are based within the EEA and are authorised by their home state. Otherwise, the FSMA and RAO provisions have supranational effect, over foreign companies, if marketed towards or sold to a person within the UK.

---

16 Financial Conduct Authority, Depositaries, first published 8 June 2016, last updated 28 January 2019, www.fca.org.uk/firms/aifmd/depositaries, last accessed 4 March 2019.
17 Financial Conduct Authority, UK AIFM marketing and passporting, first published 8 June 2016, last updated 28 January 2019, www.fca.org.uk/firms/aifmd/uk-aifm/marketing-passporting, last accessed 4 March 2019.

RESTRICTIONS OF MARKETING AN ICO WHICH IS A CIS OR AN AIF

7.42   Section 21 of FSMA states that: 'a person must not, in the course of business, communicate an invitation or inducement to engage in investment activity unless the promotion has been made or approved by an authorised person or it is directed at a person who falls into one of the exempt categories of recipient and meets a series of tests'. Consequently, without authorisation, or an applicable exemption, marketing the regulated ICO is prohibited.

7.43   Further, sections 89 and 90 of the Financial Services Act 2012 ('2012 Act') prohibit misleading statements (s 89) and misleading impressions (s 90) with respect to a regulated ICO. Under section 89 of the 2012 Act, a token issuer would be committing a criminal offence if it knowingly or recklessly made a false or misleading statement, or dishonestly concealed any material facts, with the intention of inducing, or it was reckless as to whether it might induce, another person to enter into, or refrain from entering into, a relevant agreement (for example, an agreement to subscribe for tokens).

Similarly, a token issuer would commit an offence under section 90 of the 2012 Act if a false or misleading impression was created as to the market in, or the price or value of, a relevant investment, in order to induce another person to acquire or subscribe for investments such as tokens.

7.44   A person found guilty of either offence in the Crown Court could be sentenced to seven years' imprisonment or an unlimited fine, or both.

THE LIMITED APPROACH OF THE EUROPEAN UNION

7.45   There is no explicit ICO regulation or direction which provides overarching governance within the EU. The European Securities and Markets Authority ('ESMA') has issued two statements which constitute the extent of specific regulatory oversight, from the EU, on a supranational level.

7.46   Both statements were issued on 13 November 2017: the first alerted investors to the risks involved in investing in ICOs;[18] and the second alerted firms, involved in ICOs, of the need to meet regulatory requirements.[19]

7.47   The alert to investors described ICOs, in a similar manner to the FCA, as: 'highly speculative investments'. ESMA warned investors that there was a lack of protection available with regard to investments in ICOs and that there was a possibility of losing the entirety of their investment:

> 'ESMA stresses that ICOs are extremely risky and highly speculative investments. Investors should realise that they are exposed to the following risks when investing in ICOs:

18 www.esma.europa.eu/sites/default/files/library/esma50-157-829_ico_statement_investors.pdf.
19 www.esma.europa.eu/sites/default/files/library/esma50-157-828_ico_statement_firms.pdf.

- Unregulated space, vulnerable to fraud or illicit activities – Depending on how they are structured, ICOs may not be captured by the existing rules and may fall outside of the regulated space. Some ICOs may be used for fraudulent or illicit activities, with several recent ICOs having been identified as frauds, while ESMA cannot exclude that some are being used for money laundering purposes. In the case where an ICO does not fall under the scope of EU laws and regulations, investors cannot benefit from the protection that these laws and regulations provide;

- High risk of losing all of the invested capital – The vast majority of ICOs are launched by businesses that are at a very early stage of development. Those businesses have an inherently high risk of failure. Many of the coins or tokens that are being issued have no intrinsic value other than the possibility to use them to access or use a service/product that is to be developed by the issuer. There is no guarantee that the services/products will be successfully developed and, even assuming that the project is successful, any eventual benefit may be extremely low relative to the invested capital;

- Lack of exit options and extreme price volatility – Investors may not be able to trade their coins or tokens or to exchange them for traditional currencies, such as the Euro. Not all the coins or tokens are traded on virtual currency exchanges and when they are, like virtual currencies, their price may be extremely volatile. Many of those exchanges are unregulated and vulnerable to market price manipulation and fraudulent activities. Investors may be exposed to the lack of exit options or not be able to redeem their coin or token for a prolonged period;

- Inadequate information – The information that is made available to investors, e.g. in so-called white papers, is in most cases unaudited, incomplete, unbalanced or even misleading. It typically puts the emphasis on the potential benefits but not the risks. It is technical and not easily comprehensible. Investors may therefore not understand the risks that they are taking and make investments that are not appropriate to their needs; and

- Flaws in the technology – The distributed ledger or blockchain technology that underpins the coins or tokens is still largely untested. There may be flaws in the code or programs that are used to create, transfer or store the coins or tokens. Investors may not be able to access or control their coins or tokens, or the coins or tokens may be stolen, e.g., in case of a hack. More generally, the technology may not function quickly and securely, e.g. during peaks of activity.'

7.48   In the alert to firms, ESMA went further than the FCA, stating that, when coins or tokens qualified as a financial instrument, it was likely that the firms involved in the ICO would be conducting regulated investment activities. However, like the FCA, ESMA stressed that whether an ICO falls within the regulated sphere very much depends on how it is structured:

'ESMA reminds firms involved in ICOs of their obligations under EU regulation

Firms involved in ICOs must give careful consideration as to whether their activities constitute regulated activities. If their activities constitute a regulated activity, firms have to comply with the relevant legislation and any failure to comply with the applicable rules would constitute a breach.

Depending on how they are structured, ICOs may fall outside of the scope of the existing rules and hence outside of the regulated space. However, where the coins or tokens qualify as financial instruments it is likely that the firms involved in ICOs conduct regulated investment activities, such as placing, dealing in or advising on financial instruments or managing or marketing collective investment schemes.

Moreover, they may be involved in offering transferable securities to the public. The key EU rules listed below are then likely to apply.

Please note that what follows is a high-level summary of the key applicable EU legislation. It is not intended to be an exhaustive account of the applicable rules nor of the requirements laid down in these legislations. In addition, national rules may apply.

It is the duty of the firms themselves to consider the regulatory framework, seeking the necessary permissions and meeting the applicable requirements.

Prospectus Directive

The Prospectus Directive (PD) aims to ensure that adequate information is provided to investors by companies when raising capital in the EU. It requires publication of a prospectus before the offer of transferable securities to the public or the admission to trading of such securities on a regulated market situated or operating within a Member State, unless certain exclusions or exemptions apply. In particular, the PD specifies that the prospectus shall contain the necessary information which is material to an investor for making an informed assessment of the facts and that the information shall be presented in an easily analysable and comprehensible form. The PD does not directly specify who should draw up the prospectus but requires that the party responsible for the information (being at least the issuer, the offeror, the party seeking admission to trading or the guarantor) is specified in the prospectus. Depending on how the ICO is structured, the coins or tokens could, potentially, fall within the definition of a transferable security, and could therefore necessitate the publication of a prospectus which will be subject to approval by a Competent Authority.

The Markets in Financial Instruments Directive

The Markets in Financial Instruments Directive (MiFID) aims to create a single market for investment services and activities and to ensure a high degree of harmonised protection for investors in financial instruments. A firm that provides investment services/activities in relation to financial instruments as defined by MiFID needs to comply with MiFID requirements. In the case of ICOs, where the coin or token qualifies as a financial instrument, the process by which a coin or token is created, distributed or traded is likely to involve some MiFID activities/services, such as placing, dealing in or advising on financial instruments. The organisational requirements, the conduct of business rules and the transparency requirements laid down in MiFID would then apply, depending in some cases on the services provided.

Alternative Investment Fund Managers Directive

The Alternative Investment Fund Managers Directive (AIFMD) lays down the rules for the authorisation, ongoing operation and transparency of the managers of alternative investment funds (AIFMs) which manage and/or market alternative investment funds (AIFs) in the Union. Depending on how it is structured, an ICO scheme could qualify as an AIF, to the extent that it is used to raise capital from a number of investors, with a view to investing it in accordance with a defined investment policy. Firms involved in ICOs may therefore need to comply with AIFMD rules. In particular, AIFMD provides for capital, operational and organisational rules and transparency requirements.

Fourth Anti-Money Laundering Directive

The Fourth Anti-Money Laundering Directive prohibits money laundering and terrorist financing. It applies to firms including credit institutions and financial institutions, the latter including MiFID investment firms, collective investment undertakings marketing their units or shares and firms providing certain services offered by credit institutions without being one. The Directive requires firms to carry out due diligence on customers and to have in place appropriate record-keeping and other internal procedures. Firms have an obligation to report any suspicious activity and to co-operate with any investigations by relevant public authorities.'

7.49   Financial instruments which fall within the EU regulatory regimes would likely be required to comply with the Markets in Financial Instruments Directive ('MiFID'), the Alternative Investment Fund Managers Directive ('AIFMD') and the Fourth Anti-Money Laundering Directive ('MLD4').

7.50   Although ESMA has mentioned the Prospectus Directive, this relates to the offer of securities and is unlikely to relate to the issue of tokens under an ICO (see Article 1(2)(a): '2. This Directive shall not apply to: (a) units issued by collective investment undertakings other than the closed-end type').

7.51   The requirements of MiFID are contained within **Chapter 4**, and AIFMD is discussed above.

7.52   MLD4 came into force on 26 June 2017, and provided a new threshold for which customer due diligence ('CDD') must occur. CDD is now required by anyone trading goods in cash with a value over €10,000 (previously €15,000). ICO tokens traded for €10,000 or more, or for the sterling, dollar, or potential cryptocurrency equivalent, must be subject to CDD.

7.53   MLD4 also enhanced requirements with regard to local politically exposed persons ('PEPs'). Previously, it was only foreign PEPs which required greater scrutiny. The Directive does not prevent ICO tokens from being sold to those who could be considered PEPs within the jurisdiction, but it does require further questioning in relation to the source of funds used. PEPs should not be refused access to an ICO on the basis of their status. This would be 'contrary to the letter and spirit of this Directive and of the revised FATF Recommendations'.[20]

7.54   Most significantly, any corporate or legal entity involved with an ICO will be required to maintain an accurate and current register of beneficial ownership, which must be provided to the relevant regulatory authority (in the UK, the FCA). The information on beneficial ownership will be held by each

---

20 Directive (EU) 2015/849 of the European Parliament and of the Council of 20 May 2015 on the prevention of the use of the financial system for the purposes of money laundering or terrorist financing, amending Regulation (EU) No 648/2012 of the European Parliament and of the Council, and repealing Directive 2005/60/EC of the European Parliament and of the Council and Commission Directive 2006/70/EC, Note (33).

member state in a central register that will be accessible to banks, law firms and 'any person or organisation that can demonstrate a legitimate interest'.[21]

7.55 The central register of beneficial ownership will contain the names, dates of birth, nationality, country of residence and the nature and extent of the beneficial owners' interests in the transaction.

7.56 MLD4 has removed the automatic exemptions for enhanced CDD previously enjoyed by: credit or financial institutions subject to the requirements of the Money Laundering Directive or similarly compliant local legislation; companies whose securities are listed on a regulated market subject to specified disclosure obligations; and UK public authorities. Circumstances such as previous exemption can be used to justify simplified CDD; however, this is no longer automatic. Any decision upon simplified CDD must be reasoned and evidenced.

7.57 Companies and individuals, involved in ICO trading, should adopt a risk-based approach to their anti-money laundering considerations. MLD4 requires regulated individuals to demonstrate that: risk assessments have been undertaken and are updated; policies and procedures are in place; and, where necessary, compliance is tested by internal teams. Training is also considered to be an ongoing requirement.

7.58 Whether these Directives do apply to an ICO will be for the determination of the home state which is responsible for authorisation. There are some areas of discretion throughout the different jurisdictions, but more importantly it is for the national regulators, rather than ESMA, to determine whether a token falls within the definition of a financial instrument. It is this determination which will ultimately decide whether the national or overarching EU legislation will apply.

7.59 If the ICO is based within the UK, the guidance within this book should be considered. Until there is a decision on Brexit, companies will be able to benefit from the passporting provisions contained within EU legislation. If an ICO is based within another jurisdiction within the EU, local interpretations will need to be considered. Specific legal advice should be sought.

THE CHINESE CASE STUDY OF PROHIBITION

7.60 Prior to September 2017, Reuters reported, citing local media, that ICOs in China raised at least 2.62 billion yuan (about $400 million).[22]

---

21 Ibid, Article 30(5)(c).
22 Choudhury, Saheli Roy, *China bans companies from raising money through ICOs, asks local regulators to inspect 60 major platforms*, CNBC, 5 September 2017, www.cnbc.com/2017/09/04/chinese-icos-china-bans-fundraising-through-initial-coin-offerings-report-says.html,   last accessed 27 February 2019.

7.61   However, on 4 September 2017, seven government administrations, including the People's Bank of China, the China Securities Regulatory Commission, the China Banking Regulatory Commission and the China Insurance Regulatory Commission, issued a joint statement condemning illegal public funding through ICOs:[23]

> 'The ICO is essentially an unauthorised illegal public financing, suspected of illegal fundraising, illegal issuance of securities, illegal sale of tokens, and financial fraud, pyramid schemes and other criminal activities. The country is fully comprehensive; the new ICO financing is fully suspended; the projects that have already occurred must be judged on a case-by-case basis to combat violations.'

7.62   The People's Bank of China explained the public denouement of funding through blockchain-based currency on the basis that it was rife with fraud.[24] The immediate ban on ICOs, which included the issue of a list of 60 major Chinese ICO platforms for local financial regulatory bodies to inspect, caused the value of Bitcoin to fall by approximately 5%.[25]

7.63   The extent to which the ban was successful, though, is debatable. Speaking to CNBC's Squawk Box, Zennon Kapron, founder and director at consultancy firm Kapronasia, said:[26]

> 'The only way you can really stop bitcoin in China completely is if you shut down the internet. So the regulators are really focused on the points where bitcoin hits fiat currency.[27] The current regulation that's being talked about is banning bitcoin exchanges, which would cut out a lot of the trade flows we're seeing in China right now and the exchanges around bitcoin.'

Kapron added, 'So we'll likely see them focused around those activities where there is an entity or person or some kind of connection to the traditional financial system that they can control'.

---

23 Yuxi, Wu, *Exclusive ICO Incorporate Mutual Gold Risk Special Rehabilitation No. 99 Document to Start Cleanup and Rectification* (独家IICO纳入互金风险专项整治99号文启动清理整顿), Caixin, 4 September 2017, http://finance.caixin.com/2017-09-04/101140069.html, last accessed 27 February 2019.

24 Cheng, Leng and Yujian, Wu, *China Claws Back at Cryptocurrencies With Ban on Initial Coin Offerings*, Caixin, English, 4 September 2017, www.caixinglobal.com/2017-09-04/china-claws-back-at-cryptocurrencies-with-ban-on-initial-coin-offerings-101140498.html?sourceEntityId=101140069, last accessed 27 February 2017.

25 Choudhury, Saheli Roy, *China bans companies from raising money through ICOs, asks local regulators to inspect 60 major platforms*, CNBC, 5 September 2017, www.cnbc.com/2017/09/04/chinese-icos-china-bans-fundraising-through-initial-coin-offerings-report-says.html, last accessed 27 February 2019.

26 Choudhury, Saheli Roy, *Governments want to control cryptocurrencies – but there's a danger to too many rules*, CNBC, 12 September 2017, www.cnbc.com/2017/09/12/regulators-are-turning-their-attention-to-cryptocurrencies.html, last accessed 27 February 2019.

27 Fiat money is a currency without intrinsic value that has been established as money, often by government regulation. Fiat money does not have use value, and has value only because a government maintains its value, or because parties engaging in exchange agree on its value.

7.64   In a controlled economy, ICOs, or any crowdfunding, may represent an unacceptable risk to the state's power. Like Taizo Son said, ICOs 'democratize' venture financing. Investors should therefore take into account the potential risk of subsequent, but retrospective, legislative oversight if they are considering investing in an ICO in a jurisdiction that could be considered more interventionist.

Chapter 8

The Internet of Things

INTRODUCTION

8.1   It is estimated that by 2020 there will be over 200 billion connected sensors[1] contained within 30 billion Internet of Things ('IoT') devices.[2] By 2025, the estimated market value for the IoT will be between $2.7 and $6.2 trillion per year.[3]

8.2   The IoT is not, however, the future but the present. In 1999, Kevin Ashton, a British-born technology pioneer, then working for Procter & Gamble (P&G), devised a presentation titled 'Internet of Things'.[4] At the time, this was merely a snappy title to include the newly fashionable 'internet'. However, Ashton went on to develop the phrase, and predicted that home sensors would one day inform choices in all aspects of our lives: 'We're consuming so many things without thinking about them – energy, plastic, paper, calories. I can envision a ubiquitous sensor network, a platform for real-time feedback that will enhance the comfort, security, and control of our lives'.[5]

What is the IoT?

8.3   In simple terms, the IoT is a network of physical devices that are able to exchange data. At its most basic, IoT devices permit remote monitoring or control of previously 'dumb' devices (for example, turning your house lights on and off with your mobile telephone). However, many IoT devices now contain a sensor[6] that can be programmed to detect data inputs, whether it is physical movement, atmospheric circumstances or biometric information.

1   Bajarin, Tim, *The Next Big Thing for Tech: The Internet of Everything*, TIME, 13 January 2014, http://time.com/539/the-next-big-thing-for-tech-the-internet-of-everything (last accessed 19 September 2018).
2   Nordrum, Amy, *Popular Internet of Things Forecast of 50 Billion Devices by 2020 Is Outdated* https://spectrum.ieee.org/tech-talk/telecom/internet/popular-internet-of-things-forecast-of-50-billion-devices-by-2020-is-outdated, 18 August 2016 (last accessed 19 September 2018).
3   Manyika, James; Chui, Michael; Bughin, Jacques; Dobbs, Richard; Bisson, Peter; and Marrs, Alex, *Disruptive Technologies: Advances That Will Transform Life, Business, And The Global Economy (51)*, Mckinsey & Co., May 2013.
4   Ashton, Kevin, *That 'Internet of Things' Thing*, www.rfidjournal.com/articles/view?4986, 22 June 2009 (last accessed 19 September 2018).
5   Goetz, Thomas, *Harnessing the Power of Feedback Loops*, www.wired.com/2011/06/ff_feedbackloop/all/1/ (19 June 2011) (last accessed 19 September 2018).
6   Microelectronmechanical systems (MEMS) sensors.

8.4   A good example of this is Hive, from British Gas. At its most basic level, the Hive App allows for remote control of household heating and lighting. However, through the thermostat, data is collected and analysed by the Hive App, which allows comparison of energy usage over time or with those in your local area. Again, this is a basic use of the data collected through a sensor.

8.5   The possibilities for data use extend well beyond simple comparison into the sphere of psychological profiling through the use of IoT devices. Data regarding electricity usage can reveal a person's movements (whether they are at home or not), habits (sleeping and eating patterns) and their leisure activities. One research project determined, with 96% accuracy, the television programme or film that a person was watching from monitoring the electrical signals emanating from the person's house.[7] The higher the number of sensor inputs, the larger the pool of data, and the greater the inferences which can be drawn.

8.6   Since the beginning of the decade, the cost of sensors has fallen from $25 to less than a $1 a unit.[8] The fall in the cost of sensors used to gather information, coupled with the growth of 'big data' analytics, has led to innovation in 'old' technology for a comparative advantage to companies and a benefit for consumers. With only the fewest exceptions, every home within the United Kingdom (UK) has a gas and/or electric meter. The 'Smart Meter' is the IoT version designed to gather data for the more efficient distribution of gas and electricity across the UK. By 2020, the UK Government wants all 26 million homes in the UK to have been offered the use of a Smart Meter.[9]

8.7   Trying to list the IoT devices available would be an impossible task. On the date of writing, the list would constitute half the book and, on the date of publication, it would already be out-of-date. Limiting the consideration of IoT devices to the area of health and fitness, there are four broad categories of device which illustrate the diverse use of the IoT:[10]

i.   Countertop Devices (such as weight scales and blood pressure monitors) are common, commercially purchased devices which link to a mobile app or computer. The Aria weight scale, for example, maps weight, body fat percentage and Body Mass Index (BMI) to a mobile telephone app. The

---

7 Enev, Miro; Gupta, Sidhant; Kohno, Tadayoshi; and Patel, Shwetak, *Televisions, Video Privacy, and Powerline Electromagnetic Interference*, In Proceedings of the 18th ACM conference on Computer and communications security (CCS '11). ACM, New York, NY, USA, 537-550. DOI=http://dx.doi.org/10.1145/2046707.2046770 (last accessed 20 September 2018).

8 Wolfe, Alexander, *Little MEMS Sensors Make Big Data Sing*, ORACLE VOICE, FORBES, 10 June 2013, www.forbes.com/sites/oracle/2013/06/10/little-mems-sensors-make-big-data-sing/ (last accessed 19 September 2018).

9 Smart Energy GB, About the rollout: 'The government wants energy suppliers to install smart meters in every home in England, Wales and Scotland. There are more than 26 million homes for the energy suppliers to get to, with the goal of every home being offered a smart meter by 2020', www.smartenergygb.org/en/smart-future/about-the-rollout (last accessed 19 September 2018).

10 Peppet, Scott R., *Regulating the Internet of Things: First Steps Toward Managing Discrimination, Privacy, Security and Consent*, Texas Law Review [Vol. 93:85 2014].

device is designed to be used occasionally in conjunction with its sister product, the Fitbit, as part of a program towards healthier living.

ii. Wearable Sensors are also commercially, and now readily, available. Fitbit and Nike+ are electronic pedometers that track steps taken, distances walked, calories burned, and heart rate. On 26 February 2018, Fitbit recorded 25.4 million active users over 86 countries. These figures can be considered to be reliable, as Fitbit is able to actively record data from their users minute-by-minute through their Fitbit software.

iii. Intimate Contact Sensors are currently used more for medical or research purposes than commercially available; however, these are increasingly being used by professional sports people.[11] Similar to wearable sensors, intimate contact sensors are embedded into bandages, medical tape or skins. These are also called 'epidermal electronics'. The increased surface area over which the sensors are placed provides for great variety in data to be obtained, including heart rate, brain activity, body temperature, hydration levels, and exposure to ultraviolet radiation.[12]

iv. Ingestible and Implantable Sensors are currently not for commercial use, but are increasingly being used within medical research. Medtronic, an Israeli medical technology company, has developed PillCamm (a pill-sized camera used to detect bleeding and other problems within the gastro-intestinal tract) and SmartPill (an ingestible capsule that measures pressure, pH levels and temperature as it travels through the body). The use of IoT Pacemakers, an implantable device, has been controversial, and, in 2017, attracted attention from the US Food and Drug Administration ('FDA') due to security concerns.

8.8   The IoT appears to be a new frontier in which there can be great commercial success. Those seeking to exploit the advantages intrinsic within IoT devices, either as a purchaser or a manufacturer, must however be aware of the security concerns regarding IoT devices.

Security problems with the IoT

8.9   In November 2018, printers across the world showed their support for Felix 'PewDiePie' Kjellberg, the Swedish star of the most subscribed YouTube channel available at the time. Without notice, 50,000 printers began printing

---

11 GlobalSportsJobs.com, *Important Considerations for Athletes in the Boom of Wearable Sensor Technology*, www.globalsportsjobs.com/article/important-considerations-for-athletes-int-he-boom-of-wearable-sensor-technology, 1 June 2016 (last accessed 20 September 2018).

12 Grobart, Sam, *MC10's BioStamp: The New Frontier of Medical Diagnostics*, BLOOMBERG BUSINESSWEEK, 13 June 2013, www.bloomberg.com/news/articles/2013-06-13/mc10s-biostamp-the-new-frontier-of-medical-diagnostics (last accessed 24 June 2019).

leaflets urging support for the vlogger while suggesting that a rival YouTube channel be ignored.[13]

Whether you are using a printer connected to a network, a wireless projector in an office conference room, or have a smart fridge in the company kitchen, owners and directors must understand the security concerns related to IoT devices. This is not a problem solely for the IT Department. Your IT Administrator is very unlikely to have purchased the new 'up-to-date' kitchen equipment, or be responsible for any remote access to the heating and air conditioning. However, these are potential access points for a determined 'hacker' looking to infiltrate a firm's systems, and if there is a breach, it is the board of directors who will have to notify the Information Commissioner's Office ('ICO') and to answer to the shareholders.

8.10 IoT devices are designed to be convenient in use, as well as to obtain and transmit data wirelessly. This imposes a physical restriction on the device's form. IoT devices must, in general, be small (or at least no bigger than their 'dumb' comparison) and battery powered. This intrinsically imposes a potential for security weakness. The processing power necessary for cyber security is not generally conducive with the microprocessors used in small-form IoT devices. There is simply not enough computational power to undertake the desired IoT task and protect the device through, for example, encryption. Battery power is also an issue. Separate security measures will draw upon the device's power, which lessens battery life or increases the size of the device to incorporate a larger battery.

8.11 Researchers have been exploring the security vulnerabilities of embedded systems for a number of years. In 2010, General Motors introduced a feature to enable car owners to manipulate the locks of a car, and start the car's engine, from anywhere in the world using a smartphone. The feature utilised General Motors' OnStar telematics system, which was standard in every US Ford from 2007. A team of researchers at Oakland University published a study demonstrating that, using these embedded systems, the car's brakes, engine and accelerator could be manipulated, potentially with malice.[14]

8.12 In November 2013, Symantec discovered an Internet worm that targeted over 100,000 IoT devices, including smart televisions, wireless speakers and internet-connected security cameras.[15] The aim of the worm was to produce 'ThingBots', the IoT equivalent of 'Botnets'. A hacker who has taken over an IoT device can use the device to perform a distributed denial-of-service (DDoS) attack, steal data, send spam, or allow the attacker to access the device and its connection. In January 2014, Pointproof uncovered the first mass use of IoT

13 Perekalin, Alex, 'Printers gone mad', Kaspersky Daily, 5 December 2018, www.kaspersky. co.uk/blog/hacked-printer-pewdiepie/14859/ (last accessed 24 June 2019).
14 Armstrong QC, Dean; Hyde, Dan; Thomas, Sam, *Cyber Security: Law and Practice*, LexisNexis, Bristol, 2017, at §7.08.
15 Hayasshi, Kaoru, *Linux Worm Targeting Hidden Devices*, 27 November 2013 www.symantec. com/connect/blogs/linux-worm-targeting-hidden-devices (last accessed 20 September 2018).

devices to send out malicious emails. 750,000 malicious email communications were sent from more than 100,000 everyday consumer items, including home-networking routers, connected multimedia centres, televisions and at least one refrigerator. The emails in this case were mostly spam which were immediately detected.[16]

8.13 There is little incentive for the manufacturers of IoT devices to consider cybersecurity. In many cases, there is insufficient knowledge, in-house, to incorporate security into a design. The engagement of external cybersecurity consultants is an additional cost that the majority of manufacturers would seek to avoid if possible. The physical incorporation of security measures also represents an additional cost. Consequently, many IoT devices will represent a weak point within a company's network.

How does a director mitigate this security concern?

8.14 When considering the IoT, there are five ways to improve security.

8.15 Five points of security:

1. Ensure that there is an 'air gap' between IoT devices and critical network infrastructure

   An 'air gap' is a measure to physically isolate one network from unsecured networks, such as the internet or an unsecured local area network. For example, office administrative systems, which might include company email, office printing and/or wireless conference working, should be separate from systems dealing with payments or collections, and in which intellectual property or confidential information are stored. You do not need to know how to create or maintain the air gap (that is for your IT Department), but knowing the questions to ask may ensure that your IT Department remain focused on protecting critical systems.

2. Ensure that administrative access is secure

   IT administrators are the gatekeepers to your IT systems. Invariably, these employees will have access to the most sensitive areas of your network systems, and will be able to cross any air gaps in place. Multi-factorial authentication should be applied to all administrative accounts, including test accounts used by the IT Department for beta testing.

3. Vet third parties who install or maintain IoT devices, whether physically or remotely

   The printer repairman will often be able to move unnoticed throughout your office space. However, maintenance of your IoT printer can now be

---

16 Proofpoint, *Proofpoint Uncovers Internet of Things (IoT) Cyberattack*, 16 January 2014, www.proofpoint.com/us/proofpoint-uncovers-internet-things-iot-cyberattack (last accessed 20 September 2018).

monitored remotely, off-site, at the premises of the third party installer. Proper due diligence includes ensuring that the security measures at this company are sufficient. An external threat who infiltrates their system will potentially be able to access yours through the IoT device. Request a breakdown of the security in place to prevent cyberattack.

4.   Train staff to maintain appropriate security with regard to the IoT devices they bring to work

'Bring your own device' ('BYOD') policies are now common among office working; however, these often do not extend to the IoT devices which employees bring to work. IoT wearables,[17] in particular those with higher processing power, may connect directly to a wireless network. Even those that connect through a Smartphone App are a potential security risk. Seek to limit the number and type of devices that staff link to the company network. Smartphones contain security protocols, and are necessary in the work environment. Personal health monitors or cameras, far less so, and perhaps should not be permitted to access the company Wi-Fi.

5.   Ensure that the latest version of IoT firmware is installed

Just because it does not look like a computer does not mean that installing the latest updates and patches is unnecessary. Allowing a computer to run on antiquated operating systems rather than the latest update dramatically increases the likelihood of a security breach. Similarly this applies to IoT devices. An IoT device will generally run on 'Universal Plug and Play' ('UPnP') to allow easy connectivity. UPnP can be turned off for increased security; but, if UPnP is permitted, you must ensure that firmware is up-to-date to provide the highest level of security possible.

These steps are the beginning, rather than the conclusion, for cybersecurity. IoT devices are now simply part of a matrix of potential cyber threats, both internal and external. If a company director has a concern regarding the robustness of their systems, it is incumbent upon them to seek proper advice.

Who owns the data collected through the IoT?

8.16   The growth of IoT devices, predominantly through the low-cost incorporation of internet-connected sensors into existing products, has raised a number of questions that governments and regulators are only just beginning to consider: Who owns the data generated through an IoT device? How can that data be used? Can the data be commoditised and sold to a third party, either with or without the consent of the user? If it can be sold with consent, what form of consent is required? And can the purchaser of data have a different purpose from the original collector?

---

17 An IoT wearable can include a FitBit or similar pedometer but can also include smart watches, which have greater processing power and can more readily be used as an infiltration device if unsecured.

8.17   These are merely the questions which arise in the private sector. To what extent is a state actor, whether the police or the security services, permitted to collate data from separate IoT devices and use this information to profile an individual? If the state were permitted unfettered access to all individuals' IoT devices, not only could almost everyone be constantly under surveillance but those deemed 'criminal' or 'a terrorist' could be impacted in such a way to negate any 'threat'.

8.18   It is unsurprising that different jurisdictions have reacted to the rise of the IoT with a variety of measures, dependent upon the political practicalities within the jurisdiction. It would be impossible within an entire book, let alone a single chapter, to address every country's regulatory approach to the IoT. For example, the Chinese extension of the Great Fire Wall would alone generate more potential questions than answers. Therefore, we have sought to explain the legal and regulatory position within the United Kingdom (UK), and within our two biggest trading partners: the European Union (EU) and the United States of America (US).

UK regulation of the IoT

8.19   The UK's appetite for IoT devices is strong. Estimates show that every household in the UK owns at least 10 internet-connected devices, and this is expected to increase to 15 devices by 2020. Consequently, there may be more than 420 million IoT devices in use across the UK within three years.[18]

8.20   On 7 March 2018, the UK Government, as part of its National Cyber Security Strategy,[19] published *Secure by Design: Improving the cyber security of consumer Internet of Things Report* ('The Report')[20] in order to meet the potential vulnerabilities of IoT networks in the UK.

8.21   The focus of the Report was the introduction of a draft Code of Practice for Industry on Consumer IoT ('The Code').[21] Consumer IoT is defined as 'consumer purchased "off the shelf" IoT devices; IoT devices used and installed "in the home" and the associated services linked to these devices'.[22]

---

18 Department for Digital, Culture, Media & Sport, National Cyber Security Centre, and Margot James MP, *Press release: New measures to boost cyber security in millions of internet-connected devices*, 7 March 2018 www.gov.uk/government/news/new-measures-to-boost-cyber-security-in-millions-of-internet-connected-devices (last accessed 29 September 2018).
19 https://assets.publishing.service.gov.uk/government/uploads/system/uploads/attachment_data/file/567242/national_cyber_security_strategy_2016.pdf.
20 https://assets.publishing.service.gov.uk/government/uploads/system/uploads/attachment_data/file/686089/Secure_by_Design_Report_.pdf.
21 Ibid, Chapter 4.
22 Ibid, Annex 8, 8.3.

8.22   The Code is designed to be applied throughout the IoT sector, specifically for device manufacturers,[23] IoT service providers,[24] mobile application developers,[25] and retailers.[26] The Code is designed to improve the security of consumer IoT products and associated services, and it provides practical guidance, listed in order of importance, for the IoT sector to apply.

8.23   A summary of the Code is provided below. These steps should be considered by any company supplying IoT devices, with the top three addressed as a matter of priority:

8.24

I.	No default passwords
All IoT device passwords must be unique and resettable, and suppliers must avoid universal default values. The Mirai malware (botnet) utilised common default credentials (universal usernames and passwords: admin/admin), which consumers often failed to change. Device manufacturers must ensure that each device is supplied with a unique default password.	
II.	**Implement a vulnerability disclosure policy**
All companies that provide internet-connected devices and services must provide a public point of contact as part of a vulnerability disclosure policy in order that security researchers and others are able to report issues. Disclosed vulnerabilities should be acted on in a timely manner.	
III.	**Keep software updated**
All software components in internet-connected devices should be securely updateable. Updates must be timely and not impact on the functioning of the device. The Code requires that suppliers publish an 'end-of-life' policy which states the minimum period for which updates will be received. An explanation must be provided for the reason why updates will not be provided.	
IV.	**Securely store credentials and security-sensitive data**
Any credentials must be stored securely within services and on devices. Hardcoded credentials in device software, which can be easily discovered through reverse engineering, are not acceptable. Security-sensitive data should be stored securely.[27]	

---

23 'The entity that creates an assembled final internet-connected product. A final product may contain the products of many other different manufacturers.' Ibid, 4.5.
24 'Companies that provide services such as networks, cloud storage and data transfer which are packaged as part of IoT solutions. Internet-connected devices may be offered as part of the service.' Ibid, 4.5.
25 'Entities that develop and provide applications which run on mobile devices. These are often offered as a way of interacting with devices as part of an IoT solution.' Ibid, 4.5.
26 'The sellers of internet-connected products and associated services to consumers.' Ibid, 4.5.
27 National Institute of Standards and Technology (NIST) Special Publication 800-63B: 'Digital Identity Guidelines, Authentication and Lifecycle Management, 2017' suggests that best practice includes the use of cryptographic keys and initialisation vectors, with credentials stored within a Trusted Execution Environment (see: https://pages.nist.gov/800-63-3/sp800-63b.html).

V.	Communicate securely
Appropriate encryption should be used for data relevant to the security of the device.	
VI.	**Minimise exposed attack surfaces**
Processer, user or program access should be restricted to only the information necessary for the legitimate purpose, and no more ('Principle of least privilege'). Unnecessary code or hardware which exposes the device should be minimised.	
VII.	**Ensure software integrity**
The consumer, or a company administrator, should be notified if an unauthorised change or reboot is detected.	

VIII.	Ensure that personal data is protected
The processing of personal data must be in accordance with data protection law. Within the UK, this will be in accordance with the Data Protection Act 2018. Within the EU, the General Data Protection Regulation (GDPR) will apply.	
IX.	**Make systems resilient to outages**
The IoT device or service should continue to function despite operational issues.	
X.	**Monitor system telemetry[28] data**
All telemetry data, such as usage and measurement data, should be monitored for security anomalies (but only if this data is collected).	
XI.	**Make it easy for consumers to delete personal data**
Consumers should be provided with clear instructions which allow for the deletion of their personal data.	
XII.	**Make installation and maintenance of devices easy**
Installation and maintenance should require minimal steps and should follow best security practice.	
XIII.	**Validate input data**
Data input via user interfaces and transferred via application programming interfaces ('APIs') or between networks in services and devices must be validated.	

8.25   The Code is currently voluntary, although the Executive Summary threatens that, if the market is slow to adopt, the guidelines may be made compulsory through law. If the Code remains voluntary, non-compliance will

---

28 In this context, 'telemetry' means wireless data transfer. An IoT device which suddenly has a spike in data transfer may have been hacked as a result of the external threat gaining access to the device or subsequently using the device. The Code requires that this telemetry is monitored to detect these spikes, but only if this data is already being collected. The Code does not require additional monitoring, as this may be contrary to the privacy of the user.

be very difficult to enforce. The National Cyber Security Centre ('NCSC'), the centrepiece of the National Cyber Security Strategy, provides advice and support for the public and private sector in how to avoid computer security threats, but it currently has no enforcement function. It is unlikely that the NCSC's parent organisation, GCHQ, would seek to enforce a voluntary Code. GCHQ's capabilities include: the collection and analysis of communications and data; and a range of online strategies to cause real-world effect. GCHQ does not employ enforcement officers, for example, to physically enter company premises or to ensure real-world compliance with a voluntary Code.

8.26 However, organisations supplying IoT products and services that collect and process personal data will be subject to the requirements of the Data Protection Act 2018 ('DPA') (Code VIII). These companies will need to consider data protection requirements carefully, and take steps to address the risks posed to individuals' privacy, as the ICO does have enforcement power with regard to Code VIII.

8.27 The DPA brings the General Data Protection Regulation ('GDPR') into domestic law, and nominates the ICO as the body delegated to ensure compliance. Any data controller or processer in the UK is required to abide by the principles within the DPA.

8.28 The ICO's first enforcement notice was served against AggregateIQ Data Services (AIQ) on 6 July 2018.[29] The ICO contacted AIQ with regard to the processing of personal data by AIQ on behalf of UK political organisations: VoteLeave, BeLeave, Veterans for Britain, and the DUP Vote to Leave. AIQ were provided with personal data (names and email addresses) as a consequence of their contract with these organisations, and they used this data to target political advertising and messages on social media. The ICO concluded that AIQ had processed personal data unlawfully (contrary to Articles 5(1)(a) and 6 of the GDPR), for a purpose beyond that for which it was collected (contrary to Article 5(1)(b)), and without due regard to data minimisation (contrary to Article 5(1)(c)).

8.29 AIQ have been required to 'cease processing any personal data of UK or EU citizens obtained from UK political organisations or otherwise for the purposes of data analytics, political campaigning or any other advertising purposes'.[30]

8.30 This enforcement notice was not against an IoT-related company. However, it does provide some insight to future potential ICO actions. AIQ are a Canadian company but the ICO has determined that, because AIQ's processing of personal data relates to monitoring data subjects' behaviour taking place within the EU, the company is subject to GDPR under its territorial scope provisions at Article 3(2)(b). IoT-related companies, which process personal data of UK citizens, will likely fall under the DPA regardless of whether their physical location is within the EU.

---

29 https://ico.org.uk/media/2259362/r-letter-ico-to-aiq-060718.pdf.
30 Ibid, Annex 1.

8.31   In order to comply with Article 5 of the GDPR, device manufacturers and IoT service providers must provide consumers with clear and transparent information about how their personal data is being used, by whom, and for what purposes, for each device and service. This also applies to any third parties that may be involved (including advertisers).

8.32   Where personal data is processed on the basis of consumers' consent, this must be validly and lawfully obtained, in order to meet the requirements of Article 7 of the GDPR, with those consumers being given the opportunity to withdraw it at any time. Consumers should also be provided with guidance on how to securely set up their device, as well as how they may eventually securely dispose of it.

8.33   The following practical steps may be of some assistance:

THE DATA PROTECTION ACT 2018 AND THE IoT PRACTICAL GUIDANCE
A. **Revise your data handling policy** to provide clear and transparent information to consumers about what personal data devices and services process, the organisations that process this data, and the lawful basis on which the processing takes place (lawful bases for processing of personal data are contained within Article 6 of the GDPR).
B. **Consider data protection at the beginning of product development.** Building privacy and security into the product lifecycle from the design phase, and continuing throughout production, will ensure 'Data protection by design and by default' (Article 25 of the GDPR).
C. **Ensure appropriate technical and organisational measures are in place** to protect any personal data, including processes to ensure the confidentiality, integrity, availability and resilience of processing systems and services, and regular testing to ensure the effectiveness of such measures.
D. **Appropriate technical and organisation measures must be reasonable.** This may vary depending upon the state of the art, the costs of implementation and the nature, scope, context and purposes of processing, as well as the risk of varying likelihood and severity for the rights and freedoms of natural persons (Article 32 of the GDPR).
E. **Use a data protection impact assessment ('DPIA') as a tool to help comply with data protection obligations.** When designing a device, product or service that processes personal data, a DPIA will allow you to identify and fix any data protection issues at an early stage of any new project or development, and will help you to meet your customers' expectations around privacy. This will also help to demonstrate compliance if there is any complaint or concern.
F. **Consider cybersecurity and data protection together.** Involve your IT team who are responsible for cybersecurity in the design process. If you have a resource within the company, try to use them.

> G. **Retailers should be aware of the steps taken by device manufacturers and IoT service providers.** This will allow retailers to accurately explain the personal data that will be processed, the purpose for that processing, and the lawful basis for processing. In addition, this would provide for good customer service.

8.34 There are strong suggestions that the voluntary Code is insufficient to meet the security concerns raised by the IoT. In January 2018, F-Secure published a report titled *Internet of Things: Pinning down the IoT*, warning of a 'dystopian future' if governments did not seek to regulate IoT devices.[31] Following the publication of the Code, Ken Munro, an analyst at security firm Pen Test Partners, suggested that this bleak view of the future had not been avoided by an unenforceable set of principles that many reputable manufacturers were already following:[32]

> 'Without "teeth", this standard is meaningless. Manufacturers who already play fast and loose with our security to make a quick buck from us won't change anything.'

8.35 The governance of personal data will (hopefully) be effectively secured through the ICO, regardless of the Code. Many IoT devices will be concerned with processing personal data, which extends beyond merely names and addresses to location data, or online identifiers such as an IP address. The issue becomes more important when there is an IoT device that does not process personal data as part of its design. The most basic IoT devices are simple network-linked remote controls, but these could still be used by a determined hacker as part of a distributed denial of service (DDoS) attack, in which multiple devices are used to attack a single endpoint (think Mirai and Reaper malware). The critics of the Code are correct. A voluntary code is unlikely to demand compliance from manufacturers concerned with profit, with the impact extending beyond those who have purchased their specific IoT device.

EU REGULATION OF THE IOT

8.36 If UK regulation is 'toothless', regulation by the EU is becoming increasingly sharp. GDPR is already in force; the ePrivacy Regulation[33] is on its way; and on 29 May 2018 the European Commission proposed the Cybersecurity Certification Framework.[34] In conjunction, it is believed that no IoT device would be able to fall into a European lacuna where it is not regulated.

---

31 https://fsecureconsumer.files.wordpress.com/2018/01/f-secure_pinning-down-the-iot_final.pdf.

32 Horgan, Robert, PCR, *UK government's new IoT security guidelines slammed as 'meaningless' by tech experts*, 7 March 2018, www.pcr-online.biz/features/uk-governments-new-iot-security-guidelines-slammed-as-meaningless-by-tech-experts (last accessed 1 October 2018).

33 Formally the Regulation of the European Parliament and of the Council concerning the respect for private life and the protection of personal data in electronic communications and repealing Directive 2002/58/EC (Regulation on Privacy and Electronic Communications).

34 Formally Proposal 9350/18 (29 May 2018), Title III Cybersecurity Certification Framework, Article 43, ¶ 2.

8.37 In addition, the Network Infrastructure Security Directive ('NISD') applies to digital service providers ('DSPs') and operators of essential services ('OESs'). Generally, this is unlikely to apply directly to the IoT, but it is one more piece of EU legislation in the cyber sphere.

EU LEGISLATION AND THE IoT		
EU LEGISLATION	**IN FORCE**	**DOES IT APPLY TO THE IoT?**
GPDR	Yes	Yes – if your IoT device processes personal data
NISD	Yes	Unlikely – Directive applies to DSPs and OESs only
ePrivacy Regulation	No	Yes
Cybersecurity Certification Framework	No	Very likely but legislation only in proposal stage

How does GDPR apply to the IoT?

8.38 IoT devices which process personal data would have to meet the requirements contained within GDPR. Personal data is not restricted to names and addresses (for example, GDPR mentions a range of identifiers as online identifiers, including Radio Frequency Identification ('RFID') tags) so, in many instances, IoT devices will need to comply with the GDPR principles.

8.39 If GDPR does apply, there are ten steps towards meeting compliance:

1.	**Be aware of the data you process**
Before you even consider whether GDPR applies, you must know the type of data you are processing. If the data you collect constitutes 'personal data' (and remember this extends beyond names and addresses), GDPR will apply. Consider the purpose you have for collecting that data. If the answer is not readily available, you may need to stop processing that data at all.	
2.	**Understand consent**
Consent is the first lawful basis under which data can be processed (Article 6(1)). However, the conditions for obtaining consent have been made more explicit. If you are relying upon consent, this must be demonstrable and, if achieved through a 'tick-box' request, must be in an intelligible and easily accessible form, using clear and plain language. Consent may not be the best lawful basis, as consent can be withdrawn at any time (Article 7(3)). Another lawful basis (requirement of contract or legitimate interest, for example) may be more appropriate.	
3.	**If consent is withdrawn, this applies to others with whom you trade**
If you have shared (processed) personal data with a third party on the lawful basis of consent, and continue to do so, the withdrawal of that consent will	

prevent you from sharing that data, but will also prevent the third party from processing that data. Processing prior to withdrawal of consent is unaffected (Article 7(3)). However, individuals have a right of erasure ('right to be forgotten') under Article 17. This may again impact upon an IoT firm's choice of lawful basis.

4.	Demonstrate compliance with GDPR

GDPR requires companies to record how all data is processed. This may sound like a mammoth task, but digital transfer or storage of information is almost invariably recorded. It is important to consider how it is processed and to document the considerations. If personal data of X is to be stored (processed), record in a procedure document how you are ensuring secure storage. If person Y's data is being transferred, again a procedure document needs to explain the appropriate technical measures to protect that data. If you are investigated, it is these documents and procedures which will prevent criticism.

5.	GDPR requires data protection by design and by default

Data protection by design and by default (formerly 'privacy by design') is a requirement of GDPR (Article 25). Within the IoT sector, this applies to devices, software and the back-end systems. Data security must be a consideration from inception of the IoT device, and must continue throughout the lifecycle of the product.

6.	Maintain software through regular updates

The IoT is intrinsically vulnerable. A procedure with regard to regular system updates would illustrate compliance with GDPR. Consider whether updates are required at regular meetings, which are minuted, and include a consideration of the latest intelligence and potential security threats. Illustrate that security is proactive rather than reactive.

7.	GDPR is the basis for future legislation

The EU are not going to slacken their approach to data security and compliance. As highlighted at **8.37** above, further legislation is being considered to ensure cyber systems are as secure as possible. Ignoring GDPR, or approaching compliance in a dilatory fashion, may be counterproductive in the long-run.

8.	Remember that GDPR compliance is an ongoing process

Even if you were ready for GDPR on 25 May 2018, this does not mean that you are automatically compliant now. The threats to IoT devices are evolving and your procedures must evolve as well. Regularly consider whether the data you are processing has changed. At the very least, there must be a constant assessment as to whether it remains necessary to hold personal data. If not, you should consider whether this information should be deleted. Remember, deletion is processing. When deleting information, you may wish to keep a summary of the type of personal data previously held, the date of deletion and the reason for deletion, so that this processing is recorded. Ensure data minimisation, so do not keep a greater record than is necessary.

9.	**Employ a Data Protection Officer (DPO)**

Unless you are a public authority, or an organisation whose core activities include the regular and systematic monitoring of data subjects on a wide scale, a DPO is not mandatory. However, the consideration of a DPO may be advised. Your company may not be dealing with data subjects on a 'wide scale' now, but could grow into this in the future. A DPO who understands the business from the beginning will be better prepared once you reach these levels.

10.	**Hope for the best, but prepare for the worst**

Think defensively. The preparation for an investigation, and the steps that you take towards compliance, are your defence if enforcement action is taken against you.

If there is a breach, you have 72 hours to notify the enforcement body within the jurisdiction (in the UK, it is the ICO). Being able to point towards the steps taken, both before and after the breach, at the time of notification, will place you in a better position with the regulator. Fines are heavy under GDPR (4% of worldwide turnover or €20 million, whichever is greater). Mitigation through preparation is the best way forward.

8.40   For further practical steps towards GDPR compliance, consider the ENISA report, *Baseline Security Recommendations for IoT*, or the summary of the report, at **8.51** below.

Will the ePrivacy Regulation apply to the IoT?

8.41   The ePrivacy Regulation seeks to apply the principle of confidentiality to 'current and future means of communication'. On 20 September 2018, the Council of the EU made it explicitly clear that this extended to IoT devices:[35]

> 'The use of machine-to-machine services, that is to say services involving an automated transfer of data and information between devices or software-based applications with limited or no human interaction, is emerging. While the services provided at the application-layer of such services do normally not qualify as an electronic communications service as defined in the [Directive establishing the European Electronic Communications Code], The transmission services used for the provision of machine-to-machine services regularly involves the conveyance of signals via an electronic communications network and, hence, constitutes an electronic communications service. In order to ensure full protection of the rights to privacy and confidentiality of communications, and to promote a trusted and secure Internet of Things in the digital single market, it is necessary to clarify that this Regulation, in particular the requirements relating to the confidentiality of communications, should

35 Proposal for a Regulation of the European Parliament and of the Council concerning the respect for private life and the protection of personal data in electronic communications and repealing Directive 2002/58/EC (Regulation on Privacy and Electronic Communications), 5358/17 TELECOM 12 COMPET 32 MI 45 DATAPROTECT 4 CONSOM 19 JAI 40 DIGIT 10 FREMP 3 CYBER 10 IA 12 CODEC 52, 20 September 2018, p.13, https://iapp.org/resources/article/eprivacy-regulation-september-2018-draft/ (last accessed 1 October 2018).

apply to the transmission of machine-to-machine electronic communications where carried out via an electronic communications service.'

8.42   The latest draft text of Article 5, which deals with confidentiality of electronic communications data, includes reference to 'machine-to-machine electronic communications' and will be interpreted to mean IoT devices:

'Confidentiality of electronic communications data shall apply to the transmission of machine-to-machine electronic communications where carried out via an electronic communications service.'

8.43   The ePrivacy Regulation considers electronic communications, which includes data transferred from IoT devices, as confidential. The Regulation prohibits a third party from interfering with data, including the storing, monitoring or processing of the data, unless permitted under Regulation provisions or if the user consents. The Regulation follows the consent provisions of the GDPR by requiring a clear, affirmative action, but provides additional, expanded provisions for obtaining consent to place cookies or other tracking technologies on users' devices.

8.44   Unlike the current ePrivacy Directive, which requires users to provide consent for cookies and similar technologies on each website the user visits, the Regulation proposes that users provide consent through browser settings, acknowledging that users are currently 'overloaded' with requests to provide consent. The Regulation states that the browser should provide users with a range of privacy settings, from higher settings (rejecting all cookies) to lower settings (accepting all cookies). The Regulation provides that browsers must obtain a clear, affirmative action from the user to obtain consent, and should remind users of their ability to alter privacy settings at any time. The Regulation also notes that software providers that allow electronic communications should inform users on privacy settings at the time of installation and require that users consent in order to continue with the installation.

8.45   The Regulation permits users to bring an action against any entity that violates the Regulation's provisions; this includes for both material and non-material damages. Fines from regulators will also increase, with administrative penalties for violations of the Regulation corresponding to those laid out in the GDPR, up to €10 million or 2% of the worldwide annual turnover to up to €20 million or 4% of worldwide turnover, depending on the type of violation.

8.46   The ePrivacy Regulation, when in force, will be yet another layer of compliance to be considered.

What is the Cybersecurity Certification Framework?

8.47   The Cybersecurity Certification Framework would create a single certification scheme for information communications technology ('ICT') devices. On 8 June 2018, the Council of the EU agreed on its position for the proposal of the 'Cybersecurity Act', which now allows for future deliberation within the European Parliament.[36] If the Council and the Parliament agree, the Framework will enter into legislation as part of the Cybersecurity Act.

8.48   The purpose of the Act is to create a common cybersecurity certification, which builds consumer trust in IoT products while continuing construction of a single EU digital marketplace. Speaking on behalf of the Council of the EU, Ivaylo Moskovski, Bulgarian Minister for Transport, Information Technology and Communications, stated:[37] 'We all want our devices to be secure. This new certification framework will increase trust and confidence in innovative digital solutions'.

8.49   Unless otherwise specified in EU law or member states' law, certification will be voluntary, and would include a requirement for resilience to accidental or malicious data loss or alteration. The current proposal envisages three different assurance levels – basic, substantial or high – with the basic level self-certification being possible for device manufacturers or IoT service providers.

8.50   The Cybersecurity Act would also increase the authority of the EU Agency for Network and Information Security ('ENISA') and make it a permanent EU-wide cybersecurity agency. Currently, ENISA serves as a body of experts voluntarily consulted on cybersecurity matters; however, the Act would grant ENISA powers to support both member states and EU institutions on all cybersecurity issues and to conduct cybersecurity exercises. ENISA would also be responsible for carrying out certifications of IoT products.

8.51   In November 2017, ENISA published *Baseline Security Recommendations for IoT*.[38] This is currently an advisory document, but would likely become the basis of certification if the Framework was to be enacted. Section 4 of the document provides security measures recommended in three areas:

i.   policies;

ii.   organisational, people and process measures; and

iii. technical measures.

---

36 Council of the European Union, Proposal for a Regulation of the European Parliament and of the Council on ENISA, the 'EU Cybersecurity Agency', and repealing Regulation (EU) 526/2013, and on Information and Communication Technology cybersecurity certification ('Cybersecurity Act'), 29 May 2018, http://data.consilium.europa.eu/doc/document/ST-9350-2018-INIT/en/pdf.

37 European Council, *Press release: EU to create a common cybersecurity certification framework and beef up its agency – Council agrees its position*, 8 June 2018, www.consilium.europa.eu/en/press/press-releases/2018/06/08/eu-to-create-a-common-cybersecurity-certification-framework-and-beef-up-its-agency-council-agrees-its-position/ (last accessed 2 October 2018).

38 ENISA, *Baseline Security Recommendations for IoT in the context of Critical Information Infrastructures*, November 2017, www.enisa.europa.eu/publications/baseline-security-recommendations-for-iot.

8.52 The areas of recommendations may vary in significance, depending upon a person's role within a company. IT professionals will wish to consider the technical measures, whereas policies may be more relevant to product designers. The Legal Department and Human Resources Team should consider organisational, people and process measures. Company directors, with an overarching responsibility for a product, service or firm, may be wise to consider the recommendations in their entirety.

8.53 The recommendations are worth considering in full (they span approximately six pages) but have been summarised below:

RECOMMENDATIONS	
POLICIES	
Security by design	Consider the security of the whole IoT system across the entire lifecycle. Do not allow design for power conservation to compromise security; allow for the integration of updated security; and prepare for the possibility of attacks. Consider any risks to users. For device manufacturers and IoT software developers, implement necessary test plans. For software developers, review code during implementation to reduce bugs in the final version of the product.
Privacy by design	Make privacy an integral part of the system; and perform privacy impact assessments before any new applications are launched.
Asset management	Establish and maintain asset management procedures and configuration controls for key network and information systems.
Risk and threat identification	Identify significant risks using a defence-in-depth approach; and identify the intended use and environment of a given IoT device.
ORGANISATIONAL, PEOPLE AND PROCESS MEASURES	
End-of-life support	Devise and disclose the point at which updates will be provided (end-of-life security). Monitor performance and support until the end-of-life.
Proven solutions	Use well-known protocols and algorithms, recognised by the scientific community (ie proven solutions).
Management of security	Establish procedures for security incidents, and co-ordinated disclosure of vulnerabilities, potentially through information-sharing platforms. Create a publicly disclosed mechanism for vulnerability reports (eg Bug Bounty programs).[39]

39 A deal offered by websites and software developers whereby individuals receive recognition and compensation for reporting bugs.

Security training and awareness	Train employees in good privacy and security practices, and document these activities. Establish cybersecurity roles and responsibilities for your workforce.
Third party relationships	Data processed by a third party must be protected by a data processing agreement. Only share personal data in accordance with the GDPR. For device manufacturers and IoT software developers, adopt cyber supply chain risk management policies and communicate requirements to suppliers and partners.
TECHNICAL MEASURES	
Hardware security	Use hardware that incorporates security features to strengthen the protection and integrity of the device.
Strong default security and privacy	Any applicable security features should be enabled by default, and any unused or insecure functionalities should be disabled by default. Use only hard-to-crack passwords.
Data protection and compliance	IoT stakeholders must be compliant with GDPR. Users of IoT products and services must be able to exercise their rights to information, access, erasure, rectification, data portability, restriction of processing, objection to processing, and their right not to be evaluated on the basis of automated processing.
System safety and reliability	Design with system and operational disruption in mind, preventing the system from causing an unacceptable risk of injury or physical damage. Essential features should continue to work.
Secure software / firmware updates	Maintain (automatic) firmware updates to be sent over-the-air ('OTA'). Ensure that update server is secure and updates are transmitted securely.[40]
Authentication	Maintain strong passwords and authentication schemes. Consider using two-factor or multi-factor authentication.
Authorisation	Apply the principle of least privilege within the firmware and code.
Access control – physical and environmental security	Ensure a context-based security and privacy that reflects different levels of importance. Measures for tamper protection and detection should not rely on network connectivity. Ensure device cannot be easily disassembled and that data storage is encrypted. Keep physical ports (USB) to a minimum.
Cryptography	Verify the robustness of the encryption implemented.

40 Signed by an authorised trust entity and encrypted using accepted encryption methods, and that the update package has its digital signature, signing certificate and signing certificate chain, verified by the device before the update process begins.

Secure and trusted communications	Ensure best practice communication security, and that credentials are not exposed. Guarantee data authenticity to enable reliable exchanges from data emission to data reception. Data should always be signed, and data received always through verified interconnections. IoT devices should be restrictive rather than permissive in communicating. Make intentional connections, and prevent unauthorised connections at all levels of the protocols. Apply rate limiting, controlling the traffic sent or received by a network, to reduce the risk of automated attacks.
Secure interfaces and network services	Use risk segmentation.[41] Protocols should be designed to ensure that, if a single device is compromised, it does not affect the whole set. Implement a DDoS-resistant and load-balancing infrastructure.
Secure input and output handling	Data input validation (ensuring that data is safe prior to use) and output filtering.
Logging	Log user authentication, management of accounts and access rights, modifications to security rules, and the functioning of the system. These must be preserved in durable storage.
Monitoring and auditing	Implement regular monitoring to verify the device behaviour, to detect malware and to discover integrity errors. Conduct periodic audits and reviews of security controls. Perform penetration tests biannually.

8.54 The extent to which these recommendations represent best practice, worthy of 'high' certification, or are the 'basic' level requirements under the Cybersecurity Act, is yet to be decided. Those working within the IoT sector, and who wish to trade within the EU, should consider an audit of their current position against these recommendations.

8.55 Regardless, when considering any duties which may arise under GDPR, those working in the IoT sector should consider the recommendations of ENISA. Anura Fernando is the Principal Engineer for Medical Systems Interoperability and Security at UL, and serves as a member of the US Health Care Industry Cybersecurity ('HCIC') Task Force. When asked about the ENISA report, Mr Fernando said: 'The ENISA report does a great job of explaining the cybersecurity landscape for IoT in general, with solid recommendations based on technical concerns, economics and lifecycle considerations … It shows that the EU considers these issues important enough to dedicate resources to help set the stage for the General Data Protection Regulation'.

---

41 Splitting network elements into separate components to help isolate security breaches and minimise the overall risk.

8.56   Consequently, the ENISA report should be considered a solid base from which certification could be achieved in the future, and an excellent demonstration of due diligence with regard to GDPR.

Why does the Network Infrastructure Security Directive ('NISD') not apply to the IoT?

8.57   The Cybersecurity Certification Framework is a natural extension of the NISD, and has been proposed to provide increased scrutiny in areas where the NISD does not apply. The IoT is an area in which the NISD would not automatically be considered applicable.

8.58   Currently, it is digital service providers ('DSPs') and operators of essential services ('OESs') that are held accountable for maintaining a base level of cybersecurity and reporting major security incidents to Computer Security Incident Response Teams ('CSIRTs'). The banking and energy sectors would be considered to fall within OESs, with online marketplaces, online search engines and cloud computing services generally categorised as DSPs.

8.59   The NISD includes standards to prevent data breaches and quickly and efficiently confront problems as they occur. It also calls for penalties set by each EU member state for companies that either lack sufficient security protections or fail to notify authorities of breaches.

8.60   The security requirements for DSPs and OESs include technical measures that manage the risks of cybersecurity breaches in a preventative manner, and both DSPs and OESs must provide information that allows for an in-depth assessment of their information systems and security policies. Because an OES includes any organisations whose operations engage in critical societal or economic activities that would be greatly affected in the case of a security breach, these are more heavily regulated than DSPs. It is notable, however, that DSPs which are based outside of the EU jurisdiction but which act within it are still subject to the NISD.

8.61   If the company does not fall within these definitions (DSP or OES), the NISD does not apply. The Cybersecurity Certification Framework would extend monitoring and compliance beyond OESs and DSPs to all information communications technology (ICT) devices, and would capture the IoT market.

US REGULATION OF THE IOT

8.62   There is no specific regulation for the IoT within the US. Data security is regulated at a federal level through the Federal Trade Commission ('FTC').

8.63   The FTC is an independent agency of the US government, established a century ago, in 1914, by the Federal Trade Commission Act, which was enacted to maintain competition and to prevent unfair or deceptive practices: 'Unfair methods of competition in or affecting commerce, and unfair or deceptive acts or practices in or affecting commerce, are hereby declared unlawful'.[42] Its strategic goals are to protect consumers; maintain competition; and advance organisational performance. The FTC mission statement is to protect consumers by preventing anti-competitive, deceptive, and unfair business practices, enhancing informed consumer choice and public understanding of the competitive process, and accomplishing this without unduly burdening legitimate business activity.

8.64   It is notable that the FTC is seeking to regulate the IoT in the context of existing consumer rights legislation, and has brought suits against traders under both alleged 'deceptive' (see **8.65**) and 'unfair' (see **8.70**) practices. An FTC complaint is entered into Consumer Sentinel, a secure, online database available to more than 2,000 civil and criminal law enforcement agencies in the US and abroad.

8.65   In September 2013, the FTC took its first action against an IoT manufacturer, alleging that TRENDnet, a web-enabled camera manufacturer, had marketed its SecureView cameras with the product description 'secure', when faulty software permitted open online viewing, and even listening, for those who had the camera's IP address.[43]

8.66   The FTC complaint alleged that, from at least April 2010, TRENDnet failed to use reasonable security to design and test its software, including a setting for the camera's password requirement. As a result of this failure, hundreds of consumers' private camera feeds were made public on the internet. In January 2012, a hacker exploited this flaw and made it public. Hackers posted links to the live feeds of nearly 700 of the cameras, which displayed babies asleep in their cribs, young children playing, and adults going about their daily lives. Once TRENDnet learned of this flaw, it uploaded a software patch to its website and sought to alert its customers to the need to visit the website to update their cameras.

8.67   TRENDnet and the FTC agreed terms of settlement, which also included allegations that TRENDnet transmitted user login credentials in clear, readable text over the internet, even though free software was available to secure such transmissions; and that TRENDnet's mobile applications for the cameras stored consumers' login information in clear, readable text on their mobile devices. The terms of settlement:

- prohibited TRENDnet from future misrepresentations;

---

42 Federal Trade Commission Act (Incorporating U.S. SAFE WEB Act amendments of 2006) §45. Unfair methods of competition unlawful; prevention by Commission, s 5(1).
43 Federal Trade Commission Press Release, *Marketer of Internet-Connected Home Security Video Cameras Settles FTC Charges It Failed to Protect Consumers' Privacy*, 4 September 2013, www.ftc.gov/news-events/press-releases/2013/09/marketer-internet-connected-home-security-video-cameras-settles (last accessed 25 September 2018).

- required them to establish comprehensive information security, including third-party assessment every two years for 20 years; and

- required them to notify customers with the provision of free technical support.

The Consent Order[44] carries the force of law with respect to future actions, each of which may result in a civil penalty of up to $16,000.

8.68   The TRENDnet action constituted a 'deception' case in which the FTC demonstrated that the company had violated its own statements to consumers.

8.69   A similar action was undertaken by the FTC against BREATHOMETER™, a consumer IoT breathalyser able to estimate blood alcohol content from a breath sample. In January 2017, the FTC filed an action alleging that the claim of 'accuracy' was deceptive, and that the device regularly understated blood alcohol content.[45]

8.70   In an 'unfairness' case, the FTC is required to show that the firm may injure consumers in a way that violates public policy. When the alleged perpetrator is in the context of finance or health, federal statutory requirements about data security may apply. In those cases, the FTC may seek an action regarding a trader's poor security practices. Otherwise, law suits with regard to unfairness are problematic.

8.71   As an example, in January 2017, the FTC filed a complaint against Taiwan-based computer networking equipment manufacturer D-Link Corporation and its US subsidiary, alleging that inadequate security measures had been taken by the company, which left its wireless routers and internet cameras vulnerable to hackers and put US consumers' privacy at risk.[46] The FTC alleged 'unfairness' on the basis that D-Link had failed to take reasonable steps to secure the software for their routers and IP cameras, and that the practices caused, or were likely to cause, substantial injury to consumers in the US that was not outweighed by countervailing benefits to consumers or competition.[47]

---

44 US Federal Trade Commission, In The Matter Of TRENDnet Inc., Agreement Containing Consent Order, File No. 122 3090, www.ftc.gov/sites/default/files/documents/cases/2013/09/1 30903trendnetorder.pdf (last accessed 25 September 2018).

45 Federal Trade Commission Press Release, *'Breathometer' Marketers Settle FTC Charges of Misrepresenting Ability to Accurately Measure Users' Blood Alcohol Content*, 23 January 2017, www.ftc.gov/news-events/press-releases/2017/01/breathometer-marketers-settle-ftc-charges-misrepresenting-ability (last accessed 25 September 2018).

46 Federal Trade Commission Press Release, *Device-maker's alleged failures to reasonably secure software created malware risks and other vulnerabilities*, 5 January 2017, www.ftc.gov/news-events/press-releases/2017/01/ftc-charges-d-link-put-consumers-privacy-risk-due-inadequate (last accessed 25 September 2018).

47 United States District Court Northern District of California San Francisco Division, *Federal Trade Commission (Plaintiff) -v- D-Link Corporation and D-Link Systems, Inc., (Corporations)* Complaint for Permanent Injunction and Other Equitable Relief, Case: 3:17-cv-00039, at §28–29.

8.72   On 19 September 2017, Judge James Donato from the Northern District of California dismissed three of the six counts in the FTC's complaint. Assessing the allegation of unfairness, the court dismissed the complaint, indicating that 'a mere possibility at best' did not meet the statutory requirement that the act or practice 'causes or is likely to cause substantial injury to consumers which is not reasonably avoidable by consumers themselves and not outweighed by countervailing benefits to consumers or to competition'.

8.73   The judgment is important in defining the level of evidence required for an FTC complaint. When the allegation is under alleged 'deception', the evidence available to the FTC is within the control of the trader. Assertions that cannot be robustly defended should simply not be made. Potential allegations of 'unfairness' can be avoided through an ongoing evaluation of the security measures in place, and swift action if a concern is found. The FTC can only take action, with regard to unfairness, if there is 'substantial injury' and if that injury is not 'reasonably avoidable by the consumer'. Processes, updates or patches which identify and mitigate security breaches will likely prevent substantial injury, and could also allow for consumers to rectify or avoid these breaches themselves.

8.74   Federal oversight of 'dumb' devices will extend to their IoT equivalents. In August 2017, the Food and Drug Administration ('FDA') recalled approximately 465,000 internet-connected pacemakers manufactured by Abbott Health over fears that the devices could be 'hacked'.[48]

8.75   The FDA issued a 'safety communication' on the availability of firmware updates to address cybersecurity vulnerabilities identified in Abbott's implantable cardiac pacemakers. The IoT pacemaker is implanted under the skin in the upper chest area and has connecting insulated wires (called 'leads') that go into the heart. A patient may need this device if their heartbeat is too slow or needs resynchronisation to treat heart failure. The recall extended to implanted devices, and required patients to attend a medical centre, where the pacemaker was switched to 'back-up mode' for three minutes while the firmware update was completed.

8.76   The FDA and the manufacturer, Abbott, did not recommend the prophylactic removal and replacement of affected devices; however, the company was required to:

- communicate the extent of the potential 'hack' to patients;[49]

---

48 FDA Safety Communication, Firmware Update to Address Cybersecurity Vulnerabilities Identified in Abbott's (formerly St. Jude Medical's) Implantable Cardiac Pacemakers, 29 August 2017 www.fda.gov/MedicalDevices/Safety/AlertsandNotices/ucm573669.htm (last accessed 29 September 2018).
49 '…vulnerabilities, if exploited, could allow an unauthorized user (i.e. someone other than the patient's physician) to access a patient's device using commercially available equipment. This access could be used to modify programming commands to the implanted pacemaker, which could result in patient harm from rapid battery depletion or administration of inappropriate pacing.'

- highlight the risk of installing the firmware update with the pacemaker in 'back-up mode';[50] and

- provide detailed percentages that the update would be unsuccessful.[51]

In issuing the communication, the FDA was not seeking punitive action but the communication was unlikely to have been welcomed by the directors or shareholders of Abbott.

8.77   The state approach to data protection is through 'security breach notification laws'. By 29 March 2018, all 50 states, the District of Columbia, Guam, Puerto Rico and the Virgin Islands had enacted legislation requiring private or governmental entities to notify individuals of security breaches of information involving personally identifiable information.[52] However, each state may adopt an individual approach to whether governmental notification is required, and the time period for notification. Importantly, many states also apply a 'harm threshold' under which notification is not required.[53]

So who owns the data?

8.78   Regulation of the IoT is haphazard but is growing. The US approach is to rely upon existing legislation and new security breach notification laws, whereas the EU and UK are seeking to create new methods of regulation. The EU (and the UK while it remains within the EU) are creating new statutory instruments to ensure compliance with massive incentives (fines). The UK's approach is more liberal with the imposition of a voluntary Code.

8.79   Consequently, the answer to the question, 'Who owns the data?', varies depending on your location.

8.80   In the US a 'data subject' is provided with the same rights as a consumer. At a federal level, there is currently nothing more to protect their personal data than existing consumer law. At a state level, the company is required to notify a

50 'The firmware update requires an in-person patient visit with a health care provider – it cannot be done from home via Merlin.net. The update process will take approximately 3 minutes to complete. During this time, the device will operate in backup mode (pacing at 67 beats per minute), and essential, life-sustaining features will remain available. At the completion of the update, the device will return to its pre-update settings.'
51 'As with any firmware update, there is a very low risk of an update malfunction. Based on St. Jude Medical's previous firmware update experience, installing the updated firmware could potentially result in the following malfunctions (including the rate of occurrence previously observed): reloading of previous firmware version due to incomplete update (0.161 percent); loss of currently programmed device settings (0.023 percent); loss of diagnostic data (none reported); or complete loss of device functionality (0.003 percent).'
52 National Conference of State Legislatures, Security Breach Notification Laws, 29 March 2018, www.ncsl.org/research/telecommunications-and-information-technology/security-breach-notification-laws.aspx (last accessed 29 September 2018).
53 California, Nevada, North Dakota, Minnesota, Illinois, Tennessee, New York, Georgia, Texas, Puerto Rico, and the US Virgin Islands do not have a 'harm threshold'.

data breach. However, it would be difficult to say that data is 'owned' by the data subject.

8.81   In the EU, GDPR has created a strong set of 'rights' for a data subject. These apply within the UK through the Data Protection Act 2018. These rights include the right:

- of access (Article 15);

- of rectification (Article 16);

- to erasure (Article 17);

- to restriction of processing (Article 18);

- to data portability (Article 20); and

- to object to data processing (Article 21).

In this context, it is far easier to suggest that, within the EU, the data subject is the owner of their personal data.

8.82   For those working in the IoT sector, the starting point must be to consider the inherent insecurity of IoT devices, and then the risk or harm that a security breach may generate. This will likely include a consideration of the personal data processed, in which jurisdiction, and to what extent the regulator in that jurisdiction is able to enforce compliance.

Chapter 9

Right to be forgotten and right to erasure

INTRODUCTION

9.1   On 13 May 2014, the Court of Justice of the European Union ('CJEU') legally solidified that the 'right to be forgotten' is a human right when they ruled against Google in the *Costeja* case.[1] The Court observed that not only do individuals have a right to rectify, erase or block data that is inaccurate or incomplete, but they also have a right to ensure that their personal data used by controllers is adequate, relevant, and not excessive. The Court concluded that the links to articles about Costeja González's satisfied debts were inadequate, no longer relevant, or excessive, and therefore had to be removed by Google, even though the news articles themselves could remain online.

9.2   Since that landmark decision, the law has moved on and the right to rectification and, more significantly, the right to erasure are now a central plank of the General Data Protection Regulation ('GDPR'). This came into force in all European Union jurisdictions in May 2018.

9.3   The importance of the principles which are enshrined in the GDPR cannot be overstated. It places personal data at the front and centre of data regulation going forward, and it imposes severe maximum fines for breach. Significantly, and of particular importance in terms of the likely UK exit from the European Union, the United Kingdom Parliament passed the Data Protection Act 2018 which adopted the principles of GDPR meaning that, whatever form of Brexit occurs, the European-based Regulation will continue to govern the use and misuse of personal data for UK citizens.

9.4   It would also be a mistake for those living outside Europe to dismiss the importance of the GDPR. Due to strict rules on the transfer of data to countries and parties outside of the European Union, and in an effort to ensure high standards are met and kept when using personal data across the world, those in the United States, South America and Asia are realising the importance of compliance and the consequences of non-compliance.

9.5   Whilst a detailed analysis of the provisions of GDPR is outside the scope of this work, it is of assistance to examine a few provisions in order to properly

1   Judgment in Case C-131/12 *Google Spain SL, Google Inc. v Agencia Española de Protección de Datos, Mario Costeja González.*

assess the significance of the GDPR on blockchain in particular and to examine how other decentralised ledger technologies ('DLTs') are seeking to deal with the challenges of compliance.

Right to erasure

9.6   This is an obligations-based provision codified in Article 17(1)(a)–(f) of the GDPR. It provides for personal data to be erased immediately where the data is no longer needed for the original purpose for which it was collected or where the consent has been withdrawn and there are no overriding legitimate grounds for processing that data.

Right to be forgotten

9.7   The right to be forgotten is found in Article 17(2) of the GDPR which provides that, if a data controller has made the personal data public, and if one of the above reasons for erasure exists, the data controller must take reasonable measures to inform all other controllers in data processing that all links to this personal data, as well as copies or replicates of the personal data, must be erased.

9.8   This provision takes the right to erasure one step further by providing data subjects with a remedy if their personal data is made public and where they have grounds for erasure. The onus of proving the above (ie that reasons for erasure exist) falls on the data subject first, and then the data controller is faced with the responsibility of erasure.

Fundamental issues with right to erasure/right to be forgotten and their enforcement

9.9   The fundamental problem with the GDPR and the right to erasure provisions is that they both fail to address the unequal footing on which the data controllers and the data subjects stand, from the point of collection. To put it simply, when a data subject signs up on a website/online platform, they are confronted with small boxes/pop-up forms/windows asking them to read, peruse, assess and consider a lot of fine print. Accepting this fine print commences the 'legitimate' data collection process regarding the data subject, a process that is almost invisible and automated in nature given the nature of this technology. The data is then stored in complex algorithms, anonymised, pseudonymised and encrypted, depending upon the security levels of the data controller.

9.10   Fast forward to the data subject who wishes to seek the removal of his or her data from such a website/platform. On becoming aware of reasonable grounds of erasure, the data subject, as of December 2018, has to undertake the following tasks, with limited or little assistance:

- Contact the data controller by filling in an online form and formally registering a request for erasure of data.

- Provide personal identification for the purposes of making that application.

- Provide the links which the data subject believes are in infringement of their rights.

- The data controller will then cross-check with the infringing data links whether it relates to and verifies with the identity of the person who made the request.

- The data controller may charge a fee or refuse to deal with the application if they believe that the request is excessive, manifestly false or repetitive in nature.

9.11 It is evident that the process of data removal is far more manual and long winded in nature, as compared to the nature of data collection, which is highly automated and, in most cases, encrypted.

9.12 The appetite for enforcing the obligations of the right to be forgotten was seen in January 2019 when a court of appeal in Amsterdam affirmed a first instance decision in July 2018 that a surgeon who had reportedly appeared on an 'online blacklist' was allowed to instruct Google to remove search results relating to the case. Following straight on from that decision was the news that the French regulator, CNIL, fined Alphabet's Google $57 million (€50 million) for breach of GDPR obligations.[2] The regulator said that the search engine lacked transparency and clarity in the way it informs users about its handling of personal data, and failed to properly obtain consent for personalised ads. The significance of this cannot be overstated, in that a spokesman for the regulator said:

> 'The amount decided, and the publicity of the fine, are justified by the severity of the infringements observed regarding the essential principles of the GDPR: transparency, information and consent.'

What are the consequences for DLTs and blockchain?

9.13 Given the significance of the GDPR, and the 'supposed appetite' for enforcement, the consequences for DLTs and blockchain are potentially very far reaching. One of the fundamental principles of blockchain is that any data posted on the blockchain is immutable. Thus, given the fact that the composition of a blockchain makes deletion of data impossible, how is it ever going to be possible to reconcile it with the right to erasure and/or the right to be forgotten? It is fair to say that, currently, this has sparked much debate between academics and practitioners alike. It seems that, in reality, there are only two possible ways of having a compliant blockchain arrangement and, it is submitted, neither of them are satisfactory.

---

2   www.cnil.fr/fr/la-formation-restreinte-de-la-cnil-prononce-une-sanction-de-50-millions-deuros-lencontre-de-la.

How is 'erasure' compliant with GDPR?

9.14   The definition of 'erasure' for the purposes of GDPR compliance can give us an indication as to how far blockchains or other DLTs can comply with GDPR. The question becomes, What is really meant by 'erasure', as outlined above? Does it mean 'deletion' or would it be sufficient for the purposes of the Regulation to be made permanently inaccessible?

9.15   Some might argue that, if the information existed, but was de-linked from the individual, that could be 'erasure' in fulfilment of the right to be forgotten. This argument flows from the rationale of the Court in the *Costeja* case. The roots of right to erasure/right to be forgotten stem from the *Costeja* judgment and the opinions and submissions in that case. In the judgment when the question came before the Court, the latter, in acknowledging the data subject's right to erasure/right to be forgotten, based its decision and heavy reliance on the principle of 'de-linking' of search results (or what can be called the principle of invisibility), ie removing the link between the infringing article and the data subject so that the infringing article/information would not show up. It follows, therefore, that 'erasure' at that time could be construed as meaning removal of the link between the infringing information and the data subject. To apply that logic to blockchain/DLT, de-linking would mean making sure that information on the blockchain or other DLTs does not associate or link to a user/data subject. Therefore, de-linking for the purposes of blockchain could be argued by some as GDPR compliance. However, in practice, this argument raises many questions.

9.16   On the internet, there is a clear demarcation between a data controller and data subject as the data is stored centrally and, once the data subject exercises their right to erasure/right to be forgotten, the data is removed/de-linked so that it does not show up. Full compliance with GDPR is therefore, in the view of the authors, impossible in this situation. The issue with blockchain is the absence of a central database.

Example

A person makes a request of right to erasure/right to be forgotten/de-link and that request, in order to be erased, would have to pass through all the nodes where the information is secured and require the confirmation of deletion across all the nodes on the blockchain or other DLTs, and overall de-linking once all the nodes have given their confirmation.

What types of data stored on the blockchain are caught by GDPR?

9.17   As has been stated, where data has purportedly been pseudonymised, it still falls within the definition of personal data contained in Article 4 of the GDPR. On the blockchain, there are two types of data stored:

- transactional data; and

- public keys.

9.18 Encrypted data can be accessed with the correct encryption keys, thus keeping it within the ambit of GDPR. The Article 29 Working Party considers encryption as a pseudonymisation (see **9.23** below) technique, not something which counts as anonymisation, ie 'irreversibly' preventing identification. For the same reason, transactional data comes within the scope of the Regulation, even if it has been hashed or encrypted. Public keys, although a string of letters and numbers, are still capable of identification if matched with additional information. Thus, as recital 62 of GDPR makes clear, personal data that has 'undergone pseudonymisation which could be attributed to a natural person by the use of additional information qualifies as personal data.' Since public keys are a means of identification, they are likely to be what is envisaged above.

9.19 Given the subject matter of this chapter, it is important to remember that transactional data cannot be moved 'off chain'.

Methods of data protection and data privacy

9.20 Article 4 of the GDPR defines personal data as 'any information relating to an identified or identifiable natural person ("data subject"); an identifiable natural person is one who can be identified, directly or indirectly, in particular by reference to an identifier such as a name, an identification number, location data, an online identifier or to one or more factors specific to the physical, physiological, genetic, mental, economic, cultural or social identity of that natural person'.

9.21 To protect personal data, there are various mechanisms that are more broadly available as per GDPR. It is at this point important to mention that the legislators behind the GDPR had a centralised ledger system in mind while drafting provisions for data protection. In cases of centralised ledger systems, encryption can be done by various methods. However, the problem becomes much more acute in cases of blockchain and DLTs.

9.22 The term 'hashing' is well known to users of blockchain technology. It effectively converts the data into a form whereby it cannot be returned to its original state.

What is pseudonymisation?

9.23 The process of pseudonymisation is catered for in Article 4 of the GDPR:

> '"pseudonymisation" means the processing of personal data in such a manner that the personal data can no longer be attributed to a specific data subject without the use of additional information, provided that such additional information is kept separately and is subject to technical and organisational measures to ensure that the personal data are not attributed to an identified or identifiable natural person;'

What are the effects on compliance if data is pseudonymised?

9.24   For the purposes of assessing GDPR compliance of blockchain and other DLTs, it needs to be understood that the GDPR provides its data subjects with two rights:

1.   right to be forgotten (a right that relates to 'de-linking' of information and enables an individual not to be associated, in public, with their corresponding data); and

2.   right to erasure (a right to have their data removed from the ledger).

9.25   Although these GDPR obligations are bundled together as one obligation as per legislation and *Costeja*, it needs to be understood that these are two separate obligations. In that case, the extent to which the process of pseudonymisation complies with GDPR privacy obligations all depends on which of these two rights/obligations are being considered and whether 'erasure' is to be construed widely or narrowly. It is the strong view of the authors that pseudonymisation does not meet compliance for the purposes of the GDPR.

9.26   If, for the purposes of this consideration, we are concerned about the right to be forgotten, adopting the Court's jurisprudence from *Costeja*, compliance for the blockchain/DLT means 'de-linking' of personal information of a user on the blockchain (by using technologies that restrict data subject identification), then it can be argued that pseudonymisation could potentially be GDPR-compliant, in that the personal data of a data subject on the blockchain is masked by way of encryption.

9.27   However, it seems unlikely that the process of pseudonymisation, although compliant with the 'privacy' aspect (ie the right to be forgotten), can be reconciled with the right to erasure.

9.28   If 'erasure' is construed too strictly as per the CJEU or any related superseding authority, it is highly unlikely that blockchain would be GDPR-compliant. It is more of a waiting game now, to see which version of the definition of 'erasure' the Court adopts.

9.29   Can any assistance be gained from the references in the GDPR to 'available technology' found, for example, in Article 17(2)?

9.30   It would be a bold decision by any regulator to avail blockchain of this assistance. Could it really be submitted that the whole significance of a central tenet of the GDPR (that is, the right to be forgotten) should be sidestepped because blockchains (in particular, public, permissionless blockchains) lacked the available technology to be compliant. The authors are very dubious as to the likelihood of success of that argument.

9.31   It will ultimately need resolution through legal channels and, in the authors' view, by a superior court. Some assistance can be gained from the very helpful Article 29 Working Party which envisages 'hashing' as a form of pseudonymisation (ie a protection technique as opposed to anonymisation), which takes data outside the definition of 'personal data' for the purposes of Article 4. However, although useful, this was guidance which appears to be based on the possibility of recovery of pseudonymised data and not in the context of the blockchain/GDPR conundrum. We believe that this is at the limit of reasonable interpretation. It is not a valid argument, in our view, to say that data is 'erased' if it is encrypted and only accessible by a secret key or 'hashed'. That does not constitute erasure.

9.32   A more practical suggestion, and certainly a more reliable way of seeking compliance, is to keep personal data, which is likely to be the subject of a request for erasure, off chain (but see **9.19** above concerning transactional data). This advice is not always well received by the blockchain purists, as the immutability and algorithmic nature of blockchain is what makes it so attractive for many. However, it is currently the only sure way of achieving compliance. It seems that a middle-path needs to be brokered so as to enable personal data to be on the blockchain and yet off the entire node network in a 'split storage' method. The main drawback of this solution is that, if the blockchain performs the split storage, the information is vulnerable to hacking and it limits the efficiency of blockchain.

THE RIGHT TO AMENDMENT

9.33   Article 16 of the GDPR includes the right to seek and obtain rectification from the controller. How is that to be done on the blockchain? Does the data subject seek to locate all of those responsible for the nodes? What happens in the unlikely event that they are successful? Would it be possible for the nodes to change the encrypted data in a block?

Other DLTs and GDPR compliance

9.34   Other DLTs are now being developed. It is right to say that the main driver behind these developments has been the relative slowness of transactions per second ('tps') of the more well-known applications of blockchain such as Ethereum, rather than compliance issues, but some of the developing DLTs, or purported new DLTs, do seek to resolve the issue of immutability.

9.35   There are three notable projects (and many more seeking to deal with the 'tps' issue) that purport to be compliant.

1.   Sovrin

9.36   This project differentiates between:

- data locally retained; and
- data on the public ledger.

9.37   It seeks to give control of data to what it terms the 'identity owner'. It plays up the importance of credentials which are exchanged between the identity owners and the other data users. By giving the users on the chain the power to send out data (which may or may not be personal) only when transacting for a specific purpose, Sovrin provides for the record of access to be stored on that blockchain. This record would acknowledge the data access on the blockchain and could open a Pandora's box for hackers, since the record of the access would be public and immutable.

9.38   The technical make-up of Sovrin and, indeed, the other DLTs mentioned in this chapter are outside the scope of this work, but it appears that, by stressing the importance of a high degree of trust between all users of the system, the central tenet of GDPR (control of the data subject over its own data) is supposedly achieved.

2.   LTO Network

9.39   The importance of a high level of trust is mirrored in the approach of LTO Network. The processes, called Live Contracts, sit upon a permissionless private chain. The events which occur are placed on a permissionless public chain. Significantly, with this DLT, the node of the user is the Controller, and the person who places the information is a processor. It is important to reiterate that GDPR, for the first time, places obligations on Processors but they are less onerous that those of the Controller – although they can still attract costly sanctions. What LTO Network suggests can be achieved is that any contract, internal process or third party process can be regulated, and, it asserts, automated, by a Live Contract. See also **Chapter 3** concerning smart (Live) contracts.

3.   Holochain

9.40   The most interesting development in these emerging technologies is HOLO (Holochain). This pronounces itself as 'beyond blockchain'. The data is not stored on a public ledger but is administered by agents. Each agent has, and therefore (it is said) controls, its own DNA and is shared peer to peer. It is argued and, of course, yet to be tested, that GDPR compliance is based on hApp rules (similar to dApp but centred on Holochain) and, accordingly, has an easy ability to become compliant.

9.41   Of these different DLTs, HOLO and LTO Network are effectively permissionless private chains. All of the projects discussed seek to form a hybrid approach but, significantly, away from the miners' reward model. The only major drawback with HOLO is the appointment of 'agents' which some might argue to be 'intermediaries of a central data ledger system' and therefore, by introducing a central data ledger-like intermediary, the essence of the DLT system is lost. It is logical that the agent will be considered by many to be the data controller as he will bear the responsibility of controlling the DNA (at least their own) on the network.

9.42   The desire to modernise the blockchain and particularly the speed of tps are the driving forces behind these new incarnations of DLT, but the jury may still be out on whether they can satisfy that need as well as pass the high GDPR compliance bar which has been set.

9.43   It seems likely that the blockchain and GDPR, although they set out to achieve the same objectives of providing privacy and protection in digital transactions, are now on a collision course owing to their respective objectives. GDPR, being a state-oriented and controlling legislation, seeks to take control, whereas blockchain and other DLTs seek to take that power and empower each user on the chain with the right to control their data. The ultimate resolution of this may be costly.

Chapter 10

Natural resources

INTRODUCTION

10.1   The appeal of blockchain comes from the fact that it is a distributed, decentralised, public, time-stamped and verifiable ledger.[1] With this in mind, the technology will likely have an impact across almost every aspect of the natural resources industry. The potential benefits range from real-time data registry (as gas and oil come out of the ground, or electricity is produced) to the possibility of peer-to-peer energy selling, disintermediation and the creation of a smart energy grid. These benefits are often, and first by the Energy Web Foundation ('EWF'), grouped under the headings of:

- decarbonisation;

- decentralisation;

- digitisation; and

- democratisation.[2]

10.2   What's more, these four interconnected categories are often defined as the long-term aims of blockchain implementation in the natural resources industry. They are interconnected in the sense that, for example, some aspects of digitisation would result in decarbonisation.[3] Furthermore, it is crucial for blockchain and the industry that digitisation, decentralisation, decarbonisation and democratisation are not mutually exclusive goals. Ultimately, it seems, the pursuit of decentralisation will create a more democratic market and digitisation a greener one. Moreover, if decentralisation is the primary aim for the natural resources industry, at market level, then digitisation can be seen as the means of achieving this aim.

Is blockchain the answer to the 'trilemma'?

10.3   Blockchain is perhaps the answer to the 'trilemma' that has become the central worry of energy production. The trilemma is comprised of the problems of:

1   Aitken, R. 'Smart Contracts On The Blockchain: Can Businesses Reap the Benefits?', www.forbes.com/sites/rogeraitken/2017/11/21/smart-contracts-on-the-blockchain-can-businesses-reap-the-benefits/#3774b5bc1074.
2   Basden, J. and Cottrell, M., 'How Utilities Are Using Blockchain to Modernise the Grid', *Harvard Business Review* https://hbr.org/2017/03/how-utilities-are-using-blockchain-to-modernize-the-grid.
3   Creyts, J. and Trbovich, A., 'Can blockchain help us to address the world's energy issues?', www.weforum.org/agenda/2018/01/how-can-blockchain-address-the-worlds-energy-issues/.

- security (in terms of when resources will run out);

- decarbonisation; and

- affordability.[4]

10.4   Ultimately, these problems are solvable if the aims set out by the EWF are achieved, as the hope is that decarbonisation, decentralisation, digitisation and democratisation will secure the longevity of energy production by making the industry more efficient, cleaner and cheaper. More specifically, technologies such as smart contracts (see **Chapter 3**), decentralised autonomous organisations, microgrids, real-time data registry and the creation of smart energy grids will be the technical means of achieving this, while a restructuring of the grid and movement away from traditional, centralised distribution techniques will be the philosophy behind achieving a trilemma-free energy sector. Finally, the changing landscape of the market and the movement away from the traditional consumer-distributor relationship will be central to the future of the market.

10.5   In terms of achieving these aims, there are myriad problems, some of which are an unavoidable part of the implementation of blockchain in any industry, such as:

- scalability;

- the need for new technology;

- regulatory concerns; and

- how to gain customer interest.

Meanwhile, others are unique to natural resources as an industry with high production costs and often inefficient and complex logistical systems.[5]

10.6   However, recent narratives surrounding blockchain implementation have begun to stop viewing unique industry challenges simply as negatives. Instead, when thinking realistically about implementing the technology it is important to look at the industries whose challenges are suited to blockchain. The natural resources industry, which is dominated by financial transactions, the exchange of information[6] and combined with globe-spanning and complex logistics, falls into this category.

---

4 Sandys L. et al, *Reshaping Regulation: Powering from the Future,* Graham Institute – Climate Change and the Environment, 2017.
5 Mota da Silva et al, 'Blockchain in Natural Resources: Hedging Against Volatile Prices', *TATA Consultancy Report.*
6 Belle, I., 'The architecture, engineering and construction industry and blockchain technology', *DADA 2017 International Conference on Digital Architecture.*

REGULATORY REFORM

10.7   The process of regulatory reform is often described as the largest challenge to the implementation of the technology in the industry.[7] Decentralisation, democratisation and digitisation would become more difficult to achieve by stringent or recalcitrant regulation that made blockchain unworkable. On a side note, decarbonisation is likely an inevitability, as natural resource and energy companies must look for more efficient ways of producing green energy. This aside, the question of regulatory success in the industry seems to be that both regulators and industry participators need to view regulation not as an obstacle or a challenge to overcome but rather as a necessary task to be completed which could, and should, have a positive impact on the potential uses of blockchain in the industry. And it seems that the UK will be at the forefront of this, as a country which has a reputation for leading the way in energy regulation.[8]

What is the key regulatory question?

10.8   When it comes to blockchain, the key regulatory question, or perhaps the most complex, is how to regulate peer-to-peer trading and a market in which the role of the consumer has become prosumer (ie someone who is involved in customising products for their own needs). Ideologically speaking, this is perhaps the most radical change that blockchain will bring about, as property owners become active participants in the market, buying and selling energy. Indeed, it introduces complex questions of ownership, status and simply how to regulate the increase in volume of those participating in the grid. The traditional, centralised direction of power trade, or distribution by a large corporation (one of the 'big six' in the UK, such as British Gas or EDF Energy), will be upended. With this in mind, many are asking the question as to whether blockchain will be an evolution for the industry or if it will be revolutionary. Surely, this aspect of the technology's implementation is at the heart of this question, the success of which perhaps comes down to how this transition is regulated.

What other regulatory issues need to be addressed?

10.9   In addition to this seemingly central problem, there are other regulatory issues that must be addressed. Principally these are:

- jurisdiction and how to regulate blockchains as they span the globe and regulatory boundaries;

- guarantees of service levels and performance from vendors offering blockchain platforms, and who accepts liability;

---

7   Shipworth, D., *Global Policy and Regulatory Change,* UCL Energy Institute.
8   Sandys L. et al, *Reshaping Regulation: Powering from the Future,* Graham Institute – Climate Change and the Environment, 2017.

- intellectual property;

- data privacy; and

- exit assistance, or how to leave an unalterable blockchain.

10.10 Certainly, regulation surrounding smart contracts, and their collective organisation as decentralised autonomous organisations, will need to be drafted in order to allow the technology to work efficiently.

10.11 It seems that the primary hope for blockchain, for those in the natural resources and energy sector, is that it will change the way in which we distribute energy, resulting in a cheaper and more efficient market. The advent of smart technology, including contracts and meters, will contribute to consumers becoming prosumers. That is to say, they will be able to generate and distribute their own energy, using solar panels, as well as buying from and selling back to the central grid. At first, theoretically, this will lead to a complex hybrid system involving the centralised grid as well as microgrids. Therefore, if we think of current grid distribution like a family tree, and the large intermediary energy companies as the head of a family, consumers would be first generation children. Essentially, the energy supplier of these consumers is the head of the family. The system is top down and centralised, none of the consumers interact with one another; rather, they all go through one single point of contact at the top of the tree. Whereas a system involving microgrids and peer-to-peer trading is more like a web, which is where the concept of decentralisation comes from. Each participant in the energy market is connected to one another, with no one at the centre.

10.12 Peer-to-peer trading will most likely be achieved by the use of blockchain, and possibly other technologies in combination. Ultimately, it is the point at which digitisation and decentralisation radically alter the current energy distribution hierarchy. Therefore, it is a useful starting point to examine the context surrounding blockchain and the natural resources industry, and how this relationship might be regulated.

10.13 A primary examination of the theories surrounding decentralisation, followed by an investigation of digitisation and the technology that could be used, the problems and obstacles and where regulation might be needed, will paint a picture of the possibilities for blockchain in the industry. Along the way, there are some useful case studies (where blockchain is already being implemented in the industry) to be examined, as well as a look at how the technology can be used around the market distribution phase and examples of blockchain deployment across all stages of the natural resources supply chain.

DECENTRALISATION

10.14 One of the primary reasons why blockchain is such an appropriate technology for the natural resources industry is that decentralisation is one of its innate features. That is to say, blockchain cannot be a force of centralisation.

The benefit of this decentralisation is efficiency, in terms of grid optimisation, greater power to the consumer and the reduction of energy losses. However, it also creates a complex system, involving a web of power flows and transactions, as consumers become prosumers.[9]

10.15 Blockchain creates a robust, secure and transparent distributed ledger.[10] This idea of a platform that is robust and distributed is what has led to the suggestion that the technology can bypass central authorities. Essentially, there is no singular, centralised copy of the data stored on a blockchain; rather, it is stored across nodes and validated through consensus protocols. Ultimately, devices must be in agreement about what is true, in terms of information across the blockchain, for data to be added or manipulated. This allows blockchain to certify the existence and ownership of anything that can be digitised.[11]

10.16 Currently, there is the consensus in the natural resources industry and energy sector that blockchain is the best option for the future – a future that hopes to boast a more sustainable, more efficient and cheaper energy market. The extent to which this vision can be achieved is debatable, as is the means by which it might be achieved. However, it is certain that decentralisation will be a factor of influence on the future of the natural resources and energy sector and, currently, blockchain is the best means of achieving this.

10.17 However, it would mean that these large corporations still have a significant amount of control over the grid, and the question needs to be addressed as to whether this is worth sacrificing some of the disruptive, decentralised benefits of blockchain for.

10.18 With this in mind, it is important to look at the areas of the market where decentralisation might take place, the benefits of this and obstacles to it, the regulatory questions introduced and, finally, some examples of where the technology is being utilised and the extent to which it has been successful.

AREAS OF APPLICATION

10.19 It is the market distribution stage of the natural resources industry that will be most affected by decentralisation. This new decentralised distribution system will also affect the production of energy, creating a complex system, as energy is produced at a commercial and consumer level. There is also the sense that, to some extent, blockchain will simplify distribution through the use of

---

9 Found at www.electron.org.uk/.
10 Davidson S., De Filippi, P., Potts, J., 'The Economics of Blockchain' *Public Choice Conference*, May 2016, Fort Lauderdale, United States. Proceedings of Public Choice Conference, 2016.
11 Chapron, G., 'The Environment needs Cryptogovernance', *Nature*, May 2017, www.nature.com/news/the-environment-needs-cryptogovernance-1.22023.

smart meters and the creation of a public ledger that is accessible and secure.[12] Blockchain makes the system more complex in the sense that there will be more players, ranging from start-ups to home-owning prosumers to large corporations; however, the system is also simplified by the removal of the traditional energy provider-customer relationship, as smart meters allow consumers to buy from, and interact directly with, the grid.

NON-RENEWABLES AND INTERMEDIARIES

10.20   It is most useful to first look at the aspects of simplification in the industry and what blockchain might remove (or simplify) from the industry. In the natural resources industry, distribution of materials and energy follows the passage from extraction, refining (or registry), transporting and then distribution. Oil, for example, is taken out of the ground before being refined, then it is transported and sold in consumer markets by a handful of intermediary companies who dominate a given market. When it comes to oil and gas, blockchain may usher in the end of these companies or, at the very least, instigate a significant change in their role. Ultimately, the natural resources and energy market has been commoditised at the distribution stage. In the UK, the key players in this sector of the market are known as the 'Big Six' (EDF Energy, British Gas, E.ON, NPower, Scottish Power and SSE). Evidently, the industry is heavily centralised and consumers have very limited choice on where their energy is coming from. Blockchain could alter this system as smart meters provide a secure and efficient way for consumers to buy energy directly from the grid, rather than being subject to the policy of large-scale companies that remove any autonomy from the consumer in a system that is open to monopolisation and abuse.[13] Currently, energy-transaction systems operate as countertrade, with the conventional power-generation companies being the central ledger. Ultimately, this is also less financially efficient, as energy is provided to homeowners at (increasingly competitive) fixed rates.[14]

10.21   As a result, it is easy to see why the system becomes more simple as this dominant player in the supply chain is removed. Indeed, as an industry that is capital heavy, regulated and has a complex supply chain, the natural resources industry is an ideal candidate for the technology.[15] There are examples of small-scale systems where this is being trialled with success, such as the Brooklyn Microgrid, a peer-to-peer blockchain trial which allows participants to trade solar energy. In addition to small-scale trials, there are theories on how a system might work when implemented on a wide scale. These will be considered later,

---

12 Creyts, Jon et al, 'Can blockchain help us to address the world's energy issues?', *World Economic Forum*, www.weforum.org/agenda/2018/01/how-can-blockchain-address-the-worlds-energy-issues.

13 Davidson S., De Filippi, P., Potts, J., 'The Economics of Blockchain' *Public Choice Conference*, May 2016, Fort Lauderdale, United States. Proceedings of Public Choice Conference, 2016.

14 Won Park, L. et al, 'A Sustainable Home Energy Prosumer-Chain Methodology with Energy Tags over the Blockchain', published by MDPI AG.

15 Mota da Silva et al, 'Blockchain in Natural Resources: Hedging Against Volatile Prices', *TATA Consultancy Report*.

along with their solutions as well as problems. But first it is important to examine the impact that blockchain might have on the renewables sector.

RENEWABLES AND ELECTRICITY

10.22   In terms of renewable energy sources and electricity, it is likely that blockchain will allow consumers to produce their own, as citizens become active co-producers, or prosumers.[16] The development of peer-to-peer trading in the energy market can be seen as the beginning of a movement towards micro and smart energy grids. Smart energy grids are made up of microgrids, or intelligent networks utilising renewable energy sources and high performance technology networks in order to satisfy the demand of energy from consumers.[17] Essentially, microgrids would connect users directly to a grid which would contribute to a larger smart energy grid. The most radical change would be to homeowners becoming prosumers and being able to produce and sell (rather than simply purchase) energy back to the grid or directly to other prosumers.

10.23   This is why the system has been described as more complex, even though the removal of intermediaries shortens the supply chain. In this instance, complexity is equated with an expansion of the number of players. However, such a radical change to the structure of energy distribution would require new regulation. Indeed, the questions of ownership, intellectual property, exit assistance and data privacy must be addressed.

10.24   It is useful to expand further on this concept of smart energy, in particular its role as a crucial component for the Smart City. It is perhaps a long way off, but the Smart City has been described as 'an integrated system in which human and social capital heavily interact using technology-based solutions'.[18] This system strives to use technology to solve some of the problems caused by the expansion of our cities, with the ultimate goals being efficiency, a higher quality of life and sustainability.

10.25   Microgrids are concerned with connecting participants in a city via an intelligent network which, in theory, could be done using a home configuration. In addition to this, the technology hopes to open new energy markets, ranging from simple home management systems to allowing consumers and third parties to offer their own energy resources back into the market.[19] This technology is already being used on a small scale by companies like Brooklyn Microgrid and

---

16 Wolsink, M. (2018). 'Renewables: common pool natural resources distributed generation in intelligent grids'. 1–21. Paper presented at 'Breaking the Rules – Energy Transitions as Social Innovations', Berlin, Germany.
17 Alessandra, Pieroni & Scarpato, Noemi & Di Nunzio, Luca & Fallucchi, Francesca & Raso, Mario. (2018). 'Smarter City: Smart Energy Grid based on Blockchain Technology'. International Journal on Advanced Science, Engineering and Information Technology. 8. 298. 10.18517/ijaseit.8.1.4954.
18 Ibid.
19 Ibid.

TransActiveGrid (a company concerned with blockchain-based energy distribution at the local level). What's more, examining these small-scale, unregulated trial runs of the technology will be crucial for addressing some of the regulatory questions that the technology poses, while the benefits of these microgrids is that they bring efficiency to the market by removing steps (bureaucratic steps) in the process of bringing energy from production to distribution. Ultimately, the technology brings suppliers, consumers and producers closer together, as blockchain's ability to log and store data in real time allows the producers to respond to the needs of the market in real time.[20]

CASE STUDIES

10.26   In terms of looking at the current, real-world applications of blockchain in the industry, it is perhaps first helpful to look at the prevalent theories of how this application might take place, followed by the applications themselves.

10.27   Firstly, the general trend in our power supply system is a movement towards distributed generation, smaller conversion units and renewable sources.[21] Given that the use of renewable sources, according to consensus, is an inevitability, it is most important to examine what is really meant by distributed generation and why this is happening.

Case Study 1: Wolsink

Wolsink's distributed system centres around networks of multiple, small generating units situated close to energy consumers and contributing towards a larger, intelligent grid.[22] This system is twofold, as these small systems are reliant on consumers producing energy. Ultimately, this accelerates efficiency in the energy market, as production comes from a variety of different sources. Prosumers become decision makers and influencers in the market, as their new role allows them input in terms of generation capacity, space for infrastructure and storage capacity as they become a crucial part of the installation and management of microgrids.[23] In this sense, the interest of customers is of crucial importance to the technology's implementation. Furthermore, it is this active participation that has significant implications for institutional changes in the structure of energy distribution as peer-to-peer delivery is an idea that runs in complete opposition to the traditional make-up of the power supply system.[24] As so many emerging technologies, particularly blockchain, seem to support the intelligent self-governance of

---

20 Ibid.
21 Wolsink, M. (2018). 'Renewables: common pool natural resources distributed generation in intelligent grids'. 1–21. Paper presented at 'Breaking the Rules – Energy Transitions as Social Innovations', Berlin, Germany.
22 Ibid.
23 Ibid.
24 Ibid.

energy flows, including private generation, storage and transmission, it seems only a matter of time until this regulatory question need to be answered.

10.28   It must be noted that Wolsink's presentation of a future decentralised market is perhaps not the first or the best; rather, it is useful because it paints broad theoretical strokes as opposed to looking at a specific market and the minutiae of how a system might work in this market. And, ultimately, all of the central concepts of Wolsink's system are in keeping with the aims of blockchain: decentralisation, democratisation, decarbonisation and digitisation. Importantly, it is an example of the current theories, and adds to the consensus of what the future of the market will look like. Additionally, in terms of the regulatory question, it is more important to look at the general theory that markets might fit into, especially as regulation will need to pre-date, or at least be contemporaneous with, large-scale implementation.

10.29   Despite this, it is useful to look at one specific market example of how decentralisation in the energy and natural resources sector might be implemented with blockchain.

Case Study 2: South Korea

In South Korea a range of energy companies producing hydro, central and nuclear power are all managed by the Korea Electric Power Corporation, as a single company monopolises the industry.[25] Lee Won Park, Sanghoon Lee and Hangbae Chang use the country as a case study to demonstrate how the centralisation of an energy market could be altered by the implementation of blockchain. The paper suggests that a decentralised and distributed trading system could be created on a blockchain platform to allow peer-to-peer trading in a transparent, trustworthy and secure manner.[26] Further to this, they introduce the idea of an energy tag; a smart contract that sets the conditions of every future peer-to-peer transaction in order to make them more cost-efficient. This information will be shared with multiple energy resources and home appliances democratically connected so that users benefit from high-quality, low-cost energy at all times.[27] This is a useful example as the paper is tackling a market that would be radically disrupted, due to its heavy monopolisation, while offering a radical solution. In addition to this, it demonstrates the reasons why people think decarbonisation is an inevitability with the implementation of blockchain, as the current issues with renewable energy partly come down to a question of efficiency, which the concept of 'energy tags' via smart contracts would significantly improve.

---

25 Won Park, L. et al, 'A Sustainable Home Energy Prosumer-Chain Methodology with Energy Tags over the Blockchain', published by MDPI AG.
26 Ibid.
27 Ibid.

Case Study 3: The Brooklyn Microgrid

The Brooklyn Microgrid is currently trialling a system similar to South Korea on a very small scale. The company has developed a community-powered microgrid to test the possibility of consumers selling solar energy to one another. Currently, each participant has had to invest in a computer with a blockchain node in order for their homes with solar panels to be able to sell power.[28] The first issue is scalability, as being required to buy a computer with a blockchain node does not make the technology particularly accessible. Seemingly, one of the most significant issues with a microgrid is that, currently, it is not an inclusive system and raises questions of what might happen when a person leaves or enters the microgrid, in terms of physical, digital and potential energy property. This becomes more problematic as the presence of early-stage microgrids could begin to influence house prices and where people live. Despite this, the Brooklyn Microgrid is a usefully successful example of how blockchain technology can work. Indeed, it could be used as a regulatory case study.

THE REALITY

10.30 It is important to consider the reality of what might happen in the coming years, in terms of decentralisation in the industry. Certainly, blockchain will be a disruptive force; however, many theories posed of the future of the energy and natural resources sector are just that – theories – and they often seem to forget that large, centralised corporations are not simply going to disappear. Ultimately, these companies have the resources to invest and engage with emergent technology and every one will have an innovation team. Indeed, these centralised institutions are 'digging in'; despite being vulnerable to disruption, they are protected by the existing regulations which in turn can make the market challenging for start-ups.[29] When contemplating the future of the market, they should not be ignored or forgotten, even if they do make the regulatory question more simple.

10.31 For example, the EWF provides a service specifically to meet the challenges of blockchain in the energy industry. Indeed, of the 50 companies to sign up so far, there are large energy companies as well as smaller start-ups. Ultimately, many of the conversations surrounding decentralisation and blockchain in the industry point towards the complete disruption of the role of large energy companies. While this is a possibility, it seems that the large companies, who currently have a significant share in the energy market of

---

28 Basden, J. and Cottrell, M., 'How Utilities are Using Blockchain to Modernize the Grid', https://hbr.org/2017/03/how-utilities-are-using-blockchain-to-modernize-the-grid.

29 Casey, M. J., and Vigna, P., 'In Blockchain we Trust', *MIT Technology Review,* Vol. 121, No. 3 May/June 2018.

any given country, will be the first to move, in terms of utilising blockchain technology.

10.32   The EWF states that its aim is to de-commoditise the electricity market through the active collaboration to create an open-source blockchain platform.[30]

10.33   With this in mind, it is perhaps more appropriate to look at organisations such as the EWF as possible agents of centralisation. While the EWF is a non-profit organisation, companies that sign up will have to use its open-source, scalable software and blockchain architecture. This system minimises disruption and, as a result, settles some of the issues of regulation as, in theory, the EWF would have to assume liability for those who signed up to its product.

10.34   Perhaps, the EWF is an example of the implementation of blockchain and regulation as a collaborative force and speaks to the possibility of the co-existence of new, decentralised players alongside traditional, centralised sources of natural resources contributing to a complex system.

DIGITISATION

Information storage, transparency and real-time tracking

10.35   If decentralisation is the aim of blockchain implementation, at the market and distribution stages, then digitisation is how it will be achieved. However, the implications of digitisation reach further than decentralisation, as blockchain could be beneficially implemented at every stage of the process of producing, transporting and distributing natural resources. With this in mind, the resultant benefits have been identified as reducing costs, improving productivity, and increasing trust (accommodating decentralisation can be included among these).[31]

10.36   A large proportion of blockchain's appeal comes down to its ability to store information (that is, the technology can securely store vast amounts of data in real time). For example, if you were to input your name 'Joe Bloggs' into a blockchain, it would take up the same amount of space as the entirety of James Joyce's *Ulysses*. When information is stored in a blockchain, it becomes a hash (or a representation, usually a combination of numbers and letters, of the input data) that is a fixed length. It is also important to note that, if even the smallest change is made to the input data, the output hash will be completely different. This is what makes the blockchain secure, as only the exact, unalterable original input data's hash will be accepted, making a change to the blockchain almost impossible.

---

30 Stone, M., 'The World's Top Energy Companies Look to Blockchain to "Fuse the Physical with the Virtual"', www.greentechmedia.com/articles/read/worlds-top-energy-companies-look-to-blockchain#gs.XWkHD=g.
31 Mota da Silva, F. and Jaitly, A., 'Blockchain in Natural Resources: Hedging Against Volatile Prices', *TATA Consultancy Services*.

10.37   Data storage is perhaps the use for blockchain that is easiest to imagine. What's more, it is already being used in the diamond industry, with some success. While diamonds are not energy-producing natural resources, both industries extract and refine natural products before shipping and distributing them in the market. British company Everledger is working with the diamond industry to help reduce fraud, prevent theft and solve ethical problems.[32] Everledger uses blockchain to take 40 measurements of each diamond, which are then assigned a unique identifier. This information is added to the blockchain where it becomes secure and subsequently easy to track after sales and transfers.[33] By the time a diamond arrives at the end-consumer, it is possible to know where it was mined, how it was transported and every company that touched the product along the way. This would be vital for the natural resources industry, particularly when it comes to oil, gas and coal. Often, these resources are the cause of political instability, as well as causing problems of theft, fraud and difficulty in tracking. Indeed, it is estimated that $2 billion are lost each year because of these problems in the diamond industry.[34] This is an example of blockchain optimising an aspect of the industry, but it also shows how blockchain can be its own source of regulation. Additionally, because of the nature of blockchain as transparent and secure, the technology can make it difficult to break regulations. As a result, it can be argued that it enforces the law before the fact rather than after.

10.38   The oil industry, in particular, constantly struggles against volatility of prices because of factors varying from political instability in source countries to arbitrage as assets are moved across the globe.[35] However, if assets were transparently logged in real time, it would not be possible to take advantage of the differing prices of resources in different markets.

10.39   Moreover, this aspect of the technology does have implications for the renewable sector as well. If oil and gas could be logged in real time as they are extracted from the ground, eliminating a time-consuming, expensive and human error-prone link of the supply chain, the same could be done for the solar, hydro and wind industries. Especially in the renewables sector, the process of logging energy produced is inefficient. This is another example of the inevitability of blockchain technology decarbonising the natural resources industry.

Distributed technology and the energy market

10.40   In 1997, Nick Szabo wrote a paper called 'The God Protocol' in which he came up with a theory that has since become the foundation of smart contracts. A smart contract is a decentralised piece of software capable of

32 Pearson, T., 'How Does Blockchain Technology Work?', https://hackernoon.com/how-does-blockchain-technology-work-ceeeee47eaba.
33 Ibid.
34 Carson, B. et al, 'Blockchain beyond the hype: What is the strategic business value?', www.mckinsey.com/business-functions/digital-mckinsey/our-insights/blockchain-beyond-the-hype-what-is-the-strategic-business-value.
35 Ibid.

enacting legal contracts autonomously.[36] Indeed, by placing a smart contract on a blockchain, it is no longer limited to being controlled by a single centralised party.[37] Consequently, blockchain has the potential to create a direct relationship between a natural resource producer and consumer that automatically and securely regulates the requirements of supply and payment.[38] What's more, when this idea is taken to its logical conclusion, it is another contributing factor to the consensus that the position of intermediary companies will be eradicated, or largely changed, by blockchain.

10.41   Much of the discussion around digitisation in the natural resources industry leads to conversations about the Smart City. The creation of a smart environment and the smart use of natural resources are two central pillars of this concept. The Smart City is an idealised social structure comprised of 'horizontally cumulative elements'[39] in a kind of technological egalitarianism. On a broader level, it can be defined as a system in which humans and social capital interact via technology-based solutions and the application of the Internet of Things to urban scenarios.[40]

10.42   At a technical level, creating a Smart City would involve the digitisation of the grid, the use of smart contracts and the growth of the sharing economy. In combination, these would be contributing factors to the creation of the smart energy grid which would allow the transfer of energy between properties ranging from residential houses to larger commercial spaces, as discussed, creating a sharing economy. In addition to this, these energy transfers would need to work in combination with the possibility of oil, gas and electricity orders to the home through an app which may eliminate broker fees and simplify payments.[41]

10.43   The implementation of smart contracts would be disruptive because they would alter the channels of governance within the natural resources industry. The widespread use of blockchain technology would see large-scale institutional change as power from central storage facilities is steadily replaced by (or integrated with) peer-to-peer storage and direct connection to the distribution network.[42] This movement presents questions such as, 'Who will be control of the infrastructure?', 'What exactly are they in control of?', 'Who will invest?, and 'Who collects and uses the data?'. As a result, it seems that there needs to

---

36 DuPont, Q. and Maurer, B., 'Ledgers and Laws in Blockchain', *Kings Review,* June 2015.
37 www.freshfields.com/en-gb/our-thinking/campaigns/digital/fintech/blockchain-and-smart-contracts/.
38 Pearson, T., 'How Does Blockchain Technology Work?', https://hackernoon.com/how-does-blockchain-technology-work-ceeeee47eaba.
39 Sun, J. et al, 'Blockchain-based sharing services: What blockchain technology can contribute to smart cities', K.Z.K. Financ Innov (2016) 2: 26. https://doi.org/10.1186/s40854-016-0040-y.
40 Pieroni, A. et al, 'Smarter City: Smart Energy Grid Based on Blockchain Technology', *International Journal on Advanced Science Engineering Information Technology*, March 2018.
41 Mota da Silva, F. and Jaitly, A., 'Blockchain in Natural Resources: Hedging Against Volatile Prices', *TATA Consultancy Services*.
42 Wolsink, M., 'Renewables: common pool natural resources distributed generation in intelligent grids'. 1–21. Paper presented at 'Breaking the Rules – Energy Transitions as Social Innovations', Berlin, Germany (2018).

be a structure laid out as to how this new system will be governed. For example, does governance become decentralised in the same way as the new system is? Other theories include adaptive governance, or allowing flexibility and resilience to sudden external changes, polycentric governance, or decisions taken at many different places as well as arenas and multi-level governance.[43]

10.44   The potential of smart contracts has not gone unnoticed. Currently, they are suffering from the same issues as a lot of blockchain technology: successful implementation and scalability. Clearly, there are still significant problems with the technology as, amidst the magnitude of start-ups offering their iteration of blockchain platforms, there are few succeeding. Ironically, many of these start-ups focus on making the technology accessible. For example, the now defunct Jincor was working on creating private blockchain and smart contract platforms that would allow any business to accept smart contracts and cryptocurrencies. In an interview with Forbes, Jincor CEO Vlad Kirchenko said of his platform, 'Companies can establish business relations, streamline contractual and legal procedures in a safe and easy manner. It allows entrepreneurs to embrace all the advantages of blockchain technology without the necessity to develop or adjust them on their own'.[44] Jincor was described as the 'Ethereum of business platforms' and had hoped to bring blockchain to 10,000 businesses by the end of 2018. It received substantial investment but still folded, refunding its investors after the technology presumably failed. Jincor raised capital with an initial coin offering of 35 million tokens valued at $1. This demonstrates the significant interest in smart contracts but illustrates that the technology is still not quite there. However, it does also address a regulatory issue, in that the general trend of start-ups offering platforms for blockchain demonstrates that these companies will have to accept liability for issues surrounding quality of service. The unique situation of companies being able to offer ICOs to raise funds allows for unregulated investments in a company whose technology might be unworkable.

10.45   According to McKinsey, blockchain could save businesses at least $50 billion in business-to-business transactions by 2021[45] and could allow companies to create their own systems that support their business processes and promote trust via transparency and a level of immutability (blockchain transactions are not completely irreversible in every situation). In the last decade, the cost of trust has skyrocketed, especially in the context of the dotcom bubble and the 2008 financial crisis. Blockchain reduces the possibility of erroneous valuations based on confidence. Resultantly, blockchain could reduce the cost of trust through its radical, decentralised and digital approach to accounting. Indeed, it could be a new way to structure economic organisations and, in turn, have vast regulatory implications.

43 Ibid.
44 Aitken, R., 'Smart Contracts on the Blockchain: Can businesses reap the benefits?', www.forbes.com/sites/rogeraitken/2017/11/21/smart-contracts-on-the-blockchain-can-businesses-reap-the-benefits/#3774b5bc1074.
45 Ibid.

Obstacles for blockchain in the natural resources industry and energy sector

10.46   The consensus in the energy sector is that the regulation of blockchain will not be an obstacle but a contributing factor to the technology's implementation. In terms of regulation, two factors have been identified as holding back the process. The first is the seeming need to identify a single 'silver bullet solution' to all of the regulatory questions surrounding blockchain,[46] whereas such a complex question really requires a more multi-faceted, inclusive solution approach. This 'silver bullet' idea comes from the narrative that security, affordability and decarbonisation (three of the would-be effects of blockchain implementation) are the industry's biggest challenges and are only solvable by sacrificing one for another in a trade-off situation.[47] In turn, this ideology creates a market that is progressing in different directions as companies decide which aspect of the trilemma is most important to them.[48]

Blockchain as a disruptive technology

10.47   The decentralisation of the natural resources industry at the distribution stage, as discussed, will largely be enacted by peer-to-peer trading and the use of smart contracts, as total control of the market is moved away from large-scale, centralised corporations.

10.48   In a scenario where blockchain technology sees widespread use, there would be major institutional change as power from central storage facilities begins to be replaced by peer-to-peer storage and direct connection to the distribution network.[49] During this movement, it is essential for common industry standards to be established if blockchain is going to be scalable in the industry. Clearly, it is much easier to establish these standards if a single corporation, or perhaps the government, in this case, can oversee this regulatory process.[50] However, in this instance, what could be crucial to answering this question is the response of start-ups themselves. For example, if a company offers a platform and they could accept the responsibility of helping users navigate the legal implications of using their product and introduce their own, legally binding systems to solve disputes, this would greatly simplify the process.[51] Especially in the early stages

---

46 Sandys L. et al, *Reshaping Regulation: Powering from the Future,* Graham Institute – Climate Change and the Environment, 2017.
47 Ibid.
48 Ibid.
49 Wolsink, M., 'Renewables: common pool natural resources distributed generation in intelligent grids'. 1–21. Paper presented at 'Breaking the Rules – Energy Transitions as Social Innovations', Berlin, Germany (2018).
50 Carson, B. et al, 'Blockchain beyond the hype: The strategic business value', www.mckinsey. com/business-functions/digital-mckinsey/our-insights/blockchain-beyond-the-hype-what-is-the-strategic-business-value, June 2018.
51 Aitken, R., 'Smart Contracts on the Blockchain: Can businesses reap the benefits?', www.forbes.com/sites/rogeraitken/2017/11/21/smart-contracts-on-the-blockchain-can-businesses-reap-the-benefits/#6dd45cea1074.

of implementation, if companies accepted legal liability it may prove crucial to incentivising customer participation while the wider regulatory questions are answered. Problematically, it may also make the system overly complex with vast numbers of regulatory microclimates.

Legal issues

10.49   In this section, we examine regulation, smart contracts and data privacy issues.

10.50   Digitisation brings with it significant legal implications for the natural resources industry which are largely tied up with the implementation of new technology. Certainly, organisations using blockchain will have to take into consideration what level of service they are willing to guarantee, especially bearing in mind the automated nature of the technology. Resultantly, the idea of self-execution is legally problematic, as smart contracts are enforced as soon as certain coded criteria is met. With this in mind, it is easy to question how to regulate these autonomous, automatically enforced contracts and in what manner they are, in fact, enforceable, legally speaking.[52]

10.51   It has been argued that performance assurances will depend on three considerations: risk/reward profile; the service delivery model; and how decisions are made with regard to accepting liability. Companies may well offer the technology on an 'as is' basis, without assurances that the technology will function in a reliable service.[53] With this in mind, the aspect of risk in relation to the usability of technology on a wider scale is crucial. If the technology is going to become scalable, it must be completely functioning when businesses offer it as a part of their service.

Current regulation

10.52   Currently, it seems the biggest regulatory questions facing this movement are how to regulate peer-to-peer trading and the market entry of prosumers, the legal status of data as property and the enforceability of smart contracts.

10.53   The ability of blockchain to span the globe puts it in a unique legal position, as nodes and participants of the same blockchain can be located anywhere in the world, crossing jurisdictional boundaries. This brings into question how to identify the appropriate governing law when the blockchain is

---

52 McKinlay, J. et al, 'Blockchain: background, challenges and legal issues', *DLA Piper,* www. dlapiper.com/en/denmark/insights/publications/2017/06/blockchain-background-challenges-legal-issues/.
53 Ibid.

not located in one particular place. If the technology fell under the jurisdiction of every country in which it was located, it would likely make it unusable.[54]

10.54   Ultimately, this is the kind of problem that might require the collaboration of international governing bodies to overcome. This kind of collaboration might not respect the traditional boundaries set by international law and so new, collaborative legislation will likely be required. For example, 22 EU countries signed up to a document focusing on creating a single digital economy as well as enforcing the General Data Protection Regulation in May 2018.[55] Similarly, the USA has created statutes such as the Electronic Signatures in Global and National Commerce Act and the Uniform Electronic Transactions Act, and the latter aims to support the legal basis for the integration of smart contracts.[56] It seems that, because blockchain could pose such radical changes, early organisation on a governmental and possibly international scale will be a key part of regulating the technology and the significant challenges that it poses to traditional jurisdictional boundaries.

Strong and weak smart contracts

10.55   With all this radical change in mind, digitisation and the use of smart contracts are significantly benefited by the fact that, even though they are a source of disruption, they will have a close relationship with, and perhaps aid, regulatory reform. For example, Max Raskin goes so far as to argue that smart contracts will be easily streamlined with current contract law.

10.56   Raskin centres his claim around a useful definition of strong and weak smart contracts. The argument follows that strong smart contracts have prohibitive costs of revocation and modification, while weak ones do not. In other words, if a court is able to alter a contract after it has been executed, it will be defined as a weak smart contract.[57] This creates the unique situation, which needs addressing, of how to regulate a piece of technology that must execute once it has been initiated.

10.57   With this in mind, it is possible that smart contracts could become a type of self-enforcing judicial system unto themselves. For example, if I enter into a smart contract with my neighbours to immediately purchase some electricity from their solar panels and promise to pay them by a certain date, the contract could be set up in such a way that renders my smart meter unusable if I do not pay on time. If I do not pay, I then have no access to electricity, and the punishment, so to speak, is executed by technology and agreed to before the breach of contract is committed. The judicial outcome is empirical and clear cut.

---

54 Ibid.
55 Buchanan, B., 'Building the Future of the EU: Moving Forward with International Collaboration on Blockchain', *The Journal of the British Blockchain Association*, 27 April 2018.
56 Ibid.
57 Raskin, M., 'The Law and Legality of Smart Contracts', 1 Geo. L. Tech. Rev. 305 (2017).

However, although this approach provides certainty, it does not account for the kind of eventualities or mitigating circumstances that the flexibility of the law or two parties in a normal contract might account for.

10.58   Raskin argues the solution to this must come post consequences:

> 'With a smart contract, the aggrieved party will need to go to the court to remedy a contract that has already been executed or is in the process of being performed. This is because, by definition, a strong smart contract is already executed or in the process of being executed by the time the court hears the case. So the remedy must come after the fact to undo or alter the agreement.'[58]

10.59   Therefore, smart contracts need to be strong in order to be useful. Computer code is more efficient than legal code but it comes with limitations, namely, that it is difficult to translate the ambiguity and flexibility of the legal system into a formalised language.[59] The paradoxical problem is that the strength of smart contracts lies, partly, within their security and inflexibility; however, they need to be flexible to become a force of regulation.

10.60   Raskin does go on to address this problem, offering the solution that there needs to be a method by which smart contracts can be updated to incorporate the regulatory changes that may be required.[60] It would be highly disruptive to the process of the industry if smart contracts had to be terminated because their outcomes began to diverge from the demands of the law.[61] Especially in the natural resources industry, this could bring countries to a halt. A slightly facetious example of this is using a vending machine to sell illegal goods. In itself the vending machine is not illegal, but the outcome of the process is. This is a situation that could be taken advantage of by smart contract programmers, albeit in a more nuanced manner.

10.61   Raskin's answer is that smart contracts will be written in line with existing law, as opposed to predicting regulatory updates. Although this seems to fail to address the question of how these smart contracts are then modified, he does offer a potential solution:

> 'One method to address this problem could be a system in which the relevant jurisdiction creates a publicly available database and application programming interface of relevant legal provisions. These would be provisions related to the terms of the contract. The smart contract would call these terms and be able to update those provisions in accord with the jurisdiction's update of the database.'[62]

---

58 Ibid.
59 Samer Hassan and Primavera De Filippi, 'The Expansion of Algorithmic Governance: From Code is Law to Law is Code', Field Actions Science Reports [Online], Special Issue 17, 2017, Online since 31 December 2017, connection on 30 January 2018. URL : http://journals. openedition.org/ factsreports/4518.
60 Raskin, M., 'The Law and Legality of Smart Contracts', 1 Geo. L. Tech. Rev. 305 (2017).
61 Ibid.
62 Ibid.

10.62 The solution is to have an orthodox contract alongside the smart one. Peer-to-peer trading is perhaps the regulatory sticking point of the implementation of blockchain in the natural resources industry and it relies heavily on the successful use of smart contracts. Widespread digitisation seems to be more of an inevitability, in terms of the growing use of smart meters as well as the tracking and logistical benefits, because it does not rely so heavily on customer participated decentralisation. The difficulty of the relationship comes from the manner in which smart contracts will need to work so closely with (and, indeed, become part of) regulation.

10.63 DuPont et al have usefully said:

'Seen one way, self-executing smart contracts seem to miss the whole point of contracts: that, like promises, they are made to be broken. That is to say, contacts only really get interesting in their initial formation and in their potential for breach.'[63]

10.64 Perhaps missing the point is the wrong way to describe it, but it is helpful to refer to self-executing smart contracts as contracts because of how differently they must be treated. After all, the widespread consensus is that blockchain implementation, across all industries, will result in the reconsideration of the legal devices of the ledger and, in this case, contract.[64]

10.65 As a result, the design of distributed ledgers needs to begin with a clear definition of the performance expectation of the contract. In terms of regulation, this is the crucial starting point for a distributed ledger that can store, transfer and manage value.[65] A smart contract must have a complete understanding of its own process in order for it to create the least amount of scenarios for regulatory problems.

Data privacy

10.66 Data privacy is central to blockchain as it contributes to the level of trust that the technology allows. Once something is stored in a blockchain, it is not easily alterable, which is another contributing factor to the ways in which the technology is less flexible than other systems.[66] For example, if a smart meter is programmed to deliver oil once a week to a person's home, it may then be difficult to alter this when that person moves house. The problem of entering and exiting microgrids, and how blockchain can be flexible enough to accommodate this, is one that needs consideration.

10.67 Due to current technological limitations, each house residence taking part, as a residential prosumer, in the Brooklyn Microgrid must have a computer

---

63 DuPont, Q. et al, 'Ledger and Law in the Blockchain', *Kings Review,* 23 June 2015.
64 Ibid.
65 Ibid.
66 Ibid.

specially set up for the task of being a part of the blockchain. If a participant moves house and out of the blockchain, it raises the question of how this transfer of digital property is regulated, and whether it would be possible to remain a part of the microgrid if you no longer lived in the house. A solution to this would be that the appropriate technology (often a smart meter is suggested) would move with the blockchain participant and have the ability to be flexible with the personal details of its owner.

Public or private

10.68   A possible solution to this comes with the decision between public and private blockchains[67] and which would be most prevalent in the industry. The problem with public blockchains is scalability. Blockchain networks struggle to support high volumes of participation, as seen in the outcry about Bitcoin's computational use. Currently, this is the most significant objection to using public blockchains and, in the natural resources industry, blockchains would have extremely high numbers of users. However, with private blockchains, users can be controlled by choosing who joins the network. Ultimately, private blockchains strip back some of the USPs of the technology, instead utilising the elements of efficiency and data storage rather than trust and security.

10.69   On the other hand, ironically, public blockchains are more secure. As everything is public, there is no central network and consensus is driven by who spends real world energy, making it impossible to fake and expensive to hack.[68] Public blockchains allow for transparency which can resolve problems of 'information asymmetry'; however, the concept is still a controversial one and oversharing could have unintended consequences on the market.[69]

10.70   Despite this, all transactions in the blockchain (for example, tracking a resource from production to distribution) could be public and visible within a network, appearing in chronological order. All of the participants in the blockchain could see exactly what is happening and when. In one sense, this eliminates the data privacy issue because, from production, to distributor, to consumer, everything is open. The benefit of regulation for public blockchains is that a lack of data privacy is implied in the very nature of the technology, in that there can be no privacy in a public blockchain arrangement. Theoretically, this solves the regulatory question by shifting the goal posts from an issue of regulation to one of participation – essentially, whether or not the benefits of a public blockchain are worth sacrificing for data privacy.

---

67 See definition in **Chapter 2**.
68 Pearson, T., 'How Does Blockchain Technology Work?', https://hackernoon.com/how-does-blockchain-technology-work-ceeeee47eaba.
69 Kim, K. and Kang, T., 'Does technology against corruption always lead to benefit? The potential risks and challenges of blockchain technology', OECD Global Anti-corruption and Integrity Forum, 2017.

10.71   When considering the 'public or private' question, it is important to bear in mind that, in its simplest iteration, blockchain is at its most secure. Currently, adding complexity and specific requirements to the distributed ledger can reduce the effectiveness of its security. Developers will need to resist modifying the original technology too much; otherwise, they will be required to design solutions and backup protocols, to avoid introducing vulnerabilities.[70] Ultimately, it will be much easier to regulate a secure (rather than an easily manipulated) blockchain. The responsibility in this instance lies with the developers and companies offering products. In a private blockchain, only those with permission can see the data in the chain.

Addressing some of the unique challenges of the natural resources industry

10.72   In terms of implementation, blockchain poses some unique challenges for the natural resources industry, such as scalability, crossing jurisdictional boundaries and tackling centralised institutions.

10.73   However, an examination of the manner in which it is already being used, to various degrees, within the industry can begin to contribute to answering these questions. Firstly, many of blockchain's uses are being trialled in the mining industry. Although different to the natural resources and energy industry as a whole, the extraction and distribution nature of mining makes the blockchain trials plausibly transferable. The mining industry is very similar to the non-renewables sector of the natural resources and energy industry. Ultimately, they are both industries that are largely concerned with financial transactions and the exchange of resources and information.[71]

10.74   The first example of this is automatic registration of mineral rights and intellectual property. When a mining company makes a discovery, it has to prove that it got there first as there may be others claiming precedent.[72] Blockchain would enable automatic registration of a discovery, which has the benefits of eliminating conflict over competition, it is more efficient and puts less pressure on governmental departments; a potential boon for anti-corruption. Corruption is a significant hindrance to the efficient distribution of natural resources.[73] This idea is easily adaptable to some energy sources of the natural resources industry, particularly oil and gas where competition for resources has led to political instability and conflict. Additionally, blockchain and its transparent, public nature could further help this problem.

---

70 Ibid.
71 Belle, I., 'The architecture, engineering and construction industry and blockchain technology', *DADA 2017 International Conference on Digital Architecture.*
72 Ahmed, S., 'How resource companies are using the blockchain', *SAP Industry Value Advisor, Energy and Natural Resources,* www.mining.com/web/resource-companies-using-blockchain/.
73 Kim, K. and Kang, T., 'Does technology against corruption always lead to benefit? The potential risks and challenges of blockchain technology', OECD Global Anti-corruption and Integrity Forum, 2017.

10.75 In terms of regulation, in this instance, the automation of registration may simply lead to problems not of the race for resources but of the anticipation of this race. The original registration may now have companies squabbling over resources from a much earlier stage – although, in theory, the clear-cut nature of technological registration should result in a decision being made with absolute certainty not allowing for disagreements. This is another example of how blockchain can be a force of regulation in itself.

10.76 The natural resources industry suffers from vast production costs and a large part of this is down to inefficient and complex logistical systems.[74] Blockchain is widely touted as a solution to the problems of supply chain as the industry has become more multi-layered and the world has become connected.[75] The efficiency and storage capacity of blockchain allows for the possibility of real-time data processing. For example, ports could declare and provide visibility for the movement of physical resources, allowing for greater accountability.[76]

10.77 In the shipping phase of the industry, blockchain could allow for Uber-style cargo hiring processes, an efficient solution to sourcing the right port with the correct ship, in terms of size, tonnage and specialisation.[77] Similarly, there are the possibilities of the Internet of Things hosting large amounts of data that could automate settlements and accounting in complex joint ventures, simplify cross-border payments and regulatory compliance, and reconcile amounts produced and sent to processing plants.[78]

10.78 In her paper on the architecture, engineering and construction industry, Iris Belle outlines two dilemmas for the implementation of blockchain. What's more, these two situations are transferable to the natural resources industry and both come down to the problems of flexibility that reflect on blockchain and automated technology, more generally. The first of these is how to implement the technology in situations where negotiation could be ambiguous and where often a third party, such as a lawyer, might be needed.[79] The second is when, mathematically speaking, the negotiation of the terms of a contract is difficult[80] – for example, situations such as accounting for ambiguity or unlimited flexibility dependent on how a situation progresses are difficult to automate in a smart contract. Ultimately, these situations could result in the need for retroactive action which cannot be enacted by the smart contract itself. In certain complex, ambiguous situations, the action of a smart contract could be in breach of law.

---

74 Mota da Silva et al, 'Blockchain in Natural Resources: Hedging Against Volatile Prices', *TATA Consultancy Report.*
75 Kim, K. and Kang, T., 'Does technology against corruption always lead to benefit? The potential risks and challenges of blockchain technology', OECD Global Anti-corruption and Integrity Forum, 2017.
76 Ahmed, S., 'How resource companies are using the blockchain', *SAP Industry Value Advisor, Energy and Natural Resources,* www.mining.com/web/resource-companies-using-blockchain/.
77 Ibid.
78 Ibid.
79 Belle, I., 'The architecture, engineering and construction industry and blockchain technology', *DADA 2017 International Conference on Digital Architecture.*
80 Ibid.

This is a problematic situation that would need to be made impossible by smart contract regulation. Belle argues that this goes so far as to limit the function of blockchain to instances where the entire spectrum of user behaviours can be managed and anticipated.[81]

10.79 The natural resources industry is complex because it covers significant ground, from extraction and production to distribution. As a result, there are a wide range of issues that need regulating as well as a lot of points for improvement to the industry. Ultimately, a cleaner, cheaper, distributed and more efficient natural resources industry would be a positive, and regulation should aid this movement with the implementation of blockchain.

Solutions, opportunities for regulation and conclusions

10.80 Despite the obstacles, the place for blockchain in the natural resources industry is by no means hopeless. In fact, it is quite the opposite, as companies begin to change their ideology and utilise the technology they have to tackle regulatory questions, albeit on a smaller scale. While these technological, ideological and regulatory changes might be happening slowly, the confidence of the industry seems to be with blockchain.

10.81 As mentioned, many companies are entering the blockchain market through small trial runs by implementing the technology in one aspect of their process at a time. The technology has become a fact of the sector, illustrated by the amount of events dedicated to blockchain (almost one a day around the world), the half a million new publications and 3.7 million new google search results in the last two years.[82]

10.82 In terms of small trial runs, in Austria, Wien Energie has used blockchain in the commercial sector to confirm gas trade completions using BTL Interbit's blockchain platform. Similarly, Japan and Germany, like New York, have seen trials by Eneres and Enercity aimed specifically at just customers and their interactions with energy companies. Eneres' trial, in Japan, connected 1,000 homes to a smart energy grid, which has also led to Remixpoint trialling a service which allowed consumers to pay for energy in Bitcoins. Japan is a country where bureaucracy is dominated by traditional paper-based systems, and the fact that these trials have been allowed under the law demonstrates blockchain's potential penetrability into the natural resources market.

10.83 Ultimately, these small trials will prove a useful indicator of the kinds of regulatory reform needed for the widespread application of blockchain in the industry. What's more, they may serve as useful examples as to the capacity in

81 Ibid.
82 Carson, B. et al, 'Blockchain beyond the hype: What is the strategic business value?', www.mckinsey.com/business-functions/digital-mckinsey/our-insights/blockchain-beyond-the-hype-what-is-the-strategic-business-value.

which the technology can really be used, almost like a barometer for scalability. Crucially, the technology must reach a level that means it can function amidst the already heavily regulated environment of the natural resources industry, as large-scale failures will likely lead to blockchain resistance – as was seen in Japan's difficult relationship with cryptocurrencies following the disappearance in 2014 of $450 million worth of Bitcoins handled by Mt. Gox, a company based in the country.

10.84 There are companies currently offering early adoption of blockchain technology but there are problems with early adoption concerning the offering of untrusted services. The unregulated nature of these services does not inspire the trust or confidence that blockchain promises.[83] Developers will have to offer a guaranteeable level of service when rolling out new products. A crucial part of this reliability comes with regulation in a reciprocal relationship that needs to be mutually assured and beneficial. As with many products, a central part of the blockchain initiative relies on the confidence placed in it. Vendors will be required to guarantee a reliable service, even if this means making concessions to regulators, as without regulation they will be without business.[84]

10.85 Closer to home, Electron is a British start-up looking to modernise the grid. Electron's vision of the future is the same democratic, digitised, decarbonised and decentralised energy market that the Energy Web Foundation hopes for. Central to Electron's business model is that they are looking to work with the energy sector to support their transition to smart energy and grid use. Electron's products include smart meter registration, which will massively speed up the process of switching energy supplier, a flexible trading platform and community trading projects as part of the decentralisation process. While this is not as disruptive as some proponents of the technology hope, it is an example of working with the regulatory process, rather than in direct challenge, as working with centralised companies could ultimately speed up the implementation of blockchain technology and its regulation. It is important to bear in mind that peer-to-peer trading is still possible with a centralised grid. Indeed, a centralised grid is not mutually exclusive to the implementation of blockchain. Perhaps the least desirable situation is for decentralisation to draw people away from the intermediary companies while they are still using the resources of the grid, if the central grid is still maintained by a large company – especially if these are large energy consumers or wealthy users as it will be an enormous amount of added pressure, financially, on the remaining, participating grid users.[85]

10.86 Public blockchains could be a significant positive for the implementation of the technology and its regulation, because it makes blockchain accessible. For example, the launch of Ethereum and Hyperledger has helped enable blockchain

83 Buchanan, B., 'Building the Future of the EU: Moving Forward with International Collaboration on Blockchain', *The Journal of the British Blockchain Association*, 27 April 2018.
84 Ibid.
85 Shipworth, D., 'Global policy and Regulatory Change', Blockchain Energy Forum 2018.

adopters and developers to freely build their own applications.[86] Resultantly, companies can streamline contractual and legal procedures using smart contracts and cryptocurrencies in a secure manner.[87] Ethereum and Hyperledger then become cloud service providers without being centralised. Due to the nature of blockchain, the control is decentralised and spread among peers so that no single player can stop a service or act maliciously.[88] Essentially, it is decentralised security but with a single company that is accepting liability for quality of service. In turn, this can lead to the creation of decentralised autonomous organisations with the ability to operate without the involvement of intermediaries, central authorities or one central organisation, as users are no longer reliant on these institutions for security of service. Ethereum, Hyperledger and blockchain may provide a service but they do not control the blockchains because of the nature of the technology.[89]

The legal status of data

10.87   A crucial issue with blockchain and the data it stores, in terms of legal regulation, is whether or not this data constitutes property. In terms of common law, there is no property right in the information itself; however, this changes when the information[90] is compiled. Under the Data Protection Act 2018, the data controller has to obtain the consent of the individuals if it wishes to use their personal information for a new purpose. The central problem with this comes from the shared, transparent nature of blockchain technology. The question of whether or not this 'new purpose' makes blockchain inflexible, or would require new regulation for the technology, is crucial for its application.

10.88   The level of interest and investment in blockchain technology start-ups is significant and this will only increase as the technology catches up with the theory and commercial deployments become possible.[91] Resultantly, there will be a growing need for due diligence to be carried out on start-ups and companies using the technology in novel applications. Primarily, this means that lawyers will need to understand the unique challenges that the technology poses and it might mean a modification of the due diligence process.[92] The features of blockchain as a decentralised information store, as well as its implications for intellectual property, for example, are crucial for its proper implementation. And, in terms of due diligence, they offer unique challenges that must be addressed accordingly.

---

86 Aitken, R., 'Smart Contract on the Blockchain: Can businesses reap the benefits?', www.forbes. com/sites/rogeraitken/2017/11/21/smart-contracts-on-the-blockchain-can-businesses-reap-the-benefits/#6dd45cea1074.
87 Ibid.
88 DuPont, Q. et al, 'Ledger and Law in the Blockchain', *Kings Review,* 23 June 2015.
89 Ibid.
90 Ibid.
91 Ibid.
92 Ibid.

A possible blueprint for regulation

10.89   Laura Sandys, Jeff Hardy and Professor Richard Green look to debunk both the problems surrounding the 'silver bullet solution' and the trilemma. The first point that the paper makes is that the UK has the reputation of being at the forefront of energy regulation. Secondly, it argues that the most sensible thing to do, in terms of regulation, is to ignore the trilemma.[93] Instead, the paper proposes four regulatory principles to function as a starting point to approach the question. These are as follows:

(1)   Regulate for how consumers consume, not how businesses are organised.

(2)   Regulate for system optimisation to deliver the most productive and affordable system.

(3)   Regulate to promote transparent, cost-reflective and open markets.

(4)   Regulate for where security of the system is truly at risk.[94]

10.90   What seems to be central to these four proposed regulatory principles is a considered approach. Indeed, the principles are primarily concerned with a realistic appraisal of the ideology of a new electricity market, reinforcing a consideration of consumers, a secure, efficient market that concentrates on sustainability where it is really needed. Ultimately, the paper reiterates an issue that is often attributed to decentralisation and the use of blockchain, and that is the idea of de-commoditisation. The general consensus is that, in the natural resources and energy sectors, through decentralisation, commercial interests need to take a back seat. How realistic this is, though, remains to be seen – unless, of course, it is forced into happening by blockchain and decentralisation.

10.91   The paper goes on to outline three key elements of these regulatory principles: firstly, a consideration of the consumers and how they will consume energy; secondly, the market and the public policy objectives desired for the market; and, finally, the changing risks that need to be addressed,[95] such as the grid defection referred to above, perhaps. Ultimately, once again, the emphasis is on acknowledging change and having a clear direction for regulation before the challenge is tackled.

MOVING FORWARD

10.92   The natural resources industry and energy sector clearly view blockchain as the technology of a decentralised, digitised, greener and more democratic (in terms of the market) future. In addition to this, when answering any regulatory questions surrounding the technology, it must be considered how to accommodate

---

93 Sandys L. et al, *Reshaping Regulation: Powering from the Future*, Graham Institute – Climate Change and the Environment, 2017.
94 Ibid.
95 Ibid.

blockchain's distributed nature and ability to cross jurisdictional boundaries. With this in mind, the manner in which start-ups deal with these issues in small trial runs will serve as useful case studies for some of the problems. Despite this, some of these trial runs, due to their nature as small-scale operations, will not touch on the wider problems of large-scale blockchain implementation. Finally, it is important to bear in mind that it is likely that, eventually, these unregulated trials will become detrimental to the reputation of the technology if they continue to fail, as investing in ICOs is already considered high risk.

Chapter 11

Decentralised autonomous organisations: regulation and liability

UNDERSTANDING DECENTRALISED AUTONOMOUS ORGANISATIONS

11.1   It is essential to first understand what a decentralised autonomous organisation ('DAO') is. To do that, one also needs to understand what a decentralised organisation is. These are not organisations in a conventional sense in that, whilst they do have some hallmarks of a company, they do not have people that are organised into a form of hierarchy and led, in their entirety, by the directing human mind. A decentralised organisation is a computer program that has no manager or leader. It involves users and runs on a peer-to-peer network. A peer-to-peer network means that each computer gets information from every other machine on the network rather than from one big central server. The collective contents of the network are at the command of each connected machine and enable the direct exchange of services or data between computers. In such an environment, service desktops and personal computers that make up a network become equal peers that contribute some or all of their resources to the overall computing effort. In a decentralised organisation, a set of users connect and interact with one another pursuant to a protocol which is programmed through code and is enforced on a blockchain.

11.2   Taking a decentralised organisation first, it operates under the usual concepts of a company but it has a management structure that is decentralised so that there is no board of directors or other central brain that is managing it. In the case of a decentralised organisation, the users who are interacting with each other are the ones making decisions according to the protocol that is imprinted in the code and enforced on the blockchain. The contract is imprinted in the blockchain and it maintains a record of important transactions.

11.3   An example would be that, in a conventional company, there would need to be a record of a shareholder's holdings and the ability for shareholders to cast votes on various issues. In a decentralised organisation, this would be effected via the contract which was encoded in the blockchain through the interaction of the decentralised organisation's users.

11.4   At today's evolutionary stage, a **DAO materialises as a smart contract** – a piece of code – executed on top of an increasingly opaque stack of distributed networking and consensus technology, such as the Ethereum blockchain or similar blockchains.

11.5 The diagram below provides a visual representation of a blockchain stack of Ethereum and similar blockchains:

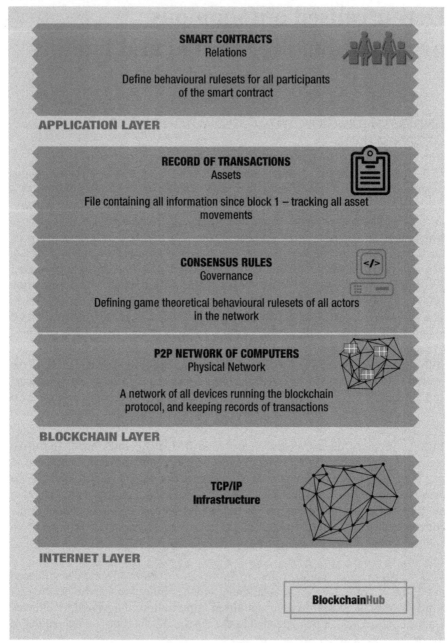

Blockchain technology stack of Ethereum and similar blockchains (inspired by Florian Glatz)

11.6 The important distinction between a decentralised organisation and a DAO is the addition of the word 'autonomous'. That means what it says. DAOs are autonomous via a combination of contracts that encode the laws and behaviours of the organisation. These are not traditional paper contracts but coded contracts (smart contracts) that have been encoded into the blockchain, thus creating one all-encompassing, comprehensive decentralised smart contract.

11.7   The effect and impact of having a comprehensive single decentralised smart contract is very important. This means that, unlike any traditional company or indeed a decentralised organisation, the DAO has no requirement for human involvement or interaction. Because everything has been pre-programmed and encoded, the decentralised autonomous organisation can automatically execute contractual clauses in the blockchain when it regards conditions as satisfied and direct itself without the need for human intervention.

11.8   Decentralised organisations and DAOs do have some aspects in common, but the important distinction is that DAOs remove the human mind from the equation as human intervention is not required in any way. In contrast, a decentralised organisation will have smart contracts but operation will be reliant on users and human intervention. When one appreciates that a DAO runs autonomously on the blockchain and is controlled entirely by its code, without direction from the human mind, one begins to appreciate the difficulties that may arise both in practical terms and also in terms of regulation. To be clear, a DAO is capable of interacting with humans in relation to its functions, but it does not need humans to function and the decisions behind the services that it provides will exclude human direction. A DAO might be thought of as a decentralised organisation that has its own brain in the form of autonomous intelligence. It will become possible, in our view, to regard a DAO as close to artificial intelligence.

THE LEGAL STATUS AND OTHER ISSUES AROUND DAOs

11.9   The DAO is a difficult concept for the law and it does not appear to have consistent recognised legal status. If we look at decentralised organisations and DAOs as generic groups, it seems clear that law has not kept pace with technology and jurisdictions do not seem able to define or address what their legal status is.

11.10   There is concern that, as technology advances, the capabilities of DAOs will increase and the combinations of smart contracts at the heart of the DAO will enable all manner of decisions to be made without human intervention. Evidently, so far as UK law is concerned, a DAO cannot be a natural person, for that would be a human. Equally, it would not be a person such as a company or partnership or any other legal entity, because it does not fulfil the conventional notions of what a legal entity is. A combination of smart contracts that effectively form the brain of an artificially intelligent construction is well beyond the current legal concept of what a legally recognised person or entity is.

11.11   It is essential to clarify and define the legal status of DAOs (and, indeed, decentralised organisations) because, without legal recognition, any investors whose investments were determined by a DAO would not have any protection under limited liability laws (ie those laws that apply to companies). If decentralised organisations continue to have no recognised legal status, individuals may be subject to personal liability because of their investments but will have no recourse against a DAO or decisions taken by it (that is, decisions in the sense of the operation of the smart contracts) because there is no person who can be sued or complained to.

11.12   The other question, of course, will be how a DAO is defined. For example, if it is deemed that a DAO is a form of general partnership, and there is some support for this view, those investors to whom tokens have been issued might owe one another fiduciary duties as partners that were not contemplated when they invested in the scheme. That risk might operate to reduce the likelihood of any investment in the first place, making decentralised organisations seem a risky bet.

11.13   In addition to DAOs making ever more sophisticated decisions due to their increased capability, there would also be the difficulty of jurisdiction. The use of smart contracts would allow DAOs to collaborate in worldwide activities but, without any recognition of their legal status or the rights of the investor, they become high risk and not a prudent investment.

RISKS

11.14   An example of the risks inherent in a DAO can be demonstrated from *The DAO*, a crowdfunded venture that is the best-known example of a DAO in action. *The DAO* was a venture capital business operated by a network of machines operating on basic principles equivalent to those that drive Bitcoin digital currency. It was designed to raise money for projects running on Ethereum blockchain, handing out funds dependent on the votes of the members. Ethereum is a form of decentralised platform with no centralised control or controller and is visible to anyone that has an internet address. It is similar to Bitcoin but arguably provides more functionality. In this instance, *The DAO* had success and this attracted multimillions of investment from around the world, but this balloon was seemingly burst when, on 12 June 2016, it was realised that an infection had found its way into the software. It was declared that, notwithstanding this, no funds were at risk.

11.15   In the background, some 50 proposals were awaiting votes as to whether to fund projects and, while attention turned to correcting the bug in the software, a hacker began to siphon *The DAO* of Ether. Ether is a form of payment made by clients of an Ethereum platform to those machines executing the requested operations. In less than a week, the hacker managed to transfer more than $3,600,000 of Ether collected from token sales. It appears that the Ether was taken from *The DAO* and dropped into software with the same structure known as a '*child DAO*'. This manoeuvre hit the price of Ether, causing it to fall from $20 to less than $13. The hacker was able to exploit a weakness in the computer code to syphon, in multiple withdrawal visits, some \$50 million. The investors, faced with a 'vehicle' blessed with considerable artificial intelligence and autonomous, seemingly irrevocable power, seemed paralysed. The solution was to convince enough humans operating *The DAO's* software platform, Ethereum, to alter the underlying code. And yet that met with resistance; the Ethereum community had vocal members who railed at the notion of interfering with *The DAO's* autonomy, viewing the hack as being the use of agreed contractual terms to the hacker's advantage. To these DAO purists, the encoded smart contracts equated to a contract, in a traditional legal sense, binding all who participated. The code was akin to law.

11.16 It should be apparent from this case study that any DAO is not beyond compromise and, in the event of a hack or malfunction, any participants in a DAO could find themselves exposed to liability as well as unable to effect any remedy or redress. The DAO is an autonomous organisation that is decentralised. There may be no contractual terms or conditions or any regulatory regime that automatically attaches, such that a situation can arise where a hacker might be able to use funds without any criminal or civil sanctions; whilst a perpetrator of an attack may then be free to act with impunity, the same cannot be said for investors who may face liability in relation to responsibilities that flow from the cyber-attack. The attack, for example, might of itself cause attention to be focused on the DAO and, if there have been breaches of laws and regulations in countries that the blockchain engages, the investors could find themselves facing actions for responsibilities they did not contemplate at the time of participating in the DAO.

11.17 Another concern is that, as the Internet of Things evolves, there will ever greater risk as smart contracts and autonomous technology controls all manner of tangibles and intangibles within our interconnected smart environment: *the car* that races away, doors locked, passengers trapped; or *the house* that is hacked, with all its interconnected content applied to the hacker's advantage. The risk that arises is not merely from the intelligence that accrues from smart contracts and code, but from the autonomy that is granted to the technology. If that autonomy is regarded as legally binding, as some argued when called upon to vary *The DAO's* underlying code, the victims of malfunction or exploitation suffer the double indignity of a loss that is proclaimed as lawful. Smart contracts can have vulnerabilities and imperfections; it is beyond the wit of man to produce perfection on every occasion. It is beyond common sense to assert that *The DAO* was unique when it failed.

11.18 As has been noted earlier in this chapter, a DAO itself is arguably not an entity with any recognised legal status, or at any rate it does not have certainty in that regard. There are some lines of argument that maintain that it is likely classified as a general partnership or, if it lacks the pre-requisite partnership elements, a joint venture. Again, this will depend on the jurisdiction that one is considering and the position may likely not be fixed, given that it will be sensitive to the laws particular to each jurisdiction. There needs to be legal certainty not only as to the legal status of the DAO but also as to the Ether tokens: are they investment contracts, and consequently securities subject to securities regulation, or not? This appears to be the likely approach if one takes the view that investors in the DAO had a reasonable expectation of profits as a result of its management by others, but there are counter-arguments that hold interests in a partnership are not securities and, again, it will depend on which jurisdictional prism we apply to form our view of what a DAO, the tokens on the Ethereum blockchain and the tokens in a DAO are *as a matter of law*.

11.19   The way through this uncertainty might be to create a form of standard legal entity that wraps around the DAO, what can be termed a 'legal wrapper'. This would be agreed upon in advance and a more conventional legal structure engineered, such that membership and shareholdings were clearly stipulated and the legal status of the wrapper was certain and safer than, say, a general partnership. To be clear, in a general partnership, its members (effectively, its partners) are deemed to *jointly* represent the DAO and are responsible and liable for its obligations, actions and omissions. In this way, members might build a shield against personal liability and have more certainty with less risk.

11.20   Given the importance of the choice of jurisdiction, one might also create a separate, traditional 'off chain' contract that stipulates which jurisdiction and law are exclusively applicable. This approach is examined in more detail in **Chapter 3** in relation to smart contracts. The contract here might also address cryptocurrency and cryptoassets under the control of the DAO, to ensure that they are subject to multiple-signature escrow wallets that the DAO members are better able to control. When one appreciates that DAOs are essentially a combination of smart contracts (or, if you prefer, a super smart contract), it follows that all the precautions required to circumvent smart contract issues will be requisite.

Appendix 1

General Data Protection Regulation

REGULATION (EU) 2016/679 OF THE EUROPEAN PARLIAMENT AND
OF THE COUNCIL

of 27 April 2016

**on the protection of natural persons with regard to the processing of personal
data and on the free movement of such data, and repealing Directive 95/46/
EC (General Data Protection Regulation)**

(Text with EEA relevance)

THE EUROPEAN PARLIAMENT AND THE COUNCIL OF THE EUROPEAN
UNION,

Having regard to the Treaty on the Functioning of the European Union, and in
particular Article 16 thereof,

Having regard to the proposal from the European Commission,

After transmission of the draft legislative act to the national parliaments,

Having regard to the opinion of the European Economic and Social Committee[1],

Having regard to the opinion of the Committee of the Regions[2],

Acting in accordance with the ordinary legislative procedure[3],

Whereas:

(1)   The protection of natural persons in relation to the processing of personal
        data is a fundamental right. Article 8(1) of the Charter of Fundamental
        Rights of the European Union (the 'Charter') and Article 16(1) of the
        Treaty on the Functioning of the European Union (TFEU) provide that
        everyone has the right to the protection of personal data concerning him
        or her.

---

1   OJ C 229, 31.7.2012, p. 90.
2   OJ C 391, 18.12.2012, p. 127.
3   Position of the European Parliament of 12 March 2014 (not yet published in the Official Journal)
    and position of the Council at first reading of 8 April 2016 (not yet published in the Official
    Journal). Position of the European Parliament of 14 April 2016.

(2)   The principles of, and rules on the protection of natural persons with regard to the processing of their personal data should, whatever their nationality or residence, respect their fundamental rights and freedoms, in particular their right to the protection of personal data. This Regulation is intended to contribute to the accomplishment of an area of freedom, security and justice and of an economic union, to economic and social progress, to the strengthening and the convergence of the economies within the internal market, and to the well-being of natural persons.

(3)   Directive 95/46/EC of the European Parliament and of the Council[4] seeks to harmonise the protection of fundamental rights and freedoms of natural persons in respect of processing activities and to ensure the free flow of personal data between Member States.

(4)   The processing of personal data should be designed to serve mankind. The right to the protection of personal data is not an absolute right; it must be considered in relation to its function in society and be balanced against other fundamental rights, in accordance with the principle of proportionality. This Regulation respects all fundamental rights and observes the freedoms and principles recognised in the Charter as enshrined in the Treaties, in particular the respect for private and family life, home and communications, the protection of personal data, freedom of thought, conscience and religion, freedom of expression and information, freedom to conduct a business, the right to an effective remedy and to a fair trial, and cultural, religious and linguistic diversity.

(5)   The economic and social integration resulting from the functioning of the internal market has led to a substantial increase in cross-border flows of personal data. The exchange of personal data between public and private actors, including natural persons, associations and undertakings across the Union has increased. National authorities in the Member States are being called upon by Union law to cooperate and exchange personal data so as to be able to perform their duties or carry out tasks on behalf of an authority in another Member State.

(6)   Rapid technological developments and globalisation have brought new challenges for the protection of personal data. The scale of the collection and sharing of personal data has increased significantly. Technology allows both private companies and public authorities to make use of personal data on an unprecedented scale in order to pursue their activities. Natural persons increasingly make personal information available publicly and globally. Technology has transformed both the economy and social life, and should further facilitate the free flow of personal data within the Union and the transfer to third countries and international organisations, while ensuring a high level of the protection of personal data.

---

4   Directive 95/46/EC of the European Parliament and of the Council of 24 October 1995 on the protection of individuals with regard to the processing of personal data and on the free movement of such data (OJ L 281, 23.11.1995, p. 31).

(7)   Those developments require a strong and more coherent data protection framework in the Union, backed by strong enforcement, given the importance of creating the trust that will allow the digital economy to develop across the internal market. Natural persons should have control of their own personal data. Legal and practical certainty for natural persons, economic operators and public authorities should be enhanced.

(8)   Where this Regulation provides for specifications or restrictions of its rules by Member State law, Member States may, as far as necessary for coherence and for making the national provisions comprehensible to the persons to whom they apply, incorporate elements of this Regulation into their national law.

(9)   The objectives and principles of Directive 95/46/EC remain sound, but it has not prevented fragmentation in the implementation of data protection across the Union, legal uncertainty or a widespread public perception that there are significant risks to the protection of natural persons, in particular with regard to online activity. Differences in the level of protection of the rights and freedoms of natural persons, in particular the right to the protection of personal data, with regard to the processing of personal data in the Member States may prevent the free flow of personal data throughout the Union. Those differences may therefore constitute an obstacle to the pursuit of economic activities at the level of the Union, distort competition and impede authorities in the discharge of their responsibilities under Union law. Such a difference in levels of protection is due to the existence of differences in the implementation and application of Directive 95/46/EC.

(10)   In order to ensure a consistent and high level of protection of natural persons and to remove the obstacles to flows of personal data within the Union, the level of protection of the rights and freedoms of natural persons with regard to the processing of such data should be equivalent in all Member States. Consistent and homogenous application of the rules for the protection of the fundamental rights and freedoms of natural persons with regard to the processing of personal data should be ensured throughout the Union. Regarding the processing of personal data for compliance with a legal obligation, for the performance of a task carried out in the public interest or in the exercise of official authority vested in the controller, Member States should be allowed to maintain or introduce national provisions to further specify the application of the rules of this Regulation. In conjunction with the general and horizontal law on data protection implementing Directive 95/46/EC, Member States have several sector-specific laws in areas that need more specific provisions. This Regulation also provides a margin of manoeuvre for Member States to specify its rules, including for the processing of special categories of personal data ('sensitive data'). To that extent, this Regulation does not exclude Member State law that sets out the circumstances for specific processing situations, including determining more precisely the conditions under which the processing of personal data is lawful.

(11)   Effective protection of personal data throughout the Union requires the strengthening and setting out in detail of the rights of data subjects and the obligations of those who process and determine the processing of personal data, as well as equivalent powers for monitoring and ensuring compliance with the rules for the protection of personal data and equivalent sanctions for infringements in the Member States.

(12)   Article 16(2) TFEU mandates the European Parliament and the Council to lay down the rules relating to the protection of natural persons with regard to the processing of personal data and the rules relating to the free movement of personal data.

(13)   In order to ensure a consistent level of protection for natural persons throughout the Union and to prevent divergences hampering the free movement of personal data within the internal market, a Regulation is necessary to provide legal certainty and transparency for economic operators, including micro, small and medium-sized enterprises, and to provide natural persons in all Member States with the same level of legally enforceable rights and obligations and responsibilities for controllers and processors, to ensure consistent monitoring of the processing of personal data, and equivalent sanctions in all Member States as well as effective cooperation between the supervisory authorities of different Member States. The proper functioning of the internal market requires that the free movement of personal data within the Union is not restricted or prohibited for reasons connected with the protection of natural persons with regard to the processing of personal data. To take account of the specific situation of micro, small and medium-sized enterprises, this Regulation includes a derogation for organisations with fewer than 250 employees with regard to record-keeping. In addition, the Union institutions and bodies, and Member States and their supervisory authorities, are encouraged to take account of the specific needs of micro, small and medium-sized enterprises in the application of this Regulation. The notion of micro, small and medium-sized enterprises should draw from Article 2 of the Annex to Commission Recommendation 2003/361/EC[5].

(14)   The protection afforded by this Regulation should apply to natural persons, whatever their nationality or place of residence, in relation to the processing of their personal data. This Regulation does not cover the processing of personal data which concerns legal persons and in particular undertakings established as legal persons, including the name and the form of the legal person and the contact details of the legal person.

(15)   In order to prevent creating a serious risk of circumvention, the protection of natural persons should be technologically neutral and should not depend on the techniques used. The protection of natural persons should apply to the processing of personal data by automated means, as well as to manual processing, if the personal data are contained or are intended to

---

5   Commission Recommendation of 6 May 2003 concerning the definition of micro, small and mediumsized enterprises (C(2003) 1422) (OJ L 124, 20.5.2003, p. 36).

be contained in a filing system. Files or sets of files, as well as their cover pages, which are not structured according to specific criteria should not fall within the scope of this Regulation.

(16) This Regulation does not apply to issues of protection of fundamental rights and freedoms or the free flow of personal data related to activities which fall outside the scope of Union law, such as activities concerning national security. This Regulation does not apply to the processing of personal data by the Member States when carrying out activities in relation to the common foreign and security policy of the Union.

(17) Regulation (EC) No 45/2001 of the European Parliament and of the Council[6] applies to the processing of personal data by the Union institutions, bodies, offices and agencies. Regulation (EC) No 45/2001 and other Union legal acts applicable to such processing of personal data should be adapted to the principles and rules established in this Regulation and applied in the light of this Regulation. In order to provide a strong and coherent data protection framework in the Union, the necessary adaptations of Regulation (EC) No 45/2001 should follow after the adoption of this Regulation, in order to allow application at the same time as this Regulation.

(18) This Regulation does not apply to the processing of personal data by a natural person in the course of a purely personal or household activity and thus with no connection to a professional or commercial activity. Personal or household activities could include correspondence and the holding of addresses, or social networking and online activity undertaken within the context of such activities. However, this Regulation applies to controllers or processors which provide the means for processing personal data for such personal or household activities.

(19) The protection of natural persons with regard to the processing of personal data by competent authorities for the purposes of the prevention, investigation, detection or prosecution of criminal offences or the execution of criminal penalties, including the safeguarding against and the prevention of threats to public security and the free movement of such data, is the subject of a specific Union legal act. This Regulation should not, therefore, apply to processing activities for those purposes. However, personal data processed by public authorities under this Regulation should, when used for those purposes, be governed by a more specific Union legal act, namely Directive (EU) 2016/680 of the European Parliament and of the Council[7]. Member States may entrust competent authorities within the

---

6   Regulation (EC) No 45/2001 of the European Parliament and of the Council of 18 December 2000 on the protection of individuals with regard to the processing of personal data by the Community institutions and bodies and on the free movement of such data (OJ L 8, 12.1.2001, p. 1).

7   Directive (EU) 2016/680 of the European Parliament and of the Council of 27 April 2016 on the protection of natural persons with regard to the processing of personal data by competent authorities for the purposes of prevention, investigation, detection or prosecution of criminal offences or the execution of criminal penalties, and the free movement of such data and repealing Council Framework Decision 2008/977/JHA (see page 89 of this Official Journal).

meaning of Directive (EU) 2016/680 with tasks which are not necessarily carried out for the purposes of the prevention, investigation, detection or prosecution of criminal offences or the execution of criminal penalties, including the safeguarding against and prevention of threats to public security, so that the processing of personal data for those other purposes, in so far as it is within the scope of Union law, falls within the scope of this Regulation.

With regard to the processing of personal data by those competent authorities for purposes falling within scope of this Regulation, Member States should be able to maintain or introduce more specific provisions to adapt the application of the rules of this Regulation. Such provisions may determine more precisely specific requirements for the processing of personal data by those competent authorities for those other purposes, taking into account the constitutional, organisational and administrative structure of the respective Member State. When the processing of personal data by private bodies falls within the scope of this Regulation, this Regulation should provide for the possibility for Member States under specific conditions to restrict by law certain obligations and rights when such a restriction constitutes a necessary and proportionate measure in a democratic society to safeguard specific important interests including public security and the prevention, investigation, detection or prosecution of criminal offences or the execution of criminal penalties, including the safeguarding against and the prevention of threats to public security. This is relevant for instance in the framework of anti-money laundering or the activities of forensic laboratories.

(20) While this Regulation applies, inter alia, to the activities of courts and other judicial authorities, Union or Member State law could specify the processing operations and processing procedures in relation to the processing of personal data by courts and other judicial authorities. The competence of the supervisory authorities should not cover the processing of personal data when courts are acting in their judicial capacity, in order to safeguard the independence of the judiciary in the performance of its judicial tasks, including decision-making. It should be possible to entrust supervision of such data processing operations to specific bodies within the judicial system of the Member State, which should, in particular ensure compliance with the rules of this Regulation, enhance awareness among members of the judiciary of their obligations under this Regulation and handle complaints in relation to such data processing operations.

(21) This Regulation is without prejudice to the application of Directive 2000/31/EC of the European Parliament and of the Council[8], in particular of the liability rules of intermediary service providers in Articles 12 to 15 of that Directive. That Directive seeks to contribute to the proper functioning of the internal market by ensuring the free movement of information society services between Member States.

---

8   Directive 2000/31/EC of the European Parliament and of the Council of 8 June 2000 on certain legal aspects of information society services, in particular electronic commerce, in the Internal Market ('Directive on electronic commerce') (OJ L 178, 17.7.2000, p. 1).

(22) Any processing of personal data in the context of the activities of an establishment of a controller or a processor in the Union should be carried out in accordance with this Regulation, regardless of whether the processing itself takes place within the Union. Establishment implies the effective and real exercise of activity through stable arrangements. The legal form of such arrangements, whether through a branch or a subsidiary with a legal personality, is not the determining factor in that respect.

(23) In order to ensure that natural persons are not deprived of the protection to which they are entitled under this Regulation, the processing of personal data of data subjects who are in the Union by a controller or a processor not established in the Union should be subject to this Regulation where the processing activities are related to offering goods or services to such data subjects irrespective of whether connected to a payment. In order to determine whether such a controller or processor is offering goods or services to data subjects who are in the Union, it should be ascertained whether it is apparent that the controller or processor envisages offering services to data subjects in one or more Member States in the Union. Whereas the mere accessibility of the controller's, processor's or an intermediary's website in the Union, of an email address or of other contact details, or the use of a language generally used in the third country where the controller is established, is insufficient to ascertain such intention, factors such as the use of a language or a currency generally used in one or more Member States with the possibility of ordering goods and services in that other language, or the mentioning of customers or users who are in the Union, may make it apparent that the controller envisages offering goods or services to data subjects in the Union.

(24) The processing of personal data of data subjects who are in the Union by a controller or processor not established in the Union should also be subject to this Regulation when it is related to the monitoring of the behaviour of such data subjects in so far as their behaviour takes place within the Union. In order to determine whether a processing activity can be considered to monitor the behaviour of data subjects, it should be ascertained whether natural persons are tracked on the internet including potential subsequent use of personal data processing techniques which consist of profiling a natural person, particularly in order to take decisions concerning her or him or for analysing or predicting her or his personal preferences, behaviours and attitudes.

(25) Where Member State law applies by virtue of public international law, this Regulation should also apply to a controller not established in the Union, such as in a Member State's diplomatic mission or consular post.

(26) The principles of data protection should apply to any information concerning an identified or identifiable natural person. Personal data which have undergone pseudonymisation, which could be attributed to a natural person by the use of additional information should be considered to be information on an identifiable natural person. To determine whether a natural person is

identifiable, account should be taken of all the means reasonably likely to be used, such as singling out, either by the controller or by another person to identify the natural person directly or indirectly. To ascertain whether means are reasonably likely to be used to identify the natural person, account should be taken of all objective factors, such as the costs of and the amount of time required for identification, taking into consideration the available technology at the time of the processing and technological developments. The principles of data protection should therefore not apply to anonymous information, namely information which does not relate to an identified or identifiable natural person or to personal data rendered anonymous in such a manner that the data subject is not or no longer identifiable. This Regulation does not therefore concern the processing of such anonymous information, including for statistical or research purposes.

(27) This Regulation does not apply to the personal data of deceased persons. Member States may provide for rules regarding the processing of personal data of deceased persons.

(28) The application of pseudonymisation to personal data can reduce the risks to the data subjects concerned and help controllers and processors to meet their data-protection obligations. The explicit introduction of 'pseudonymisation' in this Regulation is not intended to preclude any other measures of data protection.

(29) In order to create incentives to apply pseudonymisation when processing personal data, measures of pseudonymisation should, whilst allowing general analysis, be possible within the same controller when that controller has taken technical and organisational measures necessary to ensure, for the processing concerned, that this Regulation is implemented, and that additional information for attributing the personal data to a specific data subject is kept separately. The controller processing the personal data should indicate the authorised persons within the same controller.

(30) Natural persons may be associated with online identifiers provided by their devices, applications, tools and protocols, such as internet protocol addresses, cookie identifiers or other identifiers such as radio frequency identification tags. This may leave traces which, in particular when combined with unique identifiers and other information received by the servers, may be used to create profiles of the natural persons and identify them.

(31) Public authorities to which personal data are disclosed in accordance with a legal obligation for the exercise of their official mission, such as tax and customs authorities, financial investigation units, independent administrative authorities, or financial market authorities responsible for the regulation and supervision of securities markets should not be regarded as recipients if they receive personal data which are necessary to carry out a particular inquiry in the general interest, in accordance with Union or Member State law. The requests for disclosure sent by the public authorities should always be in writing, reasoned and occasional and should

not concern the entirety of a filing system or lead to the interconnection of filing systems. The processing of personal data by those public authorities should comply with the applicable data-protection rules according to the purposes of the processing.

(32) Consent should be given by a clear affirmative act establishing a freely given, specific, informed and unambiguous indication of the data subject's agreement to the processing of personal data relating to him or her, such as by a written statement, including by electronic means, or an oral statement. This could include ticking a box when visiting an internet website, choosing technical settings for information society services or another statement or conduct which clearly indicates in this context the data subject's acceptance of the proposed processing of his or her personal data. Silence, pre-ticked boxes or inactivity should not therefore constitute consent. Consent should cover all processing activities carried out for the same purpose or purposes. When the processing has multiple purposes, consent should be given for all of them. If the data subject's consent is to be given following a request by electronic means, the request must be clear, concise and not unnecessarily disruptive to the use of the service for which it is provided.

(33) It is often not possible to fully identify the purpose of personal data processing for scientific research purposes at the time of data collection. Therefore, data subjects should be allowed to give their consent to certain areas of scientific research when in keeping with recognised ethical standards for scientific research. Data subjects should have the opportunity to give their consent only to certain areas of research or parts of research projects to the extent allowed by the intended purpose.

(34) Genetic data should be defined as personal data relating to the inherited or acquired genetic characteristics of a natural person which result from the analysis of a biological sample from the natural person in question, in particular chromosomal, deoxyribonucleic acid (DNA) or ribonucleic acid (RNA) analysis, or from the analysis of another element enabling equivalent information to be obtained.

(35) Personal data concerning health should include all data pertaining to the health status of a data subject which reveal information relating to the past, current or future physical or mental health status of the data subject. This includes information about the natural person collected in the course of the registration for, or the provision of, health care services as referred to in Directive 2011/24/EU of the European Parliament and of the Council[9] to that natural person; a number, symbol or particular assigned to a natural person to uniquely identify the natural person for health purposes; information derived from the testing or examination of a body part or bodily substance, including from genetic data and biological samples; and any information on, for example, a disease, disability, disease risk,

---

9 Directive 2011/24/EU of the European Parliament and of the Council of 9 March 2011 on the application of patients' rights in crossborder healthcare (OJ L 88, 4.4.2011, p. 45).

medical history, clinical treatment or the physiological or biomedical state of the data subject independent of its source, for example from a physician or other health professional, a hospital, a medical device or an in vitro diagnostic test.

(36) The main establishment of a controller in the Union should be the place of its central administration in the Union, unless the decisions on the purposes and means of the processing of personal data are taken in another establishment of the controller in the Union, in which case that other establishment should be considered to be the main establishment. The main establishment of a controller in the Union should be determined according to objective criteria and should imply the effective and real exercise of management activities determining the main decisions as to the purposes and means of processing through stable arrangements. That criterion should not depend on whether the processing of personal data is carried out at that location. The presence and use of technical means and technologies for processing personal data or processing activities do not, in themselves, constitute a main establishment and are therefore not determining criteria for a main establishment. The main establishment of the processor should be the place of its central administration in the Union or, if it has no central administration in the Union, the place where the main processing activities take place in the Union. In cases involving both the controller and the processor, the competent lead supervisory authority should remain the supervisory authority of the Member State where the controller has its main establishment, but the supervisory authority of the processor should be considered to be a supervisory authority concerned and that supervisory authority should participate in the cooperation procedure provided for by this Regulation. In any case, the supervisory authorities of the Member State or Member States where the processor has one or more establishments should not be considered to be supervisory authorities concerned where the draft decision concerns only the controller. Where the processing is carried out by a group of undertakings, the main establishment of the controlling undertaking should be considered to be the main establishment of the group of undertakings, except where the purposes and means of processing are determined by another undertaking.

(37) A group of undertakings should cover a controlling undertaking and its controlled undertakings, whereby the controlling undertaking should be the undertaking which can exert a dominant influence over the other undertakings by virtue, for example, of ownership, financial participation or the rules which govern it or the power to have personal data protection rules implemented. An undertaking which controls the processing of personal data in undertakings affiliated to it should be regarded, together with those undertakings, as a group of undertakings.

(38) Children merit specific protection with regard to their personal data, as they may be less aware of the risks, consequences and safeguards concerned and their rights in relation to the processing of personal data. Such specific protection should, in particular, apply to the use of personal

data of children for the purposes of marketing or creating personality or user profiles and the collection of personal data with regard to children when using services offered directly to a child. The consent of the holder of parental responsibility should not be necessary in the context of preventive or counselling services offered directly to a child.

(39) Any processing of personal data should be lawful and fair. It should be transparent to natural persons that personal data concerning them are collected, used, consulted or otherwise processed and to what extent the personal data are or will be processed. The principle of transparency requires that any information and communication relating to the processing of those personal data be easily accessible and easy to understand, and that clear and plain language be used. That principle concerns, in particular, information to the data subjects on the identity of the controller and the purposes of the processing and further information to ensure fair and transparent processing in respect of the natural persons concerned and their right to obtain confirmation and communication of personal data concerning them which are being processed. Natural persons should be made aware of risks, rules, safeguards and rights in relation to the processing of personal data and how to exercise their rights in relation to such processing. In particular, the specific purposes for which personal data are processed should be explicit and legitimate and determined at the time of the collection of the personal data. The personal data should be adequate, relevant and limited to what is necessary for the purposes for which they are processed. This requires, in particular, ensuring that the period for which the personal data are stored is limited to a strict minimum. Personal data should be processed only if the purpose of the processing could not reasonably be fulfilled by other means. In order to ensure that the personal data are not kept longer than necessary, time limits should be established by the controller for erasure or for a periodic review. Every reasonable step should be taken to ensure that personal data which are inaccurate are rectified or deleted. Personal data should be processed in a manner that ensures appropriate security and confidentiality of the personal data, including for preventing unauthorised access to or use of personal data and the equipment used for the processing.

(40) In order for processing to be lawful, personal data should be processed on the basis of the consent of the data subject concerned or some other legitimate basis, laid down by law, either in this Regulation or in other Union or Member State law as referred to in this Regulation, including the necessity for compliance with the legal obligation to which the controller is subject or the necessity for the performance of a contract to which the data subject is party or in order to take steps at the request of the data subject prior to entering into a contract.

(41) Where this Regulation refers to a legal basis or a legislative measure, this does not necessarily require a legislative act adopted by a parliament, without prejudice to requirements pursuant to the constitutional order of the Member State concerned. However, such a legal basis or legislative

measure should be clear and precise and its application should be foreseeable to persons subject to it, in accordance with the case-law of the Court of Justice of the European Union (the 'Court of Justice') and the European Court of Human Rights.

(42) Where processing is based on the data subject's consent, the controller should be able to demonstrate that the data subject has given consent to the processing operation. In particular in the context of a written declaration on another matter, safeguards should ensure that the data subject is aware of the fact that and the extent to which consent is given. In accordance with Council Directive 93/13/EEC[10] a declaration of consent pre-formulated by the controller should be provided in an intelligible and easily accessible form, using clear and plain language and it should not contain unfair terms. For consent to be informed, the data subject should be aware at least of the identity of the controller and the purposes of the processing for which the personal data are intended. Consent should not be regarded as freely given if the data subject has no genuine or free choice or is unable to refuse or withdraw consent without detriment.

(43) In order to ensure that consent is freely given, consent should not provide a valid legal ground for the processing of personal data in a specific case where there is a clear imbalance between the data subject and the controller, in particular where the controller is a public authority and it is therefore unlikely that consent was freely given in all the circumstances of that specific situation. Consent is presumed not to be freely given if it does not allow separate consent to be given to different personal data processing operations despite it being appropriate in the individual case, or if the performance of a contract, including the provision of a service, is dependent on the consent despite such consent not being necessary for such performance.

(44) Processing should be lawful where it is necessary in the context of a contract or the intention to enter into a contract.

(45) Where processing is carried out in accordance with a legal obligation to which the controller is subject or where processing is necessary for the performance of a task carried out in the public interest or in the exercise of official authority, the processing should have a basis in Union or Member State law. This Regulation does not require a specific law for each individual processing. A law as a basis for several processing operations based on a legal obligation to which the controller is subject or where processing is necessary for the performance of a task carried out in the public interest or in the exercise of an official authority may be sufficient. It should also be for Union or Member State law to determine the purpose of processing. Furthermore, that law could specify the general conditions of this Regulation governing the lawfulness of personal data processing, establish specifications for determining the controller, the type of personal data which are subject to the processing, the data subjects

10 Council Directive 93/13/EEC of 5 April 1993 on unfair terms in consumer contracts (OJ L 95, 21.4.1993, p. 29).

concerned, the entities to which the personal data may be disclosed, the purpose limitations, the storage period and other measures to ensure lawful and fair processing. It should also be for Union or Member State law to determine whether the controller performing a task carried out in the public interest or in the exercise of official authority should be a public authority or another natural or legal person governed by public law, or, where it is in the public interest to do so, including for health purposes such as public health and social protection and the management of health care services, by private law, such as a professional association.

(46) The processing of personal data should also be regarded to be lawful where it is necessary to protect an interest which is essential for the life of the data subject or that of another natural person. Processing of personal data based on the vital interest of another natural person should in principle take place only where the processing cannot be manifestly based on another legal basis. Some types of processing may serve both important grounds of public interest and the vital interests of the data subject as for instance when processing is necessary for humanitarian purposes, including for monitoring epidemics and their spread or in situations of humanitarian emergencies, in particular in situations of natural and man-made disasters.

(47) The legitimate interests of a controller, including those of a controller to which the personal data may be disclosed, or of a third party, may provide a legal basis for processing, provided that the interests or the fundamental rights and freedoms of the data subject are not overriding, taking into consideration the reasonable expectations of data subjects based on their relationship with the controller. Such legitimate interest could exist for example where there is a relevant and appropriate relationship between the data subject and the controller in situations such as where the data subject is a client or in the service of the controller. At any rate the existence of a legitimate interest would need careful assessment including whether a data subject can reasonably expect at the time and in the context of the collection of the personal data that processing for that purpose may take place. The interests and fundamental rights of the data subject could in particular override the interest of the data controller where personal data are processed in circumstances where data subjects do not reasonably expect further processing. Given that it is for the legislator to provide by law for the legal basis for public authorities to process personal data, that legal basis should not apply to the processing by public authorities in the performance of their tasks. The processing of personal data strictly necessary for the purposes of preventing fraud also constitutes a legitimate interest of the data controller concerned. The processing of personal data for direct marketing purposes may be regarded as carried out for a legitimate interest.

(48) Controllers that are part of a group of undertakings or institutions affiliated to a central body may have a legitimate interest in transmitting personal data within the group of undertakings for internal administrative purposes, including the processing of clients' or employees' personal data. The general

principles for the transfer of personal data, within a group of undertakings, to an undertaking located in a third country remain unaffected.

(49) The processing of personal data to the extent strictly necessary and proportionate for the purposes of ensuring network and information security, i.e. the ability of a network or an information system to resist, at a given level of confidence, accidental events or unlawful or malicious actions that compromise the availability, authenticity, integrity and confidentiality of stored or transmitted personal data, and the security of the related services offered by, or accessible via, those networks and systems, by public authorities, by computer emergency response teams (CERTs), computer security incident response teams (CSIRTs), by providers of electronic communications networks and services and by providers of security technologies and services, constitutes a legitimate interest of the data controller concerned. This could, for example, include preventing unauthorised access to electronic communications networks and malicious code distribution and stopping 'denial of service' attacks and damage to computer and electronic communication systems.

(50) The processing of personal data for purposes other than those for which the personal data were initially collected should be allowed only where the processing is compatible with the purposes for which the personal data were initially collected. In such a case, no legal basis separate from that which allowed the collection of the personal data is required. If the processing is necessary for the performance of a task carried out in the public interest or in the exercise of official authority vested in the controller, Union or Member State law may determine and specify the tasks and purposes for which the further processing should be regarded as compatible and lawful. Further processing for archiving purposes in the public interest, scientific or historical research purposes or statistical purposes should be considered to be compatible lawful processing operations. The legal basis provided by Union or Member State law for the processing of personal data may also provide a legal basis for further processing. In order to ascertain whether a purpose of further processing is compatible with the purpose for which the personal data are initially collected, the controller, after having met all the requirements for the lawfulness of the original processing, should take into account, inter alia: any link between those purposes and the purposes of the intended further processing; the context in which the personal data have been collected, in particular the reasonable expectations of data subjects based on their relationship with the controller as to their further use; the nature of the personal data; the consequences of the intended further processing for data subjects; and the existence of appropriate safeguards in both the original and intended further processing operations.

Where the data subject has given consent or the processing is based on Union or Member State law which constitutes a necessary and proportionate measure in a democratic society to safeguard, in particular, important objectives of general public interest, the controller should be allowed to further process the personal data irrespective of the compatibility of the purposes. In any case, the application of the principles set out in this Regulation and in particular the information of the data subject on those other purposes and on his or her rights including the right to object, should be ensured. Indicating possible criminal acts or threats to public security by the controller and transmitting the relevant personal data in individual cases or in several cases relating to the same criminal act or threats to public security to a competent authority should be regarded as being in the legitimate interest pursued by the controller. However, such transmission in the legitimate interest of the controller or further processing of personal data should be prohibited if the processing is not compatible with a legal, professional or other binding obligation of secrecy.

(51) Personal data which are, by their nature, particularly sensitive in relation to fundamental rights and freedoms merit specific protection as the context of their processing could create significant risks to the fundamental rights and freedoms. Those personal data should include personal data revealing racial or ethnic origin, whereby the use of the term 'racial origin' in this Regulation does not imply an acceptance by the Union of theories which attempt to determine the existence of separate human races. The processing of photographs should not systematically be considered to be processing of special categories of personal data as they are covered by the definition of biometric data only when processed through a specific technical means allowing the unique identification or authentication of a natural person. Such personal data should not be processed, unless processing is allowed in specific cases set out in this Regulation, taking into account that Member States law may lay down specific provisions on data protection in order to adapt the application of the rules of this Regulation for compliance with a legal obligation or for the performance of a task carried out in the public interest or in the exercise of official authority vested in the controller. In addition to the specific requirements for such processing, the general principles and other rules of this Regulation should apply, in particular as regards the conditions for lawful processing. Derogations from the general prohibition for processing such special categories of personal data should be explicitly provided, inter alia, where the data subject gives his or her explicit consent or in respect of specific needs in particular where the processing is carried out in the course of legitimate activities by certain associations or foundations the purpose of which is to permit the exercise of fundamental freedoms.

(52) Derogating from the prohibition on processing special categories of personal data should also be allowed when provided for in Union or Member State law and subject to suitable safeguards, so as to protect personal data and other fundamental rights, where it is in the public interest to do so, in particular processing personal data in the field of employment law, social protection law including pensions and for health security, monitoring and alert purposes, the prevention or control of communicable diseases and other serious threats to health. Such a derogation may be made for health purposes, including public health and the management of health-care services, especially in order to ensure the quality and cost-

effectiveness of the procedures used for settling claims for benefits and services in the health insurance system, or for archiving purposes in the public interest, scientific or historical research purposes or statistical purposes. A derogation should also allow the processing of such personal data where necessary for the establishment, exercise or defence of legal claims, whether in court proceedings or in an administrative or out-of-court procedure.

(53) Special categories of personal data which merit higher protection should be processed for health-related purposes only where necessary to achieve those purposes for the benefit of natural persons and society as a whole, in particular in the context of the management of health or social care services and systems, including processing by the management and central national health authorities of such data for the purpose of quality control, management information and the general national and local supervision of the health or social care system, and ensuring continuity of health or social care and cross-border healthcare or health security, monitoring and alert purposes, or for archiving purposes in the public interest, scientific or historical research purposes or statistical purposes, based on Union or Member State law which has to meet an objective of public interest, as well as for studies conducted in the public interest in the area of public health. Therefore, this Regulation should provide for harmonised conditions for the processing of special categories of personal data concerning health, in respect of specific needs, in particular where the processing of such data is carried out for certain health-related purposes by persons subject to a legal obligation of professional secrecy. Union or Member State law should provide for specific and suitable measures so as to protect the fundamental rights and the personal data of natural persons. Member States should be allowed to maintain or introduce further conditions, including limitations, with regard to the processing of genetic data, biometric data or data concerning health. However, this should not hamper the free flow of personal data within the Union when those conditions apply to cross-border processing of such data.

(54) The processing of special categories of personal data may be necessary for reasons of public interest in the areas of public health without consent of the data subject. Such processing should be subject to suitable and specific measures so as to protect the rights and freedoms of natural persons. In that context, 'public health' should be interpreted as defined in Regulation (EC) No 1338/2008 of the European Parliament and of the Council[11], namely all elements related to health, namely health status, including morbidity and disability, the determinants having an effect on that health status, health care needs, resources allocated to health care, the provision of, and universal access to, health care as well as health care expenditure and financing, and the causes of mortality. Such processing of

11 Regulation (EC) No 1338/2008 of the European Parliament and of the Council of 16 December 2008 on Community statistics on public health and health and safety at work (OJ L 354, 31.12.2008, p. 70).

data concerning health for reasons of public interest should not result in personal data being processed for other purposes by third parties such as employers or insurance and banking companies.

(55) Moreover, the processing of personal data by official authorities for the purpose of achieving the aims, laid down by constitutional law or by international public law, of officially recognised religious associations, is carried out on grounds of public interest.

(56) Where in the course of electoral activities, the operation of the democratic system in a Member State requires that political parties compile personal data on people's political opinions, the processing of such data may be permitted for reasons of public interest, provided that appropriate safeguards are established.

(57) If the personal data processed by a controller do not permit the controller to identify a natural person, the data controller should not be obliged to acquire additional information in order to identify the data subject for the sole purpose of complying with any provision of this Regulation. However, the controller should not refuse to take additional information provided by the data subject in order to support the exercise of his or her rights. Identification should include the digital identification of a data subject, for example through authentication mechanism such as the same credentials, used by the data subject to log-in to the on-line service offered by the data controller.

(58) The principle of transparency requires that any information addressed to the public or to the data subject be concise, easily accessible and easy to understand, and that clear and plain language and, additionally, where appropriate, visualisation be used. Such information could be provided in electronic form, for example, when addressed to the public, through a website. This is of particular relevance in situations where the proliferation of actors and the technological complexity of practice make it difficult for the data subject to know and understand whether, by whom and for what purpose personal data relating to him or her are being collected, such as in the case of online advertising. Given that children merit specific protection, any information and communication, where processing is addressed to a child, should be in such a clear and plain language that the child can easily understand.

(59) Modalities should be provided for facilitating the exercise of the data subject's rights under this Regulation, including mechanisms to request and, if applicable, obtain, free of charge, in particular, access to and rectification or erasure of personal data and the exercise of the right to object. The controller should also provide means for requests to be made electronically, especially where personal data are processed by electronic means. The controller should be obliged to respond to requests from the data subject without undue delay and at the latest within one month and to give reasons where the controller does not intend to comply with any such requests.

(60) The principles of fair and transparent processing require that the data subject be informed of the existence of the processing operation and its purposes. The controller should provide the data subject with any further information necessary to ensure fair and transparent processing taking into account the specific circumstances and context in which the personal data are processed. Furthermore, the data subject should be informed of the existence of profiling and the consequences of such profiling. Where the personal data are collected from the data subject, the data subject should also be informed whether he or she is obliged to provide the personal data and of the consequences, where he or she does not provide such data. That information may be provided in combination with standardised icons in order to give in an easily visible, intelligible and clearly legible manner, a meaningful overview of the intended processing. Where the icons are presented electronically, they should be machine-readable.

(61) The information in relation to the processing of personal data relating to the data subject should be given to him or her at the time of collection from the data subject, or, where the personal data are obtained from another source, within a reasonable period, depending on the circumstances of the case. Where personal data can be legitimately disclosed to another recipient, the data subject should be informed when the personal data are first disclosed to the recipient. Where the controller intends to process the personal data for a purpose other than that for which they were collected, the controller should provide the data subject prior to that further processing with information on that other purpose and other necessary information. Where the origin of the personal data cannot be provided to the data subject because various sources have been used, general information should be provided.

(62) However, it is not necessary to impose the obligation to provide information where the data subject already possesses the information, where the recording or disclosure of the personal data is expressly laid down by law or where the provision of information to the data subject proves to be impossible or would involve a disproportionate effort. The latter could in particular be the case where processing is carried out for archiving purposes in the public interest, scientific or historical research purposes or statistical purposes. In that regard, the number of data subjects, the age of the data and any appropriate safeguards adopted should be taken into consideration.

(63) A data subject should have the right of access to personal data which have been collected concerning him or her, and to exercise that right easily and at reasonable intervals, in order to be aware of, and verify, the lawfulness of the processing. This includes the right for data subjects to have access to data concerning their health, for example the data in their medical records containing information such as diagnoses, examination results, assessments by treating physicians and any treatment or interventions provided. Every data subject should therefore have the right to know and obtain communication in particular with regard to the purposes for which

the personal data are processed, where possible the period for which the personal data are processed, the recipients of the personal data, the logic involved in any automatic personal data processing and, at least when based on profiling, the consequences of such processing. Where possible, the controller should be able to provide remote access to a secure system which would provide the data subject with direct access to his or her personal data. That right should not adversely affect the rights or freedoms of others, including trade secrets or intellectual property and in particular the copyright protecting the software. However, the result of those considerations should not be a refusal to provide all information to the data subject. Where the controller processes a large quantity of information concerning the data subject, the controller should be able to request that, before the information is delivered, the data subject specify the information or processing activities to which the request relates.

(64) The controller should use all reasonable measures to verify the identity of a data subject who requests access, in particular in the context of online services and online identifiers. A controller should not retain personal data for the sole purpose of being able to react to potential requests.

(65) A data subject should have the right to have personal data concerning him or her rectified and a 'right to be forgotten' where the retention of such data infringes this Regulation or Union or Member State law to which the controller is subject. In particular, a data subject should have the right to have his or her personal data erased and no longer processed where the personal data are no longer necessary in relation to the purposes for which they are collected or otherwise processed, where a data subject has withdrawn his or her consent or objects to the processing of personal data concerning him or her, or where the processing of his or her personal data does not otherwise comply with this Regulation. That right is relevant in particular where the data subject has given his or her consent as a child and is not fully aware of the risks involved by the processing, and later wants to remove such personal data, especially on the internet. The data subject should be able to exercise that right notwithstanding the fact that he or she is no longer a child. However, the further retention of the personal data should be lawful where it is necessary, for exercising the right of freedom of expression and information, for compliance with a legal obligation, for the performance of a task carried out in the public interest or in the exercise of official authority vested in the controller, on the grounds of public interest in the area of public health, for archiving purposes in the public interest, scientific or historical research purposes or statistical purposes, or for the establishment, exercise or defence of legal claims.

(66) To strengthen the right to be forgotten in the online environment, the right to erasure should also be extended in such a way that a controller who has made the personal data public should be obliged to inform the controllers which are processing such personal data to erase any links to, or copies or replications of those personal data. In doing so, that controller should take reasonable

steps, taking into account available technology and the means available to the controller, including technical measures, to inform the controllers which are processing the personal data of the data subject's request.

(67) Methods by which to restrict the processing of personal data could include, inter alia, temporarily moving the selected data to another processing system, making the selected personal data unavailable to users, or temporarily removing published data from a website. In automated filing systems, the restriction of processing should in principle be ensured by technical means in such a manner that the personal data are not subject to further processing operations and cannot be changed. The fact that the processing of personal data is restricted should be clearly indicated in the system.

(68) To further strengthen the control over his or her own data, where the processing of personal data is carried out by automated means, the data subject should also be allowed to receive personal data concerning him or her which he or she has provided to a controller in a structured, commonly used, machine-readable and interoperable format, and to transmit it to another controller. Data controllers should be encouraged to develop interoperable formats that enable data portability. That right should apply where the data subject provided the personal data on the basis of his or her consent or the processing is necessary for the performance of a contract. It should not apply where processing is based on a legal ground other than consent or contract. By its very nature, that right should not be exercised against controllers processing personal data in the exercise of their public duties. It should therefore not apply where the processing of the personal data is necessary for compliance with a legal obligation to which the controller is subject or for the performance of a task carried out in the public interest or in the exercise of an official authority vested in the controller. The data subject's right to transmit or receive personal data concerning him or her should not create an obligation for the controllers to adopt or maintain processing systems which are technically compatible. Where, in a certain set of personal data, more than one data subject is concerned, the right to receive the personal data should be without prejudice to the rights and freedoms of other data subjects in accordance with this Regulation. Furthermore, that right should not prejudice the right of the data subject to obtain the erasure of personal data and the limitations of that right as set out in this Regulation and should, in particular, not imply the erasure of personal data concerning the data subject which have been provided by him or her for the performance of a contract to the extent that and for as long as the personal data are necessary for the performance of that contract. Where technically feasible, the data subject should have the right to have the personal data transmitted directly from one controller to another.

(69) Where personal data might lawfully be processed because processing is necessary for the performance of a task carried out in the public interest or in the exercise of official authority vested in the controller, or on grounds of the legitimate interests of a controller or a third party, a data

subject should, nevertheless, be entitled to object to the processing of any personal data relating to his or her particular situation. It should be for the controller to demonstrate that its compelling legitimate interest overrides the interests or the fundamental rights and freedoms of the data subject.

(70) Where personal data are processed for the purposes of direct marketing, the data subject should have the right to object to such processing, including profiling to the extent that it is related to such direct marketing, whether with regard to initial or further processing, at any time and free of charge. That right should be explicitly brought to the attention of the data subject and presented clearly and separately from any other information.

(71) The data subject should have the right not to be subject to a decision, which may include a measure, evaluating personal aspects relating to him or her which is based solely on automated processing and which produces legal effects concerning him or her or similarly significantly affects him or her, such as automatic refusal of an online credit application or e-recruiting practices without any human intervention. Such processing includes 'profiling' that consists of any form of automated processing of personal data evaluating the personal aspects relating to a natural person, in particular to analyse or predict aspects concerning the data subject's performance at work, economic situation, health, personal preferences or interests, reliability or behaviour, location or movements, where it produces legal effects concerning him or her or similarly significantly affects him or her. However, decision-making based on such processing, including profiling, should be allowed where expressly authorised by Union or Member State law to which the controller is subject, including for fraud and tax-evasion monitoring and prevention purposes conducted in accordance with the regulations, standards and recommendations of Union institutions or national oversight bodies and to ensure the security and reliability of a service provided by the controller, or necessary for the entering or performance of a contract between the data subject and a controller, or when the data subject has given his or her explicit consent. In any case, such processing should be subject to suitable safeguards, which should include specific information to the data subject and the right to obtain human intervention, to express his or her point of view, to obtain an explanation of the decision reached after such assessment and to challenge the decision. Such measure should not concern a child.

In order to ensure fair and transparent processing in respect of the data subject, taking into account the specific circumstances and context in which the personal data are processed, the controller should use appropriate mathematical or statistical procedures for the profiling, implement technical and organisational measures appropriate to ensure, in particular, that factors which result in inaccuracies in personal data are corrected and the risk of errors is minimised, secure personal data in a manner that takes account of the potential risks involved for the interests and rights of the data subject and that prevents, inter alia, discriminatory effects on natural persons on the basis of racial or ethnic origin, political opinion, religion or beliefs, trade union membership, genetic or health status or sexual orientation, or that result in measures having such an effect. Automated decision-making and profiling based on special categories of personal data should be allowed only under specific conditions.

(72) Profiling is subject to the rules of this Regulation governing the processing of personal data, such as the legal grounds for processing or data protection principles. The European Data Protection Board established by this Regulation (the 'Board') should be able to issue guidance in that context.

(73) Restrictions concerning specific principles and the rights of information, access to and rectification or erasure of personal data, the right to data portability, the right to object, decisions based on profiling, as well as the communication of a personal data breach to a data subject and certain related obligations of the controllers may be imposed by Union or Member State law, as far as necessary and proportionate in a democratic society to safeguard public security, including the protection of human life especially in response to natural or manmade disasters, the prevention, investigation and prosecution of criminal offences or the execution of criminal penalties, including the safeguarding against and the prevention of threats to public security, or of breaches of ethics for regulated professions, other important objectives of general public interest of the Union or of a Member State, in particular an important economic or financial interest of the Union or of a Member State, the keeping of public registers kept for reasons of general public interest, further processing of archived personal data to provide specific information related to the political behaviour under former totalitarian state regimes or the protection of the data subject or the rights and freedoms of others, including social protection, public health and humanitarian purposes. Those restrictions should be in accordance with the requirements set out in the Charter and in the European Convention for the Protection of Human Rights and Fundamental Freedoms.

(74) The responsibility and liability of the controller for any processing of personal data carried out by the controller or on the controller's behalf should be established. In particular, the controller should be obliged to implement appropriate and effective measures and be able to demonstrate the compliance of processing activities with this Regulation, including the effectiveness of the measures. Those measures should take into account the nature, scope, context and purposes of the processing and the risk to the rights and freedoms of natural persons.

(75) The risk to the rights and freedoms of natural persons, of varying likelihood and severity, may result from personal data processing which could lead to physical, material or non-material damage, in particular: where the processing may give rise to discrimination, identity theft or fraud, financial loss, damage to the reputation, loss of confidentiality of personal data protected by professional secrecy, unauthorised reversal of pseudonymisation, or any other significant economic or social disadvantage; where data subjects might be deprived of their rights and freedoms or prevented from exercising control over their personal

data; where personal data are processed which reveal racial or ethnic origin, political opinions, religion or philosophical beliefs, trade union membership, and the processing of genetic data, data concerning health or data concerning sex life or criminal convictions and offences or related security measures; where personal aspects are evaluated, in particular analysing or predicting aspects concerning performance at work, economic situation, health, personal preferences or interests, reliability or behaviour, location or movements, in order to create or use personal profiles; where personal data of vulnerable natural persons, in particular of children, are processed; or where processing involves a large amount of personal data and affects a large number of data subjects.

(76) The likelihood and severity of the risk to the rights and freedoms of the data subject should be determined by reference to the nature, scope, context and purposes of the processing. Risk should be evaluated on the basis of an objective assessment, by which it is established whether data processing operations involve a risk or a high risk.

(77) Guidance on the implementation of appropriate measures and on the demonstration of compliance by the controller or the processor, especially as regards the identification of the risk related to the processing, their assessment in terms of origin, nature, likelihood and severity, and the identification of best practices to mitigate the risk, could be provided in particular by means of approved codes of conduct, approved certifications, guidelines provided by the Board or indications provided by a data protection officer. The Board may also issue guidelines on processing operations that are considered to be unlikely to result in a high risk to the rights and freedoms of natural persons and indicate what measures may be sufficient in such cases to address such risk.

(78) The protection of the rights and freedoms of natural persons with regard to the processing of personal data require that appropriate technical and organisational measures be taken to ensure that the requirements of this Regulation are met. In order to be able to demonstrate compliance with this Regulation, the controller should adopt internal policies and implement measures which meet in particular the principles of data protection by design and data protection by default. Such measures could consist, inter alia, of minimising the processing of personal data, pseudonymising personal data as soon as possible, transparency with regard to the functions and processing of personal data, enabling the data subject to monitor the data processing, enabling the controller to create and improve security features. When developing, designing, selecting and using applications, services and products that are based on the processing of personal data or process personal data to fulfil their task, producers of the products, services and applications should be encouraged to take into account the right to data protection when developing and designing such products, services and applications and, with due regard to the state of the art, to make sure that controllers and processors are able to fulfil their data protection obligations. The principles of data protection by design and by

185

default should also be taken into consideration in the context of public tenders.

(79) The protection of the rights and freedoms of data subjects as well as the responsibility and liability of controllers and processors, also in relation to the monitoring by and measures of supervisory authorities, requires a clear allocation of the responsibilities under this Regulation, including where a controller determines the purposes and means of the processing jointly with other controllers or where a processing operation is carried out on behalf of a controller.

(80) Where a controller or a processor not established in the Union is processing personal data of data subjects who are in the Union whose processing activities are related to the offering of goods or services, irrespective of whether a payment of the data subject is required, to such data subjects in the Union, or to the monitoring of their behaviour as far as their behaviour takes place within the Union, the controller or the processor should designate a representative, unless the processing is occasional, does not include processing, on a large scale, of special categories of personal data or the processing of personal data relating to criminal convictions and offences, and is unlikely to result in a risk to the rights and freedoms of natural persons, taking into account the nature, context, scope and purposes of the processing or if the controller is a public authority or body. The representative should act on behalf of the controller or the processor and may be addressed by any supervisory authority. The representative should be explicitly designated by a written mandate of the controller or of the processor to act on its behalf with regard to its obligations under this Regulation. The designation of such a representative does not affect the responsibility or liability of the controller or of the processor under this Regulation. Such a representative should perform its tasks according to the mandate received from the controller or processor, including cooperating with the competent supervisory authorities with regard to any action taken to ensure compliance with this Regulation. The designated representative should be subject to enforcement proceedings in the event of non-compliance by the controller or processor.

(81) To ensure compliance with the requirements of this Regulation in respect of the processing to be carried out by the processor on behalf of the controller, when entrusting a processor with processing activities, the controller should use only processors providing sufficient guarantees, in particular in terms of expert knowledge, reliability and resources, to implement technical and organisational measures which will meet the requirements of this Regulation, including for the security of processing. The adherence of the processor to an approved code of conduct or an approved certification mechanism may be used as an element to demonstrate compliance with the obligations of the controller. The carrying-out of processing by a processor should be governed by a contract or other legal act under Union or Member State law, binding the processor to the controller, setting out the subject-matter and duration of the processing, the nature and purposes

of the processing, the type of personal data and categories of data subjects, taking into account the specific tasks and responsibilities of the processor in the context of the processing to be carried out and the risk to the rights and freedoms of the data subject. The controller and processor may choose to use an individual contract or standard contractual clauses which are adopted either directly by the Commission or by a supervisory authority in accordance with the consistency mechanism and then adopted by the Commission. After the completion of the processing on behalf of the controller, the processor should, at the choice of the controller, return or delete the personal data, unless there is a requirement to store the personal data under Union or Member State law to which the processor is subject.

(82) In order to demonstrate compliance with this Regulation, the controller or processor should maintain records of processing activities under its responsibility. Each controller and processor should be obliged to cooperate with the supervisory authority and make those records, on request, available to it, so that it might serve for monitoring those processing operations.

(83) In order to maintain security and to prevent processing in infringement of this Regulation, the controller or processor should evaluate the risks inherent in the processing and implement measures to mitigate those risks, such as encryption. Those measures should ensure an appropriate level of security, including confidentiality, taking into account the state of the art and the costs of implementation in relation to the risks and the nature of the personal data to be protected. In assessing data security risk, consideration should be given to the risks that are presented by personal data processing, such as accidental or unlawful destruction, loss, alteration, unauthorised disclosure of, or access to, personal data transmitted, stored or otherwise processed which may in particular lead to physical, material or non-material damage.

(84) In order to enhance compliance with this Regulation where processing operations are likely to result in a high risk to the rights and freedoms of natural persons, the controller should be responsible for the carrying-out of a data protection impact assessment to evaluate, in particular, the origin, nature, particularity and severity of that risk. The outcome of the assessment should be taken into account when determining the appropriate measures to be taken in order to demonstrate that the processing of personal data complies with this Regulation. Where a data-protection impact assessment indicates that processing operations involve a high risk which the controller cannot mitigate by appropriate measures in terms of available technology and costs of implementation, a consultation of the supervisory authority should take place prior to the processing.

(85) A personal data breach may, if not addressed in an appropriate and timely manner, result in physical, material or non-material damage to natural persons such as loss of control over their personal data or limitation of their rights, discrimination, identity theft or fraud, financial loss, unauthorised reversal of pseudonymisation, damage to reputation, loss of

confidentiality of personal data protected by professional secrecy or any other significant economic or social disadvantage to the natural person concerned. Therefore, as soon as the controller becomes aware that a personal data breach has occurred, the controller should notify the personal data breach to the supervisory authority without undue delay and, where feasible, not later than 72 hours after having become aware of it, unless the controller is able to demonstrate, in accordance with the accountability principle, that the personal data breach is unlikely to result in a risk to the rights and freedoms of natural persons. Where such notification cannot be achieved within 72 hours, the reasons for the delay should accompany the notification and information may be provided in phases without undue further delay.

(86)   The controller should communicate to the data subject a personal data breach, without undue delay, where that personal data breach is likely to result in a high risk to the rights and freedoms of the natural person in order to allow him or her to take the necessary precautions. The communication should describe the nature of the personal data breach as well as recommendations for the natural person concerned to mitigate potential adverse effects. Such communications to data subjects should be made as soon as reasonably feasible and in close cooperation with the supervisory authority, respecting guidance provided by it or by other relevant authorities such as law-enforcement authorities. For example, the need to mitigate an immediate risk of damage would call for prompt communication with data subjects whereas the need to implement appropriate measures against continuing or similar personal data breaches may justify more time for communication.

(87)   It should be ascertained whether all appropriate technological protection and organisational measures have been implemented to establish immediately whether a personal data breach has taken place and to inform promptly the supervisory authority and the data subject. The fact that the notification was made without undue delay should be established taking into account in particular the nature and gravity of the personal data breach and its consequences and adverse effects for the data subject. Such notification may result in an intervention of the supervisory authority in accordance with its tasks and powers laid down in this Regulation.

(88)   In setting detailed rules concerning the format and procedures applicable to the notification of personal data breaches, due consideration should be given to the circumstances of that breach, including whether or not personal data had been protected by appropriate technical protection measures, effectively limiting the likelihood of identity fraud or other forms of misuse. Moreover, such rules and procedures should take into account the legitimate interests of law-enforcement authorities where early disclosure could unnecessarily hamper the investigation of the circumstances of a personal data breach.

(89)   Directive 95/46/EC provided for a general obligation to notify the processing of personal data to the supervisory authorities. While that obligation produces administrative and financial burdens, it did not in all cases contribute to improving the protection of personal data. Such indiscriminate general notification obligations should therefore be abolished, and replaced by effective procedures and mechanisms which focus instead on those types of processing operations which are likely to result in a high risk to the rights and freedoms of natural persons by virtue of their nature, scope, context and purposes. Such types of processing operations may be those which in, particular, involve using new technologies, or are of a new kind and where no data protection impact assessment has been carried out before by the controller, or where they become necessary in the light of the time that has elapsed since the initial processing.

(90)   In such cases, a data protection impact assessment should be carried out by the controller prior to the processing in order to assess the particular likelihood and severity of the high risk, taking into account the nature, scope, context and purposes of the processing and the sources of the risk. That impact assessment should include, in particular, the measures, safeguards and mechanisms envisaged for mitigating that risk, ensuring the protection of personal data and demonstrating compliance with this Regulation.

(91)   This should in particular apply to large-scale processing operations which aim to process a considerable amount of personal data at regional, national or supranational level and which could affect a large number of data subjects and which are likely to result in a high risk, for example, on account of their sensitivity, where in accordance with the achieved state of technological knowledge a new technology is used on a large scale as well as to other processing operations which result in a high risk to the rights and freedoms of data subjects, in particular where those operations render it more difficult for data subjects to exercise their rights. A data protection impact assessment should also be made where personal data are processed for taking decisions regarding specific natural persons following any systematic and extensive evaluation of personal aspects relating to natural persons based on profiling those data or following the processing of special categories of personal data, biometric data, or data on criminal convictions and offences or related security measures. A data protection impact assessment is equally required for monitoring publicly accessible areas on a large scale, especially when using optic-electronic devices or for any other operations where the competent supervisory authority considers that the processing is likely to result in a high risk to the rights and freedoms of data subjects, in particular because they prevent data subjects from exercising a right or using a service or a contract, or because they are carried out systematically on a large scale. The processing of personal data should not be considered to be on a large scale if the processing concerns personal data from patients or clients by an individual physician, other health care professional or lawyer. In such cases, a data protection impact assessment should not be mandatory.

(92)   There are circumstances under which it may be reasonable and economical for the subject of a data protection impact assessment to be broader than a single project, for example where public authorities or bodies intend to establish a common application or processing platform or where several controllers plan to introduce a common application or processing environment across an industry sector or segment or for a widely used horizontal activity.

(93)   In the context of the adoption of the Member State law on which the performance of the tasks of the public authority or public body is based and which regulates the specific processing operation or set of operations in question, Member States may deem it necessary to carry out such assessment prior to the processing activities.

(94)   Where a data protection impact assessment indicates that the processing would, in the absence of safeguards, security measures and mechanisms to mitigate the risk, result in a high risk to the rights and freedoms of natural persons and the controller is of the opinion that the risk cannot be mitigated by reasonable means in terms of available technologies and costs of implementation, the supervisory authority should be consulted prior to the start of processing activities. Such high risk is likely to result from certain types of processing and the extent and frequency of processing, which may result also in a realisation of damage or interference with the rights and freedoms of the natural person. The supervisory authority should respond to the request for consultation within a specified period. However, the absence of a reaction of the supervisory authority within that period should be without prejudice to any intervention of the supervisory authority in accordance with its tasks and powers laid down in this Regulation, including the power to prohibit processing operations. As part of that consultation process, the outcome of a data protection impact assessment carried out with regard to the processing at issue may be submitted to the supervisory authority, in particular the measures envisaged to mitigate the risk to the rights and freedoms of natural persons.

(95)   The processor should assist the controller, where necessary and upon request, in ensuring compliance with the obligations deriving from the carrying out of data protection impact assessments and from prior consultation of the supervisory authority.

(96)   A consultation of the supervisory authority should also take place in the course of the preparation of a legislative or regulatory measure which provides for the processing of personal data, in order to ensure compliance of the intended processing with this Regulation and in particular to mitigate the risk involved for the data subject.

(97)   Where the processing is carried out by a public authority, except for courts or independent judicial authorities when acting in their judicial capacity, where, in the private sector, processing is carried out by a controller whose core activities consist of processing operations that require regular and systematic monitoring of the data subjects on a large scale, or where the

core activities of the controller or the processor consist of processing on a large scale of special categories of personal data and data relating to criminal convictions and offences, a person with expert knowledge of data protection law and practices should assist the controller or processor to monitor internal compliance with this Regulation. In the private sector, the core activities of a controller relate to its primary activities and do not relate to the processing of personal data as ancillary activities. The necessary level of expert knowledge should be determined in particular according to the data processing operations carried out and the protection required for the personal data processed by the controller or the processor. Such data protection officers, whether or not they are an employee of the controller, should be in a position to perform their duties and tasks in an independent manner.

(98) Associations or other bodies representing categories of controllers or processors should be encouraged to draw up codes of conduct, within the limits of this Regulation, so as to facilitate the effective application of this Regulation, taking account of the specific characteristics of the processing carried out in certain sectors and the specific needs of micro, small and medium enterprises. In particular, such codes of conduct could calibrate the obligations of controllers and processors, taking into account the risk likely to result from the processing for the rights and freedoms of natural persons.

(99) When drawing up a code of conduct, or when amending or extending such a code, associations and other bodies representing categories of controllers or processors should consult relevant stakeholders, including data subjects where feasible, and have regard to submissions received and views expressed in response to such consultations.

(100) In order to enhance transparency and compliance with this Regulation, the establishment of certification mechanisms and data protection seals and marks should be encouraged, allowing data subjects to quickly assess the level of data protection of relevant products and services.

(101) Flows of personal data to and from countries outside the Union and international organisations are necessary for the expansion of international trade and international cooperation. The increase in such flows has raised new challenges and concerns with regard to the protection of personal data. However, when personal data are transferred from the Union to controllers, processors or other recipients in third countries or to international organisations, the level of protection of natural persons ensured in the Union by this Regulation should not be undermined, including in cases of onward transfers of personal data from the third country or international organisation to controllers, processors in the same or another third country or international organisation. In any event, transfers to third countries and international organisations may only be carried out in full compliance with this Regulation. A transfer could take place only if, subject to the other provisions of this Regulation, the conditions laid down in the provisions of this Regulation relating to the transfer of personal data to third countries

or international organisations are complied with by the controller or processor.

(102) This Regulation is without prejudice to international agreements concluded between the Union and third countries regulating the transfer of personal data including appropriate safeguards for the data subjects. Member States may conclude international agreements which involve the transfer of personal data to third countries or international organisations, as far as such agreements do not affect this Regulation or any other provisions of Union law and include an appropriate level of protection for the fundamental rights of the data subjects.

(103) The Commission may decide with effect for the entire Union that a third country, a territory or specified sector within a third country, or an international organisation, offers an adequate level of data protection, thus providing legal certainty and uniformity throughout the Union as regards the third country or international organisation which is considered to provide such level of protection. In such cases, transfers of personal data to that third country or international organisation may take place without the need to obtain any further authorisation. The Commission may also decide, having given notice and a full statement setting out the reasons to the third country or international organisation, to revoke such a decision.

(104) In line with the fundamental values on which the Union is founded, in particular the protection of human rights, the Commission should, in its assessment of the third country, or of a territory or specified sector within a third country, take into account how a particular third country respects the rule of law, access to justice as well as international human rights norms and standards and its general and sectoral law, including legislation concerning public security, defence and national security as well as public order and criminal law. The adoption of an adequacy decision with regard to a territory or a specified sector in a third country should take into account clear and objective criteria, such as specific processing activities and the scope of applicable legal standards and legislation in force in the third country. The third country should offer guarantees ensuring an adequate level of protection essentially equivalent to that ensured within the Union, in particular where personal data are processed in one or several specific sectors. In particular, the third country should ensure effective independent data protection supervision and should provide for cooperation mechanisms with the Member States' data protection authorities, and the data subjects should be provided with effective and enforceable rights and effective administrative and judicial redress.

(105) Apart from the international commitments the third country or international organisation has entered into, the Commission should take account of obligations arising from the third country's or international organisation's participation in multilateral or regional systems in particular in relation to the protection of personal data, as well as the implementation of such obligations. In particular, the third country's accession to the Council of

Europe Convention of 28 January 1981 for the Protection of Individuals with regard to the Automatic Processing of Personal Data and its Additional Protocol should be taken into account. The Commission should consult the Board when assessing the level of protection in third countries or international organisations.

(106) The Commission should monitor the functioning of decisions on the level of protection in a third country, a territory or specified sector within a third country, or an international organisation, and monitor the functioning of decisions adopted on the basis of Article 25(6) or Article 26(4) of Directive 95/46/EC. In its adequacy decisions, the Commission should provide for a periodic review mechanism of their functioning. That periodic review should be conducted in consultation with the third country or international organisation in question and take into account all relevant developments in the third country or international organisation. For the purposes of monitoring and of carrying out the periodic reviews, the Commission should take into consideration the views and findings of the European Parliament and of the Council as well as of other relevant bodies and sources. The Commission should evaluate, within a reasonable time, the functioning of the latter decisions and report any relevant findings to the Committee within the meaning of Regulation (EU) No 182/2011 of the European Parliament and of the Council[12] as established under this Regulation, to the European Parliament and to the Council.

(107) The Commission may recognise that a third country, a territory or a specified sector within a third country, or an international organisation no longer ensures an adequate level of data protection. Consequently the transfer of personal data to that third country or international organisation should be prohibited, unless the requirements in this Regulation relating to transfers subject to appropriate safeguards, including binding corporate rules, and derogations for specific situations are fulfilled. In that case, provision should be made for consultations between the Commission and such third countries or international organisations. The Commission should, in a timely manner, inform the third country or international organisation of the reasons and enter into consultations with it in order to remedy the situation.

(108) In the absence of an adequacy decision, the controller or processor should take measures to compensate for the lack of data protection in a third country by way of appropriate safeguards for the data subject. Such appropriate safeguards may consist of making use of binding corporate rules, standard data protection clauses adopted by the Commission, standard data protection clauses adopted by a supervisory authority or contractual clauses authorised by a supervisory authority. Those safeguards should ensure compliance with data protection requirements and the rights of the data subjects appropriate to processing within the Union, including

12 Regulation (EU) No 182/2011 of the European Parliament and of the Council of 16 February 2011 laying down the rules and general principles concerning mechanisms for control by Member States of the Commission's exercise of implementing powers (OJ L 55, 28.2.2011, p. 13).

the availability of enforceable data subject rights and of effective legal remedies, including to obtain effective administrative or judicial redress and to claim compensation, in the Union or in a third country. They should relate in particular to compliance with the general principles relating to personal data processing, the principles of data protection by design and by default. Transfers may also be carried out by public authorities or bodies with public authorities or bodies in third countries or with international organisations with corresponding duties or functions, including on the basis of provisions to be inserted into administrative arrangements, such as a memorandum of understanding, providing for enforceable and effective rights for data subjects. Authorisation by the competent supervisory authority should be obtained when the safeguards are provided for in administrative arrangements that are not legally binding.

(109) The possibility for the controller or processor to use standard data-protection clauses adopted by the Commission or by a supervisory authority should prevent controllers or processors neither from including the data-protection clauses in a wider contract, such as a contract between the processor and another processor, nor from adding other clauses or additional safeguards provided that they do not contradict, directly or indirectly, the standard contractual clauses adopted by the Commission or by a supervisory authority or prejudice the fundamental rights or freedoms of the data subjects. Controllers and processors should be encouraged to provide additional safeguards via contractual commitments that supplement standard protection clauses.

(110) A group of undertakings, or a group of enterprises engaged in a joint economic activity, should be able to make use of approved binding corporate rules for its international transfers from the Union to organisations within the same group of undertakings, or group of enterprises engaged in a joint economic activity, provided that such corporate rules include all essential principles and enforceable rights to ensure appropriate safeguards for transfers or categories of transfers of personal data.

(111) Provisions should be made for the possibility for transfers in certain circumstances where the data subject has given his or her explicit consent, where the transfer is occasional and necessary in relation to a contract or a legal claim, regardless of whether in a judicial procedure or whether in an administrative or any out-of-court procedure, including procedures before regulatory bodies. Provision should also be made for the possibility for transfers where important grounds of public interest laid down by Union or Member State law so require or where the transfer is made from a register established by law and intended for consultation by the public or persons having a legitimate interest. In the latter case, such a transfer should not involve the entirety of the personal data or entire categories of the data contained in the register and, when the register is intended for consultation by persons having a legitimate interest, the transfer should be made only at the request of those persons or, if they are to be the recipients, taking into full account the interests and fundamental rights of the data subject.

(112) Those derogations should in particular apply to data transfers required and necessary for important reasons of public interest, for example in cases of international data exchange between competition authorities, tax or customs administrations, between financial supervisory authorities, between services competent for social security matters, or for public health, for example in the case of contact tracing for contagious diseases or in order to reduce and/or eliminate doping in sport. A transfer of personal data should also be regarded as lawful where it is necessary to protect an interest which is essential for the data subject's or another person's vital interests, including physical integrity or life, if the data subject is incapable of giving consent. In the absence of an adequacy decision, Union or Member State law may, for important reasons of public interest, expressly set limits to the transfer of specific categories of data to a third country or an international organisation. Member States should notify such provisions to the Commission. Any transfer to an international humanitarian organisation of personal data of a data subject who is physically or legally incapable of giving consent, with a view to accomplishing a task incumbent under the Geneva Conventions or to complying with international humanitarian law applicable in armed conflicts, could be considered to be necessary for an important reason of public interest or because it is in the vital interest of the data subject.

(113) Transfers which can be qualified as not repetitive and that only concern a limited number of data subjects, could also be possible for the purposes of the compelling legitimate interests pursued by the controller, when those interests are not overridden by the interests or rights and freedoms of the data subject and when the controller has assessed all the circumstances surrounding the data transfer. The controller should give particular consideration to the nature of the personal data, the purpose and duration of the proposed processing operation or operations, as well as the situation in the country of origin, the third country and the country of final destination, and should provide suitable safeguards to protect fundamental rights and freedoms of natural persons with regard to the processing of their personal data. Such transfers should be possible only in residual cases where none of the other grounds for transfer are applicable. For scientific or historical research purposes or statistical purposes, the legitimate expectations of society for an increase of knowledge should be taken into consideration. The controller should inform the supervisory authority and the data subject about the transfer.

(114) In any case, where the Commission has taken no decision on the adequate level of data protection in a third country, the controller or processor should make use of solutions that provide data subjects with enforceable and effective rights as regards the processing of their data in the Union once those data have been transferred so that that they will continue to benefit from fundamental rights and safeguards.

(115) Some third countries adopt laws, regulations and other legal acts which purport to directly regulate the processing activities of natural and legal

persons under the jurisdiction of the Member States. This may include judgments of courts or tribunals or decisions of administrative authorities in third countries requiring a controller or processor to transfer or disclose personal data, and which are not based on an international agreement, such as a mutual legal assistance treaty, in force between the requesting third country and the Union or a Member State. The extraterritorial application of those laws, regulations and other legal acts may be in breach of international law and may impede the attainment of the protection of natural persons ensured in the Union by this Regulation. Transfers should only be allowed where the conditions of this Regulation for a transfer to third countries are met. This may be the case, inter alia, where disclosure is necessary for an important ground of public interest recognised in Union or Member State law to which the controller is subject.

(116) When personal data moves across borders outside the Union it may put at increased risk the ability of natural persons to exercise data protection rights in particular to protect themselves from the unlawful use or disclosure of that information. At the same time, supervisory authorities may find that they are unable to pursue complaints or conduct investigations relating to the activities outside their borders. Their efforts to work together in the cross-border context may also be hampered by insufficient preventative or remedial powers, inconsistent legal regimes, and practical obstacles like resource constraints. Therefore, there is a need to promote closer cooperation among data protection supervisory authorities to help them exchange information and carry out investigations with their international counterparts. For the purposes of developing international cooperation mechanisms to facilitate and provide international mutual assistance for the enforcement of legislation for the protection of personal data, the Commission and the supervisory authorities should exchange information and cooperate in activities related to the exercise of their powers with competent authorities in third countries, based on reciprocity and in accordance with this Regulation.

(117) The establishment of supervisory authorities in Member States, empowered to perform their tasks and exercise their powers with complete independence, is an essential component of the protection of natural persons with regard to the processing of their personal data. Member States should be able to establish more than one supervisory authority, to reflect their constitutional, organisational and administrative structure.

(118) The independence of supervisory authorities should not mean that the supervisory authorities cannot be subject to control or monitoring mechanisms regarding their financial expenditure or to judicial review.

(119) Where a Member State establishes several supervisory authorities, it should establish by law mechanisms for ensuring the effective participation of those supervisory authorities in the consistency mechanism. That Member State should in particular designate the supervisory authority which functions as a single contact point for the effective participation of those

authorities in the mechanism, to ensure swift and smooth cooperation with other supervisory authorities, the Board and the Commission.

(120) Each supervisory authority should be provided with the financial and human resources, premises and infrastructure necessary for the effective performance of their tasks, including those related to mutual assistance and cooperation with other supervisory authorities throughout the Union. Each supervisory authority should have a separate, public annual budget, which may be part of the overall state or national budget.

(121) The general conditions for the member or members of the supervisory authority should be laid down by law in each Member State and should in particular provide that those members are to be appointed, by means of a transparent procedure, either by the parliament, government or the head of State of the Member State on the basis of a proposal from the government, a member of the government, the parliament or a chamber of the parliament, or by an independent body entrusted under Member State law. In order to ensure the independence of the supervisory authority, the member or members should act with integrity, refrain from any action that is incompatible with their duties and should not, during their term of office, engage in any incompatible occupation, whether gainful or not. The supervisory authority should have its own staff, chosen by the supervisory authority or an independent body established by Member State law, which should be subject to the exclusive direction of the member or members of the supervisory authority.

(122) Each supervisory authority should be competent on the territory of its own Member State to exercise the powers and to perform the tasks conferred on it in accordance with this Regulation. This should cover in particular the processing in the context of the activities of an establishment of the controller or processor on the territory of its own Member State, the processing of personal data carried out by public authorities or private bodies acting in the public interest, processing affecting data subjects on its territory or processing carried out by a controller or processor not established in the Union when targeting data subjects residing on its territory. This should include handling complaints lodged by a data subject, conducting investigations on the application of this Regulation and promoting public awareness of the risks, rules, safeguards and rights in relation to the processing of personal data.

(123) The supervisory authorities should monitor the application of the provisions pursuant to this Regulation and contribute to its consistent application throughout the Union, in order to protect natural persons in relation to the processing of their personal data and to facilitate the free flow of personal data within the internal market. For that purpose, the supervisory authorities should cooperate with each other and with the Commission, without the need for any agreement between Member States on the provision of mutual assistance or on such cooperation.

(124) Where the processing of personal data takes place in the context of the activities of an establishment of a controller or a processor in the Union

and the controller or processor is established in more than one Member State, or where processing taking place in the context of the activities of a single establishment of a controller or processor in the Union substantially affects or is likely to substantially affect data subjects in more than one Member State, the supervisory authority for the main establishment of the controller or processor or for the single establishment of the controller or processor should act as lead authority. It should cooperate with the other authorities concerned, because the controller or processor has an establishment on the territory of their Member State, because data subjects residing on their territory are substantially affected, or because a complaint has been lodged with them. Also where a data subject not residing in that Member State has lodged a complaint, the supervisory authority with which such complaint has been lodged should also be a supervisory authority concerned. Within its tasks to issue guidelines on any question covering the application of this Regulation, the Board should be able to issue guidelines in particular on the criteria to be taken into account in order to ascertain whether the processing in question substantially affects data subjects in more than one Member State and on what constitutes a relevant and reasoned objection.

(125) The lead authority should be competent to adopt binding decisions regarding measures applying the powers conferred on it in accordance with this Regulation. In its capacity as lead authority, the supervisory authority should closely involve and coordinate the supervisory authorities concerned in the decision-making process. Where the decision is to reject the complaint by the data subject in whole or in part, that decision should be adopted by the supervisory authority with which the complaint has been lodged.

(126) The decision should be agreed jointly by the lead supervisory authority and the supervisory authorities concerned and should be directed towards the main or single establishment of the controller or processor and be binding on the controller and processor. The controller or processor should take the necessary measures to ensure compliance with this Regulation and the implementation of the decision notified by the lead supervisory authority to the main establishment of the controller or processor as regards the processing activities in the Union.

(127) Each supervisory authority not acting as the lead supervisory authority should be competent to handle local cases where the controller or processor is established in more than one Member State, but the subject matter of the specific processing concerns only processing carried out in a single Member State and involves only data subjects in that single Member State, for example, where the subject matter concerns the processing of employees' personal data in the specific employment context of a Member State. In such cases, the supervisory authority should inform the lead supervisory authority without delay about the matter. After being informed, the lead supervisory authority should decide, whether it will handle the case pursuant to the provision on cooperation between the

lead supervisory authority and other supervisory authorities concerned ('one-stop-shop mechanism'), or whether the supervisory authority which informed it should handle the case at local level. When deciding whether it will handle the case, the lead supervisory authority should take into account whether there is an establishment of the controller or processor in the Member State of the supervisory authority which informed it in order to ensure effective enforcement of a decision *vis-à-vis* the controller or processor. Where the lead supervisory authority decides to handle the case, the supervisory authority which informed it should have the possibility to submit a draft for a decision, of which the lead supervisory authority should take utmost account when preparing its draft decision in that one-stop-shop mechanism.

(128) The rules on the lead supervisory authority and the one-stop-shop mechanism should not apply where the processing is carried out by public authorities or private bodies in the public interest. In such cases the only supervisory authority competent to exercise the powers conferred to it in accordance with this Regulation should be the supervisory authority of the Member State where the public authority or private body is established.

(129) In order to ensure consistent monitoring and enforcement of this Regulation throughout the Union, the supervisory authorities should have in each Member State the same tasks and effective powers, including powers of investigation, corrective powers and sanctions, and authorisation and advisory powers, in particular in cases of complaints from natural persons, and without prejudice to the powers of prosecutorial authorities under Member State law, to bring infringements of this Regulation to the attention of the judicial authorities and engage in legal proceedings. Such powers should also include the power to impose a temporary or definitive limitation, including a ban, on processing. Member States may specify other tasks related to the protection of personal data under this Regulation. The powers of supervisory authorities should be exercised in accordance with appropriate procedural safeguards set out in Union and Member State law, impartially, fairly and within a reasonable time. In particular each measure should be appropriate, necessary and proportionate in view of ensuring compliance with this Regulation, taking into account the circumstances of each individual case, respect the right of every person to be heard before any individual measure which would affect him or her adversely is taken and avoid superfluous costs and excessive inconveniences for the persons concerned. Investigatory powers as regards access to premises should be exercised in accordance with specific requirements in Member State procedural law, such as the requirement to obtain a prior judicial authorisation. Each legally binding measure of the supervisory authority should be in writing, be clear and unambiguous, indicate the supervisory authority which has issued the measure, the date of issue of the measure, bear the signature of the head, or a member of the supervisory authority authorised by him or her, give the reasons for the measure, and refer to the right of an effective remedy. This should not preclude additional requirements pursuant to Member State procedural law. The adoption of a

legally binding decision implies that it may give rise to judicial review in the Member State of the supervisory authority that adopted the decision.

(130) Where the supervisory authority with which the complaint has been lodged is not the lead supervisory authority, the lead supervisory authority should closely cooperate with the supervisory authority with which the complaint has been lodged in accordance with the provisions on cooperation and consistency laid down in this Regulation. In such cases, the lead supervisory authority should, when taking measures intended to produce legal effects, including the imposition of administrative fines, take utmost account of the view of the supervisory authority with which the complaint has been lodged and which should remain competent to carry out any investigation on the territory of its own Member State in liaison with the competent supervisory authority.

(131) Where another supervisory authority should act as a lead supervisory authority for the processing activities of the controller or processor but the concrete subject matter of a complaint or the possible infringement concerns only processing activities of the controller or processor in the Member State where the complaint has been lodged or the possible infringement detected and the matter does not substantially affect or is not likely to substantially affect data subjects in other Member States, the supervisory authority receiving a complaint or detecting or being informed otherwise of situations that entail possible infringements of this Regulation should seek an amicable settlement with the controller and, if this proves unsuccessful, exercise its full range of powers. This should include: specific processing carried out in the territory of the Member State of the supervisory authority or with regard to data subjects on the territory of that Member State; processing that is carried out in the context of an offer of goods or services specifically aimed at data subjects in the territory of the Member State of the supervisory authority; or processing that has to be assessed taking into account relevant legal obligations under Member State law.

(132) Awareness-raising activities by supervisory authorities addressed to the public should include specific measures directed at controllers and processors, including micro, small and medium-sized enterprises, as well as natural persons in particular in the educational context.

(133) The supervisory authorities should assist each other in performing their tasks and provide mutual assistance, so as to ensure the consistent application and enforcement of this Regulation in the internal market. A supervisory authority requesting mutual assistance may adopt a provisional measure if it receives no response to a request for mutual assistance within one month of the receipt of that request by the other supervisory authority.

(134) Each supervisory authority should, where appropriate, participate in joint operations with other supervisory authorities. The requested supervisory authority should be obliged to respond to the request within a specified time period.

(135) In order to ensure the consistent application of this Regulation throughout the Union, a consistency mechanism for cooperation between the supervisory authorities should be established. That mechanism should in particular apply where a supervisory authority intends to adopt a measure intended to produce legal effects as regards processing operations which substantially affect a significant number of data subjects in several Member States. It should also apply where any supervisory authority concerned or the Commission requests that such matter should be handled in the consistency mechanism. That mechanism should be without prejudice to any measures that the Commission may take in the exercise of its powers under the Treaties.

(136) In applying the consistency mechanism, the Board should, within a determined period of time, issue an opinion, if a majority of its members so decides or if so requested by any supervisory authority concerned or the Commission. The Board should also be empowered to adopt legally binding decisions where there are disputes between supervisory authorities. For that purpose, it should issue, in principle by a two-thirds majority of its members, legally binding decisions in clearly specified cases where there are conflicting views among supervisory authorities, in particular in the cooperation mechanism between the lead supervisory authority and supervisory authorities concerned on the merits of the case, in particular whether there is an infringement of this Regulation.

(137) There may be an urgent need to act in order to protect the rights and freedoms of data subjects, in particular when the danger exists that the enforcement of a right of a data subject could be considerably impeded. A supervisory authority should therefore be able to adopt duly justified provisional measures on its territory with a specified period of validity which should not exceed three months.

(138) The application of such mechanism should be a condition for the lawfulness of a measure intended to produce legal effects by a supervisory authority in those cases where its application is mandatory. In other cases of cross-border relevance, the cooperation mechanism between the lead supervisory authority and supervisory authorities concerned should be applied and mutual assistance and joint operations might be carried out between the supervisory authorities concerned on a bilateral or multilateral basis without triggering the consistency mechanism.

(139) In order to promote the consistent application of this Regulation, the Board should be set up as an independent body of the Union. To fulfil its objectives, the Board should have legal personality. The Board should be represented by its Chair. It should replace the Working Party on the Protection of Individuals with Regard to the Processing of Personal Data established by Directive 95/46/EC. It should consist of the head of a supervisory authority of each Member State and the European Data Protection Supervisor or their respective representatives. The Commission should participate in the Board's activities without voting rights and the European Data Protection Supervisor should have specific voting rights.

The Board should contribute to the consistent application of this Regulation throughout the Union, including by advising the Commission, in particular on the level of protection in third countries or international organisations, and promoting cooperation of the supervisory authorities throughout the Union. The Board should act independently when performing its tasks.

(140) The Board should be assisted by a secretariat provided by the European Data Protection Supervisor. The staff of the European Data Protection Supervisor involved in carrying out the tasks conferred on the Board by this Regulation should perform its tasks exclusively under the instructions of, and report to, the Chair of the Board.

(141) Every data subject should have the right to lodge a complaint with a single supervisory authority, in particular in the Member State of his or her habitual residence, and the right to an effective judicial remedy in accordance with Article 47 of the Charter if the data subject considers that his or her rights under this Regulation are infringed or where the supervisory authority does not act on a complaint, partially or wholly rejects or dismisses a complaint or does not act where such action is necessary to protect the rights of the data subject. The investigation following a complaint should be carried out, subject to judicial review, to the extent that is appropriate in the specific case. The supervisory authority should inform the data subject of the progress and the outcome of the complaint within a reasonable period. If the case requires further investigation or coordination with another supervisory authority, intermediate information should be given to the data subject. In order to facilitate the submission of complaints, each supervisory authority should take measures such as providing a complaint submission form which can also be completed electronically, without excluding other means of communication.

(142) Where a data subject considers that his or her rights under this Regulation are infringed, he or she should have the right to mandate a not-for-profit body, organisation or association which is constituted in accordance with the law of a Member State, has statutory objectives which are in the public interest and is active in the field of the protection of personal data to lodge a complaint on his or her behalf with a supervisory authority, exercise the right to a judicial remedy on behalf of data subjects or, if provided for in Member State law, exercise the right to receive compensation on behalf of data subjects. A Member State may provide for such a body, organisation or association to have the right to lodge a complaint in that Member State, independently of a data subject's mandate, and the right to an effective judicial remedy where it has reasons to consider that the rights of a data subject have been infringed as a result of the processing of personal data which infringes this Regulation. That body, organisation or association may not be allowed to claim compensation on a data subject's behalf independently of the data subject's mandate.

(143) Any natural or legal person has the right to bring an action for annulment of decisions of the Board before the Court of Justice under the conditions provided for in Article 263 TFEU. As addressees of such decisions, the

supervisory authorities concerned which wish to challenge them have to bring action within two months of being notified of them, in accordance with Article 263 TFEU. Where decisions of the Board are of direct and individual concern to a controller, processor or complainant, the latter may bring an action for annulment against those decisions within two months of their publication on the website of the Board, in accordance with Article 263 TFEU. Without prejudice to this right under Article 263 TFEU, each natural or legal person should have an effective judicial remedy before the competent national court against a decision of a supervisory authority which produces legal effects concerning that person. Such a decision concerns in particular the exercise of investigative, corrective and authorisation powers by the supervisory authority or the dismissal or rejection of complaints. However, the right to an effective judicial remedy does not encompass measures taken by supervisory authorities which are not legally binding, such as opinions issued by or advice provided by the supervisory authority. Proceedings against a supervisory authority should be brought before the courts of the Member State where the supervisory authority is established and should be conducted in accordance with that Member State's procedural law. Those courts should exercise full jurisdiction, which should include jurisdiction to examine all questions of fact and law relevant to the dispute before them.

Where a complaint has been rejected or dismissed by a supervisory authority, the complainant may bring proceedings before the courts in the same Member State. In the context of judicial remedies relating to the application of this Regulation, national courts which consider a decision on the question necessary to enable them to give judgment, may, or in the case provided for in Article 267 TFEU, must, request the Court of Justice to give a preliminary ruling on the interpretation of Union law, including this Regulation. Furthermore, where a decision of a supervisory authority implementing a decision of the Board is challenged before a national court and the validity of the decision of the Board is at issue, that national court does not have the power to declare the Board's decision invalid but must refer the question of validity to the Court of Justice in accordance with Article 267 TFEU as interpreted by the Court of Justice, where it considers the decision invalid. However, a national court may not refer a question on the validity of the decision of the Board at the request of a natural or legal person which had the opportunity to bring an action for annulment of that decision, in particular if it was directly and individually concerned by that decision, but had not done so within the period laid down in Article 263 TFEU.

(144) Where a court seized of proceedings against a decision by a supervisory authority has reason to believe that proceedings concerning the same processing, such as the same subject matter as regards processing by the same controller or processor, or the same cause of action, are brought before a competent court in another Member State, it should contact that court in order to confirm the existence of such related proceedings. If related proceedings are pending before a court in another Member State, any court other than the court first seized may stay its proceedings or

may, on request of one of the parties, decline jurisdiction in favour of the court first seized if that court has jurisdiction over the proceedings in question and its law permits the consolidation of such related proceedings. Proceedings are deemed to be related where they are so closely connected that it is expedient to hear and determine them together in order to avoid the risk of irreconcilable judgments resulting from separate proceedings.

(145) For proceedings against a controller or processor, the plaintiff should have the choice to bring the action before the courts of the Member States where the controller or processor has an establishment or where the data subject resides, unless the controller is a public authority of a Member State acting in the exercise of its public powers.

(146) The controller or processor should compensate any damage which a person may suffer as a result of processing that infringes this Regulation. The controller or processor should be exempt from liability if it proves that it is not in any way responsible for the damage. The concept of damage should be broadly interpreted in the light of the case-law of the Court of Justice in a manner which fully reflects the objectives of this Regulation. This is without prejudice to any claims for damage deriving from the violation of other rules in Union or Member State law. Processing that infringes this Regulation also includes processing that infringes delegated and implementing acts adopted in accordance with this Regulation and Member State law specifying rules of this Regulation. Data subjects should receive full and effective compensation for the damage they have suffered. Where controllers or processors are involved in the same processing, each controller or processor should be held liable for the entire damage. However, where they are joined to the same judicial proceedings, in accordance with Member State law, compensation may be apportioned according to the responsibility of each controller or processor for the damage caused by the processing, provided that full and effective compensation of the data subject who suffered the damage is ensured. Any controller or processor which has paid full compensation may subsequently institute recourse proceedings against other controllers or processors involved in the same processing.

(147) Where specific rules on jurisdiction are contained in this Regulation, in particular as regards proceedings seeking a judicial remedy including compensation, against a controller or processor, general jurisdiction rules such as those of Regulation (EU) No 1215/2012 of the European Parliament and of the Council[13] should not prejudice the application of such specific rules.

(148) In order to strengthen the enforcement of the rules of this Regulation, penalties including administrative fines should be imposed for any infringement of this Regulation, in addition to, or instead of appropriate measures imposed by the supervisory authority pursuant to this Regulation.

13 Regulation (EU) No 1215/2012 of the European Parliament and of the Council of 12 December 2012 on jurisdiction and the recognition and enforcement of judgments in civil and commercial matters (OJ L 351, 20.12.2012, p. 1).

In a case of a minor infringement or if the fine likely to be imposed would constitute a disproportionate burden to a natural person, a reprimand may be issued instead of a fine. Due regard should however be given to the nature, gravity and duration of the infringement, the intentional character of the infringement, actions taken to mitigate the damage suffered, degree of responsibility or any relevant previous infringements, the manner in which the infringement became known to the supervisory authority, compliance with measures ordered against the controller or processor, adherence to a code of conduct and any other aggravating or mitigating factor. The imposition of penalties including administrative fines should be subject to appropriate procedural safeguards in accordance with the general principles of Union law and the Charter, including effective judicial protection and due process.

(149) Member States should be able to lay down the rules on criminal penalties for infringements of this Regulation, including for infringements of national rules adopted pursuant to and within the limits of this Regulation. Those criminal penalties may also allow for the deprivation of the profits obtained through infringements of this Regulation. However, the imposition of criminal penalties for infringements of such national rules and of administrative penalties should not lead to a breach of the principle of *ne bis in idem*, as interpreted by the Court of Justice.

(150) In order to strengthen and harmonise administrative penalties for infringements of this Regulation, each supervisory authority should have the power to impose administrative fines. This Regulation should indicate infringements and the upper limit and criteria for setting the related administrative fines, which should be determined by the competent supervisory authority in each individual case, taking into account all relevant circumstances of the specific situation, with due regard in particular to the nature, gravity and duration of the infringement and of its consequences and the measures taken to ensure compliance with the obligations under this Regulation and to prevent or mitigate the consequences of the infringement. Where administrative fines are imposed on an undertaking, an undertaking should be understood to be an undertaking in accordance with Articles 101 and 102 TFEU for those purposes. Where administrative fines are imposed on persons that are not an undertaking, the supervisory authority should take account of the general level of income in the Member State as well as the economic situation of the person in considering the appropriate amount of the fine. The consistency mechanism may also be used to promote a consistent application of administrative fines. It should be for the Member States to determine whether and to which extent public authorities should be subject to administrative fines. Imposing an administrative fine or giving a warning does not affect the application of other powers of the supervisory authorities or of other penalties under this Regulation.

(151) The legal systems of Denmark and Estonia do not allow for administrative fines as set out in this Regulation. The rules on administrative fines may be

applied in such a manner that in Denmark the fine is imposed by competent national courts as a criminal penalty and in Estonia the fine is imposed by the supervisory authority in the framework of a misdemeanour procedure, provided that such an application of the rules in those Member States has an equivalent effect to administrative fines imposed by supervisory authorities. Therefore the competent national courts should take into account the recommendation by the supervisory authority initiating the fine. In any event, the fines imposed should be effective, proportionate and dissuasive.

(152) Where this Regulation does not harmonise administrative penalties or where necessary in other cases, for example in cases of serious infringements of this Regulation, Member States should implement a system which provides for effective, proportionate and dissuasive penalties. The nature of such penalties, criminal or administrative, should be determined by Member State law.

(153) Member States law should reconcile the rules governing freedom of expression and information, including journalistic, academic, artistic and or literary expression with the right to the protection of personal data pursuant to this Regulation. The processing of personal data solely for journalistic purposes, or for the purposes of academic, artistic or literary expression should be subject to derogations or exemptions from certain provisions of this Regulation if necessary to reconcile the right to the protection of personal data with the right to freedom of expression and information, as enshrined in Article 11 of the Charter. This should apply in particular to the processing of personal data in the audiovisual field and in news archives and press libraries. Therefore, Member States should adopt legislative measures which lay down the exemptions and derogations necessary for the purpose of balancing those fundamental rights. Member States should adopt such exemptions and derogations on general principles, the rights of the data subject, the controller and the processor, the transfer of personal data to third countries or international organisations, the independent supervisory authorities, cooperation and consistency, and specific data-processing situations. Where such exemptions or derogations differ from one Member State to another, the law of the Member State to which the controller is subject should apply. In order to take account of the importance of the right to freedom of expression in every democratic society, it is necessary to interpret notions relating to that freedom, such as journalism, broadly.

(154) This Regulation allows the principle of public access to official documents to be taken into account when applying this Regulation. Public access to official documents may be considered to be in the public interest. Personal data in documents held by a public authority or a public body should be able to be publicly disclosed by that authority or body if the disclosure is provided for by Union or Member State law to which the public authority or public body is subject. Such laws should reconcile public access to official documents and the reuse of public sector information with the

right to the protection of personal data and may therefore provide for the necessary reconciliation with the right to the protection of personal data pursuant to this Regulation. The reference to public authorities and bodies should in that context include all authorities or other bodies covered by Member State law on public access to documents. Directive 2003/98/EC of the European Parliament and of the Council[14] leaves intact and in no way affects the level of protection of natural persons with regard to the processing of personal data under the provisions of Union and Member State law, and in particular does not alter the obligations and rights set out in this Regulation. In particular, that Directive should not apply to documents to which access is excluded or restricted by virtue of the access regimes on the grounds of protection of personal data, and parts of documents accessible by virtue of those regimes which contain personal data the re-use of which has been provided for by law as being incompatible with the law concerning the protection of natural persons with regard to the processing of personal data.

(155) Member State law or collective agreements, including 'works agreements', may provide for specific rules on the processing of employees' personal data in the employment context, in particular for the conditions under which personal data in the employment context may be processed on the basis of the consent of the employee, the purposes of the recruitment, the performance of the contract of employment, including discharge of obligations laid down by law or by collective agreements, management, planning and organisation of work, equality and diversity in the workplace, health and safety at work, and for the purposes of the exercise and enjoyment, on an individual or collective basis, of rights and benefits related to employment, and for the purpose of the termination of the employment relationship.

(156) The processing of personal data for archiving purposes in the public interest, scientific or historical research purposes or statistical purposes should be subject to appropriate safeguards for the rights and freedoms of the data subject pursuant to this Regulation. Those safeguards should ensure that technical and organisational measures are in place in order to ensure, in particular, the principle of data minimisation. The further processing of personal data for archiving purposes in the public interest, scientific or historical research purposes or statistical purposes is to be carried out when the controller has assessed the feasibility to fulfil those purposes by processing data which do not permit or no longer permit the identification of data subjects, provided that appropriate safeguards exist (such as, for instance, pseudonymisation of the data). Member States should provide for appropriate safeguards for the processing of personal data for archiving purposes in the public interest, scientific or historical research purposes or statistical purposes. Member States should be authorised to provide, under specific conditions and subject to appropriate

14 Directive 2003/98/EC of the European Parliament and of the Council of 17 November 2003 on the re-use of public sector information (OJ L 345, 31.12.2003, p. 90).

safeguards for data subjects, specifications and derogations with regard to the information requirements and rights to rectification, to erasure, to be forgotten, to restriction of processing, to data portability, and to object when processing personal data for archiving purposes in the public interest, scientific or historical research purposes or statistical purposes. The conditions and safeguards in question may entail specific procedures for data subjects to exercise those rights if this is appropriate in the light of the purposes sought by the specific processing along with technical and organisational measures aimed at minimising the processing of personal data in pursuance of the proportionality and necessity principles. The processing of personal data for scientific purposes should also comply with other relevant legislation such as on clinical trials.

(157) By coupling information from registries, researchers can obtain new knowledge of great value with regard to widespread medical conditions such as cardiovascular disease, cancer and depression. On the basis of registries, research results can be enhanced, as they draw on a larger population. Within social science, research on the basis of registries enables researchers to obtain essential knowledge about the long-term correlation of a number of social conditions such as unemployment and education with other life conditions. Research results obtained through registries provide solid, high-quality knowledge which can provide the basis for the formulation and implementation of knowledge-based policy, improve the quality of life for a number of people and improve the efficiency of social services. In order to facilitate scientific research, personal data can be processed for scientific research purposes, subject to appropriate conditions and safeguards set out in Union or Member State law.

(158) Where personal data are processed for archiving purposes, this Regulation should also apply to that processing, bearing in mind that this Regulation should not apply to deceased persons. Public authorities or public or private bodies that hold records of public interest should be services which, pursuant to Union or Member State law, have a legal obligation to acquire, preserve, appraise, arrange, describe, communicate, promote, disseminate and provide access to records of enduring value for general public interest. Member States should also be authorised to provide for the further processing of personal data for archiving purposes, for example with a view to providing specific information related to the political behaviour under former totalitarian state regimes, genocide, crimes against humanity, in particular the Holocaust, or war crimes.

(159) Where personal data are processed for scientific research purposes, this Regulation should also apply to that processing. For the purposes of this Regulation, the processing of personal data for scientific research purposes should be interpreted in a broad manner including for example technological development and demonstration, fundamental research, applied research and privately funded research. In addition, it should take into account the Union's objective under Article 179(1) TFEU of achieving a European Research Area. Scientific research purposes should

208

also include studies conducted in the public interest in the area of public health. To meet the specificities of processing personal data for scientific research purposes, specific conditions should apply in particular as regards the publication or otherwise disclosure of personal data in the context of scientific research purposes. If the result of scientific research in particular in the health context gives reason for further measures in the interest of the data subject, the general rules of this Regulation should apply in view of those measures.

(160) Where personal data are processed for historical research purposes, this Regulation should also apply to that processing. This should also include historical research and research for genealogical purposes, bearing in mind that this Regulation should not apply to deceased persons.

(161) For the purpose of consenting to the participation in scientific research activities in clinical trials, the relevant provisions of Regulation (EU) No 536/2014 of the European Parliament and of the Council[15] should apply.

(162) Where personal data are processed for statistical purposes, this Regulation should apply to that processing. Union or Member State law should, within the limits of this Regulation, determine statistical content, control of access, specifications for the processing of personal data for statistical purposes and appropriate measures to safeguard the rights and freedoms of the data subject and for ensuring statistical confidentiality. Statistical purposes mean any operation of collection and the processing of personal data necessary for statistical surveys or for the production of statistical results. Those statistical results may further be used for different purposes, including a scientific research purpose. The statistical purpose implies that the result of processing for statistical purposes is not personal data, but aggregate data, and that this result or the personal data are not used in support of measures or decisions regarding any particular natural person.

(163) The confidential information which the Union and national statistical authorities collect for the production of official European and official national statistics should be protected. European statistics should be developed, produced and disseminated in accordance with the statistical principles as set out in Article 338(2) TFEU, while national statistics should also comply with Member State law. Regulation (EC) No 223/2009 of the European Parliament and of the Council[16] provides further specifications on statistical confidentiality for European statistics.

---

15 Regulation (EU) No 536/2014 of the European Parliament and of the Council of 16 April 2014 on clinical trials on medicinal products for human use, and repealing Directive 2001/20/EC (OJ L 158, 27.5.2014, p. 1).

16 Regulation (EC) No 223/2009 of the European Parliament and of the Council of 11 March 2009 on European statistics and repealing Regulation (EC, Euratom) No 1101/2008 of the European Parliament and of the Council on the transmission of data subject to statistical confidentiality to the Statistical Office of the European Communities, Council Regulation (EC) No 322/97 on Community Statistics, and Council Decision 89/382/EEC, Euratom establishing a Committee on the Statistical Programmes of the European Communities (OJ L 87, 31.3.2009, p. 164).

(164) As regards the powers of the supervisory authorities to obtain from the controller or processor access to personal data and access to their premises, Member States may adopt by law, within the limits of this Regulation, specific rules in order to safeguard the professional or other equivalent secrecy obligations, in so far as necessary to reconcile the right to the protection of personal data with an obligation of professional secrecy. This is without prejudice to existing Member State obligations to adopt rules on professional secrecy where required by Union law.

(165) This Regulation respects and does not prejudice the status under existing constitutional law of churches and religious associations or communities in the Member States, as recognised in Article 17 TFEU.

(166) In order to fulfil the objectives of this Regulation, namely to protect the fundamental rights and freedoms of natural persons and in particular their right to the protection of personal data and to ensure the free movement of personal data within the Union, the power to adopt acts in accordance with Article 290 TFEU should be delegated to the Commission. In particular, delegated acts should be adopted in respect of criteria and requirements for certification mechanisms, information to be presented by standardised icons and procedures for providing such icons. It is of particular importance that the Commission carry out appropriate consultations during its preparatory work, including at expert level. The Commission, when preparing and drawing-up delegated acts, should ensure a simultaneous, timely and appropriate transmission of relevant documents to the European Parliament and to the Council.

(167) In order to ensure uniform conditions for the implementation of this Regulation, implementing powers should be conferred on the Commission when provided for by this Regulation. Those powers should be exercised in accordance with Regulation (EU) No 182/2011. In that context, the Commission should consider specific measures for micro, small and medium-sized enterprises.

(168) The examination procedure should be used for the adoption of implementing acts on standard contractual clauses between controllers and processors and between processors; codes of conduct; technical standards and mechanisms for certification; the adequate level of protection afforded by a third country, a territory or a specified sector within that third country, or an international organisation; standard protection clauses; formats and procedures for the exchange of information by electronic means between controllers, processors and supervisory authorities for binding corporate rules; mutual assistance; and arrangements for the exchange of information by electronic means between supervisory authorities, and between supervisory authorities and the Board.

(169) The Commission should adopt immediately applicable implementing acts where available evidence reveals that a third country, a territory or a specified sector within that third country, or an international organisation does not ensure an adequate level of protection, and imperative grounds of urgency so require.

(170) Since the objective of this Regulation, namely to ensure an equivalent level of protection of natural persons and the free flow of personal data throughout the Union, cannot be sufficiently achieved by the Member States and can rather, by reason of the scale or effects of the action, be better achieved at Union level, the Union may adopt measures, in accordance with the principle of subsidiarity as set out in Article 5 of the Treaty on European Union (TEU). In accordance with the principle of proportionality as set out in that Article, this Regulation does not go beyond what is necessary in order to achieve that objective.

(171) Directive 95/46/EC should be repealed by this Regulation. Processing already under way on the date of application of this Regulation should be brought into conformity with this Regulation within the period of two years after which this Regulation enters into force. Where processing is based on consent pursuant to Directive 95/46/EC, it is not necessary for the data subject to give his or her consent again if the manner in which the consent has been given is in line with the conditions of this Regulation, so as to allow the controller to continue such processing after the date of application of this Regulation. Commission decisions adopted and authorisations by supervisory authorities based on Directive 95/46/EC remain in force until amended, replaced or repealed.

(172) The European Data Protection Supervisor was consulted in accordance with Article 28(2) of Regulation (EC) No 45/2001 and delivered an opinion on 7 March 2012[17].

(173) This Regulation should apply to all matters concerning the protection of fundamental rights and freedoms *vis-à-vis* the processing of personal data which are not subject to specific obligations with the same objective set out in Directive 2002/58/EC of the European Parliament and of the Council[18], including the obligations on the controller and the rights of natural persons. In order to clarify the relationship between this Regulation and Directive 2002/58/EC, that Directive should be amended accordingly. Once this Regulation is adopted, Directive 2002/58/EC should be reviewed in particular in order to ensure consistency with this Regulation,

HAVE ADOPTED THIS REGULATION:

17 OJ C 192, 30.6.2012, p. 7.
18 Directive 2002/58/EC of the European Parliament and of the Council of 12 July 2002 concerning the processing of personal data and the protection of privacy in the electronic communications sector (Directive on privacy and electronic communications) (OJ L 201, 31.7.2002, p. 37).

CHAPTER I   GENERAL PROVISIONS

Article I   Subject-matter and objectives

1.   This Regulation lays down rules relating to the protection of natural persons with regard to the processing of personal data and rules relating to the free movement of personal data.

2.   This Regulation protects fundamental rights and freedoms of natural persons and in particular their right to the protection of personal data.

3.   The free movement of personal data within the Union shall be neither restricted nor prohibited for reasons connected with the protection of natural persons with regard to the processing of personal data.

Article 2   Material scope

1.   This Regulation applies to the processing of personal data wholly or partly by automated means and to the processing other than by automated means of personal data which form part of a filing system or are intended to form part of a filing system.

2.   This Regulation does not apply to the processing of personal data:

(a)   in the course of an activity which falls outside the scope of Union law;

(b)   by the Member States when carrying out activities which fall within the scope of Chapter 2 of Title V of the TEU;

(c)   by a natural person in the course of a purely personal or household activity;

(d)   by competent authorities for the purposes of the prevention, investigation, detection or prosecution of criminal offences or the execution of criminal penalties, including the safeguarding against and the prevention of threats to public security.

3.   For the processing of personal data by the Union institutions, bodies, offices and agencies, Regulation (EC) No 45/2001 applies. Regulation (EC) No 45/2001 and other Union legal acts applicable to such processing of personal data shall be adapted to the principles and rules of this Regulation in accordance with Article 98.

4.   This Regulation shall be without prejudice to the application of Directive 2000/31/EC, in particular of the liability rules of intermediary service providers in Articles 12 to 15 of that Directive.

Article 3   Territorial scope

1.   This Regulation applies to the processing of personal data in the context of the activities of an establishment of a controller or a processor in the Union, regardless of whether the processing takes place in the Union or not.

2. This Regulation applies to the processing of personal data of data subjects who are in the Union by a controller or processor not established in the Union, where the processing activities are related to:

   (a)   the offering of goods or services, irrespective of whether a payment of the data subject is required, to such data subjects in the Union; or

   (b)   the monitoring of their behaviour as far as their behaviour takes place within the Union.

3. This Regulation applies to the processing of personal data by a controller not established in the Union, but in a place where Member State law applies by virtue of public international law.

Article 4   Definitions

For the purposes of this Regulation:

(1)   'personal data' means any information relating to an identified or identifiable natural person ('data subject'); an identifiable natural person is one who can be identified, directly or indirectly, in particular by reference to an identifier such as a name, an identification number, location data, an online identifier or to one or more factors specific to the physical, physiological, genetic, mental, economic, cultural or social identity of that natural person;

(2)   'processing' means any operation or set of operations which is performed on personal data or on sets of personal data, whether or not by automated means, such as collection, recording, organisation, structuring, storage, adaptation or alteration, retrieval, consultation, use, disclosure by transmission, dissemination or otherwise making available, alignment or combination, restriction, erasure or destruction;

(3)   'restriction of processing' means the marking of stored personal data with the aim of limiting their processing in the future;

(4)   'profiling' means any form of automated processing of personal data consisting of the use of personal data to evaluate certain personal aspects relating to a natural person, in particular to analyse or predict aspects concerning that natural person's performance at work, economic situation, health, personal preferences, interests, reliability, behaviour, location or movements;

(5)   'pseudonymisation' means the processing of personal data in such a manner that the personal data can no longer be attributed to a specific data subject without the use of additional information, provided that such additional information is kept separately and is subject to technical and organisational measures to ensure that the personal data are not attributed to an identified or identifiable natural person;

(6)   'filing system' means any structured set of personal data which are accessible according to specific criteria, whether centralised, decentralised or dispersed on a functional or geographical basis;

(7) 'controller' means the natural or legal person, public authority, agency or other body which, alone or jointly with others, determines the purposes and means of the processing of personal data; where the purposes and means of such processing are determined by Union or Member State law, the controller or the specific criteria for its nomination may be provided for by Union or Member State law;

(8) 'processor' means a natural or legal person, public authority, agency or other body which processes personal data on behalf of the controller;

(9) 'recipient' means a natural or legal person, public authority, agency or another body, to which the personal data are disclosed, whether a third party or not. However, public authorities which may receive personal data in the framework of a particular inquiry in accordance with Union or Member State law shall not be regarded as recipients; the processing of those data by those public authorities shall be in compliance with the applicable data protection rules according to the purposes of the processing;

(10) 'third party' means a natural or legal person, public authority, agency or body other than the data subject, controller, processor and persons who, under the direct authority of the controller or processor, are authorised to process personal data;

(11) 'consent' of the data subject means any freely given, specific, informed and unambiguous indication of the data subject's wishes by which he or she, by a statement or by a clear affirmative action, signifies agreement to the processing of personal data relating to him or her;

(12) 'personal data breach' means a breach of security leading to the accidental or unlawful destruction, loss, alteration, unauthorised disclosure of, or access to, personal data transmitted, stored or otherwise processed;

(13) 'genetic data' means personal data relating to the inherited or acquired genetic characteristics of a natural person which give unique information about the physiology or the health of that natural person and which result, in particular, from an analysis of a biological sample from the natural person in question;

(14) 'biometric data' means personal data resulting from specific technical processing relating to the physical, physiological or behavioural characteristics of a natural person, which allow or confirm the unique identification of that natural person, such as facial images or dactyloscopic data;

(15) 'data concerning health' means personal data related to the physical or mental health of a natural person, including the provision of health care services, which reveal information about his or her health status;

(16) 'main establishment' means:

    (a) as regards a controller with establishments in more than one Member State, the place of its central administration in the Union, unless the decisions on the purposes and means of the processing of personal data are taken in another establishment of the controller in the Union and the latter establishment has the power to have such decisions implemented, in which case the establishment having taken such decisions is to be considered to be the main establishment;

(b) as regards a processor with establishments in more than one Member State, the place of its central administration in the Union, or, if the processor has no central administration in the Union, the establishment of the processor in the Union where the main processing activities in the context of the activities of an establishment of the processor take place to the extent that the processor is subject to specific obligations under this Regulation;

(17) 'representative' means a natural or legal person established in the Union who, designated by the controller or processor in writing pursuant to Article 27, represents the controller or processor with regard to their respective obligations under this Regulation;

(18) enterprise' means a natural or legal person engaged in an economic activity, irrespective of its legal form, including partnerships or associations regularly engaged in an economic activity;

(19) 'group of undertakings' means a controlling undertaking and its controlled undertakings;

(20) 'binding corporate rules' means personal data protection policies which are adhered to by a controller or processor established on the territory of a Member State for transfers or a set of transfers of personal data to a controller or processor in one or more third countries within a group of undertakings, or group of enterprises engaged in a joint economic activity;

(21) 'supervisory authority' means an independent public authority which is established by a Member State pursuant to Article 51;

(22) 'supervisory authority concerned' means a supervisory authority which is concerned by the processing of personal data because:

(a) the controller or processor is established on the territory of the Member State of that supervisory authority;

(b) data subjects residing in the Member State of that supervisory authority are substantially affected or likely to be substantially affected by the processing; or

(c) a complaint has been lodged with that supervisory authority;

(23) 'cross-border processing' means either:

(a) processing of personal data which takes place in the context of the activities of establishments in more than one Member State of a controller or processor in the Union where the controller or processor is established in more than one Member State; or

(b) processing of personal data which takes place in the context of the activities of a single establishment of a controller or processor in the

Union but which substantially affects or is likely to substantially affect data subjects in more than one Member State.

(24) 'relevant and reasoned objection' means an objection to a draft decision as to whether there is an infringement of this Regulation, or whether envisaged action in relation to the controller or processor complies with this Regulation, which clearly demonstrates the significance of the risks posed by the draft decision as regards the fundamental rights and freedoms of data subjects and, where applicable, the free flow of personal data within the Union;

(25) 'information society service' means a service as defined in point (b) of Article 1(1) of Directive (EU) 2015/1535 of the European Parliament and of the Council[19];

(26) 'international organisation' means an organisation and its subordinate bodies governed by public international law, or any other body which is set up by, or on the basis of, an agreement between two or more countries.

CHAPTER II   PRINCIPLES

Article 5   Principles relating to processing of personal data

1.   Personal data shall be:

(a)   processed lawfully, fairly and in a transparent manner in relation to the data subject ('lawfulness, fairness and transparency');

(b)   collected for specified, explicit and legitimate purposes and not further processed in a manner that is incompatible with those purposes; further processing for archiving purposes in the public interest, scientific or historical research purposes or statistical purposes shall, in accordance with Article 89(1), not be considered to be incompatible with the initial purposes ('purpose limitation');

(c)   adequate, relevant and limited to what is necessary in relation to the purposes for which they are processed ('data minimisation');

(d)   accurate and, where necessary, kept up to date; every reasonable step must be taken to ensure that personal data that are inaccurate, having regard to the purposes for which they are processed, are erased or rectified without delay ('accuracy');

(e)   kept in a form which permits identification of data subjects for no longer than is necessary for the purposes for which the personal data are processed; personal data may be stored for longer periods insofar as the personal data will be processed solely for archiving purposes in the public interest, scientific or historical research purposes or statistical

---

19 Directive (EU) 2015/1535 of the European Parliament and of the Council of 9 September 2015 laying down a procedure for the provision of information in the field of technical regulations and of rules on Information Society services (OJ L 241, 17.9.2015, p. 1).

purposes in accordance with Article 89(1) subject to implementation of the appropriate technical and organisational measures required by this Regulation in order to safeguard the rights and freedoms of the data subject ('storage limitation');

(f) processed in a manner that ensures appropriate security of the personal data, including protection against unauthorised or unlawful processing and against accidental loss, destruction or damage, using appropriate technical or organisational measures ('integrity and confidentiality').

2. The controller shall be responsible for, and be able to demonstrate compliance with, paragraph 1 ('accountability').

Article 6 Lawfulness of processing

1. Processing shall be lawful only if and to the extent that at least one of the following applies:

(a) the data subject has given consent to the processing of his or her personal data for one or more specific purposes;

(b) processing is necessary for the performance of a contract to which the data subject is party or in order to take steps at the request of the data subject prior to entering into a contract;

(c) processing is necessary for compliance with a legal obligation to which the controller is subject;

(d) processing is necessary in order to protect the vital interests of the data subject or of another natural person;

(e) processing is necessary for the performance of a task carried out in the public interest or in the exercise of official authority vested in the controller;

(f) processing is necessary for the purposes of the legitimate interests pursued by the controller or by a third party, except where such interests are overridden by the interests or fundamental rights and freedoms of the data subject which require protection of personal data, in particular where the data subject is a child.

Point (f) of the first subparagraph shall not apply to processing carried out by public authorities in the performance of their tasks.

2. Member States may maintain or introduce more specific provisions to adapt the application of the rules of this Regulation with regard to processing for compliance with points (c) and (e) of paragraph 1 by determining more precisely specific requirements for the processing and other measures to ensure lawful and fair processing including for other specific processing situations as provided for in Chapter IX.

3. The basis for the processing referred to in point (c) and (e) of paragraph 1 shall be laid down by:

    (a) Union law; or

    (b) Member State law to which the controller is subject.

The purpose of the processing shall be determined in that legal basis or, as regards the processing referred to in point (e) of paragraph 1, shall be necessary for the performance of a task carried out in the public interest or in the exercise of official authority vested in the controller. That legal basis may contain specific provisions to adapt the application of rules of this Regulation, inter alia: the general conditions governing the lawfulness of processing by the controller; the types of data which are subject to the processing; the data subjects concerned; the entities to, and the purposes for which, the personal data may be disclosed; the purpose limitation; storage periods; and processing operations and processing procedures, including measures to ensure lawful and fair processing such as those for other specific processing situations as provided for in Chapter IX. The Union or the Member State law shall meet an objective of public interest and be proportionate to the legitimate aim pursued.

4.   Where the processing for a purpose other than that for which the personal data have been collected is not based on the data subject's consent or on a Union or Member State law which constitutes a necessary and proportionate measure in a democratic society to safeguard the objectives referred to in Article 23(1), the controller shall, in order to ascertain whether processing for another purpose is compatible with the purpose for which the personal data are initially collected, take into account, inter alia:

    (a) any link between the purposes for which the personal data have been collected and the purposes of the intended further processing;

    (b) the context in which the personal data have been collected, in particular regarding the relationship between data subjects and the controller;

    (c) the nature of the personal data, in particular whether special categories of personal data are processed, pursuant to Article 9, or whether personal data related to criminal convictions and offences are processed, pursuant to Article 10;

    (d) the possible consequences of the intended further processing for data subjects;

    (e) the existence of appropriate safeguards, which may include encryption or pseudonymisation.

Article 7 Conditions for consent

1.   Where processing is based on consent, the controller shall be able to demonstrate that the data subject has consented to processing of his or her personal data.

2.   If the data subject's consent is given in the context of a written declaration which also concerns other matters, the request for consent shall be presented

in a manner which is clearly distinguishable from the other matters, in an intelligible and easily accessible form, using clear and plain language. Any part of such a declaration which constitutes an infringement of this Regulation shall not be binding.

3.   The data subject shall have the right to withdraw his or her consent at any time. The withdrawal of consent shall not affect the lawfulness of processing based on consent before its withdrawal. Prior to giving consent, the data subject shall be informed thereof. It shall be as easy to withdraw as to give consent.

4.   When assessing whether consent is freely given, utmost account shall be taken of whether, *inter alia*, the performance of a contract, including the provision of a service, is conditional on consent to the processing of personal data that is not necessary for the performance of that contract.

Article 8   Conditions applicable to child's consent in relation to information society services

1.   Where point (a) of Article 6(1) applies, in relation to the offer of information society services directly to a child, the processing of the personal data of a child shall be lawful where the child is at least 16 years old. Where the child is below the age of 16 years, such processing shall be lawful only if and to the extent that consent is given or authorised by the holder of parental responsibility over the child.

Member States may provide by law for a lower age for those purposes provided that such lower age is not below 13 years.

2.   The controller shall make reasonable efforts to verify in such cases that consent is given or authorised by the holder of parental responsibility over the child, taking into consideration available technology.

3.   Paragraph 1 shall not affect the general contract law of Member States such as the rules on the validity, formation or effect of a contract in relation to a child.

Article 9   Processing of special categories of personal data

1.   Processing of personal data revealing racial or ethnic origin, political opinions, religious or philosophical beliefs, or trade union membership, and the processing of genetic data, biometric data for the purpose of uniquely identifying a natural person, data concerning health or data concerning a natural person's sex life or sexual orientation shall be prohibited.

2.   Paragraph 1 shall not apply if one of the following applies:

(a)   the data subject has given explicit consent to the processing of those personal data for one or more specified purposes, except where Union or Member State law provide that the prohibition referred to in paragraph 1 may not be lifted by the data subject;

(b) processing is necessary for the purposes of carrying out the obligations and exercising specific rights of the controller or of the data subject in the field of employment and social security and social protection law in so far as it is authorised by Union or Member State law or a collective agreement pursuant to Member State law providing for appropriate safeguards for the fundamental rights and the interests of the data subject;

(c) processing is necessary to protect the vital interests of the data subject or of another natural person where the data subject is physically or legally incapable of giving consent;

(d) processing is carried out in the course of its legitimate activities with appropriate safeguards by a foundation, association or any other not-for-profit body with a political, philosophical, religious or trade union aim and on condition that the processing relates solely to the members or to former members of the body or to persons who have regular contact with it in connection with its purposes and that the personal data are not disclosed outside that body without the consent of the data subjects;

(e) processing relates to personal data which are manifestly made public by the data subject;

(f) processing is necessary for the establishment, exercise or defence of legal claims or whenever courts are acting in their judicial capacity;

(g) processing is necessary for reasons of substantial public interest, on the basis of Union or Member State law which shall be proportionate to the aim pursued, respect the essence of the right to data protection and provide for suitable and specific measures to safeguard the fundamental rights and the interests of the data subject;

(h) processing is necessary for the purposes of preventive or occupational medicine, for the assessment of the working capacity of the employee, medical diagnosis, the provision of health or social care or treatment or the management of health or social care systems and services on the basis of Union or Member State law or pursuant to contract with a health professional and subject to the conditions and safeguards referred to in paragraph 3;

(i) processing is necessary for reasons of public interest in the area of public health, such as protecting against serious cross-border threats to health or ensuring high standards of quality and safety of health care and of medicinal products or medical devices, on the basis of Union or Member State law which provides for suitable and specific measures to safeguard the rights and freedoms of the data subject, in particular professional secrecy;

(j) processing is necessary for archiving purposes in the public interest, scientific or historical research purposes or statistical purposes in accordance with Article 89(1) based on Union or Member State law which shall be proportionate to the aim pursued, respect the essence of the right to data protection and provide for suitable and specific measures to safeguard the fundamental rights and the interests of the data subject.

3.   Personal data referred to in paragraph 1 may be processed for the purposes referred to in point (h) of paragraph 2 when those data are processed by or under the responsibility of a professional subject to the obligation of professional secrecy under Union or Member State law or rules established by national competent bodies or by another person also subject to an obligation of secrecy under Union or Member State law or rules established by national competent bodies.

4.   Member States may maintain or introduce further conditions, including limitations, with regard to the processing of genetic data, biometric data or data concerning health.

Article 10   Processing of personal data relating to criminal convictions and offences

Processing of personal data relating to criminal convictions and offences or related security measures based on Article 6(1) shall be carried out only under the control of official authority or when the processing is authorised by Union or Member State law providing for appropriate safeguards for the rights and freedoms of data subjects. Any comprehensive register of criminal convictions shall be kept only under the control of official authority.

Article 11   Processing which does not require identification

1.   If the purposes for which a controller processes personal data do not or do no longer require the identification of a data subject by the controller, the controller shall not be obliged to maintain, acquire or process additional information in order to identify the data subject for the sole purpose of complying with this Regulation.

2.   Where, in cases referred to in paragraph 1 of this Article, the controller is able to demonstrate that it is not in a position to identify the data subject, the controller shall inform the data subject accordingly, if possible. In such cases, Articles 15 to 20 shall not apply except where the data subject, for the purpose of exercising his or her rights under those articles, provides additional information enabling his or her identification.

CHAPTER III   RIGHTS OF THE DATA SUBJECT

SECTION I   TRANSPARENCY AND MODALITIES

Article 12   Transparent information, communication and modalities for the exercise of the rights of the data subject

1.   The controller shall take appropriate measures to provide any information referred to in Articles 13 and 14 and any communication under Articles 15 to 22 and 34 relating to processing to the data subject in a concise,

transparent, intelligible and easily accessible form, using clear and plain language, in particular for any information addressed specifically to a child. The information shall be provided in writing, or by other means, including, where appropriate, by electronic means. When requested by the data subject, the information may be provided orally, provided that the identity of the data subject is proven by other means.

2.   The controller shall facilitate the exercise of data subject rights under Articles 15 to 22. In the cases referred to in Article 11(2), the controller shall not refuse to act on the request of the data subject for exercising his or her rights under Articles 15 to 22, unless the controller demonstrates that it is not in a position to identify the data subject.

3.   The controller shall provide information on action taken on a request under Articles 15 to 22 to the data subject without undue delay and in any event within one month of receipt of the request. That period may be extended by two further months where necessary, taking into account the complexity and number of the requests. The controller shall inform the data subject of any such extension within one month of receipt of the request, together with the reasons for the delay. Where the data subject makes the request by electronic form means, the information shall be provided by electronic means where possible, unless otherwise requested by the data subject.

4.   If the controller does not take action on the request of the data subject, the controller shall inform the data subject without delay and at the latest within one month of receipt of the request of the reasons for not taking action and on the possibility of lodging a complaint with a supervisory authority and seeking a judicial remedy.

5.   Information provided under Articles 13 and 14 and any communication and any actions taken under Articles 15 to 22 and 34 shall be provided free of charge. Where requests from a data subject are manifestly unfounded or excessive, in particular because of their repetitive character, the controller may either:

(a)   charge a reasonable fee taking into account the administrative costs of providing the information or communication or taking the action requested; or

(b)   refuse to act on the request.

The controller shall bear the burden of demonstrating the manifestly unfounded or excessive character of the request.

6.   Without prejudice to Article 11, where the controller has reasonable doubts concerning the identity of the natural person making the request referred to in Articles 15 to 21, the controller may request the provision of additional information necessary to confirm the identity of the data subject.

7.   The information to be provided to data subjects pursuant to Articles 13 and 14 may be provided in combination with standardised icons in order to give in an easily visible, intelligible and clearly legible manner a meaningful

overview of the intended processing. Where the icons are presented electronically they shall be machine-readable.

8. The Commission shall be empowered to adopt delegated acts in accordance with Article 92 for the purpose of determining the information to be presented by the icons and the procedures for providing standardised icons.

SECTION 2 INFORMATION AND ACCESS TO PERSONAL DATA

Article 13 Information to be provided where personal data are collected from the data subject

1. Where personal data relating to a data subject are collected from the data subject, the controller shall, at the time when personal data are obtained, provide the data subject with all of the following information:

    (a) the identity and the contact details of the controller and, where applicable, of the controller's representative;

    (b) the contact details of the data protection officer, where applicable;

    (c) the purposes of the processing for which the personal data are intended as well as the legal basis for the processing;

    (d) where the processing is based on point (f) of Article 6(1), the legitimate interests pursued by the controller or by a third party;

    (e) the recipients or categories of recipients of the personal data, if any;

    (f) where applicable, the fact that the controller intends to transfer personal data to a third country or international organisation and the existence or absence of an adequacy decision by the Commission, or in the case of transfers referred to in Article 46 or 47, or the second subparagraph of Article 49(1), reference to the appropriate or suitable safeguards and the means by which to obtain a copy of them or where they have been made available.

2. In addition to the information referred to in paragraph 1, the controller shall, at the time when personal data are obtained, provide the data subject with the following further information necessary to ensure fair and transparent processing:

    (a) the period for which the personal data will be stored, or if that is not possible, the criteria used to determine that period;

    (b) the existence of the right to request from the controller access to and rectification or erasure of personal data or restriction of processing concerning the data subject or to object to processing as well as the right to data portability;

    (c) where the processing is based on point (a) of Article 6(1) or point (a) of Article 9(2), the existence of the right to withdraw consent at any time, without affecting the lawfulness of processing based on consent before its withdrawal;

(d)   the right to lodge a complaint with a supervisory authority;

(e)   whether the provision of personal data is a statutory or contractual requirement, or a requirement necessary to enter into a contract, as well as whether the data subject is obliged to provide the personal data and of the possible consequences of failure to provide such data;

(f)   the existence of automated decision-making, including profiling, referred to in Article 22(1) and (4) and, at least in those cases, meaningful information about the logic involved, as well as the significance and the envisaged consequences of such processing for the data subject.

3.   Where the controller intends to further process the personal data for a purpose other than that for which the personal data were collected, the controller shall provide the data subject prior to that further processing with information on that other purpose and with any relevant further information as referred to in paragraph 2.

4.   Paragraphs 1, 2 and 3 shall not apply where and insofar as the data subject already has the information.

Article 14   Information to be provided where personal data have not been obtained from the data subject

1.   Where personal data have not been obtained from the data subject, the controller shall provide the data subject with the following information:

(a)   the identity and the contact details of the controller and, where applicable, of the controller's representative;

(b)   the contact details of the data protection officer, where applicable;

(c)   the purposes of the processing for which the personal data are intended as well as the legal basis for the processing;

(d)   the categories of personal data concerned;

(e)   the recipients or categories of recipients of the personal data, if any;

(f)   where applicable, that the controller intends to transfer personal data to a recipient in a third country or international organisation and the existence or absence of an adequacy decision by the Commission, or in the case of transfers referred to in Article 46 or 47, or the second subparagraph of Article 49(1), reference to the appropriate or suitable safeguards and the means to obtain a copy of them or where they have been made available.

2.   In addition to the information referred to in paragraph 1, the controller shall provide the data subject with the following information necessary to ensure fair and transparent processing in respect of the data subject:

(a)   the period for which the personal data will be stored, or if that is not possible, the criteria used to determine that period;

(b)   where the processing is based on point (f) of Article 6(1), the legitimate interests pursued by the controller or by a third party;

(c)   the existence of the right to request from the controller access to and rectification or erasure of personal data or restriction of processing concerning the data subject and to object to processing as well as the right to data portability;

(d)   where processing is based on point (a) of Article 6(1) or point (a) of Article 9(2), the existence of the right to withdraw consent at any time, without affecting the lawfulness of processing based on consent before its withdrawal;

(e)   the right to lodge a complaint with a supervisory authority;

(f)   from which source the personal data originate, and if applicable, whether it came from publicly accessible sources;

(g)   the existence of automated decision-making, including profiling, referred to in Article 22(1) and (4) and, at least in those cases, meaningful information about the logic involved, as well as the significance and the envisaged consequences of such processing for the data subject.

3.   The controller shall provide the information referred to in paragraphs 1 and 2:

(a)   within a reasonable period after obtaining the personal data, but at the latest within one month, having regard to the specific circumstances in which the personal data are processed;

(b)   if the personal data are to be used for communication with the data subject, at the latest at the time of the first communication to that data subject; or

(c)   if a disclosure to another recipient is envisaged, at the latest when the personal data are first disclosed.

4.   The controller intends to further process the personal data for a purpose other than that for which the personal data were obtained, the controller shall provide the data subject prior to that further processing with information on that other purpose and with any relevant further information as referred to in paragraph 2.

5.   Paragraphs 1 to 4 shall not apply where and insofar as:

(a)   the data subject already has the information;

(b)   the provision of such information proves impossible or would involve a disproportionate effort, in particular for processing for archiving purposes in the public interest, scientific or historical research purposes or statistical purposes, subject to the conditions and safeguards referred to in Article 89(1) or in so far as the obligation referred to in paragraph

1 of this Article is likely to render impossible or seriously impair the achievement of the objectives of that processing. In such cases the controller shall take appropriate measures to protect the data subject's rights and freedoms and legitimate interests, including making the information publicly available;

(c) obtaining or disclosure is expressly laid down by Union or Member State law to which the controller is subject and which provides appropriate measures to protect the data subject's legitimate interests; or

(d) where the personal data must remain confidential subject to an obligation of professional secrecy regulated by Union or Member State law, including a statutory obligation of secrecy.

Article 15 Right of access by the data subject

1. The data subject shall have the right to obtain from the controller confirmation as to whether or not personal data concerning him or her are being processed, and, where that is the case, access to the personal data and the following information:

    (a) the purposes of the processing;

    (b) the categories of personal data concerned;

    (c) the recipients or categories of recipient to whom the personal data have been or will be disclosed, in particular recipients in third countries or international organisations;

    (d) where possible, the envisaged period for which the personal data will be stored, or, if not possible, the criteria used to determine that period;

    (e) the existence of the right to request from the controller rectification or erasure of personal data or restriction of processing of personal data concerning the data subject or to object to such processing;

    (f) the right to lodge a complaint with a supervisory authority;

    (g) where the personal data are not collected from the data subject, any available information as to their source;

    (h) the existence of automated decision-making, including profiling, referred to in Article 22(1) and (4) and, at least in those cases, meaningful information about the logic involved, as well as the significance and the envisaged consequences of such processing for the data subject.

2. Where personal data are transferred to a third country or to an international organisation, the data subject shall have the right to be informed of the appropriate safeguards pursuant to Article 46 relating to the transfer.

3. The controller shall provide a copy of the personal data undergoing processing. For any further copies requested by the data subject, the controller may charge a reasonable fee based on administrative costs.

Where the data subject makes the request by electronic means, and unless otherwise requested by the data subject, the information shall be provided in a commonly used electronic form.

4.   The right to obtain a copy referred to in paragraph 3 shall not adversely affect the rights and freedoms of others.

SECTION 3   RECTIFICATION AND ERASURE

Article 16   Right to rectification

The data subject shall have the right to obtain from the controller without undue delay the rectification of inaccurate personal data concerning him or her. Taking into account the purposes of the processing, the data subject shall have the right to have incomplete personal data completed, including by means of providing a supplementary statement.

Article 17   Right to erasure ('right to be forgotten')

1.   The data subject shall have the right to obtain from the controller the erasure of personal data concerning him or her without undue delay and the controller shall have the obligation to erase personal data without undue delay where one of the following grounds applies:

(a)   the personal data are no longer necessary in relation to the purposes for which they were collected or otherwise processed;

(b)   the data subject withdraws consent on which the processing is based according to point (a) of Article 6(1), or point (a) of Article 9(2), and where there is no other legal ground for the processing;

(c)   the data subject objects to the processing pursuant to Article 21(1) and there are no overriding legitimate grounds for the processing, or the data subject objects to the processing pursuant to Article 21(2);

(d)   the personal data have been unlawfully processed;

(e)   the personal data have to be erased for compliance with a legal obligation in Union or Member State law to which the controller is subject;

(f)   the personal data have been collected in relation to the offer of information society services referred to in Article 8(1).

2.   The controller has made the personal data public and is obliged pursuant to paragraph 1 to erase the personal data, the controller, taking account of available technology and the cost of implementation, shall take reasonable steps, including technical measures, to inform controllers which are processing the personal data that the data subject has requested the erasure by such controllers of any links to, or copy or replication of, those personal data.

3.   Paragraphs 1 and 2 shall not apply to the extent that processing is necessary:

(a)   for exercising the right of freedom of expression and information;

(b)   for compliance with a legal obligation which requires processing by Union or Member State law to which the controller is subject or for the performance of a task carried out in the public interest or in the exercise of official authority vested in the controller;

(c)   for reasons of public interest in the area of public health in accordance with points (h) and (i) of Article 9(2) as well as Article 9(3);

(d)   for archiving purposes in the public interest, scientific or historical research purposes or statistical purposes in accordance with Article 89(1) in so far as the right referred to in paragraph 1 is likely to render impossible or seriously impair the achievement of the objectives of that processing; or

(e)   for the establishment, exercise or defence of legal claims.

Article 18   Right to restriction of processing

1.   The data subject shall have the right to obtain from the controller restriction of processing where one of the following applies:

(a)   the accuracy of the personal data is contested by the data subject, for a period enabling the controller to verify the accuracy of the personal data;

(b)   the processing is unlawful and the data subject opposes the erasure of the personal data and requests the restriction of their use instead;

(c)   the controller no longer needs the personal data for the purposes of the processing, but they are required by the data subject for the establishment, exercise or defence of legal claims;

(d)   the data subject has objected to processing pursuant to Article 21(1) pending the verification whether the legitimate grounds of the controller override those of the data subject.

2.   Where processing has been restricted under paragraph 1, such personal data shall, with the exception of storage, only be processed with the data subject's consent or for the establishment, exercise or defence of legal claims or for the protection of the rights of another natural or legal person or for reasons of important public interest of the Union or of a Member State.

3.   A data subject who has obtained restriction of processing pursuant to paragraph 1 shall be informed by the controller before the restriction of processing is lifted.

Article 19   Notification obligation regarding rectification or erasure of personal data or restriction of processing

The controller shall communicate any rectification or erasure of personal data or restriction of processing carried out in accordance with Article 16, Article 17(1) and Article 18 to each recipient to whom the personal data have been disclosed, unless this proves impossible or involves disproportionate effort. The controller shall inform the data subject about those recipients if the data subject requests it.

Article 20   Right to data portability

1.   The data subject shall have the right to receive the personal data concerning him or her, which he or she has provided to a controller, in a structured, commonly used and machine-readable format and have the right to transmit those data to another controller without hindrance from the controller to which the personal data have been provided, where:

(a)   the processing is based on consent pursuant to point (a) of Article 6(1) or point (a) of Article 9(2) or on a contract pursuant to point (b) of Article 6(1); and

(b)   the processing is carried out by automated means.

2.   In exercising his or her right to data portability pursuant to paragraph 1, the data subject shall have the right to have the personal data transmitted directly from one controller to another, where technically feasible.

3.   The exercise of the right referred to in paragraph 1 of this Article shall be without prejudice to Article 17. That right shall not apply to processing necessary for the performance of a task carried out in the public interest or in the exercise of official authority vested in the controller.

4.   The right referred to in paragraph 1 shall not adversely affect the rights and freedoms of others.

SECTION 4   RIGHT TO OBJECT AND AUTOMATED INDIVIDUAL DECISION-MAKING

Article 21   Right to object

1.   The data subject shall have the right to object, on grounds relating to his or her particular situation, at any time to processing of personal data concerning him or her which is based on point (e) or (f) of Article 6(1), including profiling based on those provisions. The controller shall no longer process the personal data unless the controller demonstrates compelling legitimate grounds for the processing which override the interests, rights and freedoms of the data subject or for the establishment, exercise or defence of legal claims.

2.   Where personal data are processed for direct marketing purposes, the data subject shall have the right to object at any time to processing of personal data concerning him or her for such marketing, which includes profiling to the extent that it is related to such direct marketing.

3.   Where the data subject objects to processing for direct marketing purposes, the personal data shall no longer be processed for such purposes.

4.   At the latest at the time of the first communication with the data subject, the right referred to in paragraphs 1 and 2 shall be explicitly brought to the attention of the data subject and shall be presented clearly and separately from any other information.

5.   In the context of the use of information society services, and notwithstanding Directive 2002/58/EC, the data subject may exercise his or her right to object by automated means using technical specifications.

6.   Where personal data are processed for scientific or historical research purposes or statistical purposes pursuant to Article 89(1), the data subject, on grounds relating to his or her particular situation, shall have the right to object to processing of personal data concerning him or her, unless the processing is necessary for the performance of a task carried out for reasons of public interest.

Article 22   Automated individual decision-making, including profiling

1.   The data subject shall have the right not to be subject to a decision based solely on automated processing, including profiling, which produces legal effects concerning him or her or similarly significantly affects him or her.

2.   Paragraph 1 shall not apply if the decision:

(a)   is necessary for entering into, or performance of, a contract between the data subject and a data controller;

(b)   is authorised by Union or Member State law to which the controller is subject and which also lays down suitable measures to safeguard the data subject's rights and freedoms and legitimate interests; or

(c)   is based on the data subject's explicit consent.

3.   In the cases referred to in points (a) and (c) of paragraph 2, the data controller shall implement suitable measures to safeguard the data subject's rights and freedoms and legitimate interests, at least the right to obtain human intervention on the part of the controller, to express his or her point of view and to contest the decision.

4.   Decisions referred to in paragraph 2 shall not be based on special categories of personal data referred to in Article 9(1), unless point (a) or (g) of Article 9(2) applies and suitable measures to safeguard the data subject's rights and freedoms and legitimate interests are in place.

SECTION 5   RESTRICTIONS

Article 23   Restrictions

1.   Union or Member State law to which the data controller or processor is subject may restrict by way of a legislative measure the scope of the

obligations and rights provided for in Articles 12 to 22 and Article 34, as well as Article 5 in so far as its provisions correspond to the rights and obligations provided for in Articles 12 to 22, when such a restriction respects the essence of the fundamental rights and freedoms and is a necessary and proportionate measure in a democratic society to safeguard:

(a) national security;

(b) defence;

(c) public security;

(d) the prevention, investigation, detection or prosecution of criminal offences or the execution of criminal penalties, including the safeguarding against and the prevention of threats to public security;

(e) other important objectives of general public interest of the Union or of a Member State, in particular an important economic or financial interest of the Union or of a Member State, including monetary, budgetary and taxation a matters, public health and social security;

(f) the protection of judicial independence and judicial proceedings;

(g) the prevention, investigation, detection and prosecution of breaches of ethics for regulated professions;

(h) a monitoring, inspection or regulatory function connected, even occasionally, to the exercise of official authority in the cases referred to in points (a) to (e) and (g);

(i) the protection of the data subject or the rights and freedoms of others;

(j) the enforcement of civil law claims.

2. In particular, any legislative measure referred to in paragraph 1 shall contain specific provisions at least, where relevant, as to:

(a) the purposes of the processing or categories of processing;

(b) the categories of personal data;

(c) the scope of the restrictions introduced;

(d) the safeguards to prevent abuse or unlawful access or transfer;

(e) the specification of the controller or categories of controllers;

(f) the storage periods and the applicable safeguards taking into account the nature, scope and purposes of the processing or categories of processing;

(g) the risks to the rights and freedoms of data subjects; and

(h) the right of data subjects to be informed about the restriction, unless that may be prejudicial to the purpose of the restriction.

CHAPTER IV   CONTROLLER AND PROCESSOR

SECTION I   GENERAL OBLIGATIONS

Article 24   Responsibility of the controller

1.   Taking into account the nature, scope, context and purposes of processing as well as the risks of varying likelihood and severity for the rights and freedoms of natural persons, the controller shall implement appropriate technical and organisational measures to ensure and to be able to demonstrate that processing is performed in accordance with this Regulation. Those measures shall be reviewed and updated where necessary.

2.   Where proportionate in relation to processing activities, the measures referred to in paragraph 1 shall include the implementation of appropriate data protection policies by the controller.

3.   Adherence to approved codes of conduct as referred to in Article 40 or approved certification mechanisms as referred to in Article 42 may be used as an element by which to demonstrate compliance with the obligations of the controller.

Article 25   Data protection by design and by default

1.   Taking into account the state of the art, the cost of implementation and the nature, scope, context and purposes of processing as well as the risks of varying likelihood and severity for rights and freedoms of natural persons posed by the processing, the controller shall, both at the time of the determination of the means for processing and at the time of the processing itself, implement appropriate technical and organisational measures, such as pseudonymisation, which are designed to implement data-protection principles, such as data minimisation, in an effective manner and to integrate the necessary safeguards into the processing in order to meet the requirements of this Regulation and protect the rights of data subjects.

2.   The controller shall implement appropriate technical and organisational measures for ensuring that, by default, only personal data which are necessary for each specific purpose of the processing are processed. That obligation applies to the amount of personal data collected, the extent of their processing, the period of their storage and their accessibility. In particular, such measures shall ensure that by default personal data are not made accessible without the individual's intervention to an indefinite number of natural persons.

3.   An approved certification mechanism pursuant to Article 42 may be used as an element to demonstrate compliance with the requirements set out in paragraphs 1 and 2 of this Article.

Article 26 Joint controllers

1. Where two or more controllers jointly determine the purposes and means of processing, they shall be joint controllers. They shall in a transparent manner determine their respective responsibilities for compliance with the obligations under this Regulation, in particular as regards the exercising of the rights of the data subject and their respective duties to provide the information referred to in Articles 13 and 14, by means of an arrangement between them unless, and in so far as, the respective responsibilities of the controllers are determined by Union or Member State law to which the controllers are subject. The arrangement may designate a contact point for data subjects.

2. The arrangement referred to in paragraph 1 shall duly reflect the respective roles and relationships of the joint controllers *vis-à-vis* the data subjects. The essence of the arrangement shall be made available to the data subject.

3. Irrespective of the terms of the arrangement referred to in paragraph 1, the data subject may exercise his or her rights under this Regulation in respect of and against each of the controllers.

Article 27 Representatives of controllers or processors not established in the Union

1. Where Article 3(2) applies, the controller or the processor shall designate in writing a representative in the Union.

2. The obligation laid down in paragraph 1 of this Article shall not apply to:

   (a) processing which is occasional, does not include, on a large scale, processing of special categories of data as referred to in Article 9(1) or processing of personal data relating to criminal convictions and offences referred to in Article 10, and is unlikely to result in a risk to the rights and freedoms of natural persons, taking into account the nature, context, scope and purposes of the processing; or

   (b) a public authority or body.

3. The representative shall be established in one of the Member States where the data subjects, whose personal data are processed in relation to the offering of goods or services to them, or whose behaviour is monitored, are.

4. The representative shall be mandated by the controller or processor to be addressed in addition to or instead of the controller or the processor by, in particular, supervisory authorities and data subjects, on all issues related to processing, for the purposes of ensuring compliance with this Regulation.

5. The designation of a representative by the controller or processor shall be without prejudice to legal actions which could be initiated against the controller or the processor themselves.

Article 28   Processor

1.   Where processing is to be carried out on behalf of a controller, the controller shall use only processors providing sufficient guarantees to implement appropriate technical and organisational measures in such a manner that processing will meet the requirements of this Regulation and ensure the protection of the rights of the data subject.

2.   The processor shall not engage another processor without prior specific or general written authorisation of the controller. In the case of general written authorisation, the processor shall inform the controller of any intended changes concerning the addition or replacement of other processors, thereby giving the controller the opportunity to object to such changes.

3.   Processing by a processor shall be governed by a contract or other legal act under Union or Member State law, that is binding on the processor with regard to the controller and that sets out the subject-matter and duration of the processing, the nature and purpose of the processing, the type of personal data and categories of data subjects and the obligations and rights of the controller. That contract or other legal act shall stipulate, in particular, that the processor:

(a)   processes the personal data only on documented instructions from the controller, including with regard to transfers of personal data to a third country or an international organisation, unless required to do so by Union or Member State law to which the processor is subject; in such a case, the processor shall inform the controller of that legal requirement before processing, unless that law prohibits such information on important grounds of public interest;

(b)   ensures that persons authorised to process the personal data have committed themselves to confidentiality or are under an appropriate statutory obligation of confidentiality;

(c)   takes all measures required pursuant to Article 32;

(d)   respects the conditions referred to in paragraphs 2 and 4 for engaging another processor;

(e)   taking into account the nature of the processing, assists the controller by appropriate technical and organisational measures, insofar as this is possible, for the fulfilment of the controller's obligation to respond to requests for exercising the data subject's rights laid down in Chapter III;

(f)   assists the controller in ensuring compliance with the obligations pursuant to Articles 32 to 36 taking into account the nature of processing and the information available to the processor;

(g)   at the choice of the controller, deletes or returns all the personal data to the controller after the end of the provision of services relating to processing, and deletes existing copies unless Union or Member State law requires storage of the personal data;

(h) makes available to the controller all information necessary to demonstrate compliance with the obligations laid down in this Article and allow for and contribute to audits, including inspections, conducted by the controller or another auditor mandated by the controller.

With regard to point (h) of the first subparagraph, the processor shall immediately inform the controller if, in its opinion, an instruction infringes this Regulation or other Union or Member State data protection provisions.

4. Where a processor engages another processor for carrying out specific processing activities on behalf of the controller, the same data protection obligations as set out in the contract or other legal act between the controller and the processor as referred to in paragraph 3 shall be imposed on that other processor by way of a contract or other legal act under Union or Member State law, in particular providing sufficient guarantees to implement appropriate technical and organisational measures in such a manner that the processing will meet the requirements of this Regulation. Where that other processor fails to fulfil its data protection obligations, the initial processor shall remain fully liable to the controller for the performance of that other processor's obligations.

5. Adherence of a processor to an approved code of conduct as referred to in Article 40 or an approved certification mechanism as referred to in Article 42 may be used as an element by which to demonstrate sufficient guarantees as referred to in paragraphs 1 and 4 of this Article.

6. Without prejudice to an individual contract between the controller and the processor, the contract or the other legal act referred to in paragraphs 3 and 4 of this Article may be based, in whole or in part, on standard contractual clauses referred to in paragraphs 7 and 8 of this Article, including when they are part of a certification granted to the controller or processor pursuant to Articles 42 and 43.

7. The Commission may lay down standard contractual clauses for the matters referred to in paragraph 3 and 4 of this Article and in accordance with the examination procedure referred to in Article 93(2).

8. A supervisory authority may adopt standard contractual clauses for the matters referred to in paragraph 3 and 4 of this Article and in accordance with the consistency mechanism referred to in Article 63.

9. The contract or the other legal act referred to in paragraphs 3 and 4 shall be in writing, including in electronic form.

10. Without prejudice to Articles 82, 83 and 84, if a processor infringes this Regulation by determining the purposes and means of processing, the processor shall be considered to be a controller in respect of that processing.

Article 29 Processing under the authority of the controller or processor

The processor and any person acting under the authority of the controller or of the processor, who has access to personal data, shall not process those data except on instructions from the controller, unless required to do so by Union or Member State law.

Article 30 Records of processing activities

1. Each controller and, where applicable, the controller's representative, shall maintain a record of processing activities under its responsibility. That record shall contain all of the following information:

    (a) the name and contact details of the controller and, where applicable, the joint controller, the controller's representative and the data protection officer;

    (b) the purposes of the processing;

    (c) a description of the categories of data subjects and of the categories of personal data;

    (d) the categories of recipients to whom the personal data have been or will be disclosed including recipients in third countries or international organisations;

    (e) where applicable, transfers of personal data to a third country or an international organisation, including the identification of that third country or international organisation and, in the case of transfers referred to in the second subparagraph of Article 49(1), the documentation of suitable safeguards;

    (f) where possible, the envisaged time limits for erasure of the different categories of data;

    (g) where possible, a general description of the technical and organisational security measures referred to in Article 32(1).

2. Each processor and, where applicable, the processor's representative shall maintain a record of all categories of processing activities carried out on behalf of a controller, containing:

    (a) the name and contact details of the processor or processors and of each controller on behalf of which the processor is acting, and, where applicable, of the controller's or the processor's representative, and the data protection officer;

    (b) the categories of processing carried out on behalf of each controller;

    (c) where applicable, transfers of personal data to a third country or an international organisation, including the identification of that third country or international organisation and, in the case of transfers referred to in the second subparagraph of Article 49(1), the documentation of suitable safeguards;

(d) where possible, a general description of the technical and organisational security measures referred to in Article 32(1).

3. The records referred to in paragraphs 1 and 2 shall be in writing, including in electronic form.

4. The controller or the processor and, where applicable, the controller's or the processor's representative, shall make the record available to the supervisory authority on request.

5. The obligations referred to in paragraphs 1 and 2 shall not apply to an enterprise or an organisation employing fewer than 250 persons unless the processing it carries out is likely to result in a risk to the rights and freedoms of data subjects, the processing is not occasional, or the processing includes special categories of data as referred to in Article 9(1) or personal data relating to criminal convictions and offences referred to in Article 10.

Article 31   Cooperation with the supervisory authority

The controller and the processor and, where applicable, their representatives, shall cooperate, on request, with the supervisory authority in the performance of its tasks.

SECTION 2   SECURITY OF PERSONAL DATA

Article 32   Security of processing

1. Taking into account the state of the art, the costs of implementation and the nature, scope, context and purposes of processing as well as the risk of varying likelihood and severity for the rights and freedoms of natural persons, the controller and the processor shall implement appropriate technical and organisational measures to ensure a level of security appropriate to the risk, including inter alia as appropriate:

   (a) the pseudonymisation and encryption of personal data;

   (b) the ability to ensure the ongoing confidentiality, integrity, availability and resilience of processing systems and services;

   (c) the ability to restore the availability and access to personal data in a timely manner in the event of a physical or technical incident;

   (d) a process for regularly testing, assessing and evaluating the effectiveness of technical and organisational measures for ensuring the security of the processing.

2. In assessing the appropriate level of security account shall be taken in particular of the risks that are presented by processing, in particular from

accidental or unlawful destruction, loss, alteration, unauthorised disclosure of, or access to personal data transmitted, stored or otherwise processed.

3. Adherence to an approved code of conduct as referred to in Article 40 or an approved certification mechanism as referred to in Article 42 may be used as an element by which to demonstrate compliance with the requirements set out in paragraph 1 of this Article.

4. The controller and processor shall take steps to ensure that any natural person acting under the authority of the controller or the processor who has access to personal data does not process them except on instructions from the controller, unless he or she is required to do so by Union or Member State law.

Article 33   Notification of a personal data breach to the supervisory authority

1. In the case of a personal data breach, the controller shall without undue delay and, where feasible, not later than 72 hours after having become aware of it, notify the personal data breach to the supervisory authority competent in accordance with Article 55, unless the personal data breach is unlikely to result in a risk to the rights and freedoms of natural persons. Where the notification to the supervisory authority is not made within 72 hours, it shall be accompanied by reasons for the delay.

2. The processor shall notify the controller without undue delay after becoming aware of a personal data breach.

3. The notification referred to in paragraph 1 shall at least:

    (a) describe the nature of the personal data breach including where possible, the categories and approximate number of data subjects concerned and the categories and approximate number of personal data records concerned;

    (b) communicate the name and contact details of the data protection officer or other contact point where more information can be obtained;

    (c) describe the likely consequences of the personal data breach;

    (d) describe the measures taken or proposed to be taken by the controller to address the personal data breach, including, where appropriate, measures to mitigate its possible adverse effects.

4. Where, and in so far as, it is not possible to provide the information at the same time, the information may be provided in phases without undue further delay.

5. The controller shall document any personal data breaches, comprising the facts relating to the personal data breach, its effects and the remedial action taken. That documentation shall enable the supervisory authority to verify compliance with this Article.

Article 34   Communication of a personal data breach to the data subject

1. When the personal data breach is likely to result in a high risk to the rights and freedoms of natural persons, the controller shall communicate the personal data breach to the data subject without undue delay.

2. The communication to the data subject referred to in paragraph 1 of this Article shall describe in clear and plain language the nature of the personal data breach and contain at least the information and measures referred to in points (b), (c) and (d) of Article 33(3).

3. The communication to the data subject referred to in paragraph 1 shall not be required if any of the following conditions are met:

    (a) the controller has implemented appropriate technical and organisational protection measures, and those measures were applied to the personal data affected by the personal data breach, in particular those that render the personal data unintelligible to any person who is not authorised to access it, such as encryption;

    (b) the controller has taken subsequent measures which ensure that the high risk to the rights and freedoms of data subjects referred to in paragraph 1 is no longer likely to materialise;

    (c) it would involve disproportionate effort. In such a case, there shall instead be a public communication or similar measure whereby the data subjects are informed in an equally effective manner.

4. If the controller has not already communicated the personal data breach to the data subject, the supervisory authority, having considered the likelihood of the personal data breach resulting in a high risk, may require it to do so or may decide that any of the conditions referred to in paragraph 3 are met.

SECTION 3   DATA PROTECTION IMPACT ASSESSMENT AND PRIOR CONSULTATION

Article 35   Data protection impact assessment

1. Where a type of processing in particular using new technologies, and taking into account the nature, scope, context and purposes of the processing, is likely to result in a high risk to the rights and freedoms of natural persons, the controller shall, prior to the processing, carry out an assessment of the impact of the envisaged processing operations on the protection of personal data. A single assessment may address a set of similar processing operations that present similar high risks.

2. The controller shall seek the advice of the data protection officer, where designated, when carrying out a data protection impact assessment.

239

3.   A data protection impact assessment referred to in paragraph 1 shall in particular be required in the case of:

(a)   a systematic and extensive evaluation of personal aspects relating to natural persons which is based on automated processing, including profiling, and on which decisions are based that produce legal effects concerning the natural person or similarly significantly affect the natural person;

(b)   processing on a large scale of special categories of data referred to in Article 9(1), or of personal data relating to criminal convictions and offences referred to in Article 10; or

(c)   a systematic monitoring of a publicly accessible area on a large scale.

4.   The supervisory authority shall establish and make public a list of the kind of processing operations which are subject to the requirement for a data protection impact assessment pursuant to paragraph 1. The supervisory authority shall communicate those lists to the Board referred to in Article 68.

5.   The supervisory authority may also establish and make public a list of the kind of processing operations for which no data protection impact assessment is required. The supervisory authority shall communicate those lists to the Board.

6.   Prior to the adoption of the lists referred to in paragraphs 4 and 5, the competent supervisory authority shall apply the consistency mechanism referred to in Article 63 where such lists involve processing activities which are related to the offering of goods or services to data subjects or to the monitoring of their behaviour in several Member States, or may substantially affect the free movement of personal data within the Union.

7.   The assessment shall contain at least:

(a)   a systematic description of the envisaged processing operations and the purposes of the processing, including, where applicable, the legitimate interest pursued by the controller;

(b)   an assessment of the necessity and proportionality of the processing operations in relation to the purposes;

(c)   an assessment of the risks to the rights and freedoms of data subjects referred to in paragraph 1; and

(d)   the measures envisaged to address the risks, including safeguards, security measures and mechanisms to ensure the protection of personal data and to demonstrate compliance with this Regulation taking into account the rights and legitimate interests of data subjects and other persons concerned.

8.   Compliance with approved codes of conduct referred to in Article 40 by the relevant controllers or processors shall be taken into due account in assessing the impact of the processing operations performed by such controllers or processors, in particular for the purposes of a data protection impact assessment.

9. Where appropriate, the controller shall seek the views of data subjects or their representatives on the intended processing, without prejudice to the protection of commercial or public interests or the security of processing operations.

10. Where processing pursuant to point (c) or (e) of Article 6(1) has a legal basis in Union law or in the law of the Member State to which the controller is subject, that law regulates the specific processing operation or set of operations in question, and a data protection impact assessment has already been carried out as part of a general impact assessment in the context of the adoption of that legal basis, paragraphs 1 to 7 shall not apply unless Member States deem it to be necessary to carry out such an assessment prior to processing activities.

11. Where necessary, the controller shall carry out a review to assess if processing is performed in accordance with the data protection impact assessment at least when there is a change of the risk represented by processing operations.

Article 36   Prior consultation

1. The controller shall consult the supervisory authority prior to processing where a data protection impact assessment under Article 35 indicates that the processing would result in a high risk in the absence of measures taken by the controller to mitigate the risk.

2. Where the supervisory authority is of the opinion that the intended processing referred to in paragraph 1 would infringe this Regulation, in particular where the controller has insufficiently identified or mitigated the risk, the supervisory authority shall, within period of up to eight weeks of receipt of the request for consultation, provide written advice to the controller and, where applicable to the processor, and may use any of its powers referred to in Article 58. That period may be extended by six weeks, taking into account the complexity of the intended processing. The supervisory authority shall inform the controller and, where applicable, the processor, of any such extension within one month of receipt of the request for consultation together with the reasons for the delay. Those periods may be suspended until the supervisory authority has obtained information it has requested for the purposes of the consultation.

3. When consulting the supervisory authority pursuant to paragraph 1, the controller shall provide the supervisory authority with:

   (a) where applicable, the respective responsibilities of the controller, joint controllers and processors involved in the processing, in particular for processing within a group of undertakings;

   (b) the purposes and means of the intended processing;

   (c) the measures and safeguards provided to protect the rights and freedoms of data subjects pursuant to this Regulation;

(d)   where applicable, the contact details of the data protection officer;

(e)   the data protection impact assessment provided for in Article 35; and

(f)   any other information requested by the supervisory authority.

4.   Member States shall consult the supervisory authority during the preparation of a proposal for a legislative measure to be adopted by a national parliament, or of a regulatory measure based on such a legislative measure, which relates to processing.

5.   Notwithstanding paragraph 1, Member State law may require controllers to consult with, and obtain prior authorisation from, the supervisory authority in relation to processing by a controller for the performance of a task carried out by the controller in the public interest, including processing in relation to social protection and public health.

SECTION 4   DATA PROTECTION OFFICER

Article 37   Designation of the data protection officer

1.   The controller and the processor shall designate a data protection officer in any case where:

(a)   the processing is carried out by a public authority or body, except for courts acting in their judicial capacity;

(b)   the core activities of the controller or the processor consist of processing operations which, by virtue of their nature, their scope and/ or their purposes, require regular and systematic monitoring of data subjects on a large scale; or

(c)   the core activities of the controller or the processor consist of processing on a large scale of special categories of data pursuant to Article 9 and personal data relating to criminal convictions and offences referred to in Article 10.

2.   A group of undertakings may appoint a single data protection officer provided that a data protection officer is easily accessible from each establishment.

3.   Where the controller or the processor is a public authority or body, a single data protection officer may be designated for several such authorities or bodies, taking account of their organisational structure and size.

4.   In cases other than those referred to in paragraph 1, the controller or processor or associations and other bodies representing categories of controllers or processors may or, where required by Union or Member State law shall, designate a data protection officer. The data protection officer may act for such associations and other bodies representing controllers or processors.

5.   The data protection officer shall be designated on the basis of professional qualities and, in particular, expert knowledge of data protection law and practices and the ability to fulfil the tasks referred to in Article 39.

6.   The data protection officer may be a staff member of the controller or processor, or fulfil the tasks on the basis of a service contract.

7.   The controller or the processor shall publish the contact details of the data protection officer and communicate them to the supervisory authority.

Article 38   Position of the data protection officer

1.   The controller and the processor shall ensure that the data protection officer is involved, properly and in a timely manner, in all issues which relate to the protection of personal data.

2.   The controller and processor shall support the data protection officer in performing the tasks referred to in Article 39 by providing resources necessary to carry out those tasks and access to personal data and processing operations, and to maintain his or her expert knowledge.

3.   The controller and processor shall ensure that the data protection officer does not receive any instructions regarding the exercise of those tasks. He or she shall not be dismissed or penalised by the controller or the processor for performing his tasks. The data protection officer shall directly report to the highest management level of the controller or the processor.

4.   Data subjects may contact the data protection officer with regard to all issues related to processing of their personal data and to the exercise of their rights under this Regulation.

5.   The data protection officer shall be bound by secrecy or confidentiality concerning the performance of his or her tasks, in accordance with Union or Member State law.

6.   The data protection officer may fulfil other tasks and duties. The controller or processor shall ensure that any such tasks and duties do not result in a conflict of interests.

Article 39   Tasks of the data protection officer

1.   The data protection officer shall have at least the following tasks:

(a)   to inform and advise the controller or the processor and the employees who carry out processing of their obligations pursuant to this Regulation and to other Union or Member State data protection provisions;

(b)   to monitor compliance with this Regulation, with other Union or Member State data protection provisions and with the policies of the controller or processor in relation to the protection of personal data, including the assignment of responsibilities, awareness-raising and training of staff involved in processing operations, and the related audits;

(c)   to provide advice where requested as regards the data protection impact assessment and monitor its performance pursuant to Article 35;

(d) to cooperate with the supervisory authority;

(e) to act as the contact point for the supervisory authority on issues relating to processing, including the prior consultation referred to in Article 36, and to consult, where appropriate, with regard to any other matter.

2. The data protection officer shall in the performance of his or her tasks have due regard to the risk associated with processing operations, taking into account the nature, scope, context and purposes of processing.

SECTION 5   CODES OF CONDUCT AND CERTIFICATION

Article 40   Codes of conduct

1. The Member States, the supervisory authorities, the Board and the Commission shall encourage the drawing up of codes of conduct intended to contribute to the proper application of this Regulation, taking account of the specific features of the various processing sectors and the specific needs of micro, small and medium-sized enterprises.

2. Associations and other bodies representing categories of controllers or processors may prepare codes of conduct, or amend or extend such codes, for the purpose of specifying the application of this Regulation, such as with regard to:

(a) fair and transparent processing;

(b) the legitimate interests pursued by controllers in specific contexts;

(c) the collection of personal data;

(d) the pseudonymisation of personal data;

(e) the information provided to the public and to data subjects;

(f) the exercise of the rights of data subjects;

(g) the information provided to, and the protection of, children, and the manner in which the consent of the holders of parental responsibility over children is to be obtained;

(h) the measures and procedures referred to in Articles 24 and 25 and the measures to ensure security of processing referred to in Article 32;

(i) the notification of personal data breaches to supervisory authorities and the communication of such personal data breaches to data subjects;

(j) the transfer of personal data to third countries or international organisations; or

(k) out-of-court proceedings and other dispute resolution procedures for resolving disputes between controllers and data subjects with regard to processing, without prejudice to the rights of data subjects pursuant to Articles 77 and 79.

3.   In addition to adherence by controllers or processors subject to this Regulation, codes of conduct approved pursuant to paragraph 5 of this Article and having general validity pursuant to paragraph 9 of this Article may also be adhered to by controllers or processors that are not subject to this Regulation pursuant to Article 3 in order to provide appropriate safeguards within the framework of personal data transfers to third countries or international organisations under the terms referred to in point (e) of Article 46(2). Such controllers or processors shall make binding and enforceable commitments, via contractual or other legally binding instruments, to apply those appropriate safeguards including with regard to the rights of data subjects.

4.   A code of conduct referred to in paragraph 2 of this Article shall contain mechanisms which enable the body referred to in Article 41(1) to carry out the mandatory monitoring of compliance with its provisions by the controllers or processors which undertake to apply it, without prejudice to the tasks and powers of supervisory authorities competent pursuant to Article 55 or 56.

5.   Associations and other bodies referred to in paragraph 2 of this Article which intend to prepare a code of conduct or to amend or extend an existing code shall submit the draft code, amendment or extension to the supervisory authority which is competent pursuant to Article 55. The supervisory authority shall provide an opinion on whether the draft code, amendment or extension complies with this Regulation and shall approve that draft code, amendment or extension if it finds that it provides sufficient appropriate safeguards.

6.   Where the draft code, or amendment or extension is approved in accordance with paragraph 5, and where the code of conduct concerned does not relate to processing activities in several Member States, the supervisory authority shall register and publish the code.

7.   Where a draft code of conduct relates to processing activities in several Member States, the supervisory authority which is competent pursuant to Article 55 shall, before approving the draft code, amendment or extension, submit it in the procedure referred to in Article 63 to the Board which shall provide an opinion on whether the draft code, amendment or extension complies with this Regulation or, in the situation referred to in paragraph 3 of this Article, provides appropriate safeguards.

8.   Where the opinion referred to in paragraph 7 confirms that the draft code, amendment or extension complies with this Regulation, or, in the situation referred to in paragraph 3, provides appropriate safeguards, the Board shall submit its opinion to the Commission.

9.   The Commission may, by way of implementing acts, decide that the approved code of conduct, amendment or extension submitted to it pursuant to paragraph 8 of this Article have general validity within the Union. Those implementing acts shall be adopted in accordance with the examination procedure set out in Article 93(2).

10. The Commission shall ensure appropriate publicity for the approved codes which have been decided as having general validity in accordance with paragraph 9.

11. The Board shall collate all approved codes of conduct, amendments and extensions in a register and shall make them publicly available by way of appropriate means.

Article 41 Monitoring of approved codes of conduct

1. Without prejudice to the tasks and powers of the competent supervisory authority under Articles 57 and 58, the monitoring of compliance with a code of conduct pursuant to Article 40 may be carried out by a body which has an appropriate level of expertise in relation to the subject-matter of the code and is accredited for that purpose by the competent supervisory authority.

2. A body as referred to in paragraph 1 may be accredited to monitor compliance with a code of conduct where that body has:

   (a) demonstrated its independence and expertise in relation to the subject-matter of the code to the satisfaction of the competent supervisory authority;

   (b) established procedures which allow it to assess the eligibility of controllers and processors concerned to apply the code, to monitor their compliance with its provisions and to periodically review its operation;

   (c) established procedures and structures to handle complaints about infringements of the code or the manner in which the code has been, or is being, implemented by a controller or processor, and to make those procedures and structures transparent to data subjects and the public; and

   (d) demonstrated to the satisfaction of the competent supervisory authority that its tasks and duties do not result in a conflict of interests.

3. The competent supervisory authority shall submit the draft criteria for accreditation of a body as referred to in paragraph 1 of this Article to the Board pursuant to the consistency mechanism referred to in Article 63.

4. Without prejudice to the tasks and powers of the competent supervisory authority and the provisions of Chapter VIII, a body as referred to in paragraph 1 of this Article shall, subject to appropriate safeguards, take appropriate action in cases of infringement of the code by a controller or processor, including suspension or exclusion of the controller or processor concerned from the code. It shall inform the competent supervisory authority of such actions and the reasons for taking them.

5. The competent supervisory authority shall revoke the accreditation of a body as referred to in paragraph 1 if the conditions for accreditation are

not, or are no longer, met or where actions taken by the body infringe this Regulation.

6.   This Article shall not apply to processing carried out by public authorities and bodies.

Article 42   Certification

1.   The Member States, the supervisory authorities, the Board and the Commission shall encourage, in particular at Union level, the establishment of data protection certification mechanisms and of data protection seals and marks, for the purpose of demonstrating compliance with this Regulation of processing operations by controllers and processors. The specific needs of micro, small and medium-sized enterprises shall be taken into account.

2.   In addition to adherence by controllers or processors subject to this Regulation, data protection certification mechanisms, seals or marks approved pursuant to paragraph 5 of this Article may be established for the purpose of demonstrating the existence of appropriate safeguards provided by controllers or processors that are not subject to this Regulation pursuant to Article 3 within the framework of personal data transfers to third countries or international organisations under the terms referred to in point (f) of Article 46(2). Such controllers or processors shall make binding and enforceable commitments, via contractual or other legally binding instruments, to apply those appropriate safeguards, including with regard to the rights of data subjects.

3.   The certification shall be voluntary and available via a process that is transparent.

4.   A certification pursuant to this Article does not reduce the responsibility of the controller or the processor for compliance with this Regulation and is without prejudice to the tasks and powers of the supervisory authorities which are competent pursuant to Article 55 or 56.

5.   A certification pursuant to this Article shall be issued by the certification bodies referred to in Article 43 or by the competent supervisory authority, on the basis of criteria approved by that competent supervisory authority pursuant to Article 58(3) or by the Board pursuant to Article 63. Where the criteria are approved by the Board, this may result in a common certification, the European Data Protection Seal.

6.   The controller or processor which submits its processing to the certification mechanism shall provide the certification body referred to in Article 43, or where applicable, the competent supervisory authority, with all information and access to its processing activities which are necessary to conduct the certification procedure.

7.   Certification shall be issued to a controller or processor for a maximum period of three years and may be renewed, under the same conditions, provided that the relevant requirements continue to be met. Certification

shall be withdrawn, as applicable, by the certification bodies referred to in Article 43 or by the competent supervisory authority where the requirements for the certification are not or are no longer met.

8. The Board shall collate all certification mechanisms and data protection seals and marks in a register and shall make them publicly available by any appropriate means.

Article 43   Certification bodies

1. Without prejudice to the tasks and powers of the competent supervisory authority under Articles 57 and 58, certification bodies which have an appropriate level of expertise in relation to data protection shall, after informing the supervisory authority in order to allow it to exercise its powers pursuant to point (h) of Article 58(2) where necessary, issue and renew certification. Member States shall ensure that those certification bodies are accredited by one or both of the following:

    (a) the supervisory authority which is competent pursuant to Article 55 or 56;

    (b) the national accreditation body named in accordance with Regulation (EC) No 765/2008 of the European Parliament and of the Council[20] in accordance with EN-ISO/IEC 17065/2012 and with the additional requirements established by the supervisory authority which is competent pursuant to Article 55 or 56.

2. Certification bodies referred to in paragraph 1 shall be accredited in accordance with that paragraph only where they have:

    (a) demonstrated their independence and expertise in relation to the subject-matter of the certification to the satisfaction of the competent supervisory authority;

    (b) undertaken to respect the criteria referred to in Article 42(5) and approved by the supervisory authority which is competent pursuant to Article 55 or 56 or by the Board pursuant to Article 63;

    (c) established procedures for the issuing, periodic review and withdrawal of data protection certification, seals and marks;

    (d) established procedures and structures to handle complaints about infringements of the certification or the manner in which the certification has been, or is being, implemented by the controller or processor, and to make those procedures and structures transparent to data subjects and the public; and

---

20 Regulation (EC) No 765/2008 of the European Parliament and of the Council of 9 July 2008 setting out the requirements for accreditation and market surveillance relating to the marketing of products and repealing Regulation (EEC) No 339/93 (OJ L 218, 13.8.2008, p. 30).

(e) demonstrated, to the satisfaction of the competent supervisory authority, that their tasks and duties do not result in a conflict of interests.

3. The accreditation of certification bodies as referred to in paragraphs 1 and 2 of this Article shall take place on the basis of criteria approved by the supervisory authority which is competent pursuant to Article 55 or 56 or by the Board pursuant to Article 63. In the case of accreditation pursuant to point (b) of paragraph 1 of this Article, those requirements shall complement those envisaged in Regulation (EC) No 765/2008 and the technical rules that describe the methods and procedures of the certification bodies.

4. The certification bodies referred to in paragraph 1 shall be responsible for the proper assessment leading to the certification or the withdrawal of such certification without prejudice to the responsibility of the controller or processor for compliance with this Regulation. The accreditation shall be issued for a maximum period of five years and may be renewed on the same conditions provided that the certification body meets the requirements set out in this Article.

5. The certification bodies referred to in paragraph 1 shall provide the competent supervisory authorities with the reasons for granting or withdrawing the requested certification.

6. The requirements referred to in paragraph 3 of this Article and the criteria referred to in Article 42(5) shall be made public by the supervisory authority in an easily accessible form. The supervisory authorities shall also transmit those requirements and criteria to the Board. The Board shall collate all certification mechanisms and data protection seals in a register and shall make them publicly available by any appropriate means.

7. Prejudice to Chapter VIII, the competent supervisory authority or the national accreditation body shall revoke an accreditation of a certification body pursuant to paragraph 1 of this Article where the conditions for the accreditation are not, or are no longer, met or where actions taken by a certification body infringe this Regulation.

8. The Commission shall be empowered to adopt delegated acts in accordance with Article 92 for the purpose of specifying the requirements to be taken into account for the data protection certification mechanisms referred to in Article 42(1).

9. The Commission may adopt implementing acts laying down technical standards for certification mechanisms and data protection seals and marks, and mechanisms to promote and recognise those certification mechanisms, seals and marks. Those implementing acts shall be adopted in accordance with the examination procedure referred to in Article 93(2).

CHAPTER V TRANSFERS OF PERSONAL DATA TO THIRD COUNTRIES OR INTERNATIONAL ORGANISATIONS

Article 44 General principle for transfers

Any transfer of personal data which are undergoing processing or are intended for processing after transfer to a third country or to an international organisation shall take place only if, subject to the other provisions of this Regulation, the conditions laid down in this Chapter are complied with by the controller and processor, including for onward transfers of personal data from the third country or an international organisation to another third country or to another international organisation. All provisions in this Chapter shall be applied in order to ensure that the level of protection of natural persons guaranteed by this Regulation is not undermined.

Article 45 Transfers on the basis of an adequacy decision

1. A transfer of personal data to a third country or an international organisation may take place where the Commission has decided that the third country, a territory or one or more specified sectors within that third country, or the international organisation in question ensures an adequate level of protection. Such a transfer shall not require any specific authorisation.

2. When assessing the adequacy of the level of protection, the Commission shall, in particular, take account of the following elements:

    (a) the rule of law, respect for human rights and fundamental freedoms, relevant legislation, both general and sectoral, including concerning public security, defence, national security and criminal law and the access of public authorities to personal data, as well as the implementation of such legislation, data protection rules, professional rules and security measures, including rules for the onward transfer of personal data to another third country or international organisation which are complied with in that country or international organisation, case-law, as well as effective and enforceable data subject rights and effective administrative and judicial redress for the data subjects whose personal data are being transferred;

    (b) the existence and effective functioning of one or more independent supervisory authorities in the third country or to which an international organisation is subject, with responsibility for ensuring and enforcing compliance with the data protection rules, including adequate enforcement powers, for assisting and advising the data subjects in exercising their rights and for cooperation with the supervisory authorities of the Member States; and

    (c) the international commitments the third country or international organisation concerned has entered into, or other obligations arising from legally binding conventions or instruments as well as from its participation in multilateral or regional systems, in particular in relation to the protection of personal data.

3. The Commission, after assessing the adequacy of the level of protection, may decide, by means of implementing act, that a third country, a territory or one or more specified sectors within a third country, or an international organisation ensures an adequate level of protection within the meaning of paragraph 2 of this Article. The implementing act shall provide for a mechanism for a periodic review, at least every four years, which shall take into account all relevant developments in the third country or international organisation. The implementing act shall specify its territorial and sectoral application and, where applicable, identify the supervisory authority or authorities referred to in point (b) of paragraph 2 of this Article. The implementing act shall be adopted in accordance with the examination procedure referred to in Article 93(2).

4. The Commission shall, on an ongoing basis, monitor developments in third countries and international organisations that could affect the functioning of decisions adopted pursuant to paragraph 3 of this Article and decisions adopted on the basis of Article 25(6) of Directive 95/46/EC.

5. The Commission shall, where available information reveals, in particular following the review referred to in paragraph 3 of this Article, that a third country, a territory or one or more specified sectors within a third country, or an international organisation no longer ensures an adequate level of protection within the meaning of paragraph 2 of this Article, to the extent necessary, repeal, amend or suspend the decision referred to in paragraph 3 of this Article by means of implementing acts without retro-active effect. Those implementing acts shall be adopted in accordance with the examination procedure referred to in Article 93(2).

    On duly justified imperative grounds of urgency, the Commission shall adopt immediately applicable implementing acts in accordance with the procedure referred to in Article 93(3).

6. The Commission shall enter into consultations with the third country or international organisation with a view to remedying the situation giving rise to the decision made pursuant to paragraph 5.

7. A decision pursuant to paragraph 5 of this Article is without prejudice to transfers of personal data to the third country, a territory or one or more specified sectors within that third country, or the international organisation in question pursuant to Articles 46 to 49.

8. The Commission shall publish in the *Official Journal of the European Union* and on its website a list of the third countries, territories and specified sectors within a third country and international organisations for which it has decided that an adequate level of protection is or is no longer ensured.

9. Decisions adopted by the Commission on the basis of Article 25(6) of Directive 95/46/EC shall remain in force until amended, replaced or repealed by a Commission Decision adopted in accordance with paragraph 3 or 5 of this Article.

Article 46 Transfers subject to appropriate safeguards

1. In the absence of a decision pursuant to Article 45(3), a controller or processor may transfer personal data to a third country or an international organisation only if the controller or processor has provided appropriate safeguards, and on condition that enforceable data subject rights and effective legal remedies for data subjects are available.

2. The appropriate safeguards referred to in paragraph 1 may be provided for, without requiring any specific authorisation from a supervisory authority, by:

    (a) a legally binding and enforceable instrument between public authorities or bodies;

    (b) binding corporate rules in accordance with Article 47;

    (c) standard data protection clauses adopted by the Commission in accordance with the examination procedure referred to in Article 93(2);

    (d) standard data protection clauses adopted by a supervisory authority and approved by the Commission pursuant to the examination procedure referred to in Article 93(2);

    (e) an approved code of conduct pursuant to Article 40 together with binding and enforceable commitments of the controller or processor in the third country to apply the appropriate safeguards, including as regards data subjects' rights; or

    (f) an approved certification mechanism pursuant to Article 42 together with binding and enforceable commitments of the controller or processor in the third country to apply the appropriate safeguards, including as regards data subjects' rights.

3. Subject to the authorisation from the competent supervisory authority, the appropriate safeguards referred to in paragraph 1 may also be provided for, in particular, by:

    (a) contractual clauses between the controller or processor and the controller, processor or the recipient of the personal data in the third country or international organisation; or

    (b) provisions to be inserted into administrative arrangements between public authorities or bodies which include enforceable and effective data subject rights.

4. The supervisory authority shall apply the consistency mechanism referred to in Article 63 in the cases referred to in paragraph 3 of this Article.

5. Authorisations by a Member State or supervisory authority on the basis of Article 26(2) of Directive 95/46/EC shall remain valid until amended, replaced or repealed, if necessary, by that supervisory authority. Decisions adopted by the Commission on the basis of Article 26(4) of Directive 95/46/EC shall remain in force until amended, replaced or repealed, if necessary,

by a Commission Decision adopted in accordance with paragraph 2 of this Article.

Article 47   Binding corporate rules

1. The competent supervisory authority shall approve binding corporate rules in accordance with the consistency mechanism set out in Article 63, provided that they:

    (a) are legally binding and apply to and are enforced by every member concerned of the group of undertakings, or group of enterprises engaged in a joint economic activity, including their employees;

    (b) expressly confer enforceable rights on data subjects with regard to the processing of their personal data; and

    (c) fulfil the requirements laid down in paragraph 2.

2. The binding corporate rules referred to in paragraph 1 shall specify at least:

    (a) the structure and contact details of the group of undertakings, or group of enterprises engaged in a joint economic activity and of each of its members;

    (b) the data transfers or set of transfers, including the categories of personal data, the type of processing and its purposes, the type of data subjects affected and the identification of the third country or countries in question;

    (c) their legally binding nature, both internally and externally;

    (d) the application of the general data protection principles, in particular purpose limitation, data minimisation, limited storage periods, data quality, data protection by design and by default, legal basis for processing, processing of special categories of personal data, measures to ensure data security, and the requirements in respect of onward transfers to bodies not bound by the binding corporate rules;

    (e) the rights of data subjects in regard to processing and the means to exercise those rights, including the right not to be subject to decisions based solely on automated processing, including profiling in accordance with Article 22, the right to lodge a complaint with the competent supervisory authority and before the competent courts of the Member States in accordance with Article 79, and to obtain redress and, where appropriate, compensation for a breach of the binding corporate rules;

    (f) the acceptance by the controller or processor established on the territory of a Member State of liability for any breaches of the binding corporate rules by any member concerned not established in the Union; the controller or the processor shall be exempt from that liability, in whole or in part, only if it proves that that member is not responsible for the event giving rise to the damage;

(g) how the information on the binding corporate rules, in particular on the provisions referred to in points (d), (e) and (f) of this paragraph is provided to the data subjects in addition to Articles 13 and 14;

(h) the tasks of any data protection officer designated in accordance with Article 37 or any other person or entity in charge of the monitoring compliance with the binding corporate rules within the group of undertakings, or group of enterprises engaged in a joint economic activity, as well as monitoring training and complaint-handling;

(i) the complaint procedures;

(j) the mechanisms within the group of undertakings, or group of enterprises engaged in a joint economic activity for ensuring the verification of compliance with the binding corporate rules. Such mechanisms shall include data protection audits and methods for ensuring corrective actions to protect the rights of the data subject. Results of such verification should be communicated to the person or entity referred to in point (h) and to the board of the controlling undertaking of a group of undertakings, or of the group of enterprises engaged in a joint economic activity, and should be available upon request to the competent supervisory authority;

(k) the mechanisms for reporting and recording changes to the rules and reporting those changes to the supervisory authority;

(l) the cooperation mechanism with the supervisory authority to ensure compliance by any member of the group of undertakings, or group of enterprises engaged in a joint economic activity, in particular by making available to the supervisory authority the results of verifications of the measures referred to in point (j);

(m) the mechanisms for reporting to the competent supervisory authority any legal requirements to which a member of the group of undertakings, or group of enterprises engaged in a joint economic activity is subject in a third country which are likely to have a substantial adverse effect on the guarantees provided by the binding corporate rules; and

(n) the appropriate data protection training to personnel having permanent or regular access to personal data.

3. The Commission may specify the format and procedures for the exchange of information between controllers, processors and supervisory authorities for binding corporate rules within the meaning of this Article. Those implementing acts shall be adopted in accordance with the examination procedure set out in Article 93(2).

Article 48 Transfers or disclosures not authorised by Union law

Any judgment of a court or tribunal and any decision of an administrative authority of a third country requiring a controller or processor to transfer or disclose personal data may only be recognised or enforceable in any manner if based on an international agreement, such as a mutual legal assistance treaty, in force between the requesting third country and the Union or a Member State, without prejudice to other grounds for transfer pursuant to this Chapter.

Article 49   Derogations for specific situations

1. In the absence of an adequacy decision pursuant to Article 45(3), or of appropriate safeguards pursuant to Article 46, including binding corporate rules, a transfer or a set of transfers of personal data to a third country or an international organisation shall take place only on one of the following conditions:

    (a) the data subject has explicitly consented to the proposed transfer, after having been informed of the possible risks of such transfers for the data subject due to the absence of an adequacy decision and appropriate safeguards;

    (b) the transfer is necessary for the performance of a contract between the data subject and the controller or the implementation of pre-contractual measures taken at the data subject's request;

    (c) the transfer is necessary for the conclusion or performance of a contract concluded in the interest of the data subject between the controller and another natural or legal person;

    (d) the transfer is necessary for important reasons of public interest;

    (e) the transfer is necessary for the establishment, exercise or defence of legal claims;

    (f) the transfer is necessary in order to protect the vital interests of the data subject or of other persons, where the data subject is physically or legally incapable of giving consent;

    (g) the transfer is made from a register which according to Union or Member State law is intended to provide information to the public and which is open to consultation either by the public in general or by any person who can demonstrate a legitimate interest, but only to the extent that the conditions laid down by Union or Member State law for consultation are fulfilled in the particular case.

    Where a transfer could not be based on a provision in Article 45 or 46, including the provisions on binding corporate rules, and none of the derogations for a specific situation referred to in the first subparagraph of this paragraph is applicable, a transfer to a third country or an international organisation may take place only if the transfer is not repetitive, concerns only a limited number of data subjects, is necessary for the purposes of compelling legitimate interests pursued by the controller which are not overridden by the interests or rights and freedoms of the data subject, and the controller has assessed all the circumstances surrounding the data transfer and has on the basis of that assessment provided suitable safeguards with regard to the protection of personal data. The controller shall inform the supervisory authority of the transfer. The controller shall, in addition to providing the information referred to in Articles 13 and 14, inform the data subject of the transfer and on the compelling legitimate interests pursued.

2. A transfer pursuant to point (g) of the first subparagraph of paragraph 1 shall not involve the entirety of the personal data or entire categories of the personal data contained in the register. Where the register is intended for consultation by persons having a legitimate interest, the transfer shall be made only at the request of those persons or if they are to be the recipients.

3. Points (a), (b) and (c) of the first subparagraph of paragraph 1 and the second subparagraph thereof shall not apply to activities carried out by public authorities in the exercise of their public powers.

4. The public interest referred to in point (d) of the first subparagraph of paragraph 1 shall be recognised in Union law or in the law of the Member State to which the controller is subject.

5. In the absence of an adequacy decision, Union or Member State law may, for important reasons of public interest, expressly set limits to the transfer of specific categories of personal data to a third country or an international organisation. Member States shall notify such provisions to the Commission.

6. The controller or processor shall document the assessment as well as the suitable safeguards referred to in the second subparagraph of paragraph 1 of this Article in the records referred to in Article 30.

Article 50   International cooperation for the protection of personal data

In relation to third countries and international organisations, the Commission and supervisory authorities shall take appropriate steps to:

(a) develop international cooperation mechanisms to facilitate the effective enforcement of legislation for the protection of personal data;

(b) provide international mutual assistance in the enforcement of legislation for the protection of personal data, including through notification, complaint referral, investigative assistance and information exchange, subject to appropriate safeguards for the protection of personal data and other fundamental rights and freedoms;

(c) engage relevant stakeholders in discussion and activities aimed at furthering international cooperation in the enforcement of legislation for the protection of personal data;

(d) promote the exchange and documentation of personal data protection legislation and practice, including on jurisdictional conflicts with third countries.

CHAPTER VI   INDEPENDENT SUPERVISORY AUTHORITIES

SECTION I   INDEPENDENT STATUS

Article 51   Supervisory authority

1. Each Member State shall provide for one or more independent public authorities to be responsible for monitoring the application of this Regulation, in order to protect the fundamental rights and freedoms of natural persons in relation to processing and to facilitate the free flow of personal data within the Union ('supervisory authority').

2. Each supervisory authority shall contribute to the consistent application of this Regulation throughout the Union. For that purpose, the supervisory authorities shall cooperate with each other and the Commission in accordance with Chapter VII.

3. Where more than one supervisory authority is established in a Member State, that Member State shall designate the supervisory authority which is to represent those authorities in the Board and shall set out the mechanism to ensure compliance by the other authorities with the rules relating to the consistency mechanism referred to in Article 63.

4. Each Member State shall notify to the Commission the provisions of its law which it adopts pursuant to this Chapter, by 25 May 2018 and, without delay, any subsequent amendment affecting them.

Article 52   Independence

1. Each supervisory authority shall act with complete independence in performing its tasks and exercising its powers in accordance with this Regulation.

2. The member or members of each supervisory authority shall, in the performance of their tasks and exercise of their powers in accordance with this Regulation, remain free from external influence, whether direct or indirect, and shall neither seek nor take instructions from anybody.

3. Member or members of each supervisory authority shall refrain from any action incompatible with their duties and shall not, during their term of office, engage in any incompatible occupation, whether gainful or not.

4. Each Member State shall ensure that each supervisory authority is provided with the human, technical and financial resources, premises and infrastructure necessary for the effective performance of its tasks and exercise of its powers, including those to be carried out in the context of mutual assistance, cooperation and participation in the Board.

5. Each Member State shall ensure that each supervisory authority chooses and has its own staff which shall be subject to the exclusive direction of the member or members of the supervisory authority concerned.

6. Each Member State shall ensure that each supervisory authority is subject to financial control which does not affect its independence and that it has separate, public annual budgets, which may be part of the overall state or national budget.

Article 53 General conditions for the members of the supervisory authority

1. Member States shall provide for each member of their supervisory authorities to be appointed by means of a transparent procedure by:

   — their parliament;

   — their government;

   — their head of State; or

   — an independent body entrusted with the appointment under Member State law.

2. Each member shall have the qualifications, experience and skills, in particular in the area of the protection of personal data, required to perform its duties and exercise its powers.

3. The duties of a member shall end in the event of the expiry of the term of office, resignation or compulsory retirement, in accordance with the law of the Member State concerned.

4. A member shall be dismissed only in cases of serious misconduct or if the member no longer fulfils the conditions required for the performance of the duties.

Article 54 Rules on the establishment of the supervisory authority

1. Each Member State shall provide by law for all of the following:

   (a) the establishment of each supervisory authority;

   (b) the qualifications and eligibility conditions required to be appointed as member of each supervisory authority;

   (c) the rules and procedures for the appointment of the member or members of each supervisory authority;

   (d) the duration of the term of the member or members of each supervisory authority of no less than four years, except for the first appointment after 24 May 2016, part of which may take place for a shorter period where that is necessary to protect the independence of the supervisory authority by means of a staggered appointment procedure;

   (e) whether and, if so, for how many terms the member or members of each supervisory authority is eligible for reappointment;

(f)   the conditions governing the obligations of the member or members and staff of each supervisory authority, prohibitions on actions, occupations and benefits incompatible therewith during and after the term of office and rules governing the cessation of employment.

2.   The member or members and the staff of each supervisory authority shall, in accordance with Union or Member State law, be subject to a duty of professional secrecy both during and after their term of office, with regard to any confidential information which has come to their knowledge in the course of the performance of their tasks or exercise of their powers. During their term of office, that duty of professional secrecy shall in particular apply to reporting by natural persons of infringements of this Regulation.

SECTION 2   COMPETENCE, TASKS AND POWERS

Article 55   Competence

1.   Each supervisory authority shall be competent for the performance of the tasks assigned to and the exercise of the powers conferred on it in accordance with this Regulation on the territory of its own Member State.

2.   Where processing is carried out by public authorities or private bodies acting on the basis of point (c) or (e) of Article 6(1), the supervisory authority of the Member State concerned shall be competent. In such cases Article 56 does not apply.

3.   Supervisory authorities shall not be competent to supervise processing operations of courts acting in their judicial capacity.

Article 56   Competence of the lead supervisory authority

1.   Without prejudice to Article 55, the supervisory authority of the main establishment or of the single establishment of the controller or processor shall be competent to act as lead supervisory authority for the cross-border processing carried out by that controller or processor in accordance with the procedure provided in Article 60.

2.   By derogation from paragraph 1, each supervisory authority shall be competent to handle a complaint lodged with it or a possible infringement of this Regulation, if the subject matter relates only to an establishment in its Member State or substantially affects data subjects only in its Member State.

3.   In the cases referred to in paragraph 2 of this Article, the supervisory authority shall inform the lead supervisory authority without delay on that matter. Within a period of three weeks after being informed the lead supervisory authority shall decide whether or not it will handle the case in accordance with the procedure provided in Article 60, taking into account whether or not there is an establishment of the controller or processor in the Member State of which the supervisory authority informed it.

4. Where the lead supervisory authority decides to handle the case, the procedure provided in Article 60 shall apply. The supervisory authority which informed the lead supervisory authority may submit to the lead supervisory authority a draft for a decision. The lead supervisory authority shall take utmost account of that draft when preparing the draft decision referred to in Article 60(3).

5. Where the lead supervisory authority decides not to handle the case, the supervisory authority which informed the lead supervisory authority shall handle it according to Articles 61 and 62.

6. The lead supervisory authority shall be the sole interlocutor of the controller or processor for the cross-border processing carried out by that controller or processor.

Article 57 Tasks

1. Without prejudice to other tasks set out under this Regulation, each supervisory authority shall on its territory:

    (a) monitor and enforce the application of this Regulation;

    (b) promote public awareness and understanding of the risks, rules, safeguards and rights in relation to processing. Activities addressed specifically to children shall receive specific attention;

    (c) advise, in accordance with Member State law, the national parliament, the government, and other institutions and bodies on legislative and administrative measures relating to the protection of natural persons' rights and freedoms with regard to processing;

    (d) promote the awareness of controllers and processors of their obligations under this Regulation;

    (e) upon request, provide information to any data subject concerning the exercise of their rights under this Regulation and, if appropriate, cooperate with the supervisory authorities in other Member States to that end;

    (f) handle complaints lodged by a data subject, or by a body, organisation or association in accordance with Article 80, and investigate, to the extent appropriate, the subject matter of the complaint and inform the complainant of the progress and the outcome of the investigation within a reasonable period, in particular if further investigation or coordination with another supervisory authority is necessary;

    (g) cooperate with, including sharing information and provide mutual assistance to, other supervisory authorities with a view to ensuring the consistency of application and enforcement of this Regulation;

    (h) conduct investigations on the application of this Regulation, including on the basis of information received from another supervisory authority or other public authority;

(i) monitor relevant developments, insofar as they have an impact on the protection of personal data, in particular the development of information and communication technologies and commercial practices;

(j) adopt standard contractual clauses referred to in Article 28(8) and in point (d) of Article 46(2);

(k) establish and maintain a list in relation to the requirement for data protection impact assessment pursuant to Article 35(4);

(l) give advice on the processing operations referred to in Article 36(2);

(m) encourage the drawing up of codes of conduct pursuant to Article 40(1) and provide an opinion and approve such codes of conduct which provide sufficient safeguards, pursuant to Article 40(5);

(n) encourage the establishment of data protection certification mechanisms and of data protection seals and marks pursuant to Article 42(1), and approve the criteria of certification pursuant to Article 42(5);

(o) where applicable, carry out a periodic review of certifications issued in accordance with Article 42(7);

(p) draft and publish the criteria for accreditation of a body for monitoring codes of conduct pursuant to Article 41 and of a certification body pursuant to Article 43;

(q) conduct the accreditation of a body for monitoring codes of conduct pursuant to Article 41 and of a certification body pursuant to Article 43;

(r) authorise contractual clauses and provisions referred to in Article 46(3);

(s) approve binding corporate rules pursuant to Article 47;

(t) contribute to the activities of the Board;

(u) keep internal records of infringements of this Regulation and of measures taken in accordance with Article 58(2); and

(v) fulfil any other tasks related to the protection of personal data.

2. Each supervisory authority shall facilitate the submission of complaints referred to in point (f) of paragraph 1 by measures such as a complaint submission form which can also be completed electronically, without excluding other means of communication.

3. The performance of the tasks of each supervisory authority shall be free of charge for the data subject and, where applicable, for the data protection officer.

4. Requests are manifestly unfounded or excessive, in particular because of their repetitive character, the supervisory authority may charge a reasonable fee based on administrative costs, or refuse to act on the request. The

supervisory authority shall bear the burden of demonstrating the manifestly unfounded or excessive character of the request.

Article 58   Powers

1.   Each supervisory authority shall have all of the following investigative powers:

 (a)   to order the controller and the processor, and, where applicable, the controller's or the processor's representative to provide any information it requires for the performance of its tasks;

 (b)   to carry out investigations in the form of data protection audits;

 (c)   to carry out a review on certifications issued pursuant to Article 42(7);

 (d)   to notify the controller or the processor of an alleged infringement of this Regulation;

 (e)   to obtain, from the controller and the processor, access to all personal data and to all information necessary for the performance of its tasks;

 (f)   to obtain access to any premises of the controller and the processor, including to any data processing equipment and means, in accordance with Union or Member State procedural law.

2.   Each supervisory authority shall have all of the following corrective powers:

 (a)   to issue warnings to a controller or processor that intended processing operations are likely to infringe provisions of this Regulation;

 (b)   to issue reprimands to a controller or a processor where processing operations have infringed provisions of this Regulation;

 (c)   to order the controller or the processor to comply with the data subject's requests to exercise his or her rights pursuant to this Regulation;

 (d)   to order the controller or processor to bring processing operations into compliance with the provisions of this Regulation, where appropriate, in a specified manner and within a specified period;

 (e)   to order the controller to communicate a personal data breach to the data subject;

 (f)   to impose a temporary or definitive limitation including a ban on processing;

 (g)   to order the rectification or erasure of personal data or restriction of processing pursuant to Articles 16, 17 and 18 and the notification of such actions to recipients to whom the personal data have been disclosed pursuant to Article 17(2) and Article 19;

 (h)   to withdraw a certification or to order the certification body to withdraw a certification issued pursuant to Articles 42 and 43, or to order the certification body not to issue certification if the requirements for the certification are not or are no longer met;

(i)   to impose an administrative fine pursuant to Article 83, in addition to, or instead of measures referred to in this paragraph, depending on the circumstances of each individual case;

(j)   to order the suspension of data flows to a recipient in a third country or to an international organisation.

3.   Each supervisory authority shall have all of the following authorisation and advisory powers:

(a)   to advise the controller in accordance with the prior consultation procedure referred to in Article 36;

(b)   to issue, on its own initiative or on request, opinions to the national parliament, the Member State government or, in accordance with Member State law, to other institutions and bodies as well as to the public on any issue related to the protection of personal data;

(c)   to authorise processing referred to in Article 36(5), if the law of the Member State requires such prior authorisation;

(d)   to issue an opinion and approve draft codes of conduct pursuant to Article 40(5);

(e)   to accredit certification bodies pursuant to Article 43;

(f)   to issue certifications and approve criteria of certification in accordance with Article 42(5);

(g)   to adopt standard data protection clauses referred to in Article 28(8) and in point (d) of Article 46(2);

(h)   to authorise contractual clauses referred to in point (a) of Article 46(3);

(i)   to authorise administrative arrangements referred to in point (b) of Article 46(3);

(j)   to approve binding corporate rules pursuant to Article 47.

4.   The exercise of the powers conferred on the supervisory authority pursuant to this Article shall be subject to appropriate safeguards, including effective judicial remedy and due process, set out in Union and Member State law in accordance with the Charter.

5.   Each Member State shall provide by law that its supervisory authority shall have the power to bring infringements of this Regulation to the attention of the judicial authorities and where appropriate, to commence or engage otherwise in legal proceedings, in order to enforce the provisions of this Regulation.

6.   Each Member State may provide by law that its supervisory authority shall have additional powers to those referred to in paragraphs 1, 2 and 3. The exercise of those powers shall not impair the effective operation of Chapter VII.

Article 59 Activity reports

Each supervisory authority shall draw up an annual report on its activities, which may include a list of types of infringement notified and types of measures taken in accordance with Article 58(2). Those reports shall be transmitted to the national parliament, the government and other authorities as designated by Member State law. They shall be made available to the public, to the Commission and to the Board.

CHAPTER VII   COOPERATION AND CONSISTENCY

SECTION I   COOPERATION

Article 60   Cooperation between the lead supervisory authority and the other supervisory authorities concerned

1. The lead supervisory authority shall cooperate with the other supervisory authorities concerned in accordance with this Article in an endeavour to reach consensus. The lead supervisory authority and the supervisory authorities concerned shall exchange all relevant information with each other.

2. The lead supervisory authority may request at any time other supervisory authorities concerned to provide mutual assistance pursuant to Article 61 and may conduct joint operations pursuant to Article 62, in particular for carrying out investigations or for monitoring the implementation of a measure concerning a controller or processor established in another Member State.

3. The lead supervisory authority shall, without delay, communicate the relevant information on the matter to the other supervisory authorities concerned. It shall without delay submit a draft decision to the other supervisory authorities concerned for their opinion and take due account of their views.

4. Where any of the other supervisory authorities concerned within a period of four weeks after having been consulted in accordance with paragraph 3 of this Article, expresses a relevant and reasoned objection to the draft decision, the lead supervisory authority shall, if it does not follow the relevant and reasoned objection or is of the opinion that the objection is not relevant or reasoned, submit the matter to the consistency mechanism referred to in Article 63.

5. Where the lead supervisory authority intends to follow the relevant and reasoned objection made, it shall submit to the other supervisory authorities concerned a revised draft decision for their opinion. That revised draft decision shall be subject to the procedure referred to in paragraph 4 within a period of two weeks.

6. Where none of the other supervisory authorities concerned has objected to the draft decision submitted by the lead supervisory authority within the period referred to in paragraphs 4 and 5, the lead supervisory authority and

the supervisory authorities concerned shall be deemed to be in agreement with that draft decision and shall be bound by it.

7. The lead supervisory authority shall adopt and notify the decision to the main establishment or single establishment of the controller or processor, as the case may be and inform the other supervisory authorities concerned and the Board of the decision in question, including a summary of the relevant facts and grounds. The supervisory authority with which a complaint has been lodged shall inform the complainant on the decision.

8. By derogation from paragraph 7, where a complaint is dismissed or rejected, the supervisory authority with which the complaint was lodged shall adopt the decision and notify it to the complainant and shall inform the controller thereof.

9. Where the lead supervisory authority and the supervisory authorities concerned agree to dismiss or reject parts of a complaint and to act on other parts of that complaint, a separate decision shall be adopted for each of those parts of the matter. The lead supervisory authority shall adopt the decision for the part concerning actions in relation to the controller, shall notify it to the main establishment or single establishment of the controller or processor on the territory of its Member State and shall inform the complainant thereof, while the supervisory authority of the complainant shall adopt the decision for the part concerning dismissal or rejection of that complaint, and shall notify it to that complainant and shall inform the controller or processor thereof.

10. After being notified of the decision of the lead supervisory authority pursuant to paragraphs 7 and 9, the controller or processor shall take the necessary measures to ensure compliance with the decision as regards processing activities in the context of all its establishments in the Union. The controller or processor shall notify the measures taken for complying with the decision to the lead supervisory authority, which shall inform the other supervisory authorities concerned.

11. Where, in exceptional circumstances, a supervisory authority concerned has reasons to consider that there is an urgent need to act in order to protect the interests of data subjects, the urgency procedure referred to in Article 66 shall apply.

12. The lead supervisory authority and the other supervisory authorities concerned shall supply the information required under this Article to each other by electronic means, using a standardised format.

Article 61   Mutual assistance

1. Supervisory authorities shall provide each other with relevant information and mutual assistance in order to implement and apply this Regulation in a consistent manner, and shall put in place measures for effective cooperation with one another. Mutual assistance shall cover, in particular, information

requests and supervisory measures, such as requests to carry out prior authorisations and consultations, inspections and investigations.

2. Each supervisory authority shall take all appropriate measures required to reply to a request of another supervisory authority without undue delay and no later than one month after receiving the request. Such measures may include, in particular, the transmission of relevant information on the conduct of an investigation.

3. Requests for assistance shall contain all the necessary information, including the purpose of and reasons for the request. Information exchanged shall be used only for the purpose for which it was requested.

4. The requested supervisory authority shall not refuse to comply with the request unless:

   (a) it is not competent for the subject-matter of the request or for the measures it is requested to execute; or

   (b) compliance with the request would infringe this Regulation or Union or Member State law to which the supervisory authority receiving the request is subject.

5. The requested supervisory authority shall inform the requesting supervisory authority of the results or, as the case may be, of the progress of the measures taken in order to respond to the request. The requested supervisory authority shall provide reasons for any refusal to comply with a request pursuant to paragraph 4.

6. Requested supervisory authorities shall, as a rule, supply the information requested by other supervisory authorities by electronic means, using a standardised format.

7. Requested supervisory authorities shall not charge a fee for any action taken by them pursuant to a request for mutual assistance. Supervisory authorities may agree on rules to indemnify each other for specific expenditure arising from the provision of mutual assistance in exceptional circumstances.

8. Where a supervisory authority does not provide the information referred to in paragraph 5 of this Article within one month of receiving the request of another supervisory authority, the requesting supervisory authority may adopt a provisional measure on the territory of its Member State in accordance with Article 55(1). In that case, the urgent need to act under Article 66(1) shall be presumed to be met and require an urgent binding decision from the Board pursuant to Article 66(2).

9. The Commission may, by means of implementing acts, specify the format and procedures for mutual assistance referred to in this Article and the arrangements for the exchange of information by electronic means between supervisory authorities, and between supervisory authorities and the Board, in particular the standardised format referred to in paragraph 6 of this Article. Those implementing acts shall be adopted in accordance with the examination procedure referred to in Article 93(2).

Article 62   Joint operations of supervisory authorities

1.   The supervisory authorities shall, where appropriate, conduct joint operations including joint investigations and joint enforcement measures in which members or staff of the supervisory authorities of other Member States are involved.

2.   Where the controller or processor has establishments in several Member States or where a significant number of data subjects in more than one Member State are likely to be substantially affected by processing operations, a supervisory authority of each of those Member States shall have the right to participate in joint operations. The supervisory authority which is competent pursuant to Article 56(1) or (4) shall invite the supervisory authority of each of those Member States to take part in the joint operations and shall respond without delay to the request of a supervisory authority to participate.

3.   A supervisory authority may, in accordance with Member State law, and with the seconding supervisory authority's authorisation, confer powers, including investigative powers on the seconding supervisory authority's members or staff involved in joint operations or, in so far as the law of the Member State of the host supervisory authority permits, allow the seconding supervisory authority's members or staff to exercise their investigative powers in accordance with the law of the Member State of the seconding supervisory authority. Such investigative powers may be exercised only under the guidance and in the presence of members or staff of the host supervisory authority. The seconding supervisory authority's members or staff shall be subject to the Member State law of the host supervisory authority.

4.   Where, in accordance with paragraph 1, staff of a seconding supervisory authority operate in another Member State, the Member State of the host supervisory authority shall assume responsibility for their actions, including liability, for any damage caused by them during their operations, in accordance with the law of the Member State in whose territory they are operating.

5.   The Member State in whose territory the damage was caused shall make good such damage under the conditions applicable to damage caused by its own staff. The Member State of the seconding supervisory authority whose staff has caused damage to any person in the territory of another Member State shall reimburse that other Member State in full any sums it has paid to the persons entitled on their behalf.

6.   Without prejudice to the exercise of its rights *vis-à-vis* third parties and with the exception of paragraph 5, each Member State shall refrain, in the case provided for in paragraph 1, from requesting reimbursement from another Member State in relation to damage referred to in paragraph 4.

7.   Where a joint operation is intended and a supervisory authority does not, within one month, comply with the obligation laid down in the second

sentence of paragraph 2 of this Article, the other supervisory authorities may adopt a provisional measure on the territory of its Member State in accordance with Article 55. In that case, the urgent need to act under Article 66(1) shall be presumed to be met and require an opinion or an urgent binding decision from the Board pursuant to Article 66(2).

SECTION 2 CONSISTENCY

Article 63 Consistency mechanism

In order to contribute to the consistent application of this Regulation throughout the Union, the supervisory authorities shall cooperate with each other and, where relevant, with the Commission, through the consistency mechanism as set out in this Section.

Article 64 Opinion of the Board

1. The Board shall issue an opinion where a competent supervisory authority intends to adopt any of the measures below. To that end, the competent supervisory authority shall communicate the draft decision to the Board, when it:

    (a) aims to adopt a list of the processing operations subject to the requirement for a data protection impact assessment pursuant to Article 35(4);

    (b) concerns a matter pursuant to Article 40(7) whether a draft code of conduct or an amendment or extension to a code of conduct complies with this Regulation;

    (c) aims to approve the criteria for accreditation of a body pursuant to Article 41(3) or a certification body pursuant to Article 43(3);

    (d) aims to determine standard data protection clauses referred to in point (d) of Article 46(2) and in Article 28(8);

    (e) aims to authorise contractual clauses referred to in point (a) of Article 46(3); or

    (f) aims to approve binding corporate rules within the meaning of Article 47.

2. Any supervisory authority, the Chair of the Board or the Commission may request that any matter of general application or producing effects in more than one Member State be examined by the Board with a view to obtaining an opinion, in particular where a competent supervisory authority does not comply with the obligations for mutual assistance in accordance with Article 61 or for joint operations in accordance with Article 62.

3. In the cases referred to in paragraphs 1 and 2, the Board shall issue an opinion on the matter submitted to it provided that it has not already issued

an opinion on the same matter. That opinion shall be adopted within eight weeks by simple majority of the members of the Board. That period may be extended by a further six weeks, taking into account the complexity of the subject matter. Regarding the draft decision referred to in paragraph 1 circulated to the members of the Board in accordance with paragraph 5, a member which has not objected within a reasonable period indicated by the Chair, shall be deemed to be in agreement with the draft decision.

4. Supervisory authorities and the Commission shall, without undue delay, communicate by electronic means to the Board, using a standardised format any relevant information, including as the case may be a summary of the facts, the draft decision, the grounds which make the enactment of such measure necessary, and the views of other supervisory authorities concerned.

5. The Chair of the Board shall, without undue, delay inform by electronic means:

    (a) the members of the Board and the Commission of any relevant information which has been communicated to it using a standardised format. The secretariat of the Board shall, where necessary, provide translations of relevant information; and

    (b) the supervisory authority referred to, as the case may be, in paragraphs 1 and 2, and the Commission of the opinion and make it public.

6. The competent supervisory authority shall not adopt its draft decision referred to in paragraph 1 within the period referred to in paragraph 3.

7. The supervisory authority referred to in paragraph 1 shall take utmost account of the opinion of the Board and shall, within two weeks after receiving the opinion, communicate to the Chair of the Board by electronic means whether it will maintain or amend its draft decision and, if any, the amended draft decision, using a standardised format.

8. Where the supervisory authority concerned informs the Chair of the Board within the period referred to in paragraph 7 of this Article that it does not intend to follow the opinion of the Board, in whole or in part, providing the relevant grounds, Article 65(1) shall apply.

Article 65   Dispute resolution by the Board

1. In order to ensure the correct and consistent application of this Regulation in individual cases, the Board shall adopt a binding decision in the following cases:

    (a) where, in a case referred to in Article 60(4), a supervisory authority concerned has raised a relevant and reasoned objection to a draft decision of the lead authority or the lead authority has rejected such an objection as being not relevant or reasoned. The binding decision shall concern all the matters which are the subject of the relevant and reasoned objection, in particular whether there is an infringement of this Regulation;

(b) where there are conflicting views on which of the supervisory authorities concerned is competent for the main establishment;

(c) where a competent supervisory authority does not request the opinion of the Board in the cases referred to in Article 64(1), or does not follow the opinion of the Board issued under Article 64. In that case, any supervisory authority concerned or the Commission may communicate the matter to the Board.

2. The decision referred to in paragraph 1 shall be adopted within one month from the referral of the subject-matter by a two-thirds majority of the members of the Board. That period may be extended by a further month on account of the complexity of the subject-matter. The decision referred to in paragraph 1 shall be reasoned and addressed to the lead supervisory authority and all the supervisory authorities concerned and binding on them.

3. Where the Board has been unable to adopt a decision within the periods referred to in paragraph 2, it shall adopt its decision within two weeks following the expiration of the second month referred to in paragraph 2 by a simple majority of the members of the Board. Where the members of the Board are split, the decision shall by adopted by the vote of its Chair.

4. The supervisory authorities concerned shall not adopt a decision on the subject matter submitted to the Board under paragraph 1 during the periods referred to in paragraphs 2 and 3.

5. The Chair of the Board shall notify, without undue delay, the decision referred to in paragraph 1 to the supervisory authorities concerned. It shall inform the Commission thereof. The decision shall be published on the website of the Board without delay after the supervisory authority has notified the final decision referred to in paragraph 6.

6. The lead supervisory authority or, as the case may be, the supervisory authority with which the complaint has been lodged shall adopt its final decision on the basis of the decision referred to in paragraph 1 of this Article, without undue delay and at the latest by one month after the Board has notified its decision. The lead supervisory authority or, as the case may be, the supervisory authority with which the complaint has been lodged, shall inform the Board of the date when its final decision is notified respectively to the controller or the processor and to the data subject. The final decision of the supervisory authorities concerned shall be adopted under the terms of Article 60(7), (8) and (9). The final decision shall refer to the decision referred to in paragraph 1 of this Article and shall specify that the decision referred to in that paragraph will be published on the website of the Board in accordance with paragraph 5 of this Article. The final decision shall attach the decision referred to in paragraph 1 of this Article.

Article 66   Urgency procedure

1. In exceptional circumstances, where a supervisory authority concerned considers that there is an urgent need to act in order to protect the rights and freedoms of data subjects, it may, by way of derogation from the consistency mechanism referred to in Articles 63, 64 and 65 or the procedure referred to in Article 60, immediately adopt provisional measures intended to produce legal effects on its own territory with a specified period of validity which shall not exceed three months. The supervisory authority shall, without delay, communicate those measures and the reasons for adopting them to the other supervisory authorities concerned, to the Board and to the Commission.

2. Where a supervisory authority has taken a measure pursuant to paragraph 1 and considers that final measures need urgently be adopted, it may request an urgent opinion or an urgent binding decision from the Board, giving reasons for requesting such opinion or decision.

3. Any supervisory authority may request an urgent opinion or an urgent binding decision, as the case may be, from the Board where a competent supervisory authority has not taken an appropriate measure in a situation where there is an urgent need to act, in order to protect the rights and freedoms of data subjects, giving reasons for requesting such opinion or decision, including for the urgent need to act.

4. By derogation from Article 64(3) and Article 65(2), an urgent opinion or an urgent binding decision referred to in paragraphs 2 and 3 of this Article shall be adopted within two weeks by simple majority of the members of the Board.

Article 67   Exchange of information

The Commission may adopt implementing acts of general scope in order to specify the arrangements for the exchange of information by electronic means between supervisory authorities, and between supervisory authorities and the Board, in particular the standardised format referred to in Article 64.

Those implementing acts shall be adopted in accordance with the examination procedure referred to in Article 93(2).

SECTION 3   EUROPEAN DATA PROTECTION BOARD

Article 68   European Data Protection Board

1. The European Data Protection Board (the 'Board') is hereby established as a body of the Union and shall have legal personality.

2. The Board shall be represented by its Chair.

3. The Board shall be composed of the head of one supervisory authority of each Member State and of the European Data Protection Supervisor, or their respective representatives.

4. Where in a Member State more than one supervisory authority is responsible for monitoring the application of the provisions pursuant to this Regulation, a joint representative shall be appointed in accordance with that Member State's law.

5. The Commission shall have the right to participate in the activities and meetings of the Board without voting right. The Commission shall designate a representative. The Chair of the Board shall communicate to the Commission the activities of the Board.

6. In the cases referred to in Article 65, the European Data Protection Supervisor shall have voting rights only on decisions which concern principles and rules applicable to the Union institutions, bodies, offices and agencies which correspond in substance to those of this Regulation.

Article 69   Independence

1. The Board shall act independently when performing its tasks or exercising its powers pursuant to Articles 70 and 71.

2. Without prejudice to requests by the Commission referred to in point (b) of Article 70(1) and in Article 70(2), the Board shall, in the performance of its tasks or the exercise of its powers, neither seek nor take instructions from anybody.

Article 70   Tasks of the Board

1. The Board shall ensure the consistent application of this Regulation. To that end, the Board shall, on its own initiative or, where relevant, at the request of the Commission, in particular:

    (a) monitor and ensure the correct application of this Regulation in the cases provided for in Articles 64 and 65 without prejudice to the tasks of national supervisory authorities;

    (b) advise the Commission on any issue related to the protection of personal data in the Union, including on any proposed amendment of this Regulation;

    (c) advise the Commission on the format and procedures for the exchange of information between controllers, processors and supervisory authorities for binding corporate rules;

    (d) issue guidelines, recommendations, and best practices on procedures for erasing links, copies or replications of personal data from publicly available communication services as referred to in Article 17(2);

(e) examine, on its own initiative, on request of one of its members or on request of the Commission, any question covering the application of this Regulation and issue guidelines, recommendations and best practices in order to encourage consistent application of this Regulation;

(f) issue guidelines, recommendations and best practices in accordance with point (e) of this paragraph for further specifying the criteria and conditions for decisions based on profiling pursuant to Article 22(2);

(g) issue guidelines, recommendations and best practices in accordance with point (e) of this paragraph for establishing the personal data breaches and determining the undue delay referred to in Article 33(1) and (2) and for the particular circumstances in which a controller or a processor is required to notify the personal data breach;

(h) issue guidelines, recommendations and best practices in accordance with point (e) of this paragraph as to the circumstances in which a personal data breach is likely to result in a high risk to the rights and freedoms of the natural persons referred to in Article 34(1).

(i) issue guidelines, recommendations and best practices in accordance with point (e) of this paragraph for the purpose of further specifying the criteria and requirements for personal data transfers based on binding corporate rules adhered to by controllers and binding corporate rules adhered to by processors and on further necessary requirements to ensure the protection of personal data of the data subjects concerned referred to in Article 47;

(j) issue guidelines, recommendations and best practices in accordance with point (e) of this paragraph for the purpose of further specifying the criteria and requirements for the personal data transfers on the basis of Article 49(1);

(k) draw up guidelines for supervisory authorities concerning the application of measures referred to in Article 58(1), (2) and (3) and the setting of administrative fines pursuant to Article 83;

(l) review the practical application of the guidelines, recommendations and best practices referred to in points (e) and (f);

(m) issue guidelines, recommendations and best practices in accordance with point (e) of this paragraph for establishing common procedures for reporting by natural persons of infringements of this Regulation pursuant to Article 54(2);

(n) encourage the drawing-up of codes of conduct and the establishment of data protection certification mechanisms and data protection seals and marks pursuant to Articles 40 and 42;

(o) carry out the accreditation of certification bodies and its periodic review pursuant to Article 43 and maintain a public register of accredited bodies pursuant to Article 43(6) and of the accredited controllers or processors established in third countries pursuant to Article 42(7);

(p)   specify the requirements referred to in Article 43(3) with a view to the accreditation of certification bodies under Article 42;

(q)   provide the Commission with an opinion on the certification requirements referred to in Article 43(8);

(r)   provide the Commission with an opinion on the icons referred to in Article 12(7);

(s)   provide the Commission with an opinion for the assessment of the adequacy of the level of protection in a third country or international organisation, including for the assessment whether a third country, a territory or one or more specified sectors within that third country, or an international organisation no longer ensures an adequate level of protection. To that end, the Commission shall provide the Board with all necessary documentation, including correspondence with the government of the third country, with regard to that third country, territory or specified sector, or with the international organisation.

(t)   issue opinions on draft decisions of supervisory authorities pursuant to the consistency mechanism referred to in Article 64(1), on matters submitted pursuant to Article 64(2) and to issue binding decisions pursuant to Article 65, including in cases referred to in Article 66;

(u)   promote the cooperation and the effective bilateral and multilateral exchange of information and best practices between the supervisory authorities;

(v)   promote common training programmes and facilitate personnel exchanges between the supervisory authorities and, where appropriate, with the supervisory authorities of third countries or with international organisations;

(w)   promote the exchange of knowledge and documentation on data protection legislation and practice with data protection supervisory authorities worldwide.

(x)   issue opinions on codes of conduct drawn up at Union level pursuant to Article 40(9); and

(y)   maintain a publicly accessible electronic register of decisions taken by supervisory authorities and courts on issues handled in the consistency mechanism.

2.   Where the Commission requests advice from the Board, it may indicate a time limit, taking into account the urgency of the matter.

3.   The Board shall forward its opinions, guidelines, recommendations, and best practices to the Commission and to the committee referred to in Article 93 and make them public.

4.   The Board shall, where appropriate, consult interested parties and give them the opportunity to comment within a reasonable period. The Board shall, without prejudice to Article 76, make the results of the consultation procedure publicly available.

Article 71   Reports

1.   The Board shall draw up an annual report regarding the protection of natural persons with regard to processing in the Union and, where relevant, in third countries and international organisations. The report shall be made public and be transmitted to the European Parliament, to the Council and to the Commission.

2.   The annual report shall include a review of the practical application of the guidelines, recommendations and best practices referred to in point (l) of Article 70(1) as well as of the binding decisions referred to in Article 65.

Article 72   Procedure

1.   The Board shall take decisions by a simple majority of its members, unless otherwise provided for in this Regulation.

2.   The Board shall adopt its own rules of procedure by a two-thirds majority of its members and organise its own operational arrangements.

Article 73   Chair

1.   The Board shall elect a chair and two deputy chairs from amongst its members by simple majority.

2.   The term of office of the Chair and of the deputy chairs shall be five years and be renewable once.

Article 74   Tasks of the Chair

1.   The Chair shall have the following tasks:

    (a)   to convene the meetings of the Board and prepare its agenda;

    (b)   to notify decisions adopted by the Board pursuant to Article 65 to the lead supervisory authority and the supervisory authorities concerned;

    (c)   to ensure the timely performance of the tasks of the Board, in particular in relation to the consistency mechanism referred to in Article 63.

2.   The Board shall lay down the allocation of tasks between the Chair and the deputy chairs in its rules of procedure.

Article 75   Secretariat

1.   The Board shall have a secretariat, which shall be provided by the European Data Protection Supervisor.

2.   The secretariat shall perform its tasks exclusively under the instructions of the Chair of the Board.

3. The staff of the European Data Protection Supervisor involved in carrying out the tasks conferred on the Board by this Regulation shall be subject to separate reporting lines from the staff involved in carrying out tasks conferred on the European Data Protection Supervisor.

4. Where appropriate, the Board and the European Data Protection Supervisor shall establish and publish a Memorandum of Understanding implementing this Article, determining the terms of their cooperation, and applicable to the staff of the European Data Protection Supervisor involved in carrying out the tasks conferred on the Board by this Regulation.

5. The secretariat shall provide analytical, administrative and logistical support to the Board.

6. The secretariat shall be responsible in particular for:

    (a) the day-to-day business of the Board;

    (b) communication between the members of the Board, its Chair and the Commission;

    (c) communication with other institutions and the public;

    (d) the use of electronic means for the internal and external communication;

    (e) the translation of relevant information;

    (f) the preparation and follow-up of the meetings of the Board;

    (g) the preparation, drafting and publication of opinions, decisions on the settlement of disputes between supervisory authorities and other texts adopted by the Board.

Article 76   Confidentiality

1. The discussions of the Board shall be confidential where the Board deems it necessary, as provided for in its rules of procedure.

2. Access to documents submitted to members of the Board, experts and representatives of third parties shall be governed by Regulation (EC) No 1049/2001 of the European Parliament and of the Council[21].

CHAPTER VIII   REMEDIES, LIABILITY AND PENALTIES

Article 77   Right to lodge a complaint with a supervisory authority

1. Without prejudice to any other administrative or judicial remedy, every data subject shall have the right to lodge a complaint with a supervisory authority,

---

21 Regulation (EC) No 1049/2001 of the European Parliament and of the Council of 30 May 2001 regarding public access to European Parliament, Council and Commission documents (OJ L 145, 31.5.2001, p. 43).

in particular in the Member State of his or her habitual residence, place of work or place of the alleged infringement if the data subject considers that the processing of personal data relating to him or her infringes this Regulation.

2. The supervisory authority with which the complaint has been lodged shall inform the complainant on the progress and the outcome of the complaint including the possibility of a judicial remedy pursuant to Article 78.

Article 78   Right to an effective judicial remedy against a supervisory authority

1. Without prejudice to any other administrative or non-judicial remedy, each natural or legal person shall have the right to an effective judicial remedy against a legally binding decision of a supervisory authority concerning them.

2. Without prejudice to any other administrative or non-judicial remedy, each data subject shall have the right to a an effective judicial remedy where the supervisory authority which is competent pursuant to Articles 55 and 56 does not handle a complaint or does not inform the data subject within three months on the progress or outcome of the complaint lodged pursuant to Article 77.

3. Proceedings against a supervisory authority shall be brought before the courts of the Member State where the supervisory authority is established.

4. Where proceedings are brought against a decision of a supervisory authority which was preceded by an opinion or a decision of the Board in the consistency mechanism, the supervisory authority shall forward that opinion or decision to the court.

Article 79   Right to an effective judicial remedy against a controller or processor

1. Without prejudice to any available administrative or non-judicial remedy, including the right to lodge a complaint with a supervisory authority pursuant to Article 77, each data subject shall have the right to an effective judicial remedy where he or she considers that his or her rights under this Regulation have been infringed as a result of the processing of his or her personal data in non-compliance with this Regulation.

2. Proceedings against a controller or a processor shall be brought before the courts of the Member State where the controller or processor has an establishment. Alternatively, such proceedings may be brought before the courts of the Member State where the data subject has his or her habitual residence, unless the controller or processor is a public authority of a Member State acting in the exercise of its public powers.

Article 80 Representation of data subjects

1. The data subject shall have the right to mandate a not-for-profit body, organisation or association which has been properly constituted in accordance with the law of a Member State, has statutory objectives which are in the public interest, and is active in the field of the protection of data subjects' rights and freedoms with regard to the protection of their personal data to lodge the complaint on his or her behalf, to exercise the rights referred to in Articles 77, 78 and 79 on his or her behalf, and to exercise the right to receive compensation referred to in Article 82 on his or her behalf where provided for by Member State law.

2. Member States may provide that any body, organisation or association referred to in paragraph 1 of this Article, independently of a data subject's mandate, has the right to lodge, in that Member State, a complaint with the supervisory authority which is competent pursuant to Article 77 and to exercise the rights referred to in Articles 78 and 79 if it considers that the rights of a data subject under this Regulation have been infringed as a result of the processing.

Article 81 Suspension of proceedings

1. Where a competent court of a Member State has information on proceedings, concerning the same subject matter as regards processing by the same controller or processor, that are pending in a court in another Member State, it shall contact that court in the other Member State to confirm the existence of such proceedings.

2. Where proceedings concerning the same subject matter as regards processing of the same controller or processor are pending in a court in another Member State, any competent court other than the court first seized may suspend its proceedings.

3. Where those proceedings are pending at first instance, any court other than the court first seized may also, on the application of one of the parties, decline jurisdiction if the court first seized has jurisdiction over the actions in question and its law permits the consolidation thereof.

Article 82 Right to compensation and liability

1. Any person who has suffered material or non-material damage as a result of an infringement of this Regulation shall have the right to receive compensation from the controller or processor for the damage suffered.

2. Any controller involved in processing shall be liable for the damage caused by processing which infringes this Regulation. A processor shall be liable for the damage caused by processing only where it has not complied with obligations of this Regulation specifically directed to processors or where it has acted outside or contrary to lawful instructions of the controller.

3. A controller or processor shall be exempt from liability under paragraph 2 if it proves that it is not in any way responsible for the event giving rise to the damage.

4. Where more than one controller or processor, or both a controller and a processor, are involved in the same processing and where they are, under paragraphs 2 and 3, responsible for any damage caused by processing, each controller or processor shall be held liable for the entire damage in order to ensure effective compensation of the data subject.

5. Where a controller or processor has, in accordance with paragraph 4, paid full compensation for the damage suffered, that controller or processor shall be entitled to claim back from the other controllers or processors involved in the same processing that part of the compensation corresponding to their part of responsibility for the damage, in accordance with the conditions set out in paragraph 2.

6. Court proceedings for exercising the right to receive compensation shall be brought before the courts competent under the law of the Member State referred to in Article 79(2).

Article 83 General conditions for imposing administrative fines

1. Each supervisory authority shall ensure that the imposition of administrative fines pursuant to this Article in respect of infringements of this Regulation referred to in paragraphs 4, 5 and 6 shall in each individual case be effective, proportionate and dissuasive.

2. Administrative fines shall, depending on the circumstances of each individual case, be imposed in addition to, or instead of, measures referred to in points (a) to (h) and (j) of Article 58(2). When deciding whether to impose an administrative fine and deciding on the amount of the administrative fine in each individual case due regard shall be given to the following:

    (a) the nature, gravity and duration of the infringement taking into account the nature scope or purpose of the processing concerned as well as the number of data subjects affected and the level of damage suffered by them;

    (b) the intentional or negligent character of the infringement;

    (c) any action taken by the controller or processor to mitigate the damage suffered by data subjects;

    (d) the degree of responsibility of the controller or processor taking into account technical and organisational measures implemented by them pursuant to Articles 25 and 32;

    (e) any relevant previous infringements by the controller or processor;

    (f) the degree of cooperation with the supervisory authority, in order to remedy the infringement and mitigate the possible adverse effects of the infringement;

(g) the categories of personal data affected by the infringement;

(h) the manner in which the infringement became known to the supervisory authority, in particular whether, and if so to what extent, the controller or processor notified the infringement;

(i) where measures referred to in Article 58(2) have previously been ordered against the controller or processor concerned with regard to the same subject-matter, compliance with those measures;

(j) adherence to approved codes of conduct pursuant to Article 40 or approved certification mechanisms pursuant to Article 42; and

(k) any other aggravating or mitigating factor applicable to the circumstances of the case, such as financial benefits gained, or losses avoided, directly or indirectly, from the infringement.

3. If a controller or processor intentionally or negligently, for the same or linked processing operations, infringes several provisions of this Regulation, the total amount of the administrative fine shall not exceed the amount specified for the gravest infringement.

4. Infringements of the following provisions shall, in accordance with paragraph 2, be subject to administrative fines up to 10 000 000 EUR, or in the case of an undertaking, up to 2 % of the total worldwide annual turnover of the preceding financial year, whichever is higher:

(a) the obligations of the controller and the processor pursuant to Articles 8, 11, 25 to 39 and 42 and 43;

(b) the obligations of the certification body pursuant to Articles 42 and 43;

(c) the obligations of the monitoring body pursuant to Article 41(4).

5. Infringements of the following provisions shall, in accordance with paragraph 2, be subject to administrative fines up to 20 000 000 EUR, or in the case of an undertaking, up to 4 % of the total worldwide annual turnover of the preceding financial year, whichever is higher:

(a) the basic principles for processing, including conditions for consent, pursuant to Articles 5, 6, 7 and 9;

(b) the data subjects' rights pursuant to Articles 12 to 22;

(c) the transfers of personal data to a recipient in a third country or an international organisation pursuant to Articles 44 to 49;

(d) any obligations pursuant to Member State law adopted under Chapter IX;

(e) non-compliance with an order or a temporary or definitive limitation on processing or the suspension of data flows by the supervisory authority pursuant to Article 58(2) or failure to provide access in violation of Article 58(1).

6. Non-compliance with an order by the supervisory authority as referred to in Article 58(2) shall, in accordance with paragraph 2 of this Article,

be subject to administrative fines up to 20 000 000 EUR, or in the case of an undertaking, up to 4 % of the total worldwide annual turnover of the preceding financial year, whichever is higher.

7.	Without prejudice to the corrective powers of supervisory authorities pursuant to Article 58(2), each Member State may lay down the rules on whether and to what extent administrative fines may be imposed on public authorities and bodies established in that Member State.

8.	The exercise by the supervisory authority of its powers under this Article shall be subject to appropriate procedural safeguards in accordance with Union and Member State law, including effective judicial remedy and due process.

9.	Where the legal system of the Member State does not provide for administrative fines, this Article may be applied in such a manner that the fine is initiated by the competent supervisory authority and imposed by competent national courts, while ensuring that those legal remedies are effective and have an equivalent effect to the administrative fines imposed by supervisory authorities. In any event, the fines imposed shall be effective, proportionate and dissuasive. Those Member States shall notify to the Commission the provisions of their laws which they adopt pursuant to this paragraph by 25 May 2018 and, without delay, any subsequent amendment law or amendment affecting them.

Article 84   Penalties

1.	Member States shall lay down the rules on other penalties applicable to infringements of this Regulation in particular for infringements which are not subject to administrative fines pursuant to Article 83, and shall take all measures necessary to ensure that they are implemented. Such penalties shall be effective, proportionate and dissuasive.

2.	Each Member State shall notify to the Commission the provisions of its law which it adopts pursuant to paragraph 1, by 25 May 2018 and, without delay, any subsequent amendment affecting them.

CHAPTER IX   PROVISIONS RELATING TO SPECIFIC PROCESSING SITUATIONS

Article 85   Processing and freedom of expression and information

1.	Member States shall by law reconcile the right to the protection of personal data pursuant to this Regulation with the right to freedom of expression and information, including processing for journalistic purposes and the purposes of academic, artistic or literary expression.

2.	For processing carried out for journalistic purposes or the purpose of academic artistic or literary expression, Member States shall provide for exemptions or derogations from Chapter II (principles), Chapter III (rights of the data subject), Chapter IV (controller and processor), Chapter V (transfer of personal data to third countries or international organisations), Chapter VI (independent supervisory authorities), Chapter VII (cooperation and consistency) and Chapter IX (specific data processing situations) if they are necessary to reconcile the right to the protection of personal data with the freedom of expression and information.

3.   Each Member State shall notify to the Commission the provisions of its law which it has adopted pursuant to paragraph 2 and, without delay, any subsequent amendment law or amendment affecting them.

Article 86   Processing and public access to official documents

Personal data in official documents held by a public authority or a public body or a private body for the performance of a task carried out in the public interest may be disclosed by the authority or body in accordance with Union or Member State law to which the public authority or body is subject in order to reconcile public access to official documents with the right to the protection of personal data pursuant to this Regulation.

Article 87   Processing of the national identification number

Member States may further determine the specific conditions for the processing of a national identification number or any other identifier of general application. In that case the national identification number or any other identifier of general application shall be used only under appropriate safeguards for the rights and freedoms of the data subject pursuant to this Regulation.

Article 88   Processing in the context of employment

1.   Member States may, by law or by collective agreements, provide for more specific rules to ensure the protection of the rights and freedoms in respect of the processing of employees' personal data in the employment context, in particular for the purposes of the recruitment, the performance of the contract of employment, including discharge of obligations laid down by law or by collective agreements, management, planning and organisation of work, equality and diversity in the workplace, health and safety at work, protection of employer's or customer's property and for the purposes of the exercise and enjoyment, on an individual or collective basis, of rights and benefits related to employment, and for the purpose of the termination of the employment relationship.

2.   Those rules shall include suitable and specific measures to safeguard the data subject's human dignity, legitimate interests and fundamental rights, with particular regard to the transparency of processing, the transfer of

personal data within a group of undertakings, or a group of enterprises engaged in a joint economic activity and monitoring systems at the work place.

3. Each Member State shall notify to the Commission those provisions of its law which it adopts pursuant to paragraph 1, by 25 May 2018 and, without delay, any subsequent amendment affecting them.

Article 89 Safeguards and derogations relating to processing for archiving purposes in the public interest, scientific or historical research purposes or statistical purposes

1. Processing for archiving purposes in the public interest, scientific or historical research purposes or statistical purposes, shall be subject to appropriate safeguards, in accordance with this Regulation, for the rights and freedoms of the data subject. Those safeguards shall ensure that technical and organisational measures are in place in particular in order to ensure respect for the principle of data minimisation. Those measures may include pseudonymisation provided that those purposes can be fulfilled in that manner. Where those purposes can be fulfilled by further processing which does not permit or no longer permits the identification of data subjects, those purposes shall be fulfilled in that manner.

2. Where personal data are processed for scientific or historical research purposes or statistical purposes, Union or Member State law may provide for derogations from the rights referred to in Articles 15, 16, 18 and 21 subject to the conditions and safeguards referred to in paragraph 1 of this Article in so far as such rights are likely to render impossible or seriously impair the achievement of the specific purposes, and such derogations are necessary for the fulfilment of those purposes.

3. Where personal data are processed for archiving purposes in the public interest, Union or Member State law may provide for derogations from the rights referred to in Articles 15, 16, 18, 19, 20 and 21 subject to the conditions and safeguards referred to in paragraph 1 of this Article in so far as such rights are likely to render impossible or seriously impair the achievement of the specific purposes, and such derogations are necessary for the fulfilment of those purposes.

4. Where processing referred to in paragraphs 2 and 3 serves at the same time another purpose, the derogations shall apply only to processing for the purposes referred to in those paragraphs.

Article 90 Obligations of secrecy

1. Member States may adopt specific rules to set out the powers of the supervisory authorities laid down in points (e) and (f) of Article 58(1) in relation to controllers or processors that are subject, under Union or Member State law or rules established by national competent bodies, to an obligation

of professional secrecy or other equivalent obligations of secrecy where this is necessary and proportionate to reconcile the right of the protection of personal data with the obligation of secrecy. Those rules shall apply only with regard to personal data which the controller or processor has received as a result of or has obtained in an activity covered by that obligation of secrecy.

2.   Each Member State shall notify to the Commission the rules adopted pursuant to paragraph 1, by 25 May 2018 and, without delay, any subsequent amendment affecting them.

Article 91   Existing data protection rules of churches and religious associations

1.   Where in a Member State, churches and religious associations or communities apply, at the time of entry into force of this Regulation, comprehensive rules relating to the protection of natural persons with regard to processing, such rules may continue to apply, provided that they are brought into line with this Regulation.

2.   Churches and religious associations which apply comprehensive rules in accordance with paragraph 1 of this Article shall be subject to the supervision of an independent supervisory authority, which may be specific, provided that it fulfils the conditions laid down in Chapter VI of this Regulation.

CHAPTER X   DELEGATED ACTS AND IMPLEMENTING ACTS

Article 92   Exercise of the delegation

1.   The power to adopt delegated acts is conferred on the Commission subject to the conditions laid down in this Article.

2.   The delegation of power referred to in Article 12(8) and Article 43(8) shall be conferred on the Commission for an indeterminate period of time from 24 May 2016.

3.   The delegation of power referred to in Article 12(8) and Article 43(8) may be revoked at any time by the European Parliament or by the Council. A decision of revocation shall put an end to the delegation of power specified in that decision. It shall take effect the day following that of its publication in the *Official Journal of the European Union* or at a later date specified therein. It shall not affect the validity of any delegated acts already in force.

4.   As soon as it adopts a delegated act, the Commission shall notify it simultaneously to the European Parliament and to the Council.

5.   A delegated act adopted pursuant to Article 12(8) and Article 43(8) shall enter into force only if no objection has been expressed by either the European Parliament or the Council within a period of three months of notification of that act to the European Parliament and the Council or if, before the expiry of that period, the European Parliament and the Council have both informed

the Commission that they will not object. That period shall be extended by three months at the initiative of the European Parliament or of the Council.

Article 93   Committee procedure

1.   The Commission shall be assisted by a committee. That committee shall be a committee within the meaning of Regulation (EU) No 182/2011.

2.   Where reference is made to this paragraph, Article 5 of Regulation (EU) No 182/2011 shall apply.

3.   Where reference is made to this paragraph, Article 8 of Regulation (EU) No 182/2011, in conjunction with Article 5 thereof, shall apply.

CHAPTER XI   FINAL PROVISIONS

Article 94   Repeal of Directive 95/46/EC

1.   Directive 95/46/EC is repealed with effect from 25 May 2018.

2.   References to the repealed Directive shall be construed as references to this Regulation. References to the Working Party on the Protection of Individuals with regard to the Processing of Personal Data established by Article 29 of Directive 95/46/EC shall be construed as references to the European Data Protection Board established by this Regulation.

Article 95   Relationship with Directive 2002/58/EC

This Regulation shall not impose additional obligations on natural or legal persons in relation to processing in connection with the provision of publicly available electronic communications services in public communication networks in the Union in relation to matters for which they are subject to specific obligations with the same objective set out in Directive 2002/58/EC.

Article 96   Relationship with previously concluded Agreements

International agreements involving the transfer of personal data to third countries or international organisations which were concluded by Member States prior to 24 May 2016, and which comply with Union law as applicable prior to that date, shall remain in force until amended, replaced or revoked.

Article 97   Commission reports

1.   By 25 May 2020 and every four years thereafter, the Commission shall submit a report on the evaluation and review of this Regulation to the European Parliament and to the Council. The reports shall be made public.

2. In the context of the evaluations and reviews referred to in paragraph 1, the Commission shall examine, in particular, the application and functioning of:

    (a) Chapter V on the transfer of personal data to third countries or international organisations with particular regard to decisions adopted pursuant to Article 45(3) of this Regulation and decisions adopted on the basis of Article 25(6) of Directive 95/46/EC;

    (b) Chapter VII on cooperation and consistency.

3. For the purpose of paragraph 1, the Commission may request information from Member States and supervisory authorities.

4. In carrying out the evaluations and reviews referred to in paragraphs 1 and 2, the Commission shall take into account the positions and findings of the European Parliament, of the Council, and of other relevant bodies or sources.

5. The Commission shall, if necessary, submit appropriate proposals to amend this Regulation, in particular taking into account of developments in information technology and in the light of the state of progress in the information society.

Article 98   Review of other Union legal acts on data protection

The Commission shall, if appropriate, submit legislative proposals with a view to amending other Union legal acts on the protection of personal data, in order to ensure uniform and consistent protection of natural persons with regard to processing. This shall in particular concern the rules relating to the protection of natural persons with regard to processing by Union institutions, bodies, offices and agencies and on the free movement of such data.

Article 99   Entry into force and application

1. This Regulation shall enter into force on the twentieth day following that of its publication in the *Official Journal of the European Union*.

2. It shall apply from 25 May 2018.

This Regulation shall be binding in its entirety and directly applicable in all Member States.

Done at Brussels, 27 April 2016.

For the European Parliament	*For the Council*
The President	*The President*
M. SCHULZ	J.A. HENNIS-PLASSCHAERT

Cryptoassets Taskforce: final report (October 2018)

 HM Treasury
 FINANCIAL CONDUCT AUTHORITY
 BANK OF ENGLAND

Cryptoassets Taskforce:

final report

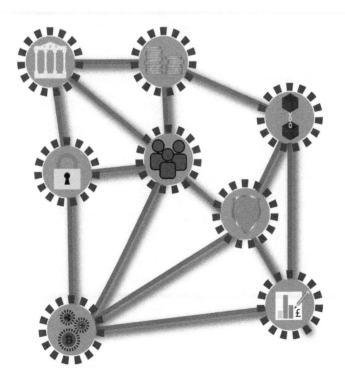

October 2018

Cryptoassets Taskforce:

final report

October 2018

ISBN 978-1-912809-13-4
PU2196

Contents

Foreword		2
Chapter 1	Introduction	4
Chapter 2	Key concepts	8
Chapter 3	Impacts of distributed ledger technology	21
Chapter 4	Impacts of cryptoassets	31
Chapter 5	Conclusions and responses	40
Annex A	The authorities' objectives	50
Annex B	Stakeholder engagement	51

1

Foreword

Cryptoassets and the distributed ledger technology (DLT) that underpins them have attracted significant attention globally. DLT has the potential to deliver substantial benefits, both in financial services and other sectors. Cryptoassets are one application of DLT, and whilst the UK market has grown, it remains small compared to some other jurisdictions, with many cryptoasset firms based outside the UK. Mainstream financial services firms are taking first steps into the market, and a small derivatives market is developing. At the same time, there is growing evidence of harm to consumers and markets.

It is against this backdrop that the Chancellor of the Exchequer launched the Cryptoassets Taskforce, consisting of HM Treasury, the Financial Conduct Authority and the Bank of England in March 2018.

The government has set out an ambition for the UK to be the world's most innovative economy, and to maintain its position as one of the leading financial centres globally.[1] The UK is well placed to achieve this, as host to a very mature and diverse domestic financial sector. This is a function of, but also relies on, the UK maintaining its international reputation as a safe and transparent place to do business in financial services; ensuring high regulatory standards in financial markets; protecting consumers; and allowing innovators in the financial sector that play by the rules to thrive, so that the benefits of new technologies can be fully realised. The Taskforce has developed a response to cryptoassets and DLT that is consistent with these objectives.

This report provides an overview of cryptoassets and the underlying technology, assesses the associated risks and potential benefits, and sets out the path forward with respect to regulation in the UK. It brings together existing work and new analysis carried out by the Taskforce, and has benefited from the contributions of stakeholders across the DLT and cryptoasset sector.[2] This has been a substantial undertaking, and the joint efforts of all three authorities – as well as valuable industry input – have been crucial in considering these issues holistically.

The Taskforce has concluded that while DLT is at an early stage of development, it has the potential to deliver significant benefits in financial services and other sectors in the future, and all three authorities will continue to support its development.

---

[1] 'UK Digital Strategy', Department for Digital, Culture, Media, and Sport, 2017, https://www.gov.uk/government/publications/uk-digital-strategy/executive-summary; 'The UK's Industrial Strategy', Department for Business, Energy, and Industrial Strategy, 2017, https://www.gov.uk/government/topical-events/the-uks-industrial-strategy; 'Fintech Sector Strategy', HM Treasury, 2018, https://assets.publishing.service.gov.uk/government/uploads/system/uploads/attachment_data/file/692874/Fintech_Sector_Strategy_print.pdf

[2] More information on the Taskforce's stakeholder engagement can be found in Annex B.

There is limited evidence of the current generation of cryptoassets delivering benefits, but this is a rapidly developing market and benefits may arise in the future. There are substantial potential risks associated with cryptoassets, and the most immediate priorities for the authorities are to mitigate the risks to consumers and market integrity, and prevent the use of cryptoassets for illicit activity. The authorities will also guard against threats to financial stability that could emerge in the future, and encourage responsible development of legitimate DLT and cryptoasset-related activity in the UK. This report sets out actions the authorities will take to deliver these objectives.

The Taskforce has concluded that strong action should be taken to address the risks associated with cryptoassets that fall within existing regulatory frameworks. Further consultation and international coordination is required for those cryptoassets that pose new challenges to traditional forms of financial regulation, and fall outside the existing regulatory framework. The authorities plan to engage with international bodies to ensure a comprehensive response.

This report lays out a clear path to establish the UK's policy and regulatory approach to cryptoassets and DLT. This is a fast-moving global market, with the technology developing and the nature of cryptoassets evolving. The authorities will keep their approach to cryptoassets and DLT under review to ensure the UK continues to support innovation, while maintaining safe and transparent financial markets.

Katharine Braddick	Andrew Bailey	Dave Ramsden
Director General, Financial Services, HM Treasury	Chief Executive Officer of the Financial Conduct Authority	Deputy Governor for Markets and Banking, Bank of England

3

Chapter 1

Introduction

1.1   In recent years, the government, the FCA and the Bank of England have undertaken work to understand the implications of cryptoassets and other applications of DLT in financial services more widely.

1.2   The government has:

- published a call for information on digital currencies and a summary of the responses. Outcomes included announcing the government's intention to apply anti-money laundering regulation to cryptoasset exchanges in the UK (2014-15).[1]

- published a report by the Government Office for Science, 'Distributed Ledger Technology: Beyond Blockchain', which set out how this technology could transform the delivery of public services and boost productivity (2016).[2]

- launched the Digital Strategy, which set out the government's ambition to make the UK the best place in the world to start and grow a digital business, including by trialling new technologies such as DLT (2017).[3]

- supported the development of DLT by investing over £10 million through Innovate UK and the research councils to support a diverse range of DLT projects; building proofs of concept to trial the use of DLT in the public sector; joining the EU Blockchain Partnership to help develop cross-border Blockchain projects in the public sector; creating a £20 million GovTech Catalyst Fund to explore technology-based solutions for public sector challenges, potentially including the use of DLT; and considering how DLT might be deployed to support new forms of financial services infrastructure through its Shared Platforms work with Deloitte.[4]

---

[1] 'Digital currencies: responses to the call for information', HM Treasury, 2015, https://assets.publishing.service.gov.uk/government/uploads/system/uploads/attachment_data/file/414040/digital_currencies_response_to_call_for_information_final_changes.pdf

[2] 'Distributed ledger technology', Beyond Blockchain', Government Office for Science, 2016, https://assets.publishing.service.gov.uk/government/uploads/system/uploads/attachment_data/file/492972/gs-16-1-distributed-ledger-technology.pdf

[3] 'UK Digital Strategy', DCMS, 2017, https://www.gov.uk/government/publications/uk-digital-strategy

[4] The UK signed the declaration on the establishment of an EU Blockchain Partnership on 10 April 2018. For further detail, see: 'Press release – European countries join Blockchain Partnership', European Commission, 2018, https://ec.europa.eu/digital-single-market/en/news/european-countries-join-blockchain-partnership; 'New support for tech to boost public sector productivity', HM Treasury, Department for Business, Energy, and Industrial Strategy, 2017, https://www.gov.uk/government/news/new-support-for-tech-to-boost-public-sector-productivity; 'Fintech Sector Strategy', HM Treasury, 2018, https://www.gov.uk/government/publications/fintech-sector-strategy

4

1.3   The FCA has established the Innovation Hub and Regulatory Sandbox to support innovation in the interests of consumers, both of which are held up as global examples of best practice. The FCA has also undertaken work to explore the potential of DLT in financial services:

- the Sandbox allows businesses to test innovative products, services, business models and delivery mechanisms in the real market, with real consumers in a controlled environment. DLT is the most popular technology tested in the Sandbox. More than one third of 89 firms that were accepted into the Sandbox used DLT and/or cryptoassets. The use of DLT appears to be rising, with further DLT sandbox tests expected in the fifth cohort. The fourth Sandbox cohort of 29 firms features 14 firms that use DLT and/or cryptoassets.[5]

- the FCA is actively exploring the use of DLT for its supervisory duties, via its RegTech initiative.[6]

- the FCA's Direct Support team provides a dedicated contact for innovative businesses that are considering applying for authorisation or a variation of permission and need support when doing so, or do not need to be authorised but could benefit from support. The team can also help businesses understand the regulatory regime and the challenges they may face when developing their innovative product or business model.

- in 2017, the FCA started a dialogue on the potential for DLT in the financial markets, and published a Discussion Paper and Feedback Statement.[7]

1.4   The Bank of England has set up a new Fintech Hub to consider the policy implications of Fintech.[8] In addition, the Bank of England has:

- published Quarterly Bulletin articles on the 'The economics of digital currencies' and 'Innovations in payment technologies', which explored the innovations of DLT (2014).[9]

- completed work with 18 firms via proof of concepts to understand how new technologies are being adopted and how they might relate to its objectives, and is embedding this approach into its business-as-usual activities. This included four DLT focused proofs-of-concept (2016-18).[10]

---

[5] The latest list of FCA's regulatory sandbox firms is available here: https://www.fca.org.uk/firms/regulatory-sandbox/regulatory-sandbox-cohort-4-businesses

[6] For further detail, see 'RegTech', FCA, 2018, https://www.fca.org.uk/firms/regtech

[7] For further detail, see: 'Feedback statement 17/4: distributed ledger technology', FCA, 2017, https://www.fca.org.uk/publications/feedback-statements/fs17-4-distributed-ledger-technology

[8] 'Open to Fintech – speech by Dave Ramsden', Bank of England, 2018, https://www.bankofengland.co.uk/speech/2018/dave-ramsden-speech-hmts-international-fintech-conference

[9] 'The economics of digital currencies', Bank of England, 2014, https://www.bankofengland.co.uk/-/media/boe/files/digital-currencies/the-economics-of-digital-currencies; 'Innovations in payment technologies and the emergence of digital currencies', Bank of England, 2014, https://www.bankofengland.co.uk/-/media/boe/files/quarterly-bulletin/2014/innovations-in-payment-technologies-and-the-emergence-of-digital-currencies.pdf

[10] 'Fintech proofs-of-concept', Bank of England, 2018, https://www.bankofengland.co.uk/research/fintech/proof-of-concept

5

- committed to ensure that the backbone of the existing payments system – the Bank of England's new RTGS service – will be compatible with DLT-based payment systems, supporting further innovation and use of DLT in financial services.[11] This includes conducting a proof-of-concept with four firms to help understand how this may be achieved (2018).[12]

- assessed the financial stability implications of cryptoassets via the Financial Policy Committee (2018).

The Cryptoassets Taskforce

1.5   In light of rapid developments in the market, the substantial potential of applications of DLT, and growing evidence of the risks associated with cryptoassets; the Chancellor of the Exchequer launched the Cryptoassets Taskforce in March 2018 as part of the government's Fintech Sector Strategy.[13]

1.6   The Taskforce has brought together HM Treasury, the FCA and the Bank of England.[14] The authorities have developed an approach to cryptoassets and DLT that:

- maintains the UK's international reputation as a safe and transparent place to do business in financial services

- ensures high regulatory standards in financial markets

- protects consumers

- guards against threats to financial stability that could emerge in the future

- allows those innovators in the financial sector that play by the rules to thrive

1.7   Parliament's Treasury Select Committee recently published a report following its Digital Currencies Inquiry, which considered similar questions to the Taskforce.[15] The Taskforce welcomes the Committee's work, and the government will formally respond in November.

Overview of the Taskforce's report

1.8   This report outlines the Taskforce's analysis and findings.

- **Chapter 2** outlines key concepts, provides an overview of the UK market, and sets out the Taskforce's framework for differentiating between types of cryptoassets and DLT. It also outlines how the current regulatory perimeter applies to different uses of cryptoassets.

---

[11] 'A blueprint for a new RTGS service for the UK', Bank of England, 2017, https://www.bankofengland.co.uk/-/media/boe/files/payments/a-blueprint-for-a-new-rtgs-service-for-the-uk.pdf

[12] 'RTGS Renewal Programme Proof of Concept: Supporting DLT Settlement Models', Bank of England, 2018, https://www.bankofengland.co.uk/news/2018/july/rtgs-renewal-programme-proof-of-concept-supporting-dlt-settlement-models

[13] 'Fintech Sector Strategy', HM Treasury, 2018, https://www.gov.uk/government/publications/fintech-sector-strategy.

[14] See Annex A for more detail on each of the authorities' objectives.

[15] The Treasury Select Committee is a Parliamentary Committee under the House of Commons. The Committee launched an inquiry into digital currencies on 22 February 2018. For the full report, see: 'Crypto-assets: Twenty-second report of session 2017-19', House of Commons Treasury Committee, 2018, https://publications.parliament.uk/pa/cm201719/cmselect/cmtreasy/910/910.pdf.

6

- **Chapter 3** considers the impact of DLT in financial services. It explores the benefits that the authorities have seen through both their work and that of innovative firms, and identifies some of the barriers to further deployment of DLT.

- **Chapter 4** assesses the risks and potential benefits associated with cryptoassets.

- **Chapter 5** sets out the Taskforce's conclusions and the actions that will be taken forward by HM Treasury, the FCA, and the Bank of England.

Chapter 2

Key concepts

Box 2.A: Summary

The current generation of DLT has its origins in the blockchain that powers Bitcoin, the first cryptoasset. However, since the development of Bitcoin in 2008, the technology and market have evolved, and cryptoassets are only one of many applications of DLT.

There is no standard form of DLT. Most DLT platforms being developed for use in financial services are different from the original Bitcoin blockchain, and are often not fully distributed or decentralised.

The Taskforce has developed a framework to distinguish between the different types and uses of cryptoassets, which supports analysis of the risks, benefits, and regulatory implications.

The Taskforce recognises that cryptoassets pose new challenges to the current regulatory framework, and the complexity of certain types of cryptoassets means it is difficult to determine whether they fall within the regulatory perimeter.

Distributed ledger technology

Key features

2.1   DLT is a type of technology that enables the sharing and updating of records in a distributed and decentralised way. Participants can securely propose, validate, and record updates to a synchronised ledger (a form of database), that is distributed across the participants.[1]

2.2   A DLT platform can be used like any conventional database that sets out who owns what, or who did what. They can store a range of data, such as ownership of existing financial assets (for example, shares), tangible assets (for example, wine, houses), or digital assets (for example, Bitcoin).

---

[1] In the context of this report, 'participant' refers to a computer participating in the operation of a DLT arrangement, otherwise known as a node.

8

Chart 2.A: Centralised and distributed ledgers[2]

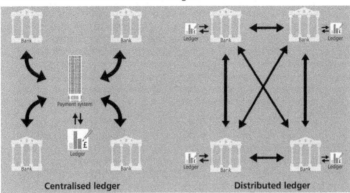

2.3   There are many different types of DLT platforms, and they usually combine elements of four common features:

- **Data distribution:** Many participants can keep a copy of the ledger, and are able to read and access the data.

- **Decentralisation of control:** Many participants can update the ledger, subject to agreed processes and controls.

- **Use of cryptography:** Cryptography may be used to identify and authenticate approved participants, confirm data records, and facilitate consensus.[3] The use of this technology is not unique to DLT.

- **Programmability/automation:** Computer-coded automation (such as smart contracts) can automatically implement the terms of an agreement, such as automatically triggering interest payments on a bond.[4]

2.4   There is no standard form of DLT. The specific combination of these features depends on what a particular DLT platform is being used for and the design choices made by developers.

2.5   The term 'blockchain' is often used interchangeably with DLT, but it refers to a specific way of structuring data on a DLT platform. Bitcoin was the first platform to use a blockchain to record information, and the first platform to combine the four common features of DLT described above. [5]

---

[2] Diagram adapted from 'The Fintech 2.0 paper: rebooting financial services', Innoventures, Santander, Oliver Wyman, Anthemis Group, 2015, https://www.finextra.com/finextra-downloads/newsdocs/the%20fintech%202%200%20paper.pdf

[3] 'Distributed ledger technology in payment, clearing and settlement', Committee on Payments and Market Infrastructures, 2017, https://www.bis.org/cpmi/publ/d157.pdf

[4] Smart contracts can carry out pre-determined commands without further human intervention.

[5] For further detail, see: 'Bitcoin: a peer-to-peer electronic cash system', Satoshi Nakomoto, 2008, https://bitcoin.org/en/bitcoin-paper

9

Permissioned and permissionless DLT

2.6   The individual technologies used in DLT are tried and tested, and some are even decades old. However, Bitcoin's unique innovation was to combine these technologies to build a decentralised network that has no central, trusted authority and which is open to anyone to participate. Networks that operate in this way are entirely '**permissionless**', so that anyone can become one of the multiple participants who maintain identical copies of the ledger. These participants employ a process known as a consensus mechanism to come to agreement on the contents of, and updates to, the ledger.[6] Bitcoin specifically uses a consensus mechanism known as 'proof of work', which is highly energy and cost intensive.[7]

2.7   In contrast, most of the DLT platforms being developed for use in financial services make significant departures from the original Bitcoin blockchain and are '**permissioned**', both in terms of who can access the network and who can update it. Access to the network is restricted to a list of known and approved parties, for example, banks who already trade with each other. The use of permissioned platforms might be preferable in some cases because financial institutions handle sensitive data and need to know who they are dealing with on the platform. There are also practical benefits to permissioned networks: if only known and trusted users are admitted to the network, the consensus mechanism used can be significantly faster and more energy and cost efficient than in permissionless systems.[8] This means that permissioned platforms avoid much of the negative environmental impact of permissionless systems.

Design choices in DLT

2.8   DLT platforms use varying degrees of distribution and decentralisation.

- **Distribution** relates to how data are shared and accessed. In permissionless platforms such as Bitcoin and many other cryptoasset platforms, any of the participants may keep a copy of the ledger,and anyone can read the data on the ledger. In permissioned platforms – which are more commonly explored in financial services - storage and access to the data is restricted to a list of known and approved participants. In addition, certain data may be shared only with a subset of participants, for example the two counterparties to a trade.

- **Decentralisation** relates to who is involved in updating the ledger. In permissionless platforms such as Bitcoin, any participant can join the network and compete to update the ledger with the latest transactions. In

---

[6] For further detail, see: 'Consensus: immutable agreement for the internet of value', KPMG, 2016, https://assets.kpmg.com/content/dam/kpmg/pdf/2016/06/kpmg-blockchain-consensus-mechanism.pdf

[7] For a more detailed description of the Bitcoin proof-of-work process, see: 'Innovations in payment technologies', Bank of England, 2014. https://www.bankofengland.co.uk/-/media/boe/files/quarterly-bulletin/2014/innovations-in-payment-technologies-and-the-emergence-of-digital-currencies.pdf. October 2018 estimates from the Digiconomist estimates the entire Bitcoin network uses just over 73kwh of electricity in a year, placing it ahead of Switzerland, Chile and Austria. For further detail, see: 'Bitcoin energy consumption index', Digiconomist, 2018. https://digiconomist.net/bitcoin-energy-consumption; and 'Bitcoin's energy usage is huge', The Guardian, 2018, https://www.theguardian.com/technology/2018/jan/17/bitcoin-electricity-usage-huge-climate-cryptocurrency

[8] For example, if all participants in a network are known, the right to update the ledger can be randomly allocated, or participants could simply agree on updates via simple majority voting. For more detail, see: 'Consensus', KPMG, 2016. https://assets.kpmg.com/content/dam/kpmg/pdf/2016/06/kpmg-blockchain-consensus-mechanism.pdf

permissioned platforms, only a group of selected, known parties may participate in the process of updating the ledger. This still requires a consensus mechanism, but is much simpler and less energy intensive.

Cryptoassets

2.9   Cryptoassets are one application of DLT. While all cryptoassets utilise some form of DLT, not all applications of DLT involve cryptoassets. The current most common cryptoassets are issued on permissionless ledgers.

2.10   There is not a single widely agreed definition of a cryptoasset. Broadly, a cryptoasset is a cryptographically secured digital representation of value or contractual rights that uses some type of DLT and can be transferred, stored or traded electronically. Examples of cryptoassets include Bitcoin and Litecoin (and other 'cryptocurrencies'), and those issued through the Initial Coin Offering (ICO) process, often referred to as 'tokens'. The market is constantly evolving, with new and different cryptoassets being developed and around 2000 currently in existence.[9]

2.11   The Taskforce considers there to be three broad types of cryptoassets:

A. **Exchange tokens** – which are often referred to as 'cryptocurrencies' such as Bitcoin, Litecoin and equivalents. They utilise a DLT platform and are not issued or backed by a central bank or other central body. They do not provide the types of rights or access provided by security or utility tokens, but are used as a means of exchange or for investment.

B. **Security tokens** – which amount to a 'specified investment' as set out in the Financial Services and Markets Act (2000) (Regulated Activities) Order (RAO).[10] These may provide rights such as ownership, repayment of a specific sum of money, or entitlement to a share in future profits. They may also be transferable securities or financial instruments under the EU's Markets in Financial Instruments Directive II (MiFID II).

C. **Utility tokens** – which can be redeemed for access to a specific product or service that is typically provided using a DLT platform.

The Taskforce's cryptoassets framework

2.12   Different cryptoassets vary significantly in the rights they grant their owners, as well as their actual and potential uses. Given the variety and complexity of applications, the Taskforce has developed a framework which takes into account the different uses of the three different types of cryptoassets identified above. Cryptoassets are typically used:

1   **As a means of exchange,** functioning as a decentralised tool to enable the buying and selling of goods and services, or to facilitate regulated payment services.

---

[9] 'All Cryptocurrencies', CoinMarketCap, as at 26.10.18, https://coinmarketcap.com/

[10] 'Regulated Activities Order - Specified investment', FCA, 2016,
   https://www.handbook.fca.org.uk/handbook/glossary/G1117.html?date=2016-03-21

11

2   **For investment,** with firms and consumers gaining direct exposure by holding and trading cryptoassets, or indirect exposure by holding and trading financial instruments that reference cryptoassets.

3   **To support capital raising and/or the creation of decentralised networks** through Initial Coin Offerings (ICOs).

2.13   While cryptoassets can be used as a means of exchange, they are not considered to be a currency or money, as both the Bank of England and the G20 Finance Ministers and Central Bank Governors have previously set out.[11] They are too volatile to be a good store of value, they are not widely-accepted as means of exchange, and they are not used as a unit of account.[12]

2.14   ICOs (or 'token sales') can be used in the creation of decentralised networks and/or as a digital way of raising funds from the public by issuing a project-specific exchange, security or utility token in exchange for an existing cryptoasset or fiat currency. Firms use ICOs as an alternative to traditional capital raising instruments, and in many cases use the funds raised to develop or improve services provided using a DLT platform. Individuals and firms typically buy ICO tokens as an investment, to secure access to a specific service, or to gain other rights attached to a token. Once issued, these cryptoassets may also be traded on a secondary market.

2.15   Chart 2.B provides a high-level overview of the three types of cryptoassets and their most common uses. These categories are not mutually exclusive – the way a cryptoasset is used, or its features, means that it could fall under several categories at any one time or at different points in its lifecycle. For example:

- A firm may use an ICO to issue a new cryptoasset to raise capital (category 3) and an investor may buy that cryptoasset for investment purposes (category 2).

- Bitcoin was originally intended as a means of exchange (category 1) and is still used as such by some. However, most current users of Bitcoin hold it for investment purposes (category 2).

2.16   The FCA will keep this framework under review and update it as necessary as the cryptoasset market continues to develop.

---

[11] For further detail, see, for example: 'The future of money – speech by Mark Carney', Bank of England, 2018, https://www.bankofengland.co.uk/speech/2018/mark-carney-speech-to-the-inaugural-scottish-economics-conference; and 'Communiqué – Finance Ministers and Central Bank Governors', G20, 2018, https://g20.org/sites/default/files/media/communique_-_fmcbg_march_2018.pdf

[12] Ibid.

12

Chart 2.B: The Taskforce's cryptoassets framework

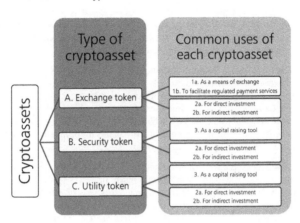

Box 2.B: Tokenisation of existing assets using DLT

The DLT that powers cryptoassets can also be used to 'tokenise' existing financial or tangible assets. Tokenisation occurs when an existing asset is recorded on a DLT platform and represented as a token in order to improve processes around trading and transfer of the asset. Depending on the underlying asset, these tokens may look similar to the types of cryptoassets discussed above.

Some taxonomies of cryptoassets draw a distinction between 'native' and 'non-native' tokens. Native tokens are intangible, non-physical assets that derive their value from the DLT platform. Non-native tokens are those which represent tangible and/or financial assets that exist elsewhere.

Many potential applications of DLT in financial services rely on this process of tokenisation. For example, a token could represent a share of ownership of a specific property (a tangible asset) or a government bond (a financial asset). In these examples, the asset (the property or government bond) has been tokenised on the DLT system, and the token represents ownership of the asset which exists outside the system.

The regulatory status of an asset or activity should not be affected by the use of DLT and the process of tokenisation, provided that doing so does not change the financial risk characteristics of the asset or the legal title to the underlying asset. If an existing asset is regulated, representing it as a token using a DLT platform should not change its regulatory status. However, the use of DLT may change the way in which regulation applies. For example, there may be differences in the systems and controls that a firm needs to have.

13

The UK cryptoasset market

2.17 Reliable and comprehensive data are not yet available, given the market is still in its early stages and developing rapidly. However, using a range of sources, the Taskforce has been able to identify that while the market has grown recently, the UK is not one of the major markets for cryptoasset trading globally.

2.18 **Cryptoassets as a means of exchange:** Cryptoassets are not widely used as a means of exchange in the UK. No major high street or online retailer accepts them as a form of payment, and only around 500 independent shops, bars and cafes around the UK accept Bitcoin.[13] Some of the few major online payment processors who accepted payment via cryptoassets have recently dropped their support.[14] There is also evidence that globally, the usage of cryptoassets for payments (rather than for investment) is declining.[15]

2.19 **Cryptoassets as a form of investment:** Data from cryptoasset exchanges shows that trading of sterling against Bitcoin makes up just 0.33% of daily global trade volumes.[16] This may partially understate the true scale of activity by UK participants in the cryptoasset market; it is currently difficult to exchange sterling directly for cryptoassets, so many active UK traders will first convert to another currency which is more widely supported. The pseudonymous nature of cryptoassets means that direct data on UK consumer holdings of, and exposure to cryptoasset markets is difficult to assess accurately. Online consumer surveys suggest that cryptoasset ownership rates among UK survey respondents are between 5-10% (in line with other G7 economies), however figures for the wider population are likely to be lower.[17]

2.20 **Cryptoassets as a form of capital raising:** The Taskforce estimates that there are 56 ICO projects in the UK that have been used for capital formation, which accounts for 4.3% of the 983 projects globally.[18] Estimates suggest that ICOs, by issuing entities in the UK, have raised $330 million, which accounts for less than one percent of the $24 billion raised globally by ICOs.[19] In general, it is not possible to see the location of the investors in ICOs, but the pattern may be quite different to the location of issuers – that is, while the proportion of funds raised through ICOs by UK entities is small relative to the global market, UK consumers may be investing in ICOs in other jurisdictions. While the total capital raised globally through ICOs increased in 2018, this appears to have been concentrated in larger token sales by

---

13 'Evidence submitted by the Bank of England – Treasury Select Committee on digital currencies', Bank of England, 2018, http://data.parliament.uk/writtenevidence/committeeevidence.svc/evidencedocument/treasury-committee/digital-currencies/written/82252.pdf

14 'Ending Bitcoin support', Stripe, 2018, https://stripe.com/blog/ending-bitcoin-support

15 'Bitcoin's use in commerce keeps falling even as volatility eases', Bloomberg, 2018, https://www.bloomberg.com/news/articles/2018-08-01/bitcoin-s-use-in-commerce-keeps-falling-even-as-volatility-eases

16 'Bitcoin trade volume by currency', CryptoCompare, as at 26.10.2018, https://www.cryptocompare.com/coins/btc/analysis/USD

17 'Global cryptocurrency survey results', Dalia Research, 2018, https://daliaresearch.com/wp-content/uploads/2018/05/2018-05-07_Pressrelease_Global_Cryptocurrency_Survey-Google-Docs.pdf; and 'Cracking the code on cryptocurrency', ING, 2018, https://think.ing.com/uploads/reports/ING_International_Survey_Mobile_Banking_2018.pdf

18 Figures based on Coinschedule market research, shared with the Taskforce on the 20.08.2018

19 This is less than ICOs issued by entities within other countries, such as the United States ($6.7 billion), Singapore ($1.3 billion), Switzerland ($1.1 billion) but more than raised by entities in Japan ($0.1 billion). This market research was undertaken by Coin Schedule on 20.08.2018 and compared against other sources including CoinDesk, Autonomous Next, Token Data and ICO tracking websites.

issuing entities outside of the UK.[20] However, the volumes raised through ICOs has been declining globally in the latter half of 2018.[21]

2.21   **UK exchanges:** There are fewer than 15 cryptoasset spot exchanges headquartered in the UK, out of a global market of 206. Only four of these spot exchanges regularly post daily individual trading volumes above $30 million, which is small relative to the global market.[22] The 12 spot exchanges with visible trading activity at the time of writing account for around 2.66% ($249 million) of daily global trading volume.[23] There are several branches of larger international exchanges operating in the UK, but these have only recently been incorporated and are yet to establish a significant footprint in the UK.

Cryptoasset market actors

2.22   A number of different actors are involved in a range of activities related to cryptoassets. The actors are constantly evolving, but the core elements are shown in Chart 2.C.

Chart 2.C: Actors in the cryptoasset market

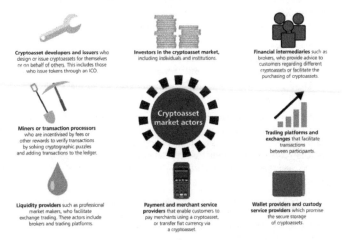

Cryptoasset developers and issuers who design or issue cryptoassets for themselves or on behalf of others. This includes those who issue tokens through an ICO.

Investors in the cryptoasset market, including individuals and institutions.

Financial intermediaries such as brokers, who provide advice to customers regarding different cryptoassets or facilitate the purchasing of cryptoassets.

Miners or transaction processors who are incentivised by fees or other rewards to verify transactions by solving cryptographic puzzles and adding transactions to the ledger.

Cryptoasset market actors

Trading platforms and exchanges that facilitate transactions between participants.

Liquidity providers such as professional market makers, who facilitate exchange trading. These actors include brokers and trading platforms.

Payment and merchant service providers that enable customers to pay merchants using a cryptoasset, or transfer fiat currency via a cryptoasset.

Wallet providers and custody service providers which promise the secure storage of cryptoassets.

---

[20] Neither Telegram or EOS, owned by Block.One, are located inside the UK. For further detail, see 'State of Blockchain 2018 Q2 report', CoinDesk, 2018, https://www.coindesk.com/research/state-of-blockchain-q2-2018/

[21] 'September ICOs 90% down from January', Autonomous Next, as at 08.10.2018, https://next.autonomous.com/thoughts/crypto-september-icos-90-down-from-january-but-venture-funding-is-ray-of-hope

[22] '24 hour volume rankings', CoinMarketCap, as at 26.10.2018, https://coinmarketcap.com/exchanges/volume/24-hour/

[23] ibid.

15

Cryptoassets and financial services regulation

2.23   Financial services regulation in the UK is broadly carried out by the FCA and the Bank of England (including through the Prudential Regulation Authority (PRA)).

- The FCA's regulation aims to protect consumers from harm, protect and enhance the integrity of the UK's financial services sector, and promote effective competition in the interest of consumers.

- The Bank of England's regulation aims to ensure the safety and soundness of firms (through the PRA) and to remove or reduce systemic risks that could pose a threat to financial stability (through the Financial Policy Committee and the Bank's supervision of Financial Market Infrastructures).

The current regulatory perimeter

2.24   The regulatory perimeter refers to the types of financial services activity to which regulation is applied. The perimeter includes specified activities and investments defined in the Financial Services and Markets Act (2000) (Regulated Activities) Order (RAO), as well as regulation set out in separate legislation such as the Payment Services Regulations 2017 (PSR). Regulated activities can also be set through EU law, which is then transposed into domestic law.

2.25   The following section and Table 2.A broadly outline how the current regulatory perimeter applies to cryptoasset-related activities, drawing on the Taskforce's framework for cryptoassets. This is a high-level analysis; a particular cryptoasset may fall under several categories, and all categories that might be relevant for that cryptoasset should be considered.

2.26   Whether and what regulation applies to a particular cryptoasset instrument or activity can only be decided on a case-by-case basis. Firms and persons involved in providing services or investments related to cryptoassets should carefully consider if their activities could involve regulated activities or the issuing of financial promotions, and must ensure they are complying with relevant legal and regulatory obligations.[24]

2.27   The FCA has been conducting enquiries into activities of unauthorised firms that are involved in some form of cryptoassets business to determine whether they are carrying on regulated activities that require FCA authorisation. If so, the FCA may investigate and take action, identifying and determining the most serious matters which pose the greatest risk to consumers. The FCA has also been encouraging regulated firms to speak to the FCA supervisors regarding cryptoasset activities they are undertaking or considering.

2.28   In addition, financial services law is not the only potentially applicable body of laws. For example, contract law, consumer law, and advertising standards may apply.

---

[24] The FCA's general guidance on the regulatory perimeter in the Perimeter Guidance Manual (PERG) may be helpful, see https://www.handbook.fca.org.uk/handbook/PERG.pdf. Firms can also contact FCA Innovate to apply for support in relation to their propositions, see https://www.fca.org.uk/firms/innovate-innovation-hub/request-support.

16

Table 2.A: Cryptoassets and the current regulatory perimeter

Common uses of cryptoassets	Within perimeter?	Detail	Most common use cases
As a means of exchange.	Depends on type of cryptoasset.	Payment services regulation under the PSR only covers activities involving fiat funds. Cryptoassets used as a means of exchange therefore do not fall within the perimeter. However, some cryptoassets used as a means of exchange may meet the definition of e-money.[25]	Exchange tokens such as Bitcoin or Litecoin can be used to enable the buying and selling of goods and services, but are not considered to be currency or money.[26] Utility tokens may be considered e-money when structured in certain ways, for example when centrally issued, and accepted by third parties as a means of exchange.
To facilitate regulated payment services.	Yes.	When cryptoassets are used to facilitate a regulated payment service as set out in the PSR, the business carrying out this service falls within the perimeter.[27]	Cryptoassets can be used as an intermediary in cross-border transactions (for example, GBP – Bitcoin – USD). Aspects of such services are regulated as money remittance under the PSR, although this will not include the cryptoasset part of the transaction.
For investment directly in cryptoassets.	Depends on type of cryptoasset and type of investor.	Direct investment in cryptoassets does not fall within the perimeter unless the cryptoasset is a security token or the	Exchange tokens such as Bitcoin, security and utility tokens can all be held as a form of investment by firms and consumers.

25 'Payment Services Regulations and Electronic Money Regulations', FCA, 2018, https://www.fca.org.uk/firms/payment-services-regulations-e-money-regulations

26 'The future of money – speech by Mark Carney', Bank of England, 2018, https://www.bankofengland.co.uk/speech/2018/mark-carney-speech-to-the-inaugural-scottish-economics-conference; and 'Communiqué

– France Ministers and Central Bank Governors', G20, 2018, https://g20.org/sites/default/files/media/communique_-_fmcbg_march_2018.pdf

27 In the UK, payment services are regulated by the Payment Services Regulations 2017 (PSR). In summary, the different types of payment services are: 1.) services enabling cash to be paid into or withdrawn from a payment account and all of the operations required for operating a payment account; 2.) execution of payment transactions - such as direct debits, credit transfers and card payments; 3.) issuing of payment instruments (for example credit or debit cards); 4.) acquiring payment transactions; 5.) money remittance 6.) account information services and 7.) payment initiation services. For further detail, see: 'Payment Services Regulations and Electronic Money Regulations', FCA, 2018, https://www.fca.org.uk/firms/payment-service-regulations-e-money-regulations

Common uses of cryptoassets	Within perimeter?	Detail	Most common use cases
		investment is made by a regulated investment vehicle.	
For indirect investment through financial instruments that reference cryptoassets.	Yes.	Financial instruments that reference cryptoassets likely fall within the perimeter. These instruments may also be financial instruments under MiFID II.[28]	Financial instruments that reference cryptoassets include contracts for difference (CFDs), options, futures, exchange traded notes, units in a collective investment scheme, or alternative investment funds.
As a capital raising tool or as part of a process designed to support a particular project, such as the creation of decentralised networks.	If a security token - yes.	Security tokens amount to a specified investment as set out in the RAO. For example, they are (or have characteristics which mean they are like) securities such as shares, bonds, or units in a collective investment scheme. They may also be transferable securities or financial instruments under MiFID II.[29]	Security tokens or utility tokens are typically issued through an ICO. Exchange tokens can also be issued through an ICO.
	If a utility token – no.	Utility tokens typically do not have the characteristics of specified investments as set out in the RAO.	

28 For further detail, see 'MiFID II', FCA, 2018. https://www.fca.org.uk/markets/mifid-ii
29 Ibid.

18

308

Other considerations for regulated firms

2.29   There are also broader considerations for regulated firms that carry out cryptoasset-related activities. Some regulatory provisions in the FCA's Handbook – such as the Principles for Business, the Senior Managers and Certification Regime, the Systems and Controls Provisions, and the Financial Promotions rules – can apply to unregulated activities in certain contexts.

- The Principles for Business are 11 high-level rules which apply to all FCA-regulated firms. Three of the Principles – those relating to the adequacy of a firm's financial resources, the adequacy of a firm's systems and controls, and the duty to deal with the FCA in an open and cooperative way – can extend to unregulated activity undertaken by regulated firms.

- The Senior Managers and Certification Regime allows the FCA to hold senior management in regulated firms to account for unregulated activities. The FCA expects these principles to apply to unregulated cryptoasset-related business being conducted by regulated firms.

- The Systems and Controls Provisions cover, amongst other things, organisational requirements, risk control, record keeping, and employee requirements.[30] The FCA has previously taken action against regulated firms carrying out unregulated activities for breaches in systems and controls.[31]

- Financial Promotions rules placed on regulated firms state that financial promotions must be fair, clear, and not misleading; give a balanced impression of the product or service; and not disguise and diminish important warning statements.

2.30   In addition to the Financial Promotions rules placed on regulated firms, there are also broader legislative restrictions in respect of financial promotions. Section 21 of the Financial Services and Markets Act 2000 (FSMA) provides that a person must not, in the course of business, communicate an invitation or inducement to engage in investment activity unless the promotion has been made or approved by an authorised person or it is exempt. Issuing a financial promotion in breach of Section 21 of FSMA is a criminal offence.

---

[30] The FCA's systems and controls provisions are primarily in the Senior Management Arrangements, Systems and Controls (SYSC) section of the FCA Handbook. For further detail, see 'FCA Handbook', https://www.handbook.fca.org.uk/handbook/SYSC/

[31] 'Press release – FCA fines five banks £1.1 billion for FX failings and announces industry-wide remediation programme', FCA, 2014, https://www.fca.org.uk/news/press-releases/fca-fines-five-banks-%C2%A311-billion-fx-failings-and-announces-industry-wide

19

Challenges posed by cryptoassets for the regulatory perimeter

2.31   There are instances in which the government reassesses the regulatory perimeter, primarily for one or more of the following reasons:

- there is evidence of regulatory arbitrage to avoid the policy intention of regulation

- prior policy decisions to exclude a particular activity produce unintended consequences that must be addressed

- future business models or use cases were not predicted or considered when the perimeter was defined, and are therefore not appropriately captured by the perimeter

2.32   The Taskforce considers that cryptoassets fall into this third category. This is a new and fast-paced market with complex and opaque products, and distinguishing whether a cryptoasset falls within regulation can be difficult.

Security tokens and other similar products

2.33   While security tokens fall within the current regulatory perimeter and it is the responsibility of firms to determine whether their activities require authorisation, the Taskforce recognises that the complexity and opacity of many cryptoassets means it is difficult to determine whether they qualify as security tokens.

2.34   The Taskforce also recognises that there may be instances in which firms issue cryptoassets that have comparable features to investments (such as those set out in the RAO) but are structured in such a way that they fall outside the regulatory perimeter (either intentionally or not). In such circumstances, it is important to consider the logical position of the perimeter to ensure that cryptoassets that are structured in similar ways and seek to achieve similar outcomes are treated in similar ways by regulators. Given the complexity and variety of cryptoasset products intended to function as investments, the Taskforce is concerned that there is not sufficient consistency of regulatory application in these circumstances.

2.35   Chapter 5 discusses in more detail how the authorities will provide further clarity on the application of regulation to security tokens, and ensure a consistent application of regulation.

Exchange tokens

2.36   While security tokens are a new form of an existing financial instrument, the Taskforce considers that exchange tokens do not meet the traditional definition of a financial instrument. However, from the perspective of consumers and investors, exchange tokens are most commonly used as a financial investment, and have no use other than as a financial investment or means of exchange. This highlights that these assets are unlike other financial services products, and do not fit neatly within existing definitions or financial regulatory frameworks.

Chapter 3

Impacts of distributed ledger technology

Box 3.A: Summary

The Taskforce considers that DLT has the potential to deliver significant benefits in financial services, as well as in a broad range of other sectors. As an emerging leader in DLT, the UK should look to capitalise on these opportunities.

DLT has the potential to enhance system resilience; improve the efficiency of end-to-end settlement processes and reporting, auditing and oversight; and enable greater automation.

However, the Taskforce considers that the technology is still in its early days, and there are some significant challenges to wider adoption.

The Taskforce does not consider there to be regulatory barriers to the adoption of DLT. The PRA and FCA will continue to take a technologically neutral approach to regulation, as well as providing a platform for innovation.

Use of DLT in the UK

3.1   The UK is an emerging leader in the development of DLT. The UK has the second largest number of DLT start-ups in the world, following the United States.[1] London also has the second highest number of DLT projects listed on code repository GitHub, just behind San Francisco.[2]

Potential benefits of DLT in financial services

3.2   Chapter 2 described four key elements of DLT: data distribution, decentralisation of control, cryptography, and programmability/automation. Using examples from the FCA's Regulatory Sandbox, the Bank of England's Fintech proofs of concept and other projects, this chapter explores how certain combinations of these elements have the potential to bring benefits in financial services to both firms and consumers. There are many more DLT use cases within financial services, and other sectors.

---

1 'State of Blockchain 2018 Q2 report', CoinDesk, 2018, https://www.coindesk.com/research/state-of-blockchain-q2-2018/; and 'Blockchain Start-up Tracker', Outlier Ventures, 2016, https://outlierventures.io/research/the-blockchain-startup-tracker/

2 'The state of the token market', Fabric Ventures, 2017, https://www.fabric.vc/report

Enhanced resilience

3.3   It may be possible to realise resilience benefits in DLT platforms which are highly distributed and decentralised. This was a theme noted by respondents to the FCA's Discussion Paper on DLT and in the Taskforce's stakeholder engagement. Maintaining copies of data that are recorded and accessed by multiple participants reduces the impact of data loss caused by an incident with any one participant. In addition, network consensus may also provide enhanced cyber resilience, as an attacker would need to take control of multiple participants to control the system. DLT can also eliminate, or reduce, central points of failure, so that if one participant in the network fails, others can continue processing.

Box 3.B: Bank of England proof of concept – transferring asset ownership

The Bank of England recognised the resilience benefits of DLT systems in one of its proofs of concept in June 2016.[3] This involved building a multi-node distributed ledger environment on the Ethereum protocol to enable the transfer of ownership of a fictional asset among several participants, including a central authority that could establish the supply of the asset and permissions to access and use the ledger. The proof of concept demonstrated that participants in the network could continue to trade the fictional asset without the central authority, removing the single point of failure of the system and considerably increasing its resilience. This work also highlighted a number of potential limitations, which were not explored in this proof of concept, but which merited further investigation, including scalability, security, privacy, interoperability and sustainability.

More efficient end-to-end settlement processes

3.4   DLT platforms can enable a wider range of participants to directly access their own immutable copy of identical data. When multiple participants can get timely access to the same, distributed but synchronised data, it provides a single source of truth. This results in more efficient end-to-end settlement processes, as it can eliminate the need for costly and slow reconciliation processes between platforms (and disputes when different systems do not tally). This benefit has been widely acknowledged, including by the European Securities and Markets Authority[4] and in the Taskforce's stakeholder engagement.

---

[3] 'Fintech Accelerator proof of concept', Bank of England, 2016, https://www.bankofengland.co.uk/research/fintech/-/media/boe/files/fintech/pwc.pdf

[4] 'Press release: ESMA assesses DLT's potential and interactions with EU rules', European Securities and Markets Authority, 2017, http://www.esma.europa.eu/press-news/esma-news/esma-assesses-dlt%E2%80%99s-potential-and-interactions-eu-rules

---

Box 3.C: FCA Regulatory Sandbox – issuance processes

One firm within the FCA's Sandbox used a permissionless DLT network to mimic the traditional issuance process for a short-term debt instrument, whilst another used a permissionless DLT network to test a platform to issue a structured product.

Both these tests demonstrated that DLT can help to streamline traditional approaches, whilst meeting legal and regulatory requirements. In a small scale test, cost reductions were achieved by a high degree of automation and by removing the need for registrars and nominees. For example, for the cost of clearing, settlement and custody of a traditionally issued product, the DLT-based solution could issue 16 equivalent products.

Due to the permissionless DLT network, ownership of an asset is recorded publicly which increases transparency for investors who, to some extent, do not rely on the issuer to hold the record of ownership anymore. This also eliminates the need for reconciliation between network participants because they share the same record of ownership, supporting more efficient settlement operations.

More efficient reporting, auditing and oversight

3.5   DLT's shared data model may reduce manual reporting within and between financial institutions, or between financial institutions and the regulators. For example, regulators could be granted access rights to consult or retrieve data stored on DLT ledgers, giving them access to one accurate and verifiable ledger in real-time.[5] Research also suggests that such uses could automate other processes, such as auditing.[6]

Box 3.D: Investment Association Digital Fund

As part of the Asset Management Taskforce, chaired by the Economic Secretary to the Treasury, the Investment Association is looking to create the UK's first digital fund. This aims to use DLT to streamline back office fund administration functions, and to increase speed and reduce cost. By reducing the number of intermediaries, a fund will make cost savings that could result in lower costs for the end investor. A DLT-enabled fund would also enable real-time clearing and settlement.[7]

---

[5] Ibid.

[6] 'Blockchain technology: a game-changer in accounting?', Deloitte, 2016,
https://www2.deloitte.com/content/dam/Deloitte/de/Documents/Innovation/Blockchain_A%20game-changer%20in%20accounting.pdf

[7] 'The Investment Management Strategy II', HM Treasury, 2017,
https://assets.publishing.service.gov.uk/government/uploads/system/uploads/attachment_data/file/665668/The_Investment_Management_Strategy_II.pdf; and 'Fintech sector strategy', HM Treasury, 2018.

23

313

Box 3.E: Regulatory Technology ('RegTech')

The FCA's RegTech team worked with the R3 consortium and two major banks in September 2017 to develop a prototype application for regulatory reporting of mortgage transaction data using the Corda DLT platform. By hosting a 'regulator node' on the network, the FCA was able to receive real-time mortgage transaction reports from the two banks in a test environment. The prototype records, executes and manages financial agreements, with DLT used to enable secure communication between participants. This collaboration demonstrated how DLT could enable continuous regulatory reporting for financial institutions at comparatively low cost.

In 2017, the FCA and Bank of England initiated a Digital Regulatory Reporting pilot, which aims to develop a prototype using a DLT network that can demonstrate the potential benefits of an end-to-end process for machine executable reporting.[8] The pilot will share the findings with industry, ask for feedback, and evaluate the potential costs and benefits of a new reporting mechanism.

Efficiency gains from automated contract tools

3.6   DLT has the potential to improve efficiency using automated reporting and smart contracts. DLT platforms built for financial services generally have a high degree of programmability, which allows them to be tailored to a specific use case. A simple example could be locking the funds for a transaction, which are then automatically released to the recipient only when specific conditions are met (for example, the confirmed delivery of goods).

---

[8] The Digital Regulatory Reporting pilot was initiated in November 2017, following a successful two-week TechSprint to examine how technology, like DLT, can make the current system of regulatory reporting more accurate, efficient and consistent. The pilot is an industry collaboration with a number of regulated firms (Santander, Lloyds, Barclays, Nationwide, NatWest and Credit Suisse), together with the University College Cork and University College London. For further detail, see 'Digital Regulatory Reporting', FCA, 2018, https://www.fca.org.uk/firms/our-work-programme/digital-regulatory-reporting

Box 3.F: Trade finance

Trade finance was frequently identified in the Taskforce's stakeholder engagement as a use case that demonstrates how DLT could speed up settlement times and increase efficiency through automation. For example, smart contracts could replace letters of credit and create a record of ownership at each step.

Stakeholders noted that the nearer-term take-up of DLT is most likely for processes such as trade finance that are old and highly paper-based.

The Hong Kong Monetary Authority and the Monetary Authority of Singapore are developing a cross-border infrastructure based on DLT to digitalise trade finance. The aim of the project is to build an information highway that will make cross-border trade and financing cheaper and safer, as well as removing the inefficiencies in the existing paper-based system.[9]

Box 3.G: FCA Regulatory Sandbox – insurance industry

Various Sandbox firms have demonstrated that DLT platforms can be used with regulated payments and e-money services to allow the deployment of smart contracts to execute transactions automatically. A Sandbox firm tested a fully automated, DLT-based flight delay insurance product. When a flight was delayed, the system would automatically trigger a pay-out in a cryptoasset or in fiat currency.

Enabling the tokenisation of existing assets

3.7   DLT platforms can enable existing assets to be 'tokenised' and represented as tokens on a DLT platform (see Box 2.B). Firms or investors may do this to gain the advantages of the technology, such as efficiency improvements from smart contracts or enhanced resilience.

3.8   Recording ownership in this way also allows fractional ownership of assets, so that users can tokenise partial units of an asset, such as property. This has the potential to lower barriers to investment, improve liquidity and tradability, and increase efficiency.

---

9 'Press release – Hong Kong and Singapore launch a joint project on cross-border trade and trade finance platform', Hong Kong Monetary Authority (HKMA), 2017, https://www.hkma.gov.hk/eng/key-information/press-releases/2017/20171115-6.shtml

Box 3.H: FCA Regulatory Sandbox – tokenisation of existing assets

A firm in the Sandbox tested the use of a DLT-enabled smart contract to allow UK private limited companies to digitally represent – or tokenise - their shares and corporate governance processes. Changes of share ownership on the firm's platform were directly updated in the Companies House register, resulting in improved efficiency and cost savings.

Challenges associated with the use of DLT

3.9   Despite a broad range of use cases, DLT is still a relatively young technology and there are a several challenges which must be overcome before it can be deployed at scale in financial services. There are both trade-offs in the design of DLT platforms and other barriers to the wider adoption of DLT.

Technological trade-offs in the design of DLT

3.10   Design choices made by DLT developers, particularly with respect to the degree of data distribution and decentralisation of control, often lead to important trade-offs that must be made between some of the features of DLT platforms. Some of the key trade-offs are between performance (for example, transaction capacity and scalability), resilience and privacy. Future technical advancements may alter these trade-offs.

Chart 3.A: Trade-offs in DLT design

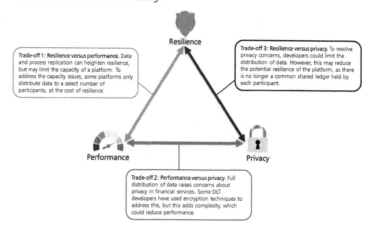

Resilience

Trade-off 1: Resilience versus performance. Data and process replication can heighten resilience, but may limit the capacity of a platform. To address the capacity issues, some platforms only distribute data to a select number of participants, at the cost of resilience.

Trade-off 3: Resilience versus privacy. To resolve privacy concerns, developers could limit the distribution of data. However, this may reduce the potential resilience of the platform, as there is no longer a common shared ledger held by each participant.

Performance

Privacy

Trade-off 2: Performance versus privacy. Full distribution of data raises concerns about privacy in financial services. Some DLT developers have used encryption techniques to address this, but this adds complexity, which could reduce performance.

26

316

Box 3.I: Privacy considerations

The potential for data to be fully distributed often leads to transparency being cited as a benefit of DLT. However, in financial services it may be better to consider the *appropriate* sharing of data, because it is rare that every participant should have access to every piece of data recorded on the platform. Platforms with the full transparency of the Bitcoin blockchain, in which every transaction amount, source, and destination is publicly visible, would be unusable for many financial services applications. Consequently, privacy of data is also important, both for commercial reasons, and because of the UK's commitment to high levels of data protection.[10]

One of the Bank of England's proofs of concept explored privacy in DLT with Chain.[11] This was an academic exercise focused on cryptographic techniques to achieve privacy in a DLT system, whilst keeping data shared amongst participants. This proof of concept found that it appears theoretically possible to configure a DLT platform in such a way that transactions remain private whilst keeping all data shared across the network. However, the trade-offs (especially with respect to scalability, speed of transaction processing, and risks around the security of the cryptographic techniques employed) would need to be further explored.

Potential barriers to the wider adoption of DLT

3.11 **Interoperability of systems:** DLT deployment is likely to be gradual, which means different platforms will need to be able to work with legacy systems, and with each other. This will require coordinated technology standards to realise many of the benefits set out earlier in this chapter.[12] The International Organisation for Standardisation (ISO) have started to develop a set of standards.[13] Coordination such as this will be important to encourage take-up on a global scale, so that there are not different standards in different jurisdictions.[14]

3.12 **Competition issues:** As with the application of other new technologies, firms' use of DLT may also raise a number of competition questions. For example, if a closed or permissioned DLT network developed to become essential infrastructure (for example in clearing and settlement) then there could be competition concerns around access.[15]

[10] See, for example: 'Data Protection Act 2018 Overview', DCMS and Home Office, 2018, https://www.gov.uk/government/publications/data-protection-act-2018-overview; and 'Guide to the General Data Protection Act (GDPR)', Information Commissioner's Office, 2018, https://ico.org.uk/for-organisations/guide-to-the-general-data-protection-regulation-gdpr/

[11] 'Fintech proof of concept', Bank of England, 2018, https://www.bankofengland.co.uk/-/media/boe/files/fintech/chain.pdf

[12] 'Press release: ESMA assesses DLT's potential and interactions with EU rules', ESMA, 2017, https://www.esma.europa.eu/press-news/esma-news/esma-assesses-dlt%E2%80%99s-potential-and-interactions-eu-rules

[13] 'ISO/TC 307 Blockchain and distributed ledger technologies', International Standards Organisation, 2016, https://www.iso.org/committee/6266604.html

[14] 'DLT in payment, clearing, and settlement', BIS, 2017, https://www.bis.org/cpmi/publ/d157.htm

[15] For further detail, see: 'Speech by Mary Starks – Blockchain: considering the risks to consumers and competition,' FCA, 2018, https://www.fca.org.uk/news/speeches/blockchain-considering-risks-consumers-and-competition

3.13   **Legal challenges**: Aside from financial services regulation, the application of DLT might also pose challenges with respect to civil law (for example, on the question of enforceability of smart contracts) and data protection (for example, the General Data Protection Regulation (GDPR)).[16] Amongst other provisions, GDPR establishes a right to erasure, which might cause tension with core features of some DLT networks that offer immutable data storage (without the technical possibility of erasure). There are particular DLT solutions, which, when compared to more traditional database technologies, claim to provide a more efficient way of complying with GDPR requirements (for example, by only sharing selective data or storing data locations rather than data files on-chain).[17] All organisations that use technologies such as DLT to process personal data must comply with the Data Protection Act 2018 and the GDPR.

3.14   **Settlement finality**: In payment systems, it is essential to know when a payment is final and irrevocable. In some versions of DLT, it can take time to ensure that all participants agree on the same version of the ledger. In rare cases, this means that a payment that appears to have been successfully completed could be 'overwritten' with a different version of the ledger. However, this is primarily a problem for permissionless platforms;[18] in permissioned platforms, consensus mechanisms can be designed to ensure that the point of final settlement is much clearer.

3.15   **Governance challenges**: DLT is by its nature a shared system. As a result, firms will have to pay careful attention to allocating responsibilities appropriately, given the absence of a central point of authority.[19] This is more of an issue for permissionless systems.

3.16   **Banking relationships**: Many stakeholders have highlighted that it is difficult for firms working in the DLT industry, including cryptoasset firms, to access banking services in the UK.

3.17   **Awareness and understanding**: Another commonly cited barrier to the effective take-up of DLT is the lack of understanding and awareness of how and when to use the technology appropriately. This may lead to situations where DLT is pursued for applications for which it is unsuitable or unnecessary, and where more traditional and established technologies may be sufficient. Conversely, because the technology is still in the early stages of development, some of the Taskforce's industry engagement noted that firms may not be aware of the range of potential applications and may therefore choose not to experiment with DLT.

---

[16] GDPR seeks to protect personal information and improve the way in which firms collect, store and process personal data. It has been effective since May 2018 and is overseen and enforced in the UK by the Information Commissioner's Office. For further detail, 'Guide to the General Data Protection Act (GDPR)', Information Commissioner's Office, 2018, https://ico.org.uk/for-organisations/guide-to-the-general-data-protection-regulation-gdpr/

[17] 'DLT FS17/04', FCA, 2017, https://www.fca.org.uk/publications/feedback-statements/fs17-4-distributed-ledger-technology

[18] This is because most permissionless platforms use consensus mechanisms such as proof of work, which offer *probabilistic settlement*: the chance of a transaction being overwritten falls over time until it is statistically close to certain that the transaction will not be overwritten.

[19] 'Discussion Paper on DLT', FCA, 2017, https://www.fca.org.uk/publication/discussion/dp17-03.pdf

Regulatory approaches to DLT

3.18   The FCA and the PRA (subject to any risks to their respective objectives) take a technologically neutral approach to regulation. Regulation is an enabler of positive innovation based on new technologies, as well as a means of containing undue risk. A technologically neutral approach means that the regulators do not mandate regulated firms to use a particular type of technology to facilitate their services.

3.19   The technology of choice will influence associated operational risks, but will not influence the regulatory status of a firm. For example, dealing in paper-based or token-based bonds will not influence the regulatory status of a firm.

3.20   Both the FCA and the Bank of England will continue to explore whether there are any unintended consequences of regulation to the innovations of new technologies, including DLT. The FCA considered this in their Discussion Paper on DLT and concluded that no changes to regulations were required.[20] The Taskforce therefore believes that the UK regulatory approach is well suited to support the development of DLT in financial services.

Box 3.J: Bank of England – RTGS renewal programme

The Bank of England has established a programme to deliver a renewed Real-Time Gross Settlement (RTGS) service.[21] RTGS holds accounts for banks, building societies and other institutions. It delivers final and risk-free settlement, by settling the net inter-bank movements arising from retail payments, and by settling high value (CHAPS) payments in real-time. RTGS is the hard infrastructure at the core of the UK payment system, processing payments of approximately £600 billion a day, equivalent to a third of annual UK GDP.

The renewed RTGS service will offer a diverse and flexible range of settlement models, to enable existing and emerging payment infrastructures to access central bank money.[22] The Bank of England has said that future forms of settlement, including those based on DLT, will be able to plug into the renewed RTGS service. This renewal of core infrastructure is intended to support private innovation.

In 2018, the Bank of England ran a proof of concept with a range of firms in order to understand how a renewed RTGS service could be capable of supporting settlement in systems operating on innovative payment technologies, such as those built on DLT.[23]

---

[20] ibid.

[21] 'The Bank of England's Real-Time-Gross-Settlement infrastructure', Bank of England, 2012, https://www.bankofengland.co.uk/-/media/boe/files/quarterly-bulletin/2012/the-boes-real-time-gross-settlement-infrastructure.pdf

[22] 'A blueprint for a new RTGS service for the UK', Bank of England, 2017, https://www.bankofengland.co.uk/-/media/boe/files/payments/a-blueprint-for-a-new-rtgs-service-for-the-uk.pdf

[23] For further detail on the outcomes of this proof of concept, see: 'RTGS renewal programme proof of concept: supporting DLT settlement models', Bank of England, 2017, https://www.bankofengland.co.uk/-/media/boe/files/payments/rtgs-renewal-programme-proof-of-concept-supporting-dlt-settlement-models.pdf

29

All participants confirmed that the planned functionality for the renewed RTGS service would enable their systems to connect and to achieve settlement in central bank money. A number of recommendations were made to ensure optimal access to central bank money, which the Bank of England will consider as part of the renewal programme.

Chapter 4
Impacts of cryptoassets

Box 4.A: Summary

Cryptoassets are not widely used in the UK, and the UK is not a major market relative to the global cryptoasset market. However, interest and activity in cryptoassets in the UK has grown over the past few years.

The Taskforce has assessed a wide range of potential benefits and risks associated with cryptoassets. It has concluded that there is limited evidence of the current generation of cryptoassets delivering benefits. However, benefits may materialise in the future, for example through the use of ICOs as a capital raising tool.

The Taskforce has concluded that cryptoassets pose a range of risks, notably to consumers (who may face large losses), market integrity (due to manipulation and other market-abuse style strategies) and financial crime. While cryptoassets currently pose no material risks to financial stability, this may change in the future.

Potential benefits of cryptoassets

4.1   Using the framework set out in Chapter 2, the Taskforce has considered whether cryptoassets present benefits when used:

- **as a means of exchange,** including by increasing the efficiency of international transfers

- **for investment,** including by widening access to new investment opportunities

- **as a capital raising tool,** including through streamlining the capital raising process

4.2   When **used as a means of exchange**, cryptoassets could allow for more efficient and cheaper transactions as a result of fewer intermediaries being involved (for example, micro-payments, simultaneous exchange and international transfers).[1] Some proponents also suggest that cryptoassets could improve the transparency and traceability of transactions; improve system resilience given the lack of a central

---

[1] Tests in the FCA's Regulatory Sandbox have demonstrated that a regulatory compliant use of cryptoassets for international transfers is possible at a small scale, and can lead to time and cost savings. For further detail, see 'Regulatory sandbox lessons learned report', FCA, 2017. https://www.fca.org.uk/publication/research-and-data/regulatory-sandbox-lessons-learned-report.pdf

system susceptible to outages; and lower barriers to entry, encouraging competition and providing, to some extent, an alternative to traditional payment services. However, these potential benefits are largely due to the use of DLT, rather than cryptoassets specifically, and would likely also apply to the use of a tokenised existing asset as a means of exchange.

4.3   When **used for investment**, proponents suggest that cryptoassets have the potential to widen access to new and different types of investment opportunities. However, the Taskforce considers that, in the current market, this broad access is likely to expose consumers to inappropriate levels of risks and exacerbate risks associated with the use of cryptoassets for illicit activity.

4.4   Evidence of the current generation of cryptoassets delivering any of these benefits is limited and many use cases are unproven at a large scale. This view was confirmed by much of the Taskforce's stakeholder engagement. The Taskforce therefore considers that, in many cases, the risks posed by the current generation of cryptoassets outweigh any potential benefits.

Cryptoassets used to support capital raising

4.5   The Taskforce has concluded that if benefits develop in the future, they are most likely to materialise through the use of ICOs as a capital raising tool. ICOs have the potential to present a range of opportunities, including:

- **Supporting innovation and competition**: Many ICOs seek to fund new, innovative business models, products and services. They may also incentivise improvements in traditional capital raising processes by introducing competition.

- **Improving efficiency**: ICOs directly link cryptoasset issuers with investors, which has the potential to make the capital raising process more streamlined, faster and cheaper, particularly for small issuances.

- **Addressing financing gaps**: Many high-risk, early stage projects struggle to raise funds. ICOs may help address these gaps by directly connecting firms and investors looking for high-risk, high-reward investments; and by allowing entrepreneurs to raise capital without needing to offer equity, in some circumstances.

- **Building a new investor and customer base:** The global accessibility of ICOs may also enable new sources of capital to be unlocked. Investors may also provide an initial customer base for new firms and create a community of early adopters for the product or service being developed.

4.6   In the current market, these benefits are most likely to accrue to developers and issuers, who can more efficiently access existing and new sources of capital. However, without appropriate protections, this is potentially to the detriment of consumers. This is discussed in more detail later in this chapter.

32

Risks associated with cryptoassets

4.7   The Taskforce has identified a range of risks associated with cryptoassets, including:

- **risks of financial crime**, including opportunities for cryptoassets to be used for illicit activity and cyber threats

- **risks to consumers**, who may buy unsuitable products, face large losses, be exposed to fraudulent activity, struggle to access market services, and be exposed to the failings of service providers

- **risks to market integrity**, which may lead to consumer losses or damage confidence in the market

- **potential implications for financial stability**, which may arise if the market grows and cryptoassets are more widely used

4.8   While most of the risks identified by the Taskforce are present across different types and uses of cryptoassets, the nature or extent of particular risks may differ.

4.9   Whilst tax was outside the Taskforce's remit, HM Treasury is working closely with HM Revenue and Customs (HMRC) to consider the tax issues raised by cryptoassets. Both authorities recognise the risks of tax avoidance and evasion arising from the increased use of cryptoassets and are continuing to review the range of enforcement tools and approaches at HMRC's disposal.

Risks of financial crime

4.10   Cryptoassets pose risks around criminal activity such as money laundering and terrorist financing because of their accessibility online, their global reach and their pseudo-anonymous nature.

4.11   The government's 2015 and 2017 National Risk Assessments of Money Laundering and Terrorist Financing (NRAs) assessed the risks associated with cryptoassets to be relatively low for both money laundering and terrorist financing, as there was little evidence of them being used to launder large amounts at high volume.[2] However, the 2017 NRA noted the role cryptoassets can play in laundering the proceeds of cyber-dependent crime (i.e. crime conducted through computer technology). Cryptoassets can also act as a method for payments between criminals and for the purchase of illicit tools or services sold online in criminal marketplaces.

4.12   Since the 2017 NRA, UK law enforcement authorities have increasingly identified cases of cryptoassets being used to launder illicit proceeds of offline crime. While the scale of this activity is unknown, certain features of cryptoassets are particularly attractive to criminals and the risks of cryptoassets being used in money laundering are expected to grow as cryptoassets become increasingly accessible.

---

[2] 'UK national risk assessment of money laundering and terrorist financing', HM Treasury and Home Office, 2015, https://assets.publishing.service.gov.uk/government/uploads/system/uploads/attachment_data/file/468210/UK_NRA_October_2015 _final_web.pdf; and 'National risk assessment of money laundering and terrorist financing', HM Treasury and Home Office, 2017, https://assets.publishing.service.gov.uk/government/uploads/system/uploads/attachment_data/file/655198/National_risk_assessme nt_of_money_laundering_and_terrorist_financing_2017_pdf_web.pdf

33

Attractive features include the anonymity afforded by cryptoasset ATMs, by peer-to-peer exchange facilities, and by the privacy features of some coins.

4.13   UK law enforcement authorities are working with international partners to continue to develop their understanding of the role cryptoassets can play in money laundering. Europol estimates that £3-4 billion is laundered using cryptoassets each year in Europe; however, this remains a small proportion of total funds laundered in Europe, which stands at £100 billion.[3] In addition, a recent Financial Action Task Force report to the G20 noted that suspicious transaction reporting linked to cryptoassets is rising globally.[4]

Risks to consumers

4.14   Cryptoassets pose a range of substantial risks to consumers, which stem from consumers purchasing unsuitable products without having access to adequate information; from fraudulent activity; and from the immaturity or failings of market infrastructures and services.

Unsuitable products and insufficient information

4.15   Consumers may suffer unexpected or large losses without regulatory protection as a result of buying cryptoasset products that are not suitable for their needs, or buying these products while being unaware of the associated risks. The high volatility of cryptoassets, which may attract investors, can also lead to substantial losses.[5]

4.16   Consumers may also invest in products that are poor value due to unclear price formation and pricing practices, high fees and difficulty in assessing fundamental value. Investment in cryptoassets could also represent an opportunity cost for some consumers, who might forego another, potentially more suitable, investment to purchase a cryptoasset product.

4.17   The key drivers of this behaviour are a search for high returns, and some consumers lacking understanding of cryptoassets and their volatility and risks. Insufficient consumer understanding stems from the complexity of these products and a lack of available information and appropriate warnings regarding the risks. Consumers may also be unaware of the limited regulatory protections for some cryptoassets and the lack of recourse to the Financial Services Compensation Scheme (FSCS) and the Financial Ombudsman Service (FOS).

4.18   The FCA has commissioned qualitative consumer research to better understand UK consumers' understanding and attitude towards cryptoassets. This research is still underway, however preliminary findings from speaking to a number of consumers about their experience of investing in cryptoassets suggest that:

---

[3] 'Criminals hide 'billions' in crypto-cash – Europol', BBC, 2018, https://www.bbc.co.uk/news/technology-43025787

[4] 'FATF report to the G20 Finance Ministers and Central Bank Governors', Financial Action Taskforce, 2018, http://www.fatf-gafi.org/media/fatf/documents/reports/FATF-Report-G20-FM-CBG-July-2018.pdf

[5] For example, in 2017, the average volatility of the top ten exchange tokens by market capitalisation was more than 25 times that of the US equities market. See: 'The future of money – speech by Mark Carney', Bank of England, 2018, https://www.bankofengland.co.uk/speech/2018/mark-carney-speech-to-the-inaugural-scottish-economics-conference

- some respondents perceived cryptoassets as a shortcut to easy money and wealth, citing 'fear of missing out' and influence from social media as reasons for investing

- some respondents tended to overestimate their knowledge of cryptoassets and the underlying technology

- because of the language and images associated with cryptoassets (such as 'mining' and 'coins'), some respondents seemed to have a sense that they were investing in tangible assets

4.19   Advertising regarding cryptoassets, which is often targeted at retail investors, is not typically fair or clear and can be misleading. Adverts often overstate benefits and rarely warn of volatility risks, the fact consumers can both grow and lose their investment, and the lack of regulation. There are also examples of regulated firms marketing cryptoasset products without clarifying that this part of their business is not regulated.

4.20   Market abuse-style activities, to which cryptoasset and related markets are vulnerable, can also result in losses for consumers (referred to in more detail in paragraph 4.30).

4.21   In addition to these risks which can be seen across different cryptoassets, certain types of cryptoassets produce some specific risks to consumers:

- **ICOs:** It can be particularly difficult for consumers to assess the risks of a particular token being issued, as the 'white paper' documents that typically accompany ICOs are not standardised and often feature exaggerated or misleading information. Given the lack of clear information, consumers may not understand that many of these projects are high-risk and at an early stage, and therefore may not suit their risk tolerance, financial sophistication or wealth.

- **Financial instruments that reference cryptoassets:** Although regulated, financial instruments that reference cryptoassets also produce some specific risks to consumers. Leveraged derivatives, such as CFDs and futures, can cause losses that go beyond the initial investment. The risk of trading losses can be exacerbated by product fees such as financing costs and spreads, as well as by a lack of transparency in the price formation of the underlying cryptoasset.

Fraudulent activity and cybercrime

4.22   Consumers are also at risk of losses resulting from fraudulent activity and deceptive practices in the cryptoasset market. In particular, the promise of high yield returns makes it easy for scammers to attract customers. A recent report by Action Fraud showed there were 203 reports of cryptoasset scams in June – July 2018, with victims reportedly losing over £2 million in total (an average of over £10,000 per person).[6] Action Fraud reported that fraudsters cold call victims and use social media platforms to advertise 'get rich quick' investments.

---

[6] 'Cryptocurrency fraud leads to £2 million worth of losses this summer', ActionFraud, 2018, https://www.actionfraud.police.uk/news/2m-lost-to-cryptocurrency-fraud-aug18

35

4.23   While fraudulent activity exists across the range of cryptoassets, it is likely to differ between types of cryptoassets. Evidence suggests there are particularly significant risks of fraudulent activity associated with ICOs. A recent study indicated that approximately 25% of ICOs could be fraudulent[7], whilst other estimates suggest that 46% of ICOs issued in 2017 have already failed.[8] In many cases investors do not receive what they were promised and issuers do not deliver the intended product or service. This is in part driven by a conflict of interest for the issuer of the ICO, who may seek to maximise the capital being raised by failing to be transparent, not providing sufficient details of the risks, and misleading consumers. In some cases, large sums of money have been raised for projects without appropriate plans or capability for delivery.

4.24   Cryptoassets also present risks to consumers through cybercrime. Cyber threats – which stem from failings on the part of exchanges and wallet providers to put in place appropriate systems and controls – can put consumers at risk of large losses. Cryptoassets are now viewed as high-value targets for theft. Both users and service providers such as wallets and exchanges are increasingly being targeted by cybercriminals, in particular to obtain the private keys which enable consumers to access and transfer their cryptoassets.[9] Some of the largest and most recent publicly-known hacks and thefts include Coincheck ($540 million stolen in January 2018), Mt Gox (nearly $500 million stolen in February 2014) and Zaif ($60 million stolen in September 2018), all in Japan, and Bithumb ($32 million stolen in June 2018) in South Korea.[10] Given the traceability of cryptoassets varies, it can be difficult for law enforcement to track stolen cryptoassets and take action against perpetrators, meaning theft and associated consumer losses are often irrecoverable.

4.25   In addition, a new but growing cybercrime threat – known as 'cryptojacking' – involves the victim's computer processing power being used to mine for cryptoassets without their explicit knowledge and permission.[11] Many internet security providers now report that cryptojacking has joined ransomware as one of the leading malware threats. One US-based software company reported that, in the first three months of 2018, new cryptojacking malware grew by 1,189%, with new ransomware threats falling by 32% from the previous quarter.[12]

---

7 'BIS Annual Economic Report', Bank for International Settlements, 2018, https://www.bis.org/publ/arpdf/ar2018e5.pdf

8 Data originally from 'TokenData', 2018, https://www.tokendata.io/, printed in 'ICOs are even riskier than you think', Bitcoin News, 2018, https://news.bitcoin.com/46-last-years-icos-failed-already/

9 The National Cyber Security Centre (NCSC) has also highlighted some of the cyber risks associated with cryptoasset storage, for further detail, see: 'Weekly threat report 2nd February 2018', NCSC, 2018, https://www.ncsc.gov.uk/report/weekly-threat-report-2nd-february-2018

10 'Coincheck: world's biggest ever digital currency 'theft'', BBC, 2018, https://www.bbc.co.uk/news/world-asia-42845505; 'MtGox gives bankruptcy details', BBC, 2014, https://www.bbc.co.uk/news/technology-26420932; 'Japan's Tech Bureau says about $60m stolen in crypto hack', Reuters, 2018, https://uk.reuters.com/article/crypto-currencies-japan-cybercrime/japans-tech-bureau-says-about-60-mln-stolen-in-crypto-hack-idUKL3N1W5692; and 'Bithumb: hackers 'rob crypto-exchange of $32m'', BBC, 2018, https://www.bbc.co.uk/news/technology-44547250

11 'The cyber threat to UK business', NCSC and National Crime Agency (NCA), 2018, http://www.nationalcrimeagency.gov.uk/publications/890-the-cyber-threat-to-uk-business-2017-2018/file

12 'McAfee Labs Threats Report', McAfee, 2018, https://www.mcafee.com/enterprise/en-us/assets/reports/rp-quarterly-threats-jun-2018.pdf

Market infrastructures and services

4.26   Risks to consumers may also result from immature market structures and failings of service providers such as exchanges, trading platforms and wallet providers.

4.27   Immature market structures and operational risk issues associated with cryptoasset exchanges, trading platforms and wallet providers may delay or deny consumers easy access to their invested funds and/or secondary market trading. This is particularly the case for less widely used cryptoassets, where there is no guarantee of liquidity in the secondary market, which makes knowing the fair price difficult and may prevent investors from selling cryptoassets and realising value.

4.28   Cryptoasset exchanges, trading platforms and wallet providers are key services required to access cryptoassets and can present risks to consumers. They may fail to put in place appropriate systems and controls, leaving consumers exposed to risks such as cybercrime (as identified in paragraph 4.24). There is also some evidence to suggest that cryptoasset exchanges, trading platforms and wallet providers are charging high and variable fees that consumers are not always made aware of. There can also be significant delays in the payment chain as a result of these service providers, which may result in consumers missing buy/sell opportunities.

Risks to market integrity

4.29   A combination of market immaturity, illiquidity and a lack of available information regarding the market give rise to concerns about market integrity. This may damage confidence and prevent both the cryptoasset market and related derivative markets from operating effectively. For cryptoassets and related markets, vulnerability to market abuse and manipulative behaviour is heightened by several factors.

- The cryptoasset market and actors are at an immature stage of development. This could mean, for example, that cryptoasset exchanges suffer from issues such as poor systems and controls, low price transparency and conflicts of interest.

- There is a lack of information about the identity of participants and their activity inherent in some instruments.

- The novel nature of the market means new abusive behaviours may arise which are not captured by current monitoring tools. Manipulation may include false signals of supply and demand (for example, wash trading, layering, and spoofing), as well as dissemination of misleading information in the media.

4.30   Market abuse-style activities pose risks to market integrity. Cryptoassets and related markets are vulnerable to such activities and there is evidence of them already occurring. Press reports indicate that individuals are using messaging applications, such as Telegram, to orchestrate 'pump and dump' schemes for cryptoassets.[13] In these arrangements, the organisers synchronise the purchase of a

---

[13] 'How traders pump and dump cryptocurrencies', UK Business Insider, 2017, http://uk.businessinsider.com/how-traders-pump-and-dump-cryptocurrencies-2017-11

selected cryptoasset, temporarily pushing up its price, encouraging excitement and further purchasing amongst other investors. Once the price has risen, the organisers then offload their cryptoassets for a profit, leaving consumers with an expensively purchased and often illiquid cryptoasset. Actors with large holdings, especially in the more illiquid cryptoassets, may also be able to use their dominant position to influence the price.

Box 4.B: Industry action to manage risks

Over the course of its stakeholder engagement, the Taskforce heard from firms and industry groups about the actions they have taken to mitigate some of the risks highlighted in this chapter. For example, some exchanges already implement anti-money laundering checks despite not yet being formally obliged to do so. In addition, some industry bodies are developing voluntary codes of conduct.

Implications for financial stability

4.31   In March 2018, the Financial Policy Committee (FPC) assessed the financial stability threats of cryptoassets and judged that existing cryptoassets do not currently pose a material risk to UK financial stability.[14] In addition, the Financial Stability Board (FSB) has judged that cryptoassets do not pose risks to global financial stability.[15] This assessment has been endorsed by the G20.[16] However, the market, industry and technology are evolving rapidly and risks to financial stability may emerge in the future.

4.32   The FPC's analysis focused on the 'transmission channels' which could transmit risks from the cryptoasset market into the formal financial system.[17] The FPC determined that, in the case of current cryptoassets, these transmission channels were not significant at this point in time but that, in certain circumstances, they could become more significant over time and therefore produce risks to financial stability. Table 4.A summarises the current situation and how these transmission channels may develop.

---

[14] 'Financial Policy Committee statement from its meeting – 12 March 2018', Financial Policy Committee (FPC), 2018, https://www.bankofengland.co.uk/statement/fpc/2018/financial-policy-committee-statement-march-2018

[15] FSB Chair's letter to G20 Finance Ministers and Central Bank Governors', Financial Stability Board (FSB), 2018, http://www.fsb.org/2018/03/fsb-chairs-letter-to-g20-finance-ministers-and-central-bank-governors/

[16] 'Communique of the G20 Finance Ministers & Central Bank Governors Meeting, 21-22 July 2018. https://g20.org/sites/default/files/media/communique-_fmcbg_july.pdf

[17] This approach follows the FPC's framework for assessing risks beyond the core banking sector, for further detail see: 'Financial Stability Report – November 2017', FPC, 2017, https://www.bankofengland.co.uk/financial-stability-report/2017/november-2017

Table 4.A: Financial stability transmission channels

Transmission channel	Current situation	Potential developments
Use of cryptoassets in payments and settlement.	Minimal use.	Work is underway in industry to overcome capacity and volatility constraints to the use of cryptoassets in payments.
		These developments are unlikely to lead to significantly greater use of cryptoassets in payments and settlement in the medium term.
Exposure of systemically important UK financial institutions to cryptoassets.	Negligible exposures.	Firms could develop direct exposure by investing directly in cryptoassets or in financial instruments that reference cryptoassets. Firms may also develop indirect exposure through relationships with exchanges or counterparty relationships with non-systemic firms exposed to cryptoassets.
		However, there does not currently appear to be an appetite from systemically important firms to take significant exposures to cryptoassets.
Links between cryptoasset markets and systemically important markets.	Limited links.	Links may develop if there is a proliferation of financial instruments that reference cryptoassets.
		However, demand to date suggests use of such products is unlikely to grow to a scale that would cause wider disruption.

39

Chapter 5
Conclusions and responses

Box 5.A: Summary

The Taskforce has concluded that DLT has the potential to deliver significant benefits in both financial services and other sectors, and all three authorities will continue to support its development.

HM Treasury, the FCA and the Bank of England will take action to mitigate the risks that cryptoassets pose to consumers and market integrity; to prevent the use of cryptoassets for illicit activity; to guard against threats to financial stability that could emerge in the future; and to encourage responsible development of legitimate DLT and cryptoasset-related activity in the UK.

In order to deliver these actions, the authorities will consult on:

- implementing one of the most comprehensive responses globally to the use of cryptoassets for illicit activity
- a potential prohibition of the sale to retail consumers of derivatives referencing certain types of cryptoassets (for example, exchange tokens)[1], including CFDs, options, futures and transferable securities
- guidance clarifying how certain cryptoassets already fall within the existing regulatory perimeter
- whether the regulatory perimeter requires extension in relation to cryptoassets that have comparable features to specified investments but that fall outside the perimeter

The Taskforce has also concluded that exchange tokens present new challenges to traditional forms of financial regulation. There is therefore a need to consider carefully how regulation could meaningfully and effectively address the risks posed by exchange tokens and what, if any, regulatory tools would be most appropriate. The government will issue a consultation in early 2019 to further explore whether and how exchange tokens and related firms such as exchanges and wallet providers could be regulated effectively, in the case that other measures outlined in this report do not adequately address all relevant risks.

In addition, the authorities will continue to:

- warn consumers of the risks of investing in cryptoassets
- monitor potential implications for financial stability

---

[1] The prospective prohibition on retail derivatives referencing certain types of cryptoassets would exclude derivatives referencing cryptoassets that qualify as securities.

40

5.1   HM Treasury, the FCA and the Bank of England are committed:

- to the UK maintaining its international reputation as a safe and transparent place to do business in financial services

- to ensuring high regulatory standards in financial markets

- to protecting consumers

- to guarding against threats to financial stability that could emerge in the future

- to allowing those innovators in the financial sector that play by the rules to thrive so that the benefits of new technologies can be fully realised

5.2   The Taskforce has developed a response to cryptoassets and DLT that is consistent with these objectives, and this chapter sets out the actions the authorities will take.

5.3   The Taskforce considers that DLT has the potential to deliver significant benefits in financial services, as well as in a broad range of other sectors. The Taskforce has also seen some evidence that certain types of cryptoassets have the potential to deliver benefits in the future, for example when used as an innovative capital raising tool. However, harnessing these potential benefits requires effective action to manage the range of risks observed in the current cryptoasset market – in particular, to consumers and market integrity, and the use of cryptoassets for illicit activity.

5.4   This is a fast-moving global market, with the technology developing and the nature of cryptoassets evolving. The authorities will keep their approach to cryptoassets and DLT under review to ensure the UK continues to support innovation while maintaining safe and transparent financial markets. **The Taskforce will convene every six months to consider developments and review the UK's approach.**

The Taskforce's response to cryptoassets

Preventing financial crime

5.5   The Taskforce has concluded that, while the use of cryptoassets for illicit activity remains low, these risks are increasing and the use of cryptoassets for money laundering is growing. The UK will not tolerate the use of cryptoassets in illicit activity, and the authorities will take strong action to address these risks by bringing all relevant firms into anti-money laundering and counter-terrorist financing (AML/CTF) regulation.

5.6   The government is developing a robust regulatory response which will address these risks by going significantly beyond the requirements set out in the EU Fifth Anti-Money Laundering Directive (5MLD), providing one of the most comprehensive responses globally to the use of cryptoassets for illicit activity. The government will consult on its proposed actions in the new year, and will legislate during 2019 to give effect to this response.

5.7   The government will bring fiat-to-cryptoasset exchange firms and custodian wallet providers within the scope of AML/CTF regulation, as required by 5MLD.

41

Following the work of the Taskforce, the government intends to broaden the UK's approach to go beyond the 5MLD requirements, and will consult on including:

- exchange services between different cryptoassets, to prevent anonymous 'layering' of funds to mask their origin

- platforms that facilitate peer-to-peer exchange of cryptoassets, which could enable anonymous transfers of funds between individuals

- cryptoasset ATMs, which could be used anonymously to purchase cryptoassets

- non-custodian wallet providers that function similarly to custodian wallet providers, which may otherwise facilitate the anonymous storage and transfer of cryptoassets. Consultation on this area will include considering issues of technological feasibility

5.8   In addition, the government will consult on whether to require firms based outside the UK to comply with these regulations when providing services to UK consumers, in order to prevent illicit actors in the UK from dealing with firms based abroad and therefore bypassing UK regulation.

5.9   The government has asked the FCA to consider taking on the role of supervising firms in fulfilling their AML/CTF obligations. The government will seek views on this through consultation before confirming the identity of the supervisor.

5.10   To date, the FCA has also been taking action in regard to regulated firms who interact with cryptoassets and associated financial crime risks. The FCA issued a letter to CEOs of all banks in June 2018, setting out appropriate practice for the handling of the financial crime risks associated with cryptoassets.[2]

5.11   Further to this domestic response, the UK is actively engaging in international discussions to ensure a global response to the risks posed by cryptoassets. The Financial Action Task Force (FATF), the global standard-setter on AML/CTF, has agreed to update its standards to apply to cryptoassets.[3] The UK will continue to be a leading voice in these discussions, and ensure that this work is progressed as a priority.

Regulating financial instruments that reference cryptoassets

5.12   The FCA has taken action where it has seen evidence of harm relating to the sale, marketing and distribution of particular derivative products. For example, the FCA supported ESMA's restrictions on the sale to retail consumers of contracts for difference (CFDs) referencing cryptoassets. This measure took effect on 1 August 2018 and will be renewed from 1 November 2018. The restriction, among other things, limits leverage on such products to 2:1, reflecting the high price volatility of these instruments. This intervention is temporary, but subject to renewal while the FCA (in parallel with other EU national competent authorities) implements its own permanent domestic interventions.

---

[2] 'Dear CEO – cryptoassets and financial crime', FCA, 2018, https://www.fca.org.uk/publication/correspondence/dear-ceo-letter-cryptoassets-financial-crime.pdf

[3] 'Regulation of virtual assets', Financial Action Task Force, 2018, http://www.fatf-gafi.org/publications/fatfrecommendations/documents/regulation-virtual-assets.html

5.13   Given concerns identified around consumer protection and market integrity in these markets, the FCA will consult on a prohibition of the sale to retail consumers of all derivatives referencing exchange tokens such as Bitcoin, including CFDs, futures, options and transferable securities. The proposed prohibition would not cover derivatives referencing cryptoassets that qualify as securities, however CFDs on securities would remain subject to ESMA's temporary restrictions and any future FCA proposals to implement permanent measures in relation to CFDs.

5.14   To ensure that the integrity of these regulated markets is maintained, the FCA will not authorise or approve the listing of a transferable security or a fund that references exchange tokens (for example, exchange-traded funds) unless it has confidence in the integrity of the underlying market and that other regulatory criteria for funds authorisation are met. Before listing any securities with cryptoassets as the underlying asset, the FCA will need to be satisfied that granting the listing would not be detrimental to investors' interests. To date, the FCA has not approved the listing of any exchange-traded products with exchange tokens as the underlying asset.

Clarifying the regulation of security tokens

5.15   Security tokens fall within the current regulatory perimeter. However, the Taskforce recognises that the novel nature of some cryptoassets and the presence of new market participants may mean the regulatory perimeter is not being correctly understood. In addition, the complexity and opacity of many cryptoassets means it is difficult to determine whether they qualify as security tokens.

5.16   To provide further clarity on the way regulation applies to security tokens, the FCA will consult on perimeter guidance by the end of 2018. This guidance will set out the FCA's interpretation of the current regulatory perimeter.

5.17   The FCA encourages prospective token issuers or other market participants, such as secondary market platforms, to consider whether their activities require authorisation. In parallel, the FCA will continue to monitor for potential breaches by entities or individuals carrying out regulated activities without the appropriate authorisation.

Consulting on extending the regulatory perimeter for ICOs

5.18   In addition, the Taskforce wants to ensure that firms do not issue cryptoassets that have comparable features to specified investments (such as shares or units in a collective investment scheme) but are structured in such a way that they avoid regulation. Activities related to such cryptoassets should be regulated in order to protect investors, eliminate fraudulent activity and ensure market integrity. Should the issuance of cryptoassets through ICOs or another distribution mechanism prove to have benefits in the future (for example, as a means of capital raising), consistent application of regulation will also enable legitimate activity to thrive in the UK.

5.19   The government will issue a consultation in early 2019 to further explore with the industry whether there are examples of such cryptoassets on the UK market and, if so, whether an extension of the regulatory perimeter is required. Subject to the outcomes of this consultation, the government stands ready to legislate to redefine and expand the perimeter if necessary. This will ensure that FCA regulation

43

333

can be applied to all cryptoassets that have comparable features to specified investments, regardless of the way they are structured.

Addressing the risks of exchange tokens

5.20   The Taskforce recognises the substantial potential risks to consumers and markets posed by investment and trading in exchange tokens such as Bitcoin and the firms that facilitate this activity, such as exchanges and wallet providers.

5.21   However, exchange tokens are unlike other financial services products, and present new challenges to traditional forms of financial regulation. There is a need to consider carefully how regulation could meaningfully and effectively address the risks posed by exchange tokens and what, if any, regulatory tools would be most appropriate.

5.22   To support the authorities in addressing these complexities, the government will issue a consultation in early 2019 to further explore whether and how exchange tokens and related firms such as exchanges and wallet providers could be regulated effectively, in the case that other measures outlined in this report do not adequately address all relevant risks.

5.23   The Taskforce also considers that a consistent international approach to respond to exchange tokens is essential, to ensure global regulatory coherence and avoid arbitrage in a market that is not confined to national boundaries and involves highly mobile actors. An internationally coordinated approach and action by other jurisdictions will also help to mitigate risks to UK consumers – many of whom invest in cryptoassets through firms based outside the UK.

Ensuring a coordinated international approach

5.24   Given the importance of international coordination, the government, the FCA and the Bank of England will continue to be actively involved in international efforts, and the UK will be a thought leader in shaping future regulatory approaches.

5.25   While work is underway through a range of international bodies to consider approaches to cryptoassets, there is a need for more integrated work to capture the full range of relevant issues and consider the particular challenges exchange tokens present for existing financial regulatory frameworks. The UK will advocate for these issues to be addressed through the G20 and G7.

5.26   The UK will continue to engage internationally through a range of fora:

- **G20 and G7 Finance Ministers and Central Bank Governors** have agreed that, while cryptoassets present risks, the underlying technology has the potential to deliver significant benefits.[4] Following these discussions, the G20 asked that the international standard setting bodies continue their work to monitor the potential risks of cryptoassets and assess multilateral

---

4 'Communique – Finance Ministers and Central Bank Governors', G20, 2018; 'Communique – Finance Ministers and Central Bank Governors', G20, 2018, https://g20.org/sites/default/files/media/communique-_fmcbg_july.pdf; and 'Chair's Summary: G7 Finance Ministers and Central Bank Governors' Meeting', G7, 2018, https://g7.gc.ca/en/g7-presidency/themes/investing-growth-works-everyone/g7-ministerial-meeting/chairs-summary-g7-finance-ministers-central-bank-governors/

responses. The UK will continue to be a leader in the G20 and G7's discussions of cryptoassets.

- **The Financial Action Task Force (FATF)**, the global standard setter on AML/CTF, has agreed to update its standards to apply to cryptoassets.[5] The UK will continue to be a leading voice in these discussions.

- The FCA is an active participant in discussions at the **International Organization of Securities Commissions** (IOSCO). As well as contributing to a consultation network of national regulators on ICOs, the FCA is chairing the organisation's Fintech Network.

- The FCA continues to engage in discussions at the European level, including with the various **European Supervisory Authorities**. In particular, the FCA is an active member of the **European Securities and Markets Authority's** taskforce on ICOs and virtual currencies.

- In August 2018, the FCA, in collaboration with 11 other overseas regulators and related organisations, published a consultation paper on the **Global Financial Innovation Network** (GFIN).[6] One of the proposed aims of this international network of regulators is to provide a forum for joint work and discussions on innovative technologies such as DLT and cryptoassets.

- The Bank of England has co-led the work of the **Financial Stability Board** to develop a global monitoring framework that will highlight risks posed by cryptoassets to financial stability.[7]

- The Prudential Regulation Authority is also actively participating in discussions with authorities internationally on the prudential regulation of cryptoassets, including at the **Basel Committee on Banking Supervision**.

- HM Treasury has led **Financial Dialogues** and **Fintech Bridges,** which have enabled the government and regulators to engage with other jurisdictions on emerging market trends and regulatory challenges, including cryptoassets. The UK has five **FinTech Bridges**, which are bilateral agreements that commit the UK to sharing FinTech policy experience and expertise with counterparts in Hong Kong, Australia, Singapore, China and the Republic of Korea.

Improving consumer awareness

5.27   The Taskforce also recognises the need to ensure UK consumers are aware of the risks of investing in cryptoassets, and the lack of regulatory protections associated with many of these products. **The authorities firmly believe that consumers should approach purchasing cryptoassets with a high degree of caution**

---

[5] 'Regulation of virtual assets', Financial Action Task Force, 2018, http://www.fatf-gafi.org/publications/fatfrecommendations/documents/regulation-virtual-assets.html

[6] 'Global Financial Innovation Network', FCA, 2018, https://www.fca.org.uk/publications/consultation-papers/global-financial-innovation-network

[7] 'Crypto-asset markets: Potential channels for future financial stability implications', Financial Stability Board, 2018, http://www.fsb.org/2018/10/crypto-asset-markets-potential-channels-for-future-financial-stability-implications/

45

and be prepared to lose money. The authorities have been taking action to warn consumers of these risks, and will continue to do so.

5.28   To date, the FCA has taken a number of steps to improve public awareness of the risks associated with all types of cryptoassets. This includes through media appearances,[8] and by issuing consumer and firm warnings about the risks of ICOs, cryptoasset derivatives, CFDs and investment scams.[9] In addition, cryptoassets have been added to the FCA's ScamSmart Warning List, a campaign that aims to help consumers over the ages of 55 falling victim to scams and investment fraud.[10]

Maintaining financial stability

5.29   While cryptoassets do not currently pose a material threat to UK or global financial stability, the Taskforce recognises that risks could emerge as the market develops and that vigilant monitoring is essential.

5.30   The Bank of England will continue to monitor market developments to identify potential implications for financial stability through the Financial Policy Committee's (FPC) monitoring of risks to financial stability, the Prudential Regulation Authority's (PRA) supervision of firms and the Bank of England's supervision of Financial Market Infrastructures.

- The FPC will act to ensure the core of the UK financial system remains resilient if linkages between crypto-assets and systemically important financial institutions or markets were to grow significantly. In the event that one or more cryptoassets were likely to become widely used for payments, or as an asset intended to store value, the FPC would require current financial stability standards to be applied to relevant payments and exchanges.

- The PRA is currently assessing the adequacy of prudential regulations, including for capital, which apply to cryptoasset-related exposures of banks, insurance companies and designated investment firms. As part of this work, the PRA issued a letter to CEOs of all PRA-regulated firms in June 2018, reminding them of the risks associated with the current generation of cryptoassets and the relevant obligations under PRA rules.[11]

- The Bank of England is also alert to potential issues related to cryptoassets as part of its supervision of Financial Market Infrastructures (FMI). The Bank has already worked with HM Treasury to widen the regulatory perimeter to include non-interbank payment systems (through the Digital

---

[8] In December 2017, FCA Chief Executive Andrew Bailey appeared on BBC Newsnight, warning that "If you want to invest in Bitcoin, be prepared to lose your money". For further detail, see 'Regulator warns Bitcoin buyers: be ready to lose all your money', BBC, 2017, https://www.bbc.co.uk/news/business-42360553

[9] 'Initial Coin Offerings', FCA, 2017, https://www.fca.org.uk/news/statements/initial-coin-offerings; 'Cryptocurrency derivatives', FCA, 2018, https://www.fca.org.uk/news/statements/cryptocurrency-derivatives; 'Consumer warning about the risks of investing in cryptocurrency CFDs', FCA, 2017, https://www.fca.org.uk/news/news-stories/consumer-warning-about-risks-investing-cryptocurrency-cfds; and 'Cryptocurrency investment scams', FCA, 2018, https://www.fca.org.uk/scamsmart/cryptocurrency-investment-scams.

[10] ScamSmart, FCA, 2018, https://www.fca.org.uk/scamsmart

[11] 'Dear CEO – existing or planned exposure to cryptoassets', Prudential Regulation Authority, 2018, https://www.bankofengland.co.uk/-/media/boe/files/prudential-regulation/letter/2018/existing-or-planned-exposure-to-crypto-assets.pdf

Economy Act 2017). This means that a payment system, including one based on DLT, whose users are not banks, can be brought under the Bank's supervision, should one become systemically important to the UK financial system. If an FMI proposed to use cryptoassets or DLT in its clearing, payments or settlement system, this would be addressed as part of the Bank of England's existing supervisory approach. In each case, the FMI would be required to show how the use of cryptoassets or DLT met relevant regulatory requirements.

Taxation

5.31   Tax was outside the Taskforce's remit, so substantive considerations of tax issues are not included in this report. However, HM Treasury is working closely with HM Revenue and Customs to consider the tax issues raised by cryptoassets.

5.32   Current guidance on the tax treatment of cryptoassets is set out on HMRC's website.[12] HMRC will further update their guidance by early 2019, drawing on the Taskforce's work.

The Taskforce's response to distributed ledger technology

5.33   While the authorities' immediate priority is to mitigate the risks associated with the current generation of cryptoassets, the Taskforce considers that other applications of DLT have the potential to deliver significant benefits in both financial services and other sectors. The authorities do not believe there are regulatory barriers to further adoption of DLT. However, the technology requires further development before it could be used at scale and before these opportunities could be realised.

5.34   The authorities will continue to encourage and enable experimentation and innovation, so that DLT and other new technologies can develop and be adopted safely in the financial system.

5.35   The regulators take a technologically neutral approach to regulation, and will continue to provide a platform for innovation to encourage the development of new technologies to support a dynamic financial system.

5.36   The FCA has accepted a significant number of DLT-based projects into its Regulatory Sandbox, and via its RegTech initiative is actively exploring the use of DLT for its supervisory duties.

5.37   The backbone of the existing payments system – the Bank of England's new RTGS service - will be compatible with DLT-based payment systems, supporting further innovation and use of DLT in financial services.

5.38   **The government is also acting to support DLT in and beyond financial services.** The government has invested over £10 million through Innovate UK and

---

[12] For VAT purposes: 'VATFIN2330', HMRC, 2016, https://www.gov.uk/hmrc-internal-manuals/vat-finance-manual/vatfin2330;

For Capital Gains Tax purposes: 'CG12100', HMRC, 2016, https://www.gov.uk/hmrc-internal-manuals/capital-gains-manual/cg12100; and

'Revenue and Customs Brief 9 (2014): Bitcoin and other cryptocurrencies', HMRC, 2014, https://www.gov.uk/government/publications/revenue-and-customs-brief-9-2014-bitcoin-and-other-cryptocurrencies.

the research councils to support a diverse range of DLT projects; created a £20 million GovTech Catalyst Fund to explore technology-based solutions for public sector challenges, potentially including the use of DLT; and is considering how DLT might be deployed to support new forms of financial services infrastructure through its Shared Platforms work with Deloitte.[13] Many government departments are also building proofs of concept to trial the use of the technology.

Next steps

5.39   **Table 5.A** sets out actions to be taken forward by HM Treasury, the FCA and the Bank of England, accordance with their remits, to further develop and implement the UK's policy and regulatory approach to cryptoassets and DLT.

Table 5.A: Actions to be taken by the authorities

Action	Owner	Timing
Developing and implementing the UK's policy and regulatory approach		
Consult on guidance for cryptoasset activities currently within the regulatory perimeter	Financial Conduct Authority	By end 2018
Consult on a potential prohibition of the sale to retail consumers of derivatives referencing certain types of cryptoassets (for example, exchange tokens), including CFDs, options, futures and transferable securities	Financial Conduct Authority	By end 2018
Consult on potential changes to the regulatory perimeter to bring in cryptoassets that have comparable features to specified investments, and explore how exchange tokens might be regulated if necessary	HM Treasury	In early 2019
Transpose the EU Fifth Anti-Money Laundering Directive and broaden the scope of AML/CTF regulation further	HM Treasury	Consultation in the new year, with legislation in 2019
Continue to assess the adequacy of the prudential regulatory framework, in conjunction with international counterparts	Prudential Regulation Authority	Ongoing
Issue revised guidance on the tax treatment of cryptoassets	HM Revenue and Customs	By early 2019
Monitoring market developments		
Continue to monitor market developments and regularly review the UK's approach	HM Treasury, Financial Conduct Authority and Bank of England	The Taskforce will convene every six months

---

[13] 'New support for tech to boost public sector productivity', HM Treasury, Department for Business, Energy, and Industrial Strategy, 2017, https://www.gov.uk/government/news/new-support-for-tech-to-boost-public-sector-productivity; 'Shared platforms' will help UK firms that face certain barriers due to the need to invest in new systems and perform complex financial services activities by creating economies of scale around the provision of these activities. For further detail, see: 'Fintech sector strategy', HM Treasury, 2018, https://www.gov.uk/government/publications/fintech-sector-strategy

48

338

Action	Owner	Timing
Continue to monitor financial stability risks	Bank of England	Ongoing
Promoting a coordinated international response		
Continue to engage internationally through the G20, G7, FATF, FSB, IOSCO, BCBS, EU, OECD and bilaterally	HM Treasury, Financial Conduct Authority and Bank of England	Ongoing
Supporting innovation with distributed ledger technology		
Enable the renewed RTGS service to be capable of interfacing with innovative payment platforms, including those based on DLT	Bank of England	Update on timing to be provided at the end of 2018
Continue to develop experience with DLT applications through the Regulatory Sandbox and support firms through the Innovate initiative	Financial Conduct Authority	Ongoing
Continue to explore the use of DLT to enable a more accurate, efficient and consistent regulatory reporting system	Financial Conduct Authority	Ongoing
Continue to consider how DLT might be deployed to support new forms of financial services Infrastructure, including in work on Shared Platforms	HM Treasury	Ongoing
Continue to identify opportunities to use DLT in the public sector, including through the cross-government Blockchain Network, the GovTech Catalyst Fund, and building proofs of concept to trial the use of the technology.	Various government departments	Ongoing
Test the potential of DLT through Field Labs, where the Digital Catapult will work with businesses, investors, and regulators in a range of areas, including in construction and the management of goods in ports.	Digital Catapult	Ongoing

Annex A
The authorities' objectives

A.1 The Taskforce has considered its approach to cryptoassets and distributed ledger technology in financial services in a holistic way by bringing together perspectives from across government, the central bank, and the financial services regulators. Each authority has its own objectives:

- HM Treasury is the government's economic and finance ministry, and is responsible for financial services policy. One of its priorities is to promote a stable and efficient financial services sector that supports growth, consumers, and businesses, including through enabling effective competition and improving outcomes for consumers.

- The FCA is the conduct regulator for 58,000 financial services firms and financial markets in the UK, and the prudential regulator for over 18,000 of those firms. Its operational objectives are to protect consumers, protect financial markets, and promote competition.

- The Bank of England is the UK's central bank and has statutory objectives to maintain monetary and financial stability. The Prudential Regulation Authority (PRA) is its regulatory arm. One of the PRA's primary objectives is to promote the safety and soundness of the firms it regulates.

50

Annex B
Stakeholder engagement

B.1 Industry engagement has formed an important part of the Taskforce's work, and the views and opinions of industry have helped to shape some of the conclusions of this report. Overall, the Taskforce met over 60 firms and other stakeholders.

B.2 It was important for the Taskforce to speak to a range of stakeholders across various sectors, to ensure it heard different perspectives.

Chart B.1 The Taskforce's stakeholder engagement

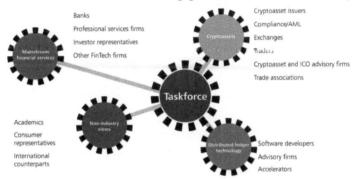

B.3 The Taskforce used its engagement to seek views on a variety of topics, including: the trajectory of the industry; the risks, benefits and underlying economic value of cryptoassets; and the UK's future regulatory approach.

B.4 Many of the issues raised by stakeholders have been cited throughout this report. Other views heard in the course of engagement are captured in Table B.1.

Table B.1: Examples of stakeholder views

Theme	Comments
Cryptoassets	• The market is continuing to evolve rapidly.
	• The current generation of cryptoassets lack clear benefits for consumers.
	• There is increasing institutional investment in this space, and many banks are starting to explore how they can interact with this growing market.
DLT	• There are many use cases demonstrating the potential benefits of DLT.
	• There is a lack of understanding of what DLT can and cannot do.
	• There are technological barriers to DLT adoption, such as governance and scalability.
	• It is difficult for DLT firms (including cryptoasset firms) to get bank accounts in the UK.
Regulatory approach	• There is a lack of regulatory clarity in the UK.
	• Regulation should be introduced to support the legitimate players in this market. It is also crucial in mitigating risks.
	• Regulatory and tax frameworks should be aligned.

HM Treasury contacts

This document can be downloaded from
www.gov.uk

If you require this information in an alternative
format or have general enquiries about
HM Treasury and its work, contact:

Correspondence Team
HM Treasury
1 Horse Guards Road
London
SW1A 2HQ

Tel: 020 7270 5000

Email: public.enquiries@hmtreasury.gov.uk

Cryptocurrencies and blockchain – Legal context and implications for financial crime, money laundering and tax evasion (European Parliament, July 2018)

This European Parliament report addresses the concern of global regulators that criminals appear to have a propensity for using cryptocurrencies as part of their criminal schemes. It focuses on financial crimes such as money laundering, terrorist financing and tax evasion which form part of a cryptocurrency misuse market thought to be valued at €7 billion. The report's research identifies anonymity as a key enabler, concluding that varying degrees of anonymity – from pseudo anonymity through to absolute anonymity – enable unregulated transactions, unmonitored movements that can launder illicit proceeds and/or evade tax.

This is then examined in the context of the Fifth Anti-Money Laundering Directive ('AMLD5') which does address the problem in part but leaves gaps that could be exploited, since miners and 'pure cryptocurrency exchanges' together with other examples are outside its scope and prone to criminal exploitation. Solutions such as expanding the scope of AMLD5, voluntary or mandatory registration of users subject to the possibility of a materiality threshold and a ban applying to elements of cryptocurrency, such as those that might render it untraceable, are all considered. Interestingly, the report concludes that blockchain has so many legitimate lawful applications that it does not merit such additional safeguards, and the focus in combatting crime should be on cryptocurrencies rather than the underlying technology.

To view the full text of the report, please follow this link: www.europarl.europa.eu/cmsdata/150761/TAX3%20Study%20on%20cryptocurrencies%20and%20blockchain.pdf.

To view AMLD5, please follow this link: https://eur-lex.europa.eu/legal-content/EN/TXT/?uri=CELEX%3A32018L0843.

Index

All references are to paragraph number or Appendix.

A

Alternative investment funds (AIFs)
initial coin offerings, 7.29–7.41
Anonymisation
right to be forgotten, 9.18
Anonymity
legal challenges, 3.15–3.18
Anti-Money Laundering Directive
see also **Money laundering**
generally, 3.23
Automation
characteristics of DLT, 2.29

B

Beenz
meaning of 'currency', 2.36
Belarus
regulatory issues, 6.43
Bitcoin
anonymity, and, 3.17
commodity, as, 2.54–2.59
crime, and, 3.13–3.16
cryptoassets, and, 3.6–3.7
cryptocurrency, as, 2.38
currency, as
EU, in, 2.57–2.58
introduction, 2.5
Genesis Block, 2.43–2.44
initial coin offerings, and, 7.5
introduction, 2.2
'medium of exchange, as, 2.52
'mining', 2.46–2.51
money laundering, and, 3.22
operation, 2.40–2.45
proof of work verification, 2.8
verification, 2.45
Blockchain
see also **Distributed ledger technology**
background, 1.1–1.4
characteristics, 2.6
creation, 2.4
crime, and, 3.13–3.16

Blockchain – *contd*
data privacy and protection, 3.26–3.28
distributed ledger technology, as
characteristics, 2.29–2.30
generally, 2.27–2.28
introduction, 1.7
meaning, 2.25–2.26
global regulation, and, 6.4–6.5
intellectual property, and
generally, 2.22–2.24
ownership of information, 3.36–3.42
introduction, 2.1–2.5
money laundering, and, 3.20–3.25
operation, 2.6–2.21
overview, 1.6
permissioned/private, 2.16–2.17
permissionless/public, 2.16
property, and, 3.46–3.48
purpose, 2.4
regulatory and legal challenges, 1.8–1.16
types, 2.16–2.17
use, 2.3–2.4
Bring your own device (BYOD) policies
Internet of Things, 8.15

C

Canada
regulatory issues, 5.1–5.8
China
initial coin offerings
regulatory approach, 7.60–7.64
regulatory philosophy, 6.11–6.18
jurisdictional issues, 6.7
regulatory philosophies, 6.11–6.18
Choice of jurisdiction
generally, 4.1–4.5
Collective investment scheme
initial coin offerings, 7.24–7.28
Commodities
cryptocurrency, and, 2.54–2.59
'Confirming'
cryptocurrency, and, 2.46

Contractual issues
smart contracts
benefits, 3.57
characteristics, 3.58–3.59
creation of legal relations, 3.60–3.61
liability, 3.62–3.66
meaning, 3.53
operation, 3.56
parties, 3.54–3.55
Crime
legal challenges, 3.13–3.19
Crowdfunding
initial coin offerings, 7.5
Cryptoassets
categories, 3.3
exchange tokens, 3.3
generally, 3.1–3.3
initial coin offerings, and, 7.5
meaning, 3.1
regulation, 3.4–3.10
security tokens, 3.3
use, 3.2
utility tokens, 3.3
Cryptocurrency
see also **Regulation**
background, 1.1–1.4
characteristics of DLT, and, 2.29
commodity, as, 2.54–2.59
'confirming', 2.46
cryptoassets, and, 3.6–3.7
'currency', 2.34–2.38
currency, as, 2.52–2.53
introduction, 2.31–2.33
Libra Coin, and, 2.60–2.66
meaning, 2.39–2.45
'mining', 2.46–2.51
money laundering, and, 3.20–3.25
regulatory and legal challenges, 1.8–1.16
Currency
cryptocurrency, and, 2.52–2.53
meaning, 2.34–2.38
Cyber Certification Framework
generally, 8.47–8.56
introduction, 8.36

D
Dash
anonymity, and, 3.17
Data distribution
characteristics of DLT, 2.29
generally, 3.26–3.28
personal data, 3.29–3.35

Data ownership
Internet of Things
generally, 8.78–8.82
introduction, 8.16–8.18
Data privacy
natural resources industry
generally, 10.66–10.67
introduction, 10.9
right to be forgotten, 9.20–9.22
Data protection
see also **General Data Protection Regulation**
Internet of Things
collection, 8.16–8.18
EU regulation, 8.38–8.40
ownership of data, 8.78–8.82
UK regulation, 8.26–8.27
US regulation, 8.77
introduction, 1.24–1.26
Data storage
natural resources industry, 10.37
Decarbonisation
generally, 10.3
regulatory reform, and, 10.7
Decentralisation
areas of application, 10.19
case studies, 10.26–10.29
characteristics of DLT, 2.29
electricity, 10.22–10.25
generally, 10.14–10.18
intermediaries, 10.20–10.21
introduction, 10.1
non-renewables, 10.20–10.21
reality for future, 10.30–10.34
regulatory reform, and, 10.7
renewables, 10.22–10.25
Decentralised autonomous organisations (DAOs)
autonomous, 11.6
generally, 11.1–11.8
global regulation, 6.3
introduction, 3.43–3.45
meaning, 11.1
overview, 1.18–1.19
legal status, 11.9–11.13
peer-to-peer network, 11.1
risks, 11.14–11.20
smart contracts, 11.4
Declaration for European Blockchain Partnership
generally, 4.6–4.9

Democratisation
generally, 10.1
regulatory reform, and, 10.7
Digital service providers (DSPs)
Internet of Things, 8.37
Digitisation
disruptive technology, 10.47–10.48
distributed technology, 10.40–10.45
generally, 10.35–10.39
information storage, 10.36
introduction, 10.1–10.2
obstacles, 10.46
regulatory reform, and, 10.7
Distributed denial of service (DDoS)
Internet of Things, 8.35
Distributed ledger technology (DLT)
blockchain as, 2.27–2.28
characteristics
generally, 2.29–2.30
introduction, 2.6
cryptoassets, and, 3.1
features, 2.29
financial services, and, 3.11
generally, 2.27–2.28
Gibraltar, and, 6.19–6.21
introduction, 2.1
meaning, 2.25–2.26
operation, 2.6–2.21
overview, 1.7
real-time gross settlement, and, 3.12
regulation, 3.11–3.12
use, 2.3
Double spend
characteristics of DLTs, 2.9

E

Electricity
renewable energy, 10.22–10.25
Encrypted data
right to be forgotten, 9.18
ePrivacy Regulation
generally, 8.41–8.46
introduction, 8.36
Erasure
compliance with GDPR, 9.14–9.16
consequences, 9.13
enforcement, 9.9–9.13
fundamental issues, 9.9–9.13
generally, 9.6
introduction, 9.1–9.2
pseudonymisation, 9.24–9.32
right to be forgotten, and, 9.7–9.8

Estonia
general approach, 4.35
regulatory philosophies, 6.43
Ethereum
cryptocurrency, as, 2.38
currency, as, 2.5
initial coin offerings, and, 7.5
proof of work verification, 2.8
EU Blockchain Observatory and Forum
generally, 4.10–4.11
EU regulation
Cyber Certification Framework, 8.47–8.56
digital service providers, 8.37
ePrivacy Regulation, 8.41–8.46
GDPR, 8.38–8.40
initial coin offerings, 7.45–7.59
Internet of Things
CCF, 8.47–8.56
DSPs, 8.37
ePrivacy Regulation, 8.41–8.46
GDPR, 8.38–8.40
introduction, 8.36–8.37
NISD, 8.57–8.61
OESs, 8.37
RFID, 8.38
jurisdictional issues, 6.6
MiFID, 4.21–4.23
MiFID II, 4.24–4.33
MiFIR, 4.24
Network Infrastructure Security Directive, 8.57–8.61
operators of essential services (OESs), 8.37
other countries, 4.34–4.68
Radio Frequency Identification (RFID), 8.38
United Kingdom, 4.12–4.20
Exchange tokens
cryptoassets, 3.3
Exclusive jurisdiction
generally, 4.2–4.4

F

Federal Trade Commission (FTC)
Internet of Things, 8.62–8.73
Financial Conduct Authority (FCA)
authorised persons, 4.18–4.20
cryptoassets, and, 3.8–3.10
generally, 4.12–4.17
initial coin offerings, and, 7.18–7.19
'regulated activities', 4.16
Flooz
meaning of 'currency', 2.36

Food and Drug Administration
Internet of Things, 8.74–8.76
France
regulatory issues, 4.36–4.40

G
General Data Protection Regulation (GDPR)
characteristics of DLTs, and, 2.21
Internet of Things
generally, 8.38–8.40
introduction, 8.36
UK, in, 8.27–8.33
introduction, 1.24–1.26
global regulation, and, 6.1–6.2
jurisdictional issues
effect, 3.50–3.52
generally, 3.49
right to amendment
effects on compliance, 9.34–9.43
Holochain, 9.40–9.43
introduction, 9.33
LTO Network, 9.39
Sovrin, 9.36–9.38
right to be forgotten
anonymisation, 9.18
consequences, 9.13
data caught by right, 9.17–9.19
data protection, 9.20–9.22
data subject, 9.20
encrypted data, 9.18
enforcement, 9.9–9.13
fundamental issues, 9.9–9.19
generally, 9.7–9.8
'hashing', 9.22
introduction, 9.1–9.5
personal data, 9.21
privacy, 9.20–9.22
pseudonymisation, 9.23–9.32
public keys, 9.17–9.18
transactional data, 9.17–9.19
right to erasure
compliance with GDPR, 9.14–9.16
consequences, 9.13
enforcement, 9.9–9.13
fundamental issues, 9.9–9.13
generally, 9.6
introduction, 9.1–9.2
pseudonymisation, 9.24–9.32
text, App 1
Genesis Block
meaning of 'cryptocurrency', 2.43–2.44

Gibraltar
regulatory issues, 6.19–6.22
Global issues
see also **Regulation**
choice of jurisdiction, 4.1–4.5
Declaration for European Blockchain Partnership, 4.6–4.9
EU Blockchain Observatory and Forum, 4.10–4.11
European Union, 4.21–4.33
introduction, 1.20
North America, 5.1–5.26
other European countries, 4.34–4.68
rest of the world, 6.1–6.52
United Kingdom, 4.12–4.20

H
Hash
characteristics of DLTs, 2.18
'Hashing'
right to be forgotten, 9.22
Holochain
right to amendment, 9.40–9.43
Hong Kong
regulatory issues, 6.23–6.24

I
Immutability
characteristics of DLTs, 2.9
India
regulatory issues, 6.25–6.35
Initial coin offerings (ICOs)
alternative investment fund, as, 7.29–7.41
China and
regulatory approach, 7.60–7.64
regulatory philosophy, 6.11–6.18
collective investment scheme, as, 7.24–7.28
crime, and, 3.16
crowdfunding, as, 7.5
cryptocurrency, as, 7.5
EU regulation, 7.45–7.59
FCA approach, 7.18–7.19
generally, 7.5–7.6
Hong Kong, and, 6.23–6.24
introduction, 7.1–7.4
investment companies, by, 7.13–7.17
meaning, 7.5–7.6
overview, 1.21
private offerings, 7.5
public offerings, 7.5
purpose, 7.6

Initial coin offerings (ICOs) – *contd*
  regulatory approach
    China, 7.60–7.64
    European Union, 7.45–7.59
    United Kingdom, 7.18–7.44
    United States, 7.7–7.17
  tokens, 7.5
  UK regulation
    alternative investment fund, as, 7.29–7.41
    collective investment scheme, as, 7.24–7.28
    FCA approach, 7.18–7.19
    generally, 7.18–7.22
    marketing restrictions, 7.42–7.44
    types, 7.23–7.41
  US regulation
    generally, 7.7–7.12
    investment companies, 7.13–7.17
  use, 7.6
Injunctions
  introduction, 1.12
Intellectual property
  generally, 2.22–2.24
  natural resources industry, 10.9
  ownership of information in blockchain, 3.36–3.42
Internet of Things (IoT)
  administrative access, 8.15
  'air gap', 8.15
  available device, 8.7
  bring your own device (BYOD) policies, 8.15
  Code of Practice, 8.20–8.25
  cost of sensors, 8.6
  countertop devices, 8.7
  Cyber Certification Framework
    generally, 8.47–8.56
    introduction, 8.36
  data ownership
    generally, 8.78–8.82
    introduction, 8.16–8.18
  data protection
    EU regulation, 8.38–8.40
    UK regulation, 8.26–8.27
    US regulation, 8.77
  Data Protection Act, 8.26–8.27
  digital service providers (DSPs), 8.37
  distributed denial of service (DDoS), 8.35
  ePrivacy Regulation
    generally, 8.41–8.46
    introduction, 8.36

Internet of Things (IoT) – *contd*
  EU regulation
    Cyber Certification Framework, 8.47–8.56
    digital service providers, 8.37
    ePrivacy Regulation, 8.41–8.46
    GDPR, 8.38–8.40
    introduction, 8.36–8.37
    Network Infrastructure Security Directive, 8.57–8.61
    operators of essential services, 8.37
    Radio Frequency Identification, 8.38
  Federal Trade Commission, 8.62–8.73
  firmware updates, 8.15
  Food and Drug Administration, 8.74–8.76
  GDPR
    generally, 8.38–8.40
    introduction, 8.36
    UK, in, 8.27–8.33
  generally, 8.3–8.8
  ingestible sensors, 8.7
  implantable sensors, 8.7
  Information Commissioner's Office, 8.26–8.30
  intimate contact sensors, 8.7
  introduction, 8.1–8.2
  market value, 8.1
  meaning, 8.3–8.8
  National Cyber Security Strategy, 8.20
  Network Infrastructure Security Directive (NISD)
    generally, 8.57–8.61
    introduction, 8.37
  operators of essential services, 8.37
  overview, 1.5
  Radio Frequency Identification, 8.38
  regulation
    European Union, 8.36–8.61
    United Kingdom, 8.19–8.35
    United States, 8.62–8.77
  security issues
    improvements, 8.15
    mitigation, 8.14–8.15
    problem areas, 8.9–8.13
  sensors, 8.6–8.7
  staff training, 8.15
  UK regulation
    Code of Practice, 8.20–8.25
    Data Protection Act, 8.26–8.27
    DDoS, 8.35
    F-secure report, 8.34
    GDPR, 8.27–8.33

Internet of Things (IoT) – *contd*
  UK regulation – *contd*
    generally, 8.19
    Information Commissioner's Office,
      8.26–8.30
    National Cyber Security Strategy, 8.20
  US regulation
    data protection, 8.77
    Federal Trade Commission, 8.62–8.73
    Food and Drug Administration, 8.74–
      8.76
  use, 8.2
  vetting third party users, 8.15
  wearables, 8.7
Investigatory powers
  introduction, 1.11
Investment companies
  initial coin offerings, 7.13–7.17
Israel
  regulatory issues, 6.36–6.38

J

Japan
  regulatory issues, 6.39–6.42
Jersey
  regulatory issues, 4.59–4.68
Jurisdictional issues
  blockchain, 6.9
  China, 6.7
  choice of jurisdiction, 4.1–4.5
  cryptocurrency, 6.9
  effect, 3.50–3.52
  Europe, 6.6
  generally, 3.49
  introduction, 6.1–6.5
  natural resources industry, 10.9
  Russia, 6.6
  United States, 6.8

K

Kazakhstan
  regulatory issues, 6.43
Kyrgyz Republic
  regulatory issues, 6.44

L

Legal challenges
  anonymity, 3.15–3.18
  contracts
    benefits, 3.57
    characteristics, 3.58–3.59
    creation of legal relations, 3.60–3.61

Legal challenges – *contd*
  contracts – *contd*
    liability, 3.62–3.66
    meaning, 3.53
    operation, 3.56
    parties, 3.54–3.55
  criminal issues, 3.13–3.19
  data privacy and protection
    generally, 3.26–3.28
    personal data, 3.29–3.35
  decentralised autonomous organisations,
    3.43–3.45
  intellectual property, 3.36–3.42
  introduction, 1.8–1.16
  jurisdictional issues
    effect, 3.50–3.52
    generally, 3.49
  money laundering, 3.20–3.25
  property issues, 3.46–3.48
Libra Coin
  cryptocurrency, and, 2.60–2.66
LTO Network
  right to amendment, 9.39

M

Malta
  regulatory issues, 4.41–4.58
Masternodes
  proof of stake verification, 2.11
Mexico
  regulatory issues, 5.9–5.16
MiFID
  Directive I, 4.21–4.23
  Directive II, 4.24–4.33
  UK post-Brexit approach, 6.22
MiFIR
  generally, 4.24
'Mining'
  generally, 2.46–2.51
  proof of work verification, 2.8
Monero
  anonymity, and, 3.17
Money laundering
  legal challenges, 3.20–3.25
**Mutual Legal Assistance Treaties
(MLATs)**
  introduction, 1.16

N

National Cyber Security Strategy
  Internet of Things, 8.20

Natural resources industry
affordability, 10.4
benefits of blockchain, 10.1
blueprint for regulation, 10.89–10.91
case studies
Brooklyn Microgrid, 10.29
introduction, 10.26–10.27
South Korea, 10.29
Wolsink, 10.27–10.29
data privacy
generally, 10.66–10.67
introduction, 10.9
data storage, 10.37
decarbonisation
generally, 10.3
regulatory reform, and, 10.7
decentralisation
areas of application, 10.19
case studies, 10.26–10.29
electricity, 10.22–10.25
generally, 10.14–10.18
intermediaries, 10.20–10.21
introduction, 10.1
non-renewables, 10.20–10.21
reality for future, 10.30–10.34
regulatory reform, and, 10.7
renewables, 10.22–10.25
democratisation
introduction, 10.1
regulatory reform, and, 10.7
digitisation
disruptive technology, 10.47–10.48
distributed technology, 10.40–10.45
generally, 10.35–10.39
information storage, 10.36
introduction, 10.1–10.2
obstacles, 10.46
regulatory reform, and, 10.7
dilemmas, 10.3–10.6
distributed technology, 10.40–10.45
disruptive technology, 10.47–10.48
electricity, 10.22–10.25
information storage, 10.36
intellectual property, 10.9
intermediaries, 10.20–10.21
introduction, 10.1–10.2
jurisdictional issues, 10.9
legal issues, 10.49–10.51
legal status of data, 10.87–10.88
non-renewables, 10.20–10.21
overview, 1.22–1.23
peer-to-peer trading, 10.8

Natural resources industry – *contd*
public/private blockchains, 10.68–10.71
reality for future, 10.30–10.34
regulation
blueprint, 10.89–10.91
challenges in industry, 10.72–10.79
generally, 10.52–10.54
regulatory issues
introduction, 10.7
key question, 10.8
other matters, 10.9–10.13
renewables, 10.22–10.25
scalability, 10.5
security, 10.3
service guarantees, 10.9
solutions and opportunities, 10.80–10.86
smart contracts
generally, 10.55–10.65
introduction, 10.10
smart technology, 10.11
status of data, 10.87–10.88
Network Infrastructure Security Directive (NISD)
generally, 8.57–8.61
introduction, 8.37
Norwich Pharmacal orders
introduction, 1.12
Nxt
proof of stake verification, 2.10

O
Operators of essential services (OESs)
Internet of Things, 8.37

P
Payment Services Regulations 2017
cryptoassets, and, 3.6–3.7
Peercoin
proof of stake verification, 2.10
Peer-to-peer (P2P)
characteristics of DLTs, 2.6
natural resources industry, 10.8
Permissioned blockchain
characteristics of DLTs, 2.16–2.17
global regulation, 6.5
Permissionless blockchain
characteristics of DLTs, 2.16
global regulation, 6.5
Personal data
right to be forgotten, 9.21
user's public key, 3.29–3.35

Privacy
natural resources industry
generally, 10.66–10.67
introduction, 10.9
right to be forgotten, 9.20–9.22
Private blockchain
characteristics of DLTs, 2.16–2.17
global regulation, 6.5
Private key
characteristics of DLTs, 2.20
Programmability
characteristics of DLT, 2.29
Proof of authority (PoA)
generally, 2.13–2.14
introduction, 2.7
Proof of stake (PoS)
generally, 2.10–2.12
introduction, 2.7
Proof of work (PoW)
generally, 2.8–2.9
introduction, 2.7
'mining', and, 2.47–2.50
Property issues
legal challenges, 3.46–3.48
Pseudonymisation
right to be forgotten
effects on compliance, 9.24–9.32
generally, 9.23
introduction, 9.18
meaning, 9.23
Public blockchain
characteristics of DLTs, 2.16
global regulation, 6.5
Public key
characteristics of DLTs, 2.20
data protection, 3.29–3.35
right to be forgotten, 9.17–9.18

R
Radio Frequency Identification (RFID)
Internet of Things, 8.38
Real-time gross settlement (RTGS)
distributed ledger technology, 3.12
Regulation
Belarus, 6.43
Canada, 5.1–5.8
challenges
cryptoassets, 3.1–3.10
distributed ledger technology, 3.11–3.12
China
jurisdictional issues, 6.7

Regulation – *contd*
China – *contd*
regulatory philosophies, 6.11–6.18
choice of jurisdiction, 4.1–4.5
cryptoassets
categories, 3.3
exchange tokens, 3.3
generally, 3.1–3.3
meaning, 3.1
regulation, 3.4–3.10
security tokens, 3.3
use, 3.2
utility tokens, 3.3
Declaration for European Blockchain
Partnership, 4.6–4.9
distributed ledger technology, 3.11–3.12
Estonia
general approach, 4.35
regulatory philosophies, 6.43
EU Blockchain Observatory and Forum,
4.10–4.11
European Union
MiFID, 4.21–4.23
MiFID II, 4.24–4.33
MiFIR, 4.24
jurisdictional issues, 6.6
other countries, 4.34–4.68
United Kingdom, 4.12–4.20
Financial Conduct Authority, by
authorised persons, 4.18–4.20
generally, 4.12–4.17
'regulated activities', 4.16
France, 4.36–4.40
Gibraltar, 6.19–6.22
global issues
choice of jurisdiction, 4.1–4.5
Declaration for European Blockchain
Partnership, 4.6–4.9
EU Blockchain Observatory and
Forum, 4.10–4.11
European Union, 4.21–4.33
North America, 5.1–5.26
other European countries, 4.34–4.68
rest of the world, 6.1–6.52
United Kingdom, 4.12–4.20
Hong Kong, 6.23–6.24
India, 6.25–6.35
initial coin offerings
China, 7.60–7.64
European Union, 7.45–7.59
United Kingdom, 7.18–7.44
United States, 7.7–7.17

Regulation – *contd*
  Internet of Things
    European Union, 8.36–8.61
    United Kingdom, 8.19–8.35
    United States, 8.62–8.77
  introduction, 1.8–1.16
  Israel, 6.36–6.38
  Japan, 6.39–6.42
  Jersey, 4.59–4.68
  jurisdictional issues
    China, 6.7
    blockchain, 6.9
    choice of jurisdiction, 4.1–4.5
    cryptocurrency, 6.9
    Europe, 6.6
    introduction, 6.1–6.5
    Russia, 6.6
    United States, 6.8
  Kazakhstan, 6.43
  Kyrgyz Republic, 6.44
  Malta, 4.41–4.58
  Mexico, 5.9–5.16
  natural resources industry
    blueprint, 10.89–10.91
    challenges in industry, 10.72–10.79
    generally, 10.52–10.54
    introduction, 10.7
    key question, 10.8
    other matters, 10.9–10.13
  North America
    Canada, 5.1–5.8
    Mexico, 5.9–5.16
    United States, 5.17–5.27
  philosophies
    Belarus, 6.43
    China, 6.11–6.18
    Estonia, 6.43
    generally, 6.10
    Gibraltar, 6.19–6.22
    Hong Kong, 6.23–6.24
    India, 6.25–6.35
    introduction, 6.9
    Israel, 6.36–6.38
    Japan, 6.39–6.42
    Kazakhstan, 6.43
    Kyrgyz Republic, 6.44
    Russia, 6.49
    South Korea, 6.45–6.48
    Switzerland, 6.50–6.52
    UK post-Brexit, 6.22
  rest of the world
    jurisdictional issues, 6.1–6.9

Regulation – *contd*
  rest of the world – *contd*
    regulatory philosophies, 6.10–6.
  Russia
    jurisdictional issues, 6.6
    regulatory philosophies, 6.49
  South Korea, 6.45–6.48
  Switzerland, 6.50–6.52
  United Kingdom
    authorised persons, 4.18–4.20
    generally, 4.12–4.17
    post-Brexit approach, 6.22
    'regulated activities', 4.16
  United States
    generally, 5.17–5.21
    jurisdictional issues, 6.8
    licensing, 5.22
    money transmission laws, 5.23
    regulatory guidance, 5.24–5.26
Right to amendment
  effects on compliance, 9.34–9.43
  Holochain, 9.40–9.43
  introduction, 9.33
  LTO Network, 9.39
  Sovrin, 9.36–9.38
Right to be forgotten
  anonymisation, 9.18
  consequences, 9.13
  data caught by right, 9.17–9.19
  data protection, 9.20–9.22
  data subject, 9.20
  encrypted data, 9.18
  enforcement, 9.9–9.13
  erasure
    compliance with GDPR, 9.14–9.16
    data caught by right, 9.17–9.19
    general right, 9.6
  fundamental issues, 9.9–9.19
  generally, 9.7–9.8
  'hashing', 9.22
  introduction, 9.1–9.5
  personal data, 9.21
  privacy, 9.20–9.22
  pseudonymisation
    effects on compliance, 9.24–9.32
    generally, 9.23
    introduction, 9.18
    meaning, 9.23
  public keys, 9.17–9.18
  transactional data, 9.17–9.19
Right to erasure
  compliance with GDPR, 9.14–9.16

Right to erasure – *contd*
consequences, 9.13
enforcement, 9.9–9.13
fundamental issues, 9.9–9.13
generally, 9.6
introduction, 9.1–9.2
pseudonymisation, 9.24–9.32
right to be forgotten, and, 9.7–9.8
Russia
jurisdictional issues, 6.6
regulatory philosophies, 6.49

S
Security issues
Internet of Things
improvements, 8.15
mitigation, 8.14–8.15
problem areas, 8.9–8.13
natural resources industry, 10.3
Security tokens
cryptoassets, 3.3
Smart contracts
benefits, 3.57
characteristics, 3.58–3.59
creation of legal relations, 3.60–3.61
decentralised autonomous organisations,
11.4
introduction, 1.17
liability, 3.62–3.66
meaning, 3.53
natural resources industry
generally, 10.55–10.65
introduction, 10.10
operation, 3.56
parties, 3.54–3.55
South Korea
regulatory issues, 6.45–6.48
Sovrin
right to amendment, 9.36–9.38
Switzerland
regulatory issues, 6.50–6.52

T
Time stamp
characteristics of DLTs, 2.18
Tokens
initial coin offerings, 7.5
Transactional data
right to be forgotten, 9.17–9.19

U
UK regulation
authorised persons, 4.18–4.20
cryptocurrencies, 4.12
derivatives, 4.15
exempt person, 4.17
foreign exchange, 4.13
generally, 4.12–4.17
initial coin offerings
alternative investment fund, as, 7.29–
7.41
collective investment scheme, as,
7.24–7.28
FCA approach, 7.18–7.19
generally, 7.18–7.22
marketing restrictions, 7.42–7.44
types, 7.23–7.41
Internet of Things
Code of Practice, 8.20–8.25
Data Protection Act, 8.26–8.27
DDoS, 8.35
F-secure report, 8.34
GDPR, 8.27–8.33
generally, 8.19
Information Commissioner's Office,
8.26–8.30
National Cyber Security Strategy,
8.20
MiFID II, and, 4.14
post-Brexit approach, 6.22
'regulated activities', 4.16
US regulation
generally, 5.17–5.21
initial coin offerings
generally, 7.7–7.12
investment companies, 7.13–7.17
Internet of Things
data protection, 8.77
Federal Trade Commission, 8.62–8.73
Food and Drug Administration, 8.74–
8.76
jurisdictional issues, 6.8
licensing, 5.22
money transmission laws, 5.23
regulatory guidance, 5.24–5.26
Utility tokens
cryptoassets, 3.3

V
Validation
characteristics of DLTs, 2.18

Validators
    proof of authority verification, 2.13–
      2.14
VeChain
    proof of stake verification, 2.11

W

Wearables
    Internet of Things, 8.7

Z

ZCash
    anonymity, and, 3.17